Human
Communication in Action

SEVENTH EDITION

GREG G. ARMFIELD
ERIC L. MORGAN

Kendall Hunt
publishing company

Cover images courtesy of Greg G. Armfield, PhD, Shelbey Quintanilla, and Ebenezer Aidoo

Kendall Hunt
publishing company

www.kendallhunt.com
Send all inquiries to:
4050 Westmark Drive
Dubuque, IA 52004-1840

Published in the United States of America

To the memory of Dr. Rebecca M. Verser,
whose passion for teaching shall continue to inspire.
May she serve as a role model for us all.

Contents

UNIT FIVE

Communication Contexts in Action　303

Section

EXERCISES　369

Unit

Editor Biographies

GREG G. ARMFIELD is an Associate Professor of Communication Studies and the Basic Course Director at New Mexico State University. He received his PhD in Communication from the University of Missouri-Columbia in 2004. His research interests include communication and sport, organizational communication, and leadership. In addition to editing five editions of this textbook, he has co-edited *The ESPN Effect* (2013) and *The ESPN Aftershock* (2019) both published by Peter Lang. In 2013 he won the NMSU Patricia Christmore Faculty Teaching award and the College of Arts and Sciences Service and Outreach award. When not teaching, working, or engaged in research he spends time with family and friends. His hobbies include sports, vintage automobiles, and fishing.

ERIC L. MORGAN is a Professor and Department Head of Communication Studies at New Mexico State University. He received his PhD in Communication from the University of Massachusetts, Amherst in 2002. His research interests include cultural/intercultural communication as well as environmental communication. He is the co-editor of the award-winning book *Environmental Communication Pedagogy and Practice*. He has won several teaching awards while at NMSU including the Donald C. Roush Award for Teaching Excellence, which is selected by students. When not teaching, researching, or otherwise working, he can normally be found outside climbing, hiking, and camping or playing music with friends and family.

Human Communication in Action

Eric L. Morgan and Greg G. Armfield

Welcome! This text is an introduction to communication, the most fundamental of all human social processes. This text is also an exploration of the exciting academic field of Communication. Communication as a phenomenon and Communication as a field both lead us to an examination of fascinating and exciting questions. Let's consider that first statement again, "Communication is the most fundamental of all human social processes." I once had a professor who said something along these lines. It was more than 20 years ago, but that thought has stayed with me in my journey through the academic field of communication. If we pause to really consider that statement, we recognize just how accurate it is. Humans are social creatures. We need each other to survive. Communication is the thing that allows us to live together as social creatures. Thus, communication is the key to survival. There is not a single thing we do together that does not include some aspect of communication. So, now that we've established the importance of communication, we hope that you will come to find the study of it as enjoyable and fascinating as we do.

This textbook is divided into five different units that will guide you through your exploration of communication. The first unit is devoted to outlining some principles of human communication including discussions of verbal and nonverbal communication, ethics, and culture and communication. The second unit focuses on public speaking. In this unit, you will encounter detailed discussions of different types of public speaking as well as some advice for becoming a competent public speaker in society. Unit Three considers the broad field of Interpersonal Communication. This unit will cover aspects of relationships as well as how we can best engage in conflict management with others. The fourth unit is on Organizational Communication. Organizational communication focuses on how the organizations of which we are part are made up of communication practices. This unit will be particularly useful as one moves into the workforce beyond college. Finally, the fifth unit provides detailed discussions of some important areas of communication. Here, you will encounter explorations of health communication, persuasion, and how digital literacy is quickly becoming a necessary skill. After all of this, however, we will have barely scratched the surface of the exciting area that is the study of human communication. Hopefully, the authors included in this textbook will inspire you to dig deeper into the wonderfully complex world of communication.

Fundamentals of Human Communication

Eric L. Morgan and Greg G. Armfield

Objectives

- ► Be able to identify the range of benefits associated with studying communication.
- ► Define communication.
- ► Characterize and apply the transactional model of communication.
- ► Apply basic principles of communication to everyday life.

When I (Morgan) was an undergraduate student in the 1990s, like many of my peers, I was not sure exactly what I wanted to do with my life. I could easily respond to questions of "what's your major?" or "what do you want to study?", but I didn't feel a strong pull to my answers. I believe it was the fourth semester of my college career when I enrolled in the basic course in Human Communication. That course changed my life. All of a sudden, I was listening to a professor having conversations about things I had been wondering about for years but had never really had the ways to express the questions. These questions and conversations about communication opened up a door to me that has proven to be endlessly fascinating. I'm extraordinarily grateful for that professor. She remains, to this day, one of the people that I look to as life-changing. She invited me into a conversation that talked about what made us human. It was a course that looked at the very mechanism of human social life. I had finally found a field of study that opened up an amazing expanse of possibility. Now, 20 plus years later, I feel like I have just started this journey. As I write this portion of the text, I cannot help but be excited for the possibilities that you will encounter.

To begin, we will explore some of the key reasons why studying communication will benefit you personally and professionally. Following this, we will explore a brief history of the systematic study of communication. This will be followed by a brief discussion of how we might define communication. Different scholars provide different definitions of communication, but we believe ours is broad enough to encompass the rich diversity of the field while also capturing the essence of what communication is. We will follow with a discussion of an important model useful in understanding the different components of communication. Finally, we will conclude with some general thoughts about how communication functions in everyday life.

WHY STUDY COMMUNICATION?

Studying communication is potentially one of the most fulfilling activities one can undertake as an undergraduate. Communication is crucial to everything we do together. Developing your understanding of communication can benefit you in powerful ways. This section will highlight some of the areas in which the study of communication has enormous potential to benefit you. Critically thinking about communication has so many positive benefits. For example, studying communication will help you create more productive and fulfilling relationships. It will provide a framework for engaging issues of diversity and culture. It gives us insight into an increasingly complex world shaped by social media and other communication technologies. It helps us understand and engage political systems and understand our own civic engagement. It gives us tools for thinking about issues of health, environment, religion, and even sports. More than all of this, however, the study of communication helps us to understand ourselves and opens new and exciting avenues for personal growth. One crucially important benefit, however, is that studying communication has enormous benefits for one's employment.

Communication and Employment

According to Tyler Omoth (2017) of the company TopResume, communication skills rank as the number one job skill that employers were looking for in 2017. Very simply he writes that "regardless of your profession, communication skills are a must" (para 3). According to the CLIMB Center (Continuous Learning for Individuals, Management, and Business) (2017) out of Portland Community College, the number one skill on their list of top 10 skills that employers look for is "strong communication skills." In their description, employers want individuals who can express themselves well and understand the importance of listening well. Scott Steinberg (2017) writing for *Parade Magazine* in an article titled "2017 Job Trends: 15 Skills Employers Are Now Looking For" writes that "Top hires will exhibit superior ability to listen, write, and speak." Almost certainly there are statistics on this in virtually every list or conversation of what employers are looking for in employees. It is certainly vitally important to be trained vocationally; however, when it comes to actually practicing the skills you learned for your chosen profession, communication becomes the paramount skill.

Communication and Personal Growth

The study of communication is imminently practical for one's personal life. The ways in which we form relationships, manage relationships, and even dissolve certain relationships are all accomplished through communication processes. Likewise, through communication, we can better understand how our family relationships exist and play out over time. Developing communication skills also helps us when navigating interpersonal conflicts. Years ago, I (Morgan) delved into the world of conflict mediation, particularly for workplace conflicts. One of the great joys of this work is seeing how communication can solve problems that arise in the workplace and lead to more productive relationships and more productive working environments. When one undertakes a study of communication, one quickly becomes familiar with all areas that communication impacts. For example, when studying communication and culture, students quickly gain a broader appreciation of themselves as whole new worlds of how people live open up to them.

Communication and Diversity and Inclusion

The society in which we live is becoming increasingly diverse. As this occurs, we are also continually changing how we, as a society, engage with issues of diversity. A driving question through all of this is "how can we engage in communication that is broadly inclusive of various identities and positions in society?" This question will be addressed, in part, in the later section on ethics and communication. Another important question to ask is "why is the study of communication important for better understanding issues of diversity and inclusion?" For the answer to this, we can consider the words of Fallon Murphy, president of the Black Student Association and Communication Studies major at New Mexico State University. She states the following:

> I think everyone creates meaning in different ways, and they make sense of things differently depending on their identity and back-grounds. The ability to understand [different communication patterns] is productive and important in diversifying environments and in being more inclusive in whatever you're doing. If you understand that people communicate differently, you can understand who they are better.

From these words, we see that communication and diversity concerns are intimately intertwined. Ms. Murphy also spoke of another key concern regarding the relationship between communication and diversity, specifically about the importance of understanding diversity in communication patterns. She reminds us that communication patterns and even emotions are produced within contexts that are dependent on background and identity. Thus, understanding the role of communication in diversity will make for a more accepting and inclusive situation.

A BRIEF HISTORY OF PEOPLE STUDYING COMMUNICATION

Across the U.S. and increasingly in other parts of the world, university students are required to take courses in communication. At the university where the authors of this text work, this course is known as a general education course. These courses exist because one of the guiding principles of higher education is that in order for one to count as being educated, an individual should have a broad and general knowledge base across a variety of areas. This principle dates back all the way to the Ancient Greeks, where the formal study of rhetoric began. In this classical tradition, understanding oratorical traditions and their impact was a critical portion of a person's education.

In fact, the art, practice, and study of public speaking have been around for mil-lennia. This study has been strongly linked to both personal empowerment and even societal development. The Ancient Egyptians, for example, highly valued eloquent speech; so much so, in fact, that they had a deity named Hu that personified elo-quent speech. Likewise, one of the attributes of the pharaohs was said to be eloquence (Hutto, 2002). Fox (1983) argues that Egyptian rhetorical practices were closely linked to being a good and proper person. In addition, Gray (1946) points out that in order for speech to be considered eloquent in this Ancient Egyptian context, one had to be fair and honest. Indeed, one's persuasiveness, among the Ancient Egyptians, was grounded in humility and modesty in speech.

ORATORY

the art, practice, and study of public speaking.

The Ancient Greeks were also closely associated with the study of rhetorical practice and linking that study to how people ought to be in society (Jaffe, 2010). It was with the Greeks that we find the first formal teaching of public speech. In the fifth century B.C.E., Corax and his student Tisius embarked on a campaign in the city-state of Syracuse to teach people the principles of public address so that citizens could petition the ruler for grievances. Corax was the first to give lessons on public speaking with an emphasis on persuasion. Corax presented the idea that persuasion was much more likely to be accomplished when the speaker could best present the probability of truth (Smith, 1921). The tale of Corax and his pupil Tisius is actually shrouded in mystery, but it has been passed down through the ages as a way to discuss the beginnings of public speech teaching.

Of course, no discussion of the Greek association with oratory can occur without reference to Socrates, his student Plato, and Plato's student Aristotle. Each of these philosophers argued that public speech should be practiced as a way to arrive at truth (Brydon & Scott, 1994). Closely associated with Aristotle and other Greek rhetoricians are the Five Canons of Rhetoric (Brydon & Scott, 1994). These are principles of good persuasive public speaking. Briefly they include the following:

- ▶ Invention—figuring out the different ways that persuasion may occur;
- ▶ Arrangement—putting the argument together in an effective and potentially successful way;
- ▶ Style—being able to use eloquent language in the presentation of the argument;
- ▶ Memory—being able to speak extemporaneously (more on this later); and,
- ▶ Delivery—being able to use appropriate gestural and vocal enthusiasm in one's delivery.

Interestingly these canons overlap with the Roman tradition where we find some of the strongest discussions of the role of public speaking in society. The great orator, Cicero, once asked this pointed question about the role of public speaking in society. *Quid tam porro regiu, tam liberale, tam munificium, quam opem ferre supplicibus, excitare afflictus, dare sabutam, liberare periculus, retinere hominess in civitate?* (What function again is so kingly, so worthy of the free, so generous, as to bring help to the suppliant, to raise up those that are cast down, to bestow security, to set free from peril, to maintain men in their civil rights?) (Sutton, 1942, p. 24). Cicero asked this question to support his argument that oratory was vital to the interests of the state. It reminds us that it is through the power of public oratory that society is constituted and shaped. Cicero also taught that morality and honesty needed to be in harmony with speech (Remer, 2009). A century following Cicero, another Roman, Quintilian, wrote "vir bonus, dicendi peritus," which translates into a good person who is skilled in speaking (The Latin Library, 2010). Some scholars argue that this means that the ideal orator is a good person. While true, I also believe that there was a strong cultural belief that what counted as a good person was one who was skilled in oratory. In this way, it was a value of society, just like being honest or trustworthy might be in today's society.

These are just three historical examples of how communication was valued, studied, and celebrated throughout society. While these examples represent a classical approach to understanding the role of human communication, we could also attend to the many other traditions of communication study throughout time. In fact, studying diverse traditions of communication allows us to broaden our understanding in powerful ways. We will touch on some of this in the later sections on culture and communication. For now, let's turn our attention to how we can define communication.

DEFINING COMMUNICATION

Dr. Armfield and I define communication as follows: **Communication** *is a social process in which individuals exchange messages using symbols and other nonverbal cues in order to generate meaning in various contexts.* This definition encompasses the breadth and complexity of what communication is and can be, at least when looking at communication from a social scientific perspective. To explore this definition a bit more, let's take a look at each of the components.

First, this definition reminds us that communication is a process. Not only that, communication is a complex process. What does it mean to say that something is a process? When we say that communication is a process, we mean that communication is not a *thing*. It is not an object. In fact, when we communicate we are constantly coordinating and managing how we create meaning with others (Cronen, Chen, & Pearce, 1988). This coordination is oftentimes highly synchronized with our communication partners. When things are going well, we often do not realize just what an accomplishment this is. In order to communicate we have to attend to the other person, the environment, the broader context, the messages we are generating and those that the other person is generating, and our emotions, among many other things. Sometimes things can go wrong during this process. When this happens, we oftentimes find ourselves questioning some aspect of the process of communication. For example, we might question what we said, if we understood what the other person said, or even what our goals were in communicating in a particular way. There are so many aspects of communication that pinpointing just when things go wrong can sometimes be difficult.

At this point, it is probably worth mentioning that in the field of communication and in this class we use the term communication (without an "s"). Doing this consistently keeps our attention on the process aspect of communication. The term "communications" can be used as a way to refer to telecommunications, which is really only about the transmission of messages through some sort of technology (Lindsey, 2016). It could also be used to refer to a specific act of communication as in saying, "the President sent the following communications to his cabinet." Neither of these uses of the term communications means what we mean when we say communication.

The definition of communication presented here provides us with a way to investigate communication in powerful ways. Another useful approach to defining communication comes in the perspective we can take toward the phenomenon. Pearce (2007) utilizes a grammatical metaphor to discuss two different perspectives. You may be familiar with the idea of first ("I"), second ("you"), and third ("he, she, or it") person when describing pronouns and verb conjugation. The distinction that Pearce uses is between viewing communication from the first-person perspective versus the third-person perspective. If we treat communication from the third-person perspective, as if we were looking at communication as something outside of ourselves, then we might notice that communication looks like a game in which the conversational partners take turns speaking. What would happen, however, if I were to ask you to define communication based on your experience of it? Does communication always feel like a game of back-and-forth with your conversational partners? Probably not. Rather, communication is likely experienced as a process of coordinating and managing your goals within a number of contexts.

By way of example, imagine the following scenario. You are sitting at the student union building drinking a cup of coffee and studying for an upcoming exam. At the table next to you are two international students from Japan. The two students are having a conversation in Japanese, a language that you do not speak. If I were to ask you to describe the conversation, what would you say? You might at first think that you cannot say anything about the conversation because you can't understand the words of the conversation. However, you would certainly notice some things. For example, you would probably notice that the two students were taking turns at speaking. In fact, because you cannot understand anything in this situation, you might be able to identify all those aspects that go into communication that are not the words themselves. From this perspective, communication looks like a game, or a highly synchronized dance, or some sort of coordinated, cooperative action. Now, if you were to try to participate in the conversation, it might look, sound, and feel like a completely different phenomenon. For example, if you do not speak Japanese, it would be hard to participate in an effortless way. You would probably be focused on trying to figure out how to establish a shared code so that you could come to some mutual understanding. I present this point to highlight just how complex communication can be. Using our definition of communication to understand the above scenario, it is possible to investigate the social process that is communication, the verbal and nonverbal messages that go into it, and the ways that meaning is generated throughout the whole process.

To conclude this portion on defining communication, let's take a look at the etymology of the term as a way to remind us of what studying communication is really about. A quick look into the etymology of the word shows that the word ultimately comes from Latin through French and borrowed into English around 1400 C.E. The Latin verb *communicare* essentially means the process of making something common. This is a great way to conceive of what we are doing with communication. We are, in essence, trying to find commonality with others. In order to get a better understanding of what communication is, the following portion will explain a particularly useful model of communication.

A MODEL OF HUMAN COMMUNICATION PROCESSES

Now that we have explored the definition of communication, we can turn our attention to what communication might look like if we tried to depict it in a model. As scholars began systematically examining human communication from a "third-person" perspective, it became clear that communication consisted of numerous aspects. Understanding these different aspects and how they related to one another allowed us to more fully grasp the complexity of the communication process. In the early days of this effort, two engineers, Shannon and Weaver (1948) published a piece titled *A Mathematical Theory of Communication* that showed how some of these aspects might go together. They provided a simplistic model that focused on a source, a receiver, a channel, and noise. The source was the origination of the communication act. The receiver was the recipient of the message, and the channel was the thing that transmitted the message. Noise was anything that could potentially interfere with a message. This model helped us to understand the importance of channels and the clarity of a message or message fidelity.

In 1970, communication theorist Dean Barnlund published a much more complex model of communication that took into account many other features of the communication process. This model came to be known as the transactional model of communication. The elements of the transactional model include the following: (1) source/receiver, (2) message, (3) channel, (4) noise, (5) encoding/decoding, (6) feedback loops, and (7) context (Barnlund, 1970). From this perspective, communication is modeled as consisting of two communicators who engage in both sending and receiving *simultaneously*. During conversations, naturally, one communicator will function primarily as a sender while the other will function as a receiver. In a conversation, these roles will switch quickly and with little effort provided that both communicators share the same code (i.e., language as well as rules for the conduct and interpretation of other communicative cues).

These communicators will be engaged in exchanging messages. A **message** is something that is assumed to invoke meaning in the other person. As Pittenger, Hockett, and Danehy (1960) stated long ago, these messages tend to come in "packages" of both verbal and nonverbal cues or signals. These messages will be sent via a channel. A **channel** is anything over which communication flows. You are likely quite familiar with certain types of channels associated with telecommunications such as a channel on television or the radio. In our modern era, these channels transmit digital data as opposed to analog. In the same way that telecommunications channels are pathways for data flow, so are channels in the everyday, face-to-face communication. We will discuss different types of channels in later sections of this unit; however, for now, we can understand that there are numerous channels that we use in communication with others. The **feedback** loops associated with the transactional model draw our attention to the message flow from the person acting primarily as the receiver and sending messages back. While these flows can often seem relatively coordinated, there are times when something interferes with the flow.

This interference is known as **noise**. In general, we can think about four different types of noise including physical noise, physiological noise, psychological noise, and semantic noise (Lindsey, 2016). Physical noise is anything physical in the environment that impedes the message flow. This could be a loud noise or some other occurrence that interrupts the fidelity of the message. Physiological noise is noise created by our sense of our bodies while in communication. For example, we may be tired or hungry or feeling some strong emotion. This can interfere with the ways we both send and receive messages. Psychological noise occurs when we are distracted by our thoughts. There are many situations in which we find ourselves communicating while also thinking about other things happening. Another form of psychological noise occurs when we find ourselves thinking about what we are going to say rather than actually listening to the other person. This will be discussed later in the book in the section on listening. Finally, semantic noise refers to interference due to our inability to understand what is being said. An obvious example is if you do not have a full grasp of a language that is being used while conversing. A more common form of semantic noise, however, occurs when one does not understand the ways that language is being used. For instance, if you've ever read something written in English, but the level of the writing was so inaccessible that you did not have any idea what was being communicated, then you have experienced semantic noise.

The transactional model is also useful in that it includes the psychological processes that underlie message development and reception. These processes are known as encoding and decoding respectively. **Encoding** occurs whenever a communicator forms a message prior to sending the message. Essentially, this entails taking thoughts or ideas and placing them into a "code" that is (at least partially) shared with others. Perhaps the code we most often think of during this process is language. When you produce spoken language, you are only able to do so after encoding the message. The other process discussed here is decoding. **Decoding** is the interpretation of the message. Decoding requires that we first perceive stimuli, then organize that stimuli into meaningful formats, evaluate that stimuli, and ultimately make it relevant to our experience, either specifically or more broadly.

MESSAGE

encoded information that is assumed to invoke meaning in another.

CHANNEL

anything over which communication flows.

FEEDBACK

messages generated in response to other messages.

NOISE

anything that interferes with message flow and its role in meaning generation.

ENCODING

formulating thoughts, ideas, and/or feelings into messages.

DECODING

interpreting a message.

CONTEXT

the physical,
cultural, relational,
and historical
environment in which
communication
occurs.

Finally, and perhaps most importantly, the transactional model includes context. **Context** refers to the physical, cultural, relational, and historical environment in which communication occurs. Physical places impact how we generate and assign meaning to messages. If you are in a classroom or a place of worship or a house, the things said will likely be different and the understanding based on being in these places will also be different. Our cultural backgrounds provide the framework for all of communication and the generation of meaning. This will be discussed in the last three sections of this unit. The relationship we have with another person is also a critical aspect of the context. There is so much to be said about this aspect that we devote an entire unit to understanding the relationships we have and how communication both impacts and is impacted by that. Finally, I use "historical context" to refer generally to when something is said. Broadly speaking, there are certain ways that we communicate today that would be found odd years prior. However, our own development can also play a role in how we understand communication. As you might have noticed, communication is a profoundly complex process. The transactional model is one way that we can come to understand a little bit of the process.

The Transactional Model of Human Communication

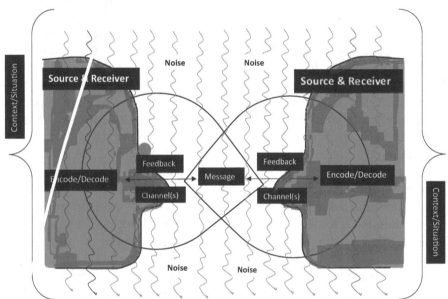

Adapted from the National Communication Association (2019)

BASIC PRINCIPLES OF HUMAN COMMUNICATION

Celebrated communication scholar, Joseph DeVito (2014), writes about a number of basic principles of human communication. Understanding these can help us in our everyday interactions. He writes that communication exhibits certain characteristics that, when understood, help us to navigate the complex world of communication. For example, DeVito reminds us that communication is purposeful and involves choices. When we communicate we often do so to achieve some sort of goal. According to Lindsey (2016), these goals include such things as communicating to inform, to persuade, to form and maintain relationships, to manage conflict, and to make decisions. These goals will form the basis of later units and sections of this textbook. Another basic principle is that communication is ambiguous. This means that while we often believe we know what things mean or what people intended, things can remain pretty murky. Certainly nonverbal communication cues exhibit this property, but ambiguity is also a major part of verbal communication. In fact, much communication is motivated to seek clarity and reduce the amounts of ambiguity (see Berger & Calabrese, 1975). A third principle discussed by DeVito is that communication always has a power dimension. As communication scholars, we are often interested in how communication creates and perpetuates various types of power dynamics.

In 1967, Watzlawick, Beavin, and Jackson published a foundational text in the area of communication. In this book, these scholars outline principles of communication that are used to this day. One powerful insight they provide is that communication always exists on two dimensions: a content dimension and a relational dimension. The content dimension refers to the information being communicated. Whenever we understand something or some behavior as signifying something else, then we are paying attention to the content dimension. Communication also has a relational dimension. Each time we engage in communication we are sending messages, to be sure, but we are also "commenting" on the relationship we have with our conversational partners. Lindsey (2016) explains the relational dimension by noting that how we say something will communicate our attitude toward the other person, just as much as the content. Recognizing these two features of communication helps us in assessing our own communication behaviors at a very broad level. For example, if I were to have a conversation that went poorly, I may start to ask what went wrong. It may be something about the message itself, or it may be that the person understood our relationship differently because of the way I said something. One last item on this issue, which points to the importance of both the content and the relational dimension. Today, quite a bit of our telecommunication is conducted via text messaging. Have you ever been confused by a text because you didn't have access to the relational dimension cues of a message? The answer is almost assuredly, yes. Knowing this, we can now strategize about how we might include some relational cues to help with our meaning.

The last cluster of characteristics that we will discuss here is a reminder that communication is **inevitable**, **irreversible**, and **unrepeatable** (DeVito, 2014). We may already know this, and we have certainly experienced this in action, but it is important to remember. To say that communication is *inevitable* means that when we find ourselves in an *interactive situation*, communication will occur. An interactive situation is one in which we find ourselves aware of the presence of another. If we are aware that another person is present in some way, then communication has the potential of occurring. This was summarized by Watzlawick, Beavin, and Jackson (1967) with the phrase, "one cannot not communicate." This principle reminds us that we are always potentially sending messages even if we do not intend to do so.

The second principle in this cluster is that communication is irreversible (DeVito, 2014). The most obvious example of how communication is *irreversible* comes with computer-mediated communication. While you probably already know this, it bears repeating that you cannot "take back" e-mails that you intended not to send or texts that were worded inappropriately. Electronic communication is irreversible. Face-to-face communication is also irreversible. Often it seems that the messages in face-to-face communication fade quickly, but the impact of their role in generating meaning lingers. Sometimes we say things that we do not mean. While unfortunate, we simply cannot say "I take it back" and go on as if nothing is different. The best we can do is try to manage the situation. We will discuss some skills that might be helpful in these situations in later sections of the textbook.

The third and final principle to be discussed is that communication is *unrepeatable* (DeVito, 2014). This seems like an odd one to consider at first because we might think that we can simply say the same thing twice. Remember the above discussion about content and relationship dimensions of communication. While the content may be the same, how you say something, the situation in which you say something, and the state of being of both yourself and your conversational partner will be different. Because contexts always change, communication always changes. Thus, it is important that we develop skills to be flexible in our communication practices. I often use the example of planning out conversations before actually having them. It's likely that you have done this before. The question to ask though is, have you ever had a conversation go exactly the way it was planned? Probably not. The lesson here is that we need to continually develop our understanding of communication so that we can better navigate the constantly changing communication landscape.

CONCLUSION

As we learned above, communication is a complex and fascinating process. There are so many dimensions and pieces to the puzzle. What we've discussed here barely scratches the surface. In fact, communication is a broad area that draws together scholars interested in a wide array of areas. Within this breadth, the community of scholars and practitioners that are communication specialists come to understand communication in its entirety. The academic study of communication as a field is *necessarily* broad because communication is an inherent part of every single sphere of human social life. Scholars in communication are interested in exploring what communication is and how it functions in a wide variety of contexts. To give you a quick sense of the diversity of scholarship in the field of Communication, a quick look at the website for the National Communication Association reveals 48 different divisions (NCA, 2018). These are 48 different areas of "substantive inquiry" that scholars from all around the world systematically investigate through research and seek to teach to others. This textbook covers the main areas that make up the field of Communication. As we move forward we will explore exciting areas such as how culture and communication work together, public speaking, interpersonal communication, organizational communication, health communication, and even discussions of digital literacy. We sincerely hope that this inspires you to explore the wonderfully exciting world of communication beyond a single class.

Discussion Questions

1. Think about a typical day. How often are you engaged in communication with others? What are the different contexts? Who is involved? What are your goals in each of these conversations?

2. How does your communication change depending on context and conversational partners?

3. Think of the 10 best communicators you know. What makes them good communicators? Think of the 10 worst communicators you know. What makes them bad communicators?

4. Considering your own communication tendencies, what types of skills do you believe you could work on?

5. What are some metaphors or similes of communication that you can think of? In other words, complete the following sentence:

    Communication is like _____.

    What aspects of communication are highlighted in this metaphor?

6. Have you ever found yourself in a situation in which your conversation may have gone poorly? Using the transactional model, can you explain what might have gone wrong?

7. Is it possible for one to not communicate?

References

Barnlund, D. (1970). A transactional model of communication. In J. Akin, A. Goldberg, G. Myers, & J. Stewart (Eds.), *Language behavior: A book of readings in communication.* The Hague: Mouton.

Berger, C. R., & Calabrese, R. J. (1975). Some explorations in initial interaction and beyond: A developmental theory of interpersonal communication. *Human Communication Research, 1,* 99–112.

Brydon, S. R., & Scott, M. D. (1994). *Between one and many: The art and science of public speaking.* Mountain View, CA: Mayfield Publishing Co.

CLIMB Professional Development and Training (2017, July). 10 top skills that employers are looking for in employees (2017 edition). Retrieved from http://climb.pcc.edu/blog/10-top-skills-that-employers-are-looking-for-in-employees-2017-edition

Cronen, V. E., Chen, V., & Pearce, W. B. (1988). Coordinated management of meaning: A critical theory. In Y. Y. Kim and W. B. Gudykunst (Eds.), *Theories in intercultural communication* (pp. 66–98). Newbury Park, CA: Sage Publications.

DeVito, J. (2014). *Essentials of human communication* (8th ed.). Boston, MA: Pearson.

Fox, M. V. (1983). Ancient Egyptian rhetoric. *Rhetorica, 1*(1), 9–22.

Gray, G. W. (1946). The 'precepts of Kagemni and Ptah-hotep.' *The Quarterly Journal of Speech, 32*(4), 446–454.

Hutto, D. (2002). Ancient Egyptian rhetoric in the Old and Middle Kingdoms. *Rhetorica, 20*(3), 213–233.

Jaffe, C. (2010). *Public speaking: Concepts and skills for a diverse society* (6th ed.). Boston, MA: Wadsworth Cengage Learning.

The Latin Library. (2010). *Quintillian Institutio Oratoria XII.* Retrieved from http://www.thelatinlibrary.com/quintilian/quintilian.institutio12.shtml

Lindsey, A. E. (2016). What is communication? In G. G. Armfield & E. L. Morgan (Eds.), *Human communication in action* (6th ed., pp. 3–16). Dubuque, IA: Kendall Hunt Publishing.

National Communication Association. (2019). What is communication? Retrieved from https://www.natcom.org/about-nca/what-communication

Omoth, T. (2017). The top 5 job skills that employers are looking for in 2017. Retrieved from https://www.topresume.com/career-advice/the-top-5-job-skills-that-employers-are-looking-for-in-2017

Pearce, W. B. (2007). *Making social worlds: A communication perspective.* Malden, MA: Blackwell Publishing.

Pittenger, R. E., Hockett, C. F., & Danehy, J. J. (1960). *The first five minutes.* Ithaca, NY: Paul Martineau.

Remer, G. (2009). Rhetoric as a balancing of ends: Cicero and Machiavelli. *Philosophy and Rhetoric, 42*(1), 1–28.

Shannon, C. E., & Weaver, W. (1948). *A mathematical theory of communication.* Urbana, IL: The University of Illinois Press.

Smith, B. (1921). Corax and probability. *The Quarterly Journal of Speech, 7*(1), 13–42.

Steinberg, S. (2017, February). 2017 job trends: 15 skills employers are now looking for. *Parade Magazine.* Retrieved from https://parade.com/538769/scott_steinberg/2017-job-trends-15-skills-employers-are-now-looking-for/

Sutton, E. W. (1942). *Cicero in twenty-eight volumes. De Oratore.* Cambridge, MA: Harvard University Press.

Watzlawick, P., Beavin, J., & Jackson, D. D. (1967). *Pragmatics of human communication: A study of interactional patterns, pathologies, and paradoxes.* New York: Norton.

Verbal Communication: Types and Characteristics

Eric L. Morgan

Objectives

▶ Define verbal communication.
▶ Gain familiarity with different types of verbal communication.
▶ Characterize and describe the building blocks of language.
▶ Apply concepts of verbal communication to experiences with language.

When most people think of communication, in general, they normally think of aspects of verbal communication. It should be stated though that verbal communication is by no means the only type of communication in which we engage, nor is it even the most common type of communication in which we engage. However, that said, for many people, verbal communication represents an important type of communication. This section is devoted to exploring the various features and functions of verbal communication with special attention paid to language. I will first discuss what verbal communication is and what characterizes this type of communication. This will be followed by a discussion of how language functions in our lives.

WHAT IS VERBAL COMMUNICATION?

Defining verbal communication is actually quite simple. We will use the following easy definition: verbal communication is our use of symbols. To understand what this means, we should define what a symbol is. Simply stated, a symbol is anything that stands for something else. Symbols are important for understanding communication in general. We will come back to them later in this section and in the book. It's likely that you can come up with a number of examples of symbols. Flags of nations are good examples. A flag is normally a piece of cloth with some sort of design on it. However, a community of people have agreed that the piece of cloth in question will stand for the country. Engagement and wedding rings are also good examples of symbols. Take the engagement ring for instance. Throughout much of the United States, as well as in other parts of the world, the intention to marry is symbolized by a rock. Words, be they written, spoken, or signed, are also symbols. If I say the word communication, that sound invokes within you a sense of something. The sounds that make up the word communication, at least in English, strung together in that order come to stand

VERBAL COMMUNICATION

our use of symbols to generate meaning.

SYMBOL

anything that represents something else. It is arbitrary yet conventional.

for something else. What those sounds stand for is the subject of this book and of the course you are taking. So, in sum, verbal communication is our use of symbols and symbols are things that represent other things. Easy, right? Well, what those symbols stand for and how symbols come to stand for the things they do is not simple at all. It is a process that leads us to two important characteristics of symbols.

Communication scholar Brad Hall (2005) states that symbols are both arbitrary and conventional. The term arbitrary refers to the relationship that symbols have with the things they represent. More specifically, it means that symbols do not have a natural relationship with the things they represent. In other words, there is no natural or physical reason that any one symbol must represent the thing that it does. Rather, this relationship is established by agreement within communities. A good way to demonstrate the arbitrariness of symbols is to look across languages. Take, for instance, the word "table" in English. In Spanish, the word used to refer to the same thing is *mesa*. These two words are not related. They don't look or sound anything alike, yet they stand for the same thing. The point is that there is no natural reason that a flat surface normally with legs of some sort used for eating upon or placing things upon must be called a table or mesa. Rather, English speakers and Spanish speakers agree within their respective linguistic communities that this is what these sounds will mean. This brings us to the next point, which is that symbols are conventional. This means that while there is no natural agreement, any one individual within a language community cannot simply go about assigning new meanings to words or make up new words to refer to things that the community has already agreed upon. To demonstrate this point, one could simply choose to call boys "girls" and girls "boys" for a day. It's likely that this would create a lot of confusion because that would violate the language community's "agreement."

TYPES OF VERBAL COMMUNICATION

To gain a better sense of what constitutes verbal communication, it will be useful to discuss different types of verbal communication. To do this, we turn to communication scholar Robbin Crabtree (personal communication) for assistance. She argues that we can divide communication behavior along certain dimensions. The first dimension is whether communication is verbal or nonverbal. Nonverbal communication will be discussed in Section Four of this unit. As we established in the previous section, verbal communication systems use symbols. Nonverbal communication systems do not. Nonverbal communication also exhibits other characteristics, which we will not get into here. However, if we see a type of communication behavior in which symbols are being used, then we know we are dealing with verbal communication. We know, however, that there are numerous ways people can go about using symbols. So, our next question will be whether or not the vocal apparatus of humans is being used to produce these symbols. Thus, we have a vocal/nonvocal dimension. The grid in Figure 1.2 shows us four categories for thinking about types of communication behavior. In this section, we will deal with verbal and vocal communication as well as verbal and nonvocal communication.

If you think carefully, you'll realize that many of us use verbal and vocal communication all the time. Indeed there is only one type of communication behavior that fits this category, and that is speaking. In fact, in this category, we are only concerned with the words that people form when they are speaking. Everything else we do with our voice is actually a part of nonverbal communication.

Figure **1.2**

	VERBAL	**NONVERBAL**
VOCAL	Speaking	Paralanguage (Vocalics)
NONVOCAL	Writing Sign Language(s) Emblems	Appearance Facial Communication Kinesics Proxemics Haptics Olfactics Chronemics Silence

The verbal/nonvocal category embodies three types of behavior. The first is something you are also quite familiar with—writing. Often, people assume that because writing does not use the voice, it is not verbal communication. However, writing clearly uses symbols, so it is a type of verbal communication. Writing is interesting in that it seeks to represent spoken language, but it can only do so in an imperfect fashion. You might experience this problem when you try to e-mail somebody and express frustration. While we have words to write that can approach this expression, we lack, in large part, the nonverbal component that expresses emotion. For writing to work, it requires a visual representation of language. This is known as an **orthography**. Any orthography simply summarizes spoken language. For instance, you know that there are 26 letters in the English alphabet. Does that mean that there are only 26 sounds in the English language? The answer, of course, is no. Rather, when we write we combine those 26 letters that represent some sounds to represent most of what we can say.

The second type of communication behavior that falls into the verbal/nonvocal category is a special type of gesture known as an **emblem**. These gestures have direct translations into a linguistic system. For example, among many U.S. American English speakers, holding one's index finger and middle finger up with the palm facing outward translates directly to "peace." Why is this the case? Well, who knows why? It's a symbol and thus arbitrary. In fact, not too long ago this gesture more commonly represented victory. Particularly, victory in World War II. Thus, we see that this gesture is functioning symbolically and is therefore a type of verbal communication. Another example that many people are familiar with can be described in a bumper sticker I recently saw. This bumper sticker read, "Horn broken, watch for finger." The finger in question is likely the middle finger held extended. I'll trust that you know what this refers to and leave it at that. The more interesting question is how I knew which finger (and therefore which gesture) was being referenced in this bumper sticker. The reason is because I'm a member of the linguistic community that shares a conventional meaning for this emblem.

The third type of communication behavior that can be described as both verbal and nonvocal is sign language. Sign language is used by many people, but it is mostly associated with those who are deaf or hard of hearing. I should state at the outset here that there are many sign languages. One common misconception is that there is a single universal sign language that all deaf and hard of hearing people use throughout the world. This is not the case at all. The most commonly used form of sign language in the United States is American Sign Language (ASL). However, there are other

ORTHOGRAPHY

a spelling system used to represent a language.

EMBLEM

a gesture that has a direct translation.

forms used throughout the United States as well such as Signed English or Pidgin Signed English. American Sign Language, as it is practiced today, is related to French Sign Language with approximately 60% of all American signs tracing their origin to French signs (Gannon, 1981). The reason for this has to do with the history of deaf education in the United States. Two individuals in particular—Laurent Clerc and the Reverend Thomas H. Gallaudet—were instrumental in shaping deaf education and, thus, American Sign Language. Clerc taught deaf children in France and was himself deaf. Gallaudet was not deaf, but because of personal history desired to start a school for the deaf in America. Gallaudet traveled to France where he met and became good friends with Clerc. He convinced Clerc to travel back to America to help found the first school for deaf Americans in Hartford, Connecticut. It's likely that Clerc, Gallaudet, and the other teachers at this school combined formalized French signs with already existing American signs. This system of sign language spread to other schools for the deaf and hard of hearing and became known as American Sign Language (Gannon, 1981). While there were concerted efforts to suppress this language, American Sign Language has persisted and is a fully functional linguistic system.

CHARACTERISTICS OF VERBAL COMMUNICATION

Now that we've determined what constitutes verbal communication, we can further our understanding of this form of communication by examining what characterizes it. While any one system of verbal communication will be characterized by numerous features, there are several characteristics that cut across all systems. Linguistic anthropologist Dell Hymes (1962) once wrote that in considering all language systems, three assumptions can be made to help us better understand them. The first assumption is that language systems are structured or patterned in specific ways. This allows much larger numbers of people to communicate than would normally be the case without it. It also allows us to study these systems over time (called diachronic analysis) and to determine how the systems are constructed (called synchronic analysis). This study leads us to a better understanding of communication and increased effectiveness. The second assumption to be made is that these systems are diverse. By this, Hymes draws our attention to the many different methods humans have created to accomplish this feat of verbal communication. The diversity assumption also shows us that the manners in which people use language create distinct social worlds. Finally, Hymes notes that all linguistic systems are social. There are two dimensions to this last one, which is perhaps the most important. The first is that verbal communication systems are used to create social bonds between people. Indeed without communication, we would not have the relationships we do. The second is that verbal communication systems are products of social agreement. Recall the discussion of symbols being conventional. For symbols to work, there needs to be some degree of agreement about meaning among community members. These three broad assumptions start us down the path to a deeper understanding of verbal communication; however, they are not the only understandings to be had. In fact, there are a number of other characteristics that all verbal communication systems share. Four of these characteristics (structure, displacement, self-reflexivity, and context) will be discussed in turn.

Structure of Verbal Communication

All verbal communication systems, as symbolic systems, are structured. We knew this already from Hymes, but the question of how these systems are structured still remains. Linguists, linguistic anthropologists, and communication scholars have a variety of ways to discuss this structure. One helpful way to understand this is through the concept of rules. Verbal communication structure is governed by sets of rules that all language users know and share. There are rules that tell us how to string words together, rules that tell us how to change verbs so that they agree with their subjects (a process called conjugation), even rules that tell us how to refer to more than one thing at a time (i.e., forming plurals). These rules of grammar are called **syntactic rules**. Rules that tell us what certain words and combinations of sounds mean are called **semantic rules**. The most basic rules guiding the structure of verbal communication system, though, are called **phonological rules** (Adler & Rodman, 2006). They tell us how to string certain sounds together. For example, in English, only certain sounds can be placed together to form a sound that other English speakers will understand as meaningful. The sound represented by an s can be combined with quite a few other sounds in English, such as those represented by c, h, l, m, n, p, qu, t, w, or any vowel. It cannot, however, be combined with sounds like "b," or "z." These basic sounds that comprise a language are known as **phonemes**. Phonemes actually are the smallest unit of potentially meaningful sound in a particular language. They do not, however, carry meaning on their own. Humans are capable of producing all sorts of sounds when speaking a language; however, only a certain set of these sounds will be used to produce a specific language. English, for example, uses approximately 44 different phonemes when spoken. I say approximately because of variation in accents. Some languages use far more phonemes than 44 (such as the Xhosan languages spoken in Southern Africa) and some use far less than 44 (such as Hawaiian). I should state here that although there are differences in the number of phonemes used to produce language, all languages are equally complex, a point we will return to later in this section.

It doesn't matter which language is at issue, all phonemes are combined to produce units of meaning in a language. The smallest unit of meaning in a language is known as a **morpheme**. Sometimes a single word is a morpheme, and sometimes a single word has more than one morpheme. As mentioned before, the rules guiding the production of meaning through morphemes are known as semantic rules. One common morphemic combination in English occurs when we form plurals. For example, I can say the word "elephant." This word represents only one morpheme. If I wanted to refer to more than one elephant, I would need to add an s, thereby creating elephants. The *s* in this sense carries the meaning, "more than one of." The problem though is that the s can't stand on its own as meaningful, so where does that leave us with morphemes? Well, in this case the "s" represents what is called a bounded morpheme. In other words, the "s" is a morpheme that only becomes a morpheme when bounded to a regular morpheme. One-word morphemes are relatively common in English. Other languages, like Inuktitut (spoken among the Inuit) or German, string morphemes together much more readily.

People who are learning languages often learn these three types of rules first as they are the most basic. However, no language exists outside of its usage by people, and another set of rules guides this practice. These are known as pragmatic rules, and they guide the appropriate use of speech. For example, in the informal use of American English, one might say to another, "What's up?" From a pragmatic standpoint, the other person, provided they share the same system of rules, knows that this question is not to be taken literally. Rather, the person will hear that phrase as a request for information about his or her well-being and activity. More often than not, the response will be "not much." From a literal standpoint, this exchange doesn't make

SYNTACTIC RULES

Rules of grammar and structure.

SEMANTIC RULES

Rules that guide meaning.

PHONOLOGICAL RULES

Rules that guide how sounds are put together in a meaningful way.

PHONEME

the smallest unit of potentially meaningful sound in a language.

MORPHEME

smallest unit of meaning in a language.

a lot of sense. There are, of course, lots of things that are "up" from the speakers. The speakers though are engaging in a type of verbal communication that, if they know the correct rules, is accomplishing the social function of greeting.

Verbal Communication Exhibits Displacement

In discussing this characteristic, scholars will often simply say that language is abstract (Drake, 2007); however, using the term displacement tells us how language is abstract. This characteristic of verbal communication is a consequence of symbol usage. Recall that symbols stand for other things. Because of this, we can talk about things that are "not here" and "not now." This is a distinguishing characteristic between verbal communication and nonverbal communication. Nonverbal communication refers to all the different types of communication that are not linguistic (or symbolic) in nature. The different types, many of which will be discussed in a following section, are listed in Figure 1.2. Because we can use symbols to refer to things that are not physically or temporally present, we can use them to refer to abstract ideas. Thus, our ability to discuss ideas such as "freedom" or "liberty" or "spirituality" is a direct result of this characteristic of verbal communication.

Verbal Communication Is Self-Reflexive

Similar to the previous characteristic, this refers to verbal communication's ability to refer to itself. In this way, verbal communication "reflects" itself. Why is this important? Probably the most important reason is that, through self-reflection, verbal communication creates social worlds and social realities. For example, have you ever been part of a conversation that begins with one person saying, "We need to talk." Because of the pragmatic rules of communication, many speakers of American English know that this phrase will create a context in which a relationship or another weighty issue will be discussed. So, using communication to refer to communication creates a context that is important for many people. We can also view this characteristic in another sense. Any time we use verbal communication, we reflect ourselves. For example, if I have a conversation about sports with a friend, then I am reflecting an aspect of my identity as a "sports fan."

Verbal Communication Is Contextual

Earlier, I mentioned that language is always used in particular contexts. It is these contexts that give us clues as to meaning. Meaning is never fully carried in just the words used, but is also a product of features of the context. For example, I may have a conversation with a friend in which the friend is telling me an unbelievable story. At the end of the story, I may utter the phrase, "Get out of town!" Because of the context, the friend will likely hear this as a simple statement of surprise and not an actual demand for the friend to leave town. The context of the conversation provided this sense of meaning. In the first section of this unit, we describe different types of contexts that impact communication. These contexts work together to provide us with a sense of meaning concerning verbal communication.

CONCLUSION

In summary, verbal communication can be defined as "our use of symbols." Symbols are defined as anything that represents something else. They are both arbitrary, yet conventional. Symbolic systems (i.e., verbal communication systems) such as language exhibit a number of distinguishing characteristics. We know, for instance, that these systems are diverse and thus function to create diverse social worlds. We know that they are structured and patterned through a number of types of rules. We also know now that these systems are productive through their complexity and that they exhibit displacement and are self-reflexive. Now it is time to turn our attention to how these systems function in our daily lives. Before that, though, let's take a brief tour through languages of the world.

A LANGUAGE INTERLUDE

How many languages are spoken in the world today? This is an interesting question for a number of reasons, not the least of which is the further question, "What counts as a language?" Putting aside that debate for the time being, scholars estimate that there are approximately 6,500 languages left in the world today (Gordon, 2005). This sounds like a lot, but in fact this number is continually shrinking. Some historical linguists believe that there may have once been close to 10,000 languages spoken. There are many reasons why languages die out, and with each loss comes a loss of an incredibly complex (see previous section) system for organizing human experience. We will not dwell here on the death of language, but for further reading on the matter, Mark Abley's (2003) book *Spoken Here: Travels Among Threatened Languages* is an easy-to-read and useful treatment of the subject.

Of the 6,500 languages left, what is the most commonly spoken language? The answer coincides with the most populated country on earth, China. Mandarin Chinese is spoken by about one in seven people on earth. While English is spreading quite rapidly due to its status as a language of commerce, only about one third of the number of people that speak Mandarin speak English as their first language. Even then, English only comes in at about the third or fourth most commonly spoken language in the world. Spanish has about an equal number of speakers (Ash, 2003). So, what's the second most commonly spoken language in the world? This is where the problem of what counts as a language comes into play. Ash states that it is Hindustani, which refers to both Hindi and Urdu. Some speakers of Hindi and of Urdu can understand much of what the other is saying, but in Pakistan it is written in modified Arabic script while in India it is written in Devanagari script. So does that mean it is two different languages? That's a debate for scholars to have. The important thing is that a large number of people use this linguistic system. Rounding out the 10 most commonly spoken languages are English, Spanish, Bengali, Arabic, Portuguese, Russian, Japanese, and German. What's interesting about this is that about half of the world's population speaks one of these languages natively. That means that the other 6,490 languages are spoken by the other half of the world's population. Certainly there are other languages with large numbers of speakers, like French or Malay or Thai. That means that the vast majority of languages are spoken by relatively few people. In some places, this makes for quite a linguistically diverse climate. For example, in the highlands of Papua New Guinea an estimated 892 different languages are spoken although the population is only 3.9 million (Anderson, 2008).

1. How many different languages do you encounter in your day-to-day activities? What are they? Are you able to communicate a few phrases in all these languages?

2. Consider the section on phonemes and morphemes. Research a language that you do not speak, and try to produce sounds that are not part of your normal language use. How difficult was this to do? Why do you think that is?

Abley, M. (2003). *Spoken here: Travels among threatened languages.* Boston, MA: Houghton Mifflin.

Adler, R. B., & Rodman, G. (2006). *Understanding human communication* (9th ed.). New York: Oxford University Press.

Anderson, S. R. (2008). How many languages are there in the world? Linguistic Society of America. Retrieved from http://www.lsadc.org/info/ling-faqs-howmany.cfm

Ash, R. (2003). *The top 10 of everything 2004.* London: DK Publishing.

Drake, L. E. (2007). Language and meaning. In E. Morgan & A. E. Lindsey (Eds.), *Principle and practice in human communication: A reader and workbook for COMM 265.* Dubuque, IA: Kendall Hunt Publishing.

Gannon, J. R. (1981). Deaf heritage: A narrative history of deaf America. Silver Spring, MD: National Association of the Deaf.

Gordon, R. J. (Ed.). (2005). *Ethnologue: Languages of the world* (15th ed.). Dallas, TX: SIL International.

Hall, B. J. (2005). Among cultures: The challenge of communication. Belmont, CA: Wadsworth Cengage.

Hymes, D. (1962). The ethnography of speaking. In T. Gladwin and W. Sturtevant (Eds.), Anthropology and human behavior. Washington, DC: Anthropological Society of Washington.

Verbal Communication: Functions

Eric L. Morgan

Objectives

- ▶ Characterize different functions of verbal communication.
- ▶ Apply concepts of verbal communication to lived experiences of identity.
- ▶ Describe linguistic relativity.

FUNCTIONS OF VERBAL COMMUNICATION

One way we can better understand verbal communication systems is to understand how we use them. This is known as a functional approach. Most scholars of language would agree that people use language to accomplish certain things. In fact, there was an entire school of linguistics, known as the Prague School, devoted to studying language from the perspective of how language functions. We will discuss three primary functions of language. In short, we use language (1) to refer to the world around us, (2) to create and maintain groups, and (3) to influence thought.

The Referential Function

It seems rather obvious to state that we use language to refer to the world. For instance, I can point to a chair and say "chair." Voilà, I have just used language to reference the world. However, as with most things, this seemingly simple act can become quite complex when we think about how this referencing gets done. This process of referencing is called **signification**. Colapietro (1993) defines signification as "the process by which signs and therefore meaning are generated or produced" (p. 181). Entire bodies of scholarly work, philosophies, theories, and literatures have been devoted to understanding how it is that humans do this. To keep things simple, I'll rely mostly on the ideas of the famous Swiss linguist, Ferdinand Saussure (1986). [A quick note about Saussure—Ferdinand Saussure was actually a historical and structural linguist (Sampson, 1980). His ideas are being presented here to show how language functions to reference the world. His *Course in General Linguistics* is actually a compilation of his notes put together by former students after his death in 1913.]

SIGNIFICATION

the process by which signs are produced, thereby generating meaning.

SIGN

the whole that is made up of the signifier and the signified.

DENOTATION

the most commonly held meaning of a sign in a linguistic community.

CONNOTATION

meaning generated from people's association with a particular sign, often emotionally charged.

The basic unit of concern within signification is the **sign**. A sign is basically a relationship between two other concepts, the signifier and the signified. The signifier is the expression of the sign. So, the word dog, for instance, is a signifier. It signifies the signified. Now, it's commonly heard that the signified is the thing in the world to which the signifier refers. This is actually not the case. Rather, the signified is the concept of the thing in the world. So, when I say "dog," I'm actually signifying the concept of a dog, not the actual furry creature itself. In essence, the sign is a three-part relationship among the signifier, the signified, and the object (see Figure 1.3).

This basic signification process is how we use language to refer to the world. It is the basic building block for creating meaning. When we wonder what words mean, we are concerned with the signifier/signified relationship. This meaning, though, can occur at a number of levels. Linguists typically discuss two types of meaning—denotation and connotation. **Denotation** refers to the most commonly held meaning for a particular sign. For example, when I utter the word cat, I can be fairly confident that the large majority of English speakers will know to what that word refers. Occasionally, people will say that denotation refers to the dictionary meaning of a word. This is only correct to the extent that dictionaries are books that document the most commonly held meanings of words. Another type of meaning is known as connotation. **Connotation** is the meaning of signs that comes from our personal experiences with the phenomenon or even with the sign itself. Often, connotative meaning is described as a personal meaning. Connotative meaning can be described using the notion of a semantic differential (Osgood, May, & Miron, 1975). Osgood and his colleagues were psychologists who researched the meaning of symbols across cultures. Osgood was interested in determining if there were any meanings that were universal across all cultures. He found that there seems to be three dimensions of meanings that all people use in developing connotative meaning—an evaluative dimension, a potency dimension, and an activity dimension. Given a particular sign, people will evaluate the meaning as good or bad, determine how potent the sign is in terms of how strong or weak it is, and determine how active the sign is in terms of whether it is slow or fast. Generally speaking, these dimensions can be applied to any phenomenon as a way to characterize connotation. Connotation, however, is broader than these three dimensions and is perhaps more easily understood as how we make personal sense of a sign.

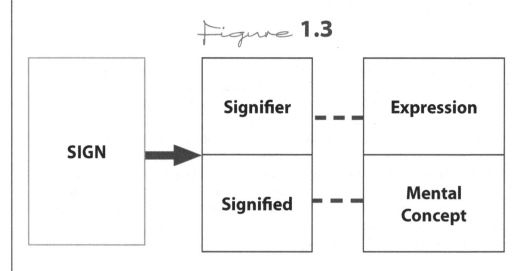

Figure **1.3**

The Group Creation and Maintenance Function

We use language to create and maintain the groups to which we belong. These groups are important to us for a number of reasons. They provide a mechanism of social support, a sense of belonging, and they give us a sense of our identity. All such groups, however, are a product of the ways people communicate them into existence. Group members are group members to the extent that they know the appropriate use of language for a particular group. As an example, try this exercise. Think of any group to which you belong. Now, think about how the communication you use within that group is different from any other group to which you belong. You'll likely find striking differences across all your group memberships. If you are a member of a religious group, then that group will likely use language not found in your school study groups. Naturally, there will be some overlap, but these specific ways of communicating, in a sense, create the groups in the first place.

We have a number of terms to describe the specialized vocabularies found in groups. A term that you may be familiar with is jargon. **Jargon** is a specialized vocabulary associated with a particular profession. For example, doctors use a particular vocabulary that others in the medical profession know. Because of this, they are able to accomplish their role as doctor. Lawyers speak "legalese," educators have their IEPs, engineers have their thermal dynamics, broadcast journalists have their CG's and b-roll, and so forth. Any profession will have a jargon associated with it, and one's success at that profession is dependent, in part, on mastering that jargon. Another term with which you might be familiar is slang. **Slang** refers to a common form of language used by any group as it differs from the formal version of the language. Everyone uses slang, and everyone uses different types of slang. One way to demonstrate this is to consider how one uses language differently between family members and peer group members. Ask yourself this simple question, "Do you talk the same way to your friends as you do to an elderly relative?" Perhaps some of you do, but I would suspect that, for the majority, this is not the case. Both types of language use can be considered slang, but they mark the groups differently. More specifically, the difference used here could be considered one of register. **Register**, in this sense, refers to the level of formality within a language. A third type of language to consider here is argot. **Argot** refers to a highly specialized and often secret language. It functions the same way slang and jargon do, but in specific contexts. For example, groups that regulate their membership to a large degree will sometimes use special words that only members are allowed to know. This has two consequences. It excludes non-members from the group based on linguistic knowledge, and it strengthens the group from the member's standpoint.

Finally, within this category of types of language are dialect and accent. Dialect refers to a way of using language including colloquialisms, euphemisms, and other turns of phrase that are shared by a relatively large community of language users. The differences between American English and British English are often ones of dialect. The differences are not so great that Americans and Britons cannot understand one another, but there are distinct differences in the way language is used. This example also serves to illustrate accent. Accent refers to the pronunciation of a language. Clearly, Americans and Britons differ in how the English language is spoken. Southerners in the United States are often said to speak with a "drawl" or a "twang." These are accent differences. The turns of phrase that are used in certain parts of the United States, but not in others, could be said to be differences in dialect. The point, though, is that when people use dialects they are marking themselves as a member of a certain group.

JARGON

a specialized vocabulary associated with a profession.

SLANG

an informal use of language.

REGISTER

the level of formality of language as it is spoken.

ARGOT

a highly specialized and often secret language.

Language and Identity

IDENTITY

how we see ourselves in relation to others; self-construal.

AVOWAL

who we say we are.

ASCRIPTION

who others say we are.

This function of verbal communication leads us to consider the relationship of language to our identities. **Identity** basically refers to how we see ourselves in relation to others. It is a concept that scholars have studied a great deal. While there are numerous approaches to the study of identity, the one we will discuss here is a communicative approach (Carbaugh, 1996; Collier & Thomas, 1988; Hall, Covarrubias, & Kirschbaum, 2018). Identity from this standpoint is viewed as an outcome of communication. In other words, we are who we are because of how we communicate with others. A few concepts may help us to get a better sense of this perspective. Two processes are associated with the communication of identity. First is the process of **avowal**. This is basically who I say I am. Second is the process of **ascription**. This is basically who you say I am. Sometimes these coincide, but other times they do not. For example, I can avow that I am a professor, but to actually hold that identity in a meaningful way in society, others would have to ascribe that same identity to me. Luckily they do. As I mentioned, there are times when who we say we are does not coincide with who others say we are. It's at these moments that we must negotiate our identities through communication. One interesting example of how the interplay of avowal and ascription works comes in the form of the self-fulfilling prophecy. Take my sister for example. As an elementary and secondary education student, she was consistently told that she was bad at math. Over time, she came to believe this about herself, and this became a part of her identity. Because people told her she was bad at math, conditions were created in which she could perform "being bad at math." She is, however, not bad at math. In fact, I have witnessed her provide mathematical help to her children in ways that are effective, productive, and quite insightful. To this day, though, if you asked her, she would still say she that she is bad at math. This can be quite frustrating from an educator's standpoint. A lot of students believe that they are bad at something, and because of this belief they enact being bad at whatever it is. The point here is that our identities come about from the interactions we have with other people.

Let's extend this notion a bit further. I mentioned in the previous paragraph that I am a professor and that others ascribed this identity to me. While this is the case, I can't simply stop there. Rather, I have to continually perform the role of being a professor for people to keep ascribing me this identity. This is known as role performance (Hall, 2005). But what is it that I am performing? In order to successfully perform the role of professor, I need to understand what society expects of professors and act accordingly. This role, then, has a set of role expectations (Hall, 2005). So, to perform appropriately the role of professor, I need to do things like teach classes, research, write, lecture, advise, serve on committees, and so forth. If I do not fulfill these expectations, then I will be performing the role of professor poorly, and it is likely that I wouldn't be able to claim this identity for very long.

The relation of language use to identity is a complex one. I've been discussing an occupational identity with the professor example. We have numerous other identities as well. In fact, we can divide all of our identities (all of which are a product of communication) into three levels: personal, relational, and communal (Hall, Covarrubias, et al., 2005). The personal level of identity is how we and others see ourselves as individuals. You may think of yourself as an outgoing person. This distinguishes you, in part, from other people, yet it also requires others to help create the situations for you to be outgoing. You also need to understand what it means to be outgoing in a particular culture (role expectations) and to be able to act in an outgoing manner (role performance). The relational level of identity refers to the identities we have that are defined by relations. Previously, I mentioned my biological sister. This is a relational identity in that one can only be a biological sister if one has a sibling. Thus, the identity is defined in terms of the relationship. Once again, what it means to hold this identity will vary across cultures and is a product of our communication. Finally, a communal identity is one that is held in common with a large number of people. One's nationality or religious affiliation is a good example of this level of identity. Now that we know how language is related to the creation of groups, let's turn to an interesting function and debate.

The Influencing Thought Function

If you were to survey the history of linguistics, you would find that a large number of scholars were somewhat preoccupied by a particular relationship. This relationship is between thought and language. We call this relationship **linguistic relativity** (LR). Because I, like many others, have found this idea particularly intriguing, what follows is a somewhat lengthy discussion of this novel idea.

LINGUISTIC RELATIVITY

the idea that language, through habitual use, will predispose us to perceive the world in particular ways.

Linguistic relativity can be summarized by stating that diverse languages affect the thought(s) of their speakers (Lucy, 1992). More specifically, it is the idea that the languages we speak predispose us, through habitual use, to perceive the world in a particular way (Whorf, 1956/1997). This idea is quite often referred to as the Sapir-Whorf Hypothesis, a term that is highly misleading. Furthermore, scholars will often write about a strong version of the hypothesis and a weak version of the hypothesis. The strong version is that languages determine how we think. So, because I'm an English speaker, I will think like other English speakers. The weak version is that languages influence and shape our thoughts, but do not necessarily determine our thoughts. Linguistic relativity is actually much closer to the "weak" version, at least as it was conceived by Sapir and Whorf. To gain some clarity, let's explore the development of this idea.

The Development of Linguistic Relativity

Various scholars (Gumperz & Levinson, 1996; Kaye, 1997; Lucy, 1992) attribute the origins of linguistic relativity to a variety of philosophers from the early and middle part of the 19th century. Among these philosophers are Herder, Hume, and von Humboldt. Linguistic relativity is particularly resonant for von Humboldt, who was primarily concerned with issues of nationalism and how people formed themselves into "nations." Von Humboldt (1988) came to the conclusion that a people and their language were inseparable, and consequently that their language and psychic characteristics were equally inseparable. As such, it might better be said that "linguistic determinacy" is particularly resonant for von Humboldt. Indeed, in the seventh chapter of his work titled *On Language*, von Humboldt argues that the minds of a people are completely inseparable from the languages they speak. He further explains that the spirit of a people is manifest in their language so that the "spirit" of a language will most certainly be part and parcel of a speaker's spirit. Von Humboldt ultimately argues that thought is formed of language. His formulation of linguistic relativity is of a particularly strong bent, arguing that language determines thought. Because language plays this deterministic role, it could be said that speakers of the same language essentially think the same. Therefore, for von Humboldt, it was possible to locate the various "nations" of the world by the variety of languages spoken. His argument in summary: One language → one system of thought → one people. This is a highly problematic assertion, particularly in today's world; however, the point is not to take issue with von Humboldt's hierarchy of language, but to rather suggest that it is with him that linguistic relativity gains a solid foothold in the overall scheme of philosophical thought. Indeed, this idea that language and thought, while not being the same thing, could also not be separated, enjoyed much currency in philosophical circles (Wittgenstein, 1972). It was, however, never really developed through empirical study until it came to the shores of the United States with Franz Boas.

Franz Boas is often credited with founding the field of anthropology in its current four-part manifestation. Indeed he has done work in each of the subfields—physical, social/cultural, linguistic, archaeology—except for archaeology. Many of his students came to be the primary movers and shakers in anthropology. They included Ruth Benedict, Margaret Mead, and Edward Sapir to name but a few. Needless to say, the influence of Boas was quite profound. In his most cited linguistic work, *Introduction to the Handbook of Native American Languages*, Boas (1911/1991) lays out his approach to culture and language. He even tackles language and thought. Boas was not nearly the linguistic determinist that von Humboldt was. Indeed, he remained skeptical of even highly qualified linguistic relative positions until his death (Lucy, 1992). That said, the claims he advanced regarding the study of ethnolinguistics had a profound impact on Edward Sapir who would later treat linguistic relativity more systematically. In his work, Boas describes a framework (providing examples from many Native American languages) of how to conduct ethnolinguistic studies. This framework allows him to begin to consider the relationship among language, culture, and thought. For Boas, it was clear that languages classify our sensory experiences. In other words, a person's sensual experience of something is categorized by the language we speak. From this, it follows that different languages categorize different experiences differently. This is obvious if languages are taken to be structurally different in form and meaning, a point made more strongly by Sapir (1949). A third observation made by Boas was that language, unlike other ethnological phenomena, rarely rises to the level of consciousness. The importance of this idea is that classifications of experience based on language are almost always covert, and, as such, do not allow for much secondary interpretation. The linguistic classification of the world, then, will be seen by speakers of a particular language as natural, a point considered by Whorf (1956/1997). Boas did not take language to be formative of thought as von Humboldt did. In fact, he merely suggested that language reflected the psychic lives of people. Thus, through the study of language, it becomes possible to examine the psychology of a people. These ideas were further developed by his pupil, Edward Sapir.

Most linguists today, even those who are skeptical of linguistic relativity, believe that Sapir was a genius when it came to linguistic description. Indeed Sapir is probably responsible for the shape that most linguistic anthropological studies take. One key addition that Sapir made to the arguments of Boas was in regard to the structure of language. For instance, Sapir argued simply that languages formed formal oppositions and that this indicated a distinction in meaning (Mandelbaum, 1984). This characterization of language immediately conjoins form and meaning. Thus, it is easy to suggest that the languages people speak, because they differ in form, will lead to differences in meaning. Sapir also proposed that language did not merely reflect the thought of its speaker, but rather began to shape that thought as well. Given this, culture began to play a larger role in the relationship between language and thought. Lucy (1992) argues that while Sapir began to approach the idea that language influenced thought and that language could influence culture, he ultimately believed much as his esteemed mentor did—that language was affected by cultural processes more than vice versa. This, however, may not be the case. In the introduction to his book *Language: An Introduction to the Study of Speech*, Sapir (1949) argues that he is "inclined to believe that [language] antedated even the lowliest developments of material culture, that these developments, in fact, were not strictly possible until language, the tool of significant expression had itself taken shape" (p. 23).

In this passage, Sapir argues a position that not only approaches the linguisticality of thought, but clearly states his attitude toward the influence of language on culture. This position can be further seen in the following famous quote (thanks to Whorf):

> Language is a guide to 'social reality.' . . . [Language] powerfully conditions all our thinking about social problems and processes. Human beings do not live in the objective world alone, nor alone in the world of social activity as ordinarily understood, but are very much at the mercy of the particular language which has become the medium of expression for their society. It is quite an illusion to imagine that one adjusts to reality essentially without the use of language and that language is merely an incidental means of solving specific problems of communication or reflection. The fact of the matter is that the "real world" is to a large extent unconsciously built upon the language habits of the group . . . We see and hear and otherwise experience very largely as we do because the language habits of our community predispose certain choices of interpretation (Sapir, 1949/1984, p. 162).

This frequently cited passage suggests that people do not live in reality outside of language. Therefore, the languages we speak clearly have an influence on the way we go about constructing that social world. As such, Sapir argues, language can be seen as a "guide to social reality." If language is a guide, and if Sapir is to remain consistent with his idea that formal distinctions in language lead to formal distinctions in meaning, then language must have some sort of formative influence on culture. This is the case particularly if we are to take culture to be located in and accessible through symbolic practice (Geertz, 1973; Schneider, 1976; see also Sections 6 through 8 of this unit). Sapir's influence in this area is certainly great. His linguistic studies of Native American languages lend general empirical support to some versions of linguistic relativity. Unfortunately, Sapir stopped short of working through this concept in its entirety. It is interesting to consider what would have happened if circumstances had allowed the relationship between Sapir and one of his students to develop further in this area. The student was Benjamin Lee Whorf.

Whorf is perhaps one of the most maligned characters in all of linguistics (see Cameron, 1999). Several reasons could be given for this, not the least of which is that some linguists see Whorf 's profession as fire insurance inspector to be demeaning toward the discipline. Why is Whorf such a controversial figure? The answer lies in the fact that he provided the most clear-cut description of linguistic relativity and that he further argued to support it with empirical data from his own comparative linguistic work. Although Whorf was not an official member of the academy, his work, even during his lifetime, was well respected by many linguists of the day. Indeed, Sapir even gave him an "A" on his groundbreaking work, written as a student, on Mayan hieroglyphic systems. In 1956, his major works and a full bibliography were collected into a volume titled *Language, Thought and Reality*. In that volume, Whorf presents several articles that are particularly relevant to the formulation of linguistic relativity. The most relevant, "The Relationship Between Habitual Thought and Language," provides a convincing argument for the notion that the grammars we use condition us to see the world in a particular way.

In this article, Whorf is concerned with how languages constantly classify information and the implications for that on thought. After presenting some interesting anecdotes from his work as a fire insurance inspector, Whorf provides a systematic comparison of SAE (Standard Average European) languages and Hopi. One point of comparison Whorf made is between rather covert categories. The notion of the covert aspects of language were particularly important to Whorf as it was within these that he argued language most influenced thought. For example, one could take the case of plurality and numeration. In SAE languages, there are two types of plurals, imagined and real. Real plurals occur when we see and objectively experience multiple instances of the same object. For instance, one could objectively encounter and experience one, two, or three pencils simultaneously. Imagined plurals are metaphorical aggregates such that a singular instance of something can be objectively experienced, but the plural manifestation of that instance must be imagined (Whorf, 1956/1997, p. 139). Whorf uses the example of 1 day versus 10 days. One can experience a single day, but "10 days" cannot be experienced objectively. Rather, the plural of days must be imagined. The Hopi language does not allow for imagined plurals as does English. The implication, therefore, is that Hopi speakers, through the habitual use of language, will perceive these phenomena differently. Whorf uses this and other comparisons to make the point that languages must necessarily structure the world in terms of its grammatical rules. The argument follows that as fundamentally different as SAE languages and Hopi are, the world will necessarily be structured differently grammatically.

The other key point to this is the notion of "habitual thought." Because the use of language will classify the world according to its own grammatical sense, and because language use will rarely rise to the level of consciousness, humans will habitually experience the world according to linguistic classification. The power of habit as it relates to language use should not be underestimated. Certainly, many scholars argue that habitual use of racist or sexist language impacts peoples' perceptions of others (Adler & Rodman, 2006; Drake, 2007). Thus, the relationship between thought and language is one of heavy influence of the latter on the former.

It is important to notice the nature of both Sapir's and Whorf's claim at this point. Sapir argues that our experience of the world is largely associated with our "language habits." He stops well short of saying that our thought is determined by language. Notice his turn of phrase when explicating this. He writes, "We see and hear and otherwise experience very largely as we do because the language habits of our community predispose certain choices of interpretation" (Sapir, 1949/1984, p. 162). Language is seen as habitual and those habits will predispose (not determine) speakers to a certain set of choices about how to interpret the world in which the speaker finds him- or herself. Whorf further develops the notion of "habitual thought" and is indeed more forceful than Sapir, but he still stops well shy of a linguistically determined precipice. Indeed, scholars who present Sapir and Whorf as linguistic determinists are guilty of misreading these scholars. In a footnote in one of Whorf's (1956/1997) articles, he notes,

> some have supposed thinking to be entirely linguistic. Watson I believe holds or held this view. . . . His error lies in going the whole hog; also, perhaps, in not realizing or at least not emphasizing that the linguistic aspect of thinking is not a biologically organized process, 'speech' or 'language,' but a cultural organization (p. 66).

Unfortunately, much criticism of Whorf and linguistic relativity has been leveled against the determinist position. However, as Lucy (1992) says, no one really believes the strong version (linguistic determinism) and no one really disagrees with the weak version (linguistic relativity). This is all to say that linguistic relativity has been a key source of concern for a long time and for numerous people. Too often, this complex relationship is simply boiled down to two versions of the hypothesis. Doing this, however, can be misleading and does not further our understanding of verbal communication.

CONCLUSION

Congratulations! You've just made it through a lot of material about verbal communication. There's a lot of information in these two sections, but it barely scratches the surface of all that we know about the complex human ability to use language. I hope that you will take some of these ideas and explore them further. These ideas covered the basic definition of verbal communication, followed by a discussion of what characterizes this type of communication. After this, we discussed languages in general and concluded with a lengthy discussion of how language functions in our lives. In summary, we now know that verbal communication is our use of symbols. Symbols are things that represent something else. While symbols are arbitrary, that does not mean that we can simply make them up and have them be effective. This is because symbols and their meanings are also conventional, meaning that large communities of people have to agree on particular meanings. While speaking is clearly a form of verbal communication, there are other types as well. Writing is one; emblems are another. One interesting type of nonvocal but verbal type of communication is sign language. All of these types of verbal communication exhibit certain characteristics. Hymes (1962) reminds us of three key characteristics. First, verbal communication is structured through rules. We discussed four different types of rules including phonological, semantic, syntactic, and pragmatic rules. Second, Hymes reminds us that verbal communication systems are diverse. This diversity was illustrated in the section on languages and how commonly they are spoken. Finally, Hymes reminds us that verbal communication systems are social. This means that we use language to form social bonds with one another. It also refers to the fact that languages require social agreement if they are to function effectively. There are, of course, other characteristics of language as well. For instance, languages are also productive because, through their complexity, they have the ability to generate novel ideas and experiences. Languages also exhibit displacement in that they can refer to abstract concepts that are neither physically nor temporally emplaced. Languages are self-reflexive; they have the ability to refer to themselves and thus create new situations as well as to reflect the "selves" of the speakers no matter what is being said. Finally, we discussed how languages are always used within contexts and that these contexts directly impact the meaning of communication.

Turning from the characteristics of language, we explored in depth how it functions. First, we revisited the referential function and discussed how it is that words come to mean what they do through a process called signification. Second, we discussed the various ways that languages create and maintain groups and how these groups impact our own identities. Finally, we discussed the intriguing relationship between human thought and human language.

Now that you know about these basic ideas, you will be better able to see the effects of language in your own life as well as to use language more effectively. I hope you have gained an appreciation for the complexity of something that is often taken for granted. Language is more than a simple tool used to refer to the world. It also directly impacts our very thoughts and identities, and it is the mechanism through which we accomplish most of what we do. By way of conclusion, I would simply leave you with a request. Learn another language. In doing so, each of the ideas presented here will become more real, but beyond that, I am confident you will have access to a completely new way of looking at the world.

Discussion Questions

1. What are some specific terms that you use only with certain groups? Try to identify examples of jargon, slang, and possibly argot in your life.

2. Consider the section on language and identity. What labels do you use to describe yourself? How have those labels shifted over time? How have you used language to shape who you are?

3. Do you think it is possible to think without language?

4. Find an example of language use that clearly prompts us to think about a situation in ways that may not encompass the entire complexity of the situation.

References

Adler, R. B., & Rodman, G. (2006). *Understanding human communication* (9th ed.). New York: Oxford University Press.

Boas, F. (1911/1991). Introduction to handbook of American Indian languages. In P. Holder (Ed.), *Introduction to handbook of American Indian languages and Indian linguistic families of America North of Mexico.* Lincoln, NE: University of Nebraska Press.

Cameron, D. (1999). Linguistic relativity: Benjamin Lee Whorf and the return of the repressed. *Critical Quarterly, 41*(2), 153.

Carbaugh, D. (1996). *Situating selves: The communication of social identities in American scenes.* Albany, NY: SUNY Press.

Colapietro, V. M. (1993). *Glossary of semiotics.* New York: Paragon House.

Collier, M. J., & Thomas, M. (1988). Cultural identity: An interpretive perspective. In Y. Y. Kim and W. B. Gudykunst (Eds.), *Theories in Intercultural Communication* (pp. 99–122). Newbury Park, CA: Sage Publications.

Drake, L. E. (2007). Language and meaning. In E. Morgan & A. E. Lindsey (Eds.), *Principle and practice in human communication: A reader and workbook for COMM 265.* Dubuque, IA: Kendall Hunt Publishing.

Geertz, C. (1973). *The interpretation of cultures.* New York: Basic Books.

Gumperz, J. J., & Levinson, S. C. (Eds.). (1996). *Rethinking linguistic relativity.* Cambridge: Cambridge University Press.

Hall, B. J. (2005). *Among cultures: The challenge of communication.* Belmont, CA: Thompson Wadworth.

Hall, B. J., Covarrubias, P., & Kirschbaum, K. A. (2018). *Among cultures: The challenge of communication.* New York: Routledge.

Hymes, D. (1962). The ethnography of speaking. In T. Gladwin & W. Sturtevant (Eds.), *Anthropology and human behavior.* Washington, DC: Anthropological Society of Washington.

Kaye, A. S. (1997). Language diversity and thought: A reformulation of the linguistic relativity hypothesis (book review). *International Journal of American Linguistics, 63*(2), 275–278.

Lucy, J. A. (1992). *Language diversity and thought: A reformulation of the linguistic relativity hypothesis.* Cambridge: Cambridge University Press.

Mandelbaum, D. G. (Ed.). (1984). Introduction. *Selected writings in language, culture, and personality.* Berkeley, CA: University of California Press.

Osgood, C. E., May, W. H., & Miron, M. S. (1975). *Cross-cultural universals of meaning.* Urbana, IL: University of Illinois Press.

Sampson, G. (1980). Schools of linguistics. Stanford, CA: Stanford University Press.

Sapir, E. (1933). *Language. Encyclopedia of social sciences.* New York: Macmillan.

Sapir, E. (1949). *Language: An introduction to the study of speech.* San Diego, CA: Harcourt, Brace and Company.

Sapir, E. (1984). *Selected writings in language, culture, and personality.* D. G. Mandelbaum (Ed.). Berkeley, CA: University of California Press.

Saussure, F. (1986). *Course in general linguistics.* Chicago, IL: Open Court.

Schneider, D. (1976). Notes toward a theory of culture. In K. H. Basso & H. A. Selby (Eds.), *Meaning in anthropology.* Albuquerque, NM: University of New Mexico Press.

Von Humboldt, W. (1988). *On language: The diversity of human language structure and its influence on the mental development of mankind.* Cambridge: Cambridge University Press.

Whorf, B. L. (1956/1997). *Language, thought, and reality: Selected writings of Benjamin Lee Whorf.* J. B. Carroll (Ed.). Cambridge, MA: The MIT Press.

Wittgenstein, L. (1972). *Philosophical investigations.* Oxford: Blackwell.

Nonverbal Communication

Eric L. Morgan

Objectives

- ► Be able to define and describe nonverbal communication and its characteristics.
- ► Be able to characterize the different channels of nonverbal communication.
- ► Be able to apply concepts associated with nonverbal communication to everyday life.

In other sections of the text, you will have read about characteristics and functions of verbal communication. Verbal communication represents only a portion of the entire breadth of communication behaviors. All the other communication behaviors can be classified as nonverbal communication. Nonverbal communication, simply put is any communication behavior that is nonlinguistic in nature. Another way to define nonverbal communication would be to say that it is the generation of meaning through the display and interpretation of cues that are not explicitly part of verbal communication systems (meaning that these cues are not words or some other arbitrary symbol). These definitions are vague, but they will become clearer when we dive into an exploration of the different types (or channels) of nonverbal communication behaviors. Throughout this presentation, we will also present the different ways that nonverbal communication functions. The goal of this brief module is to provide you with an introduction into the world of nonverbal communication and invite you to seek out further opportunities to study this fascinating area of human communication.

NONVERBAL COMMUNICATION

any communication behavior that is nonlinguistic in nature.

CHARACTERISTICS OF NONVERBAL COMMUNICATION

As with verbal communication, nonverbal communication exhibits a number of characteristics. These characteristics help us to understand the wide breadth of channels and types of behaviors that can be called "nonverbal." Essentially, we can characterize nonverbal communication as being multi-channeled, continuous, and ambiguous. Let's examine each one briefly in reverse order.

To say that nonverbal communication is *ambiguous* means that we often do not have a clear sense of what a particular nonverbal behavior might mean (with the exception of emblems). In this way, a single act of nonverbal communication would not be considered symbolic in the same ways that symbols were discussed in the sections on verbal communication. For example, I regularly hear people complain that others have misread their facial expressions. Sometimes, people are just thinking about something, but the look on their face might suggest to others that something is wrong or that they are angry. Although any one act of nonverbal communication may be considered ambiguous, these behaviors play a critical role in how we create messages and thus generate meaning with others.

Nonverbal communication is also *continuous*. This characteristic draws our attention to the fact that nonverbal communication is potentially ongoing. Whereas verbal communication is made up of discrete units (phonemes, morphemes, words, etc.), it is hard to say what a single act of nonverbal communication might be. Certainly, we can emphasize certain nonverbal behaviors, such as when we smile, but that smile comes amid a whole host of other facial expressions. The continuous nature of nonverbal communication is made more clear when we consider the sheer amount of types of channels and behaviors that exist. For example, even if we are focusing on performing a particular type of nonverbal behavior, our appearance is still communicating something, our posture is communicating something, how close or far away from someone communicates something, and on and on. This leads us nicely to the third characteristic of nonverbal communication.

Nonverbal communication is *multi-channeled*, which means that it flows over numerous channels simultaneously. Contrast this with verbal communication, which typically flows over a single channel. We could divide the vast array of nonverbal channels in a number of ways. What I present below, however, focuses on some of the major areas of research when it comes to nonverbal communication. I should state clearly here that the chart and the discussion below is not exhaustive. To illustrate this point, we could consider the communicative dimensions of virtually anything. Doing so would be to focus on nonverbal communication.

These are just some specific characteristics of nonverbal communication. We could also discuss at length the various functions of nonverbal communication in terms of what we accomplish communicatively. This discussion would require an entire book in itself (and there are plenty out there!). Along these lines though, and for our purposes, I would like to briefly discuss how nonverbal messages interact with our verbal messages (DeVito, 2014). Understanding this function allows us to dive into the complexity of communication as a whole. DeVito argues that nonverbal communication interacts with messages in six ways. First, we use nonverbal communication to **accent** what is being said. If we want to emphasize something, we can use aspects of paralanguage (discussed below) to accomplish that. Second, we use nonverbal communication to **complement** what is being said. Smiling while telling a funny story, for example. Third, nonverbal communication **contradicts** our verbal communication at times. Have you ever told someone you were fine when you weren't? If the person knew that you were not fine, it is likely because they were able to read your nonverbal cues. Fourth, we use nonverbal communication to **control** an interaction. This is the case with regulators, a type of gesture discussed below. Fifth, we can use nonverbal communication to **repeat** the verbal message. For example, you might indicate "hurry up" with your hand as well as your words. Finally, we use nonverbal communication to **substitute** for the verbal message. Nodding your head to indicate "yes" is a classic example. Now that we have a sense of some general ideas about nonverbal communication, let's dive into the fascinating world of the different channels.

CHANNELS OF NONVERBAL COMMUNICATION

In the sections focused on verbal communication, we provide a small table that helps organize our thinking about the different types of communication behavior. We will continue with that table here to help organize our understanding of nonverbal communication behavior (see below). Recall the discussion from Section One of this unit on channels of communication. A **communication channel** is anything over which communication flows. As such, the following types of behaviors can be considered channels of nonverbal communication:

COMMUNICATION CHANNEL

anything over which communication flows.

	VERBAL	**NONVERBAL**
VOCAL	Speaking	Paralanguage (Vocalics)
NONVOCAL	Writing Sign Language(s) Emblems	Appearance Facial Communication Kinesics Proxemics Haptics Olfactics Chronemics Silence

Nonverbal and Vocal Communication Behaviors

Paralanguage (Vocalics)

Frequently, the term "nonverbal" is treated as synonymous with "nonvocal," suggesting that anything we use our vocal chords to produce results is verbal communication. However, this is not the case. There are many types of behaviors we produce with our vocal chords that are not part of the verbal communication system, such as writing. In general, we can refer to these nonverbal behaviors as "vocalics" or "paralanguage." These behaviors include those that typically (but not always!) accompany the words we speak. Devito (2014) divides these behaviors into three categories including vocal characterizers, vocal qualifiers, and vocal segregates. Vocal characterizers include behaviors such as laughing, crying, screaming, yelling (without words), sighing, and so forth. Essentially, these behaviors characterize our emotional states. Vocal qualifiers are those behaviors that accompany the words we produce, although these behaviors do not necessarily have morphemic qualities (meaning that the behaviors are not generally understood as carrying meaning in and of themselves, although they certainly impact how meaning is generated). These behaviors include such aspects of communication behavior as rate of speech, tone of voice, pitch, intonation, and so forth. Finally, vocal segregates include those vocalizations that we produce in the midst of utterances. Examples of these behaviors in English would include such sounds as "umm," "uhh," or "ahh." Quite frequently these are used to "hold the floor" when one is speaking. In other words, it is quite common to hear these from a speaker when that same speaker wishes to continue speaking, but does not want to stop vocalizing so as to be able to continue speaking in the immediate future.

These behaviors are interesting in that they play a critical role in structuring our conversation. Conversation is so much more than simply exchanging verbal messages.

We can think of conversation as a coordinated "dance" between at least two partners. In order to successfully engage in conversation, we have to attend to the other person's verbal messages, their nonverbal cues, the context, and noise at a minimum (remember the transactional model of communication here). When it comes to paralanguage, we often use these to help regulate such conversational features as when we can take a turn at speaking, the length of our utterances, pauses. At times, these behaviors help us generate meaning from the overall conversational event.

Nonverbal and Nonvocal Communication Behaviors

This category includes the greatest variety of communication behaviors or nonverbal communication channels. Because of this, these behaviors are the subject of the most study within nonverbal communication. There are different ways to divide the categories of channels, but for our purposes here, we will focus on eight different types.

Kinesics

KINESICS

the study of gestures and their role in communication.

Kinesics refers to the gestures we use when we communicate. Oftentimes when people think about nonverbal communication or "body language," kinesic behaviors are what they have in mind. A gesture is a movement of the body that communicates some aspect of feeling or intention (Knapp & Hall, 1992). One way to better understand how gestures operate is to consider the various types of behaviors that make up this category (see the following table). We can differentiate these types according to how they function in communication. These distinctions are widely used throughout the field of communication and are attributed to the groundbreaking work of Ekman and Friesen (1969).

Illustrators	Gestures performed with verbal messages that illustrate what is being said
Regulators	Gestures that regulate conversation or the verbal behavior of another
Adaptors	Gestures that manipulate some part of the speaker's body
Affect Displays	Gestures that display some sort of emotion

One special category of gestures are known as emblems. You may recognize this from the previous sections on verbal communication. Because emblems have direct translations within a particular cultural context, they function as a part of the verbal communication system. However, these are also gestures that function like the ones listed in the table above. When considering emblems and their role in communication, it can be useful to distinguish among speech-independent gestures and speech-related gestures (Knapp & Hall, 1992). A speech-independent gesture is one that does not rely on speech in order to make sense. Thus, emblems are speech-independent. Because of this, the meanings associated with emblems vary across cultures. A thumbs-up sign in the U.S. may mean something entirely different in a different part of the world. The problem lies in that we sometimes think of speech-independent gestures as being universal. This is not the case and can lead to intercultural misunderstandings.

Touch

The term **haptics** refers to the use of touch in order to communicate. With this channel of nonverbal communication, we can come to understand just how important touch is when it comes to generating meaning. In fact, Knapp and Hall (1992) argue that touch or "tactile communication" may be the most basic form of human communication. Given this, there has been a large amount of research on the role of touch in human development (Knapp & Hall). While we do not have an opportunity to review the literature on touch and human development here, it should be noted that most research agrees that touching is vitally important during infancy for the development of a child (Knapp & Hall). The question becomes, then, what types of things do we communicate with our touch? One useful way to approach this is to utilize Heslin and Alper's (1983) taxonomy of touch behaviors as presented in the chart below.

Functional-Professional	Occurs when a person must touch another as part of their profession. A hairstylist for example. This touch accomplishes some task.
Social-Polite	This type of touch is used to acknowledge another in some way, but it is still impersonal. For example, a handshake.
Friendship-Warmth	This type of touch communicates friendship or some other type of emotional intimacy associated with friendship. It can frequently be misunderstood depending on context.
Love-Intimacy	This type of touch frequently communicates love and a strong emotional and physical intimacy. The other person is understood as the object of love. This touch is often unique to a particular person.
Sexual Arousal	This type of touch may be a part of other types of touch, but it is strongly associated with sexual intimacy.

It is important to understand that touch plays a different role in communicating intent and feeling. Our touching behavior also indicates a particular type of relationship. That said, it is vitally important to realize that touch and the messages it communicates varies across cultures.

HAPTICS

the study of how touch is used to communicate.

Cosmic squirrel/Shutterstock.com

PROXEMICS

studying how
space is used in
communication.

Space

The term **proxemics** refers to the ways we use personal space to communicate. We all have a sense of how to use space to generate particular meanings. For example, you have likely experienced a time when someone violated your sense of appropriateness concerning personal space. Perhaps someone stood too close to you for your comfort while waiting in line, or perhaps the person in front of you was standing too far away and, thus, you understood that person to not be in line. These are some obvious examples, of course, but the point remains that personal space communicates. One of the first scholars to articulate the role of personal space in communication was anthropologist Edward Hall (1959; 1966). In his book *The Hidden Dimension*, Hall discusses the various ways that humans use space to create meaning. One of his main contributions to this study was his articulation of interpersonal space zones. These zones, Hall argued, played a role in how meaning was generated between people.

Hall's Space Zones	
Intimate Space	0–18 inches
Casual-Personal Space	18 inches to 4 feet
Social-Consultative Space	4 feet to 12 feet
Public Space	Over 12 feet

While these space zones indicate particular types of actions associated with various activities, Hall, himself cautioned against generalizing these zones across cultures. Furthermore, these zones can be "negotiated" between conversational partners depending on the relationship, the context, the environment, shared activity, and so forth. The point here is that we manipulate our personal space in order to communicate different messages. As with all nonverbal behaviors, culture plays a major role in how space is perceived and used in communication. Some people from some cultural systems stand much closer together when talking, while others stand further apart. These behaviors are learned through the enculturation process and become a backdrop to our everyday communicative life. While most of the time we don't really perceive a problem, when our personal space is violated, we do tend to notice rather quickly.

Another area of concern treating space as communication is with territoriality (Altman, 1975). Territoriality refers to how we use our physical environment to communicate. Knapp and Hall (1992) provide the following definition, "[territoriality] means behavior characterized by identification with a geographic area in a way that

indicates ownership and defense of this territory against 'invaders'" (p. 149). So, territoriality is not just space, it is more about how we behave in relation to space. In general, we can talk about three types of territory that are associated with different ways we behave. **Primary territory** refers to spaces that are very clearly designated as yours. You can often claim ownership of these spaces. **Secondary territory** refers to spaces that you can't claim as your own, but have become associated with you. One good example of how secondary territory works is when students sit in the same place each time for class. While a student cannot claim any ownership of that seat, the rest of the class quickly understands that it is associated with that person. Finally, **public territory** refers to a space that everyone is able to use. These territories often have rules of behavior associated with them. These are just a couple of interesting points about how space is used to communicate.

Physical Appearance

Our physical appearance communicates a great deal about us. Indeed, we spend enormous amounts of effort and energy in manipulating our appearance in order to generate particular meanings for other individuals. Perhaps the most often changed aspect of our physical appearance is our clothing. What we wear, either by choice or not, communicates some aspect of the self. What meanings do you hold regarding certain types of clothing? Some simple examples of how clothing communicates can be found in uniforms. It is likely that if you see someone wearing a police officer's uniform that you will automatically assume that this person plays a particular role in society, one in which a person who wears that uniform has the authority to enforce laws. The same goes for any type of uniform. Wearing it means that the person is performing certain roles, and presumably that person knows the range of role expectations associated with that role. Another interesting example of how clothing communicates can be found in religious dress. Throughout the world, there are many religious practitioners that signal their adherence to their religious tradition through dress. A great example here is the hijab. A hijab is a headscarf that many Muslim women wear. These pieces of clothing hold significant religious meaning for those who wear them as well as the communities in which they are understood to communicate some degree of adherence to a particular faith tradition. Another example of religious dress may include robes and vestments for certain members of the clergy, particularly in Christian traditions.

Clothing is an important part of the ways in which physical appearance communicates; however, there are other aspects as well. For example, we could investigate how meaning is associated with particular body types. We could also delve into what is considered beautiful within a particular society and how those notions are portrayed in media.

© Inspiring/Shutterstock.com

Smell

The term olfactics refers to how smell communicates. We don't often consider the role of smell in our communication, but it is clear that smell is a key part of generating meaning. Consider how many things in your life are perfumed in some way? Much of what we consider "clean" or "sanitary" and therefore "safe" has to do with the way things smell. From cleaning supplies, to laundry detergent, to dish soap, to body soap, to shampoos and conditioners, to deodorants, to perfumes and colognes, so much of the products we interact with in everyday life play a part in how we manipulate smells. Another interesting aspect of smell and communication concerns the relationship between various smells and our memories. There has been an enormous amount of research looking into this relationship (see Baker, 2014 for an easy to read overview of this research). Much of this research concerns the psychology of memory and how sometimes these memories are "triggered" by certain odors. Oftentimes, these odors will invoke certain emotions, which can then lead us to communicate in different ways. For our purposes, we are interested in how meaning associated with memories is connected to the smells in our environment.

Facial Communication

If I asked you to communicate that you are sad, what is the first thing you would do? Most likely you would change your facial expression. Facial expressions are critical in our communication with others, particularly to the extent that they are used to express emotion. In fact, it is hard to conceive of the communication of emotion outside of using facial expressions. This subject has been the focus of a great deal of research. For example, two influential psychologists conducted a great deal of research on the universality of facial expressions. The underlying question here is whether facial expressions are the same in what they represent for all humans. If this is the case, it is quite remarkable given that virtually no human behavior is completely universal. It turns out that, in fact, facial expressions are universal (Ekman & Friesen, 1975; 1987; Hall, Covarrubias, & Kirschbaum, 2018). While there is some disagreement among researchers in terms of the number of universally expressed emotions, in general, we can say that the emotions of happiness, sadness, anger, surprise, disgust, and fear are universally expressed. While these emotions may all be expressed the same across cultures and societies, they are not all valued the same, nor do they occur for the same reasons. Rather, we apply different rules for the display of emotion across cultures.

These rules are called cultural display rules. For example, one may find something funny (thereby leading to happiness) in one cultural system, whereas others may orient to that same thing with disgust. Furthermore, the ways we value certain emotions (as communicated through facial expressions) differs across cultures. One interesting example compared Japanese and U.S. American students in terms of how they rated smiling and neutral faces (Matsumoto & Kudoh, 1993). The U.S. American students rated the smiling face as more attractive and more intelligent than the neutral face. The Japanese students, on the other hand, rated the smiling face as more sociable, but not more attractive. They also rated the neutral face as more intelligent.

Facial expressions also play a role in how we interact with ourselves. Cappella (1993) discusses the facial feedback hypothesis. This hypothesis states that we can influence our emotions by using certain facial expressions. You have probably heard it said that if you are sad, try to smile and you will cheer up. This is, in essence the facial feedback hypothesis. While there are definitely some benefits to smiling (such as lowering your heart rate and reducing stress), it remains unclear whether forcing a smile can actually make you happy. There is sufficient evidence, however, to say

SADNESS   CONTEMPT   SURPRISE

ANGER   DISGUST   FEAR

HAPPINESS   NEUTRAL   LOVE

© Plateresca/Shutterstock.com

that using certain facial expressions can influence how we feel (Burgoon, Guerrero, & Floyd, 2010).

Eye Behavior or Gaze

We use our eyes in communication an enormous amount. Research that focuses on the communication dimensions of eye behavior is known as **oculesics**. However, many scholars simply refer to our "gaze" as a way to talk about how we use our eyes to communicate. Consider all the ways in which you have paid attention to someone's eyes and assigned some sort of meaning to that. We use our eyes to communicate emotion, to communicate power, to communicate respect, among many other types of messages. We also use our eyes to create psychological space when necessary. Let's focus on this idea of communicating respect. In many U.S. American contexts, respect is tightly associated with direct eye contact. We hear this cultural rule in such statements as "Look at me when I'm talking to you!" Even in public speaking situations, consistent eye contact is often said to be a mark of good public speaking. In these cases, direct eye contact is associated with showing that one is paying attention, and is therefore, providing respect. In other contexts, such as among some indigenous communities, the proper way to communicate respect is to not provide direct eye contact. This can create a situation of intercultural miscommunication, depending

OCULESICS

the study of how our eye behavior impacts communication.

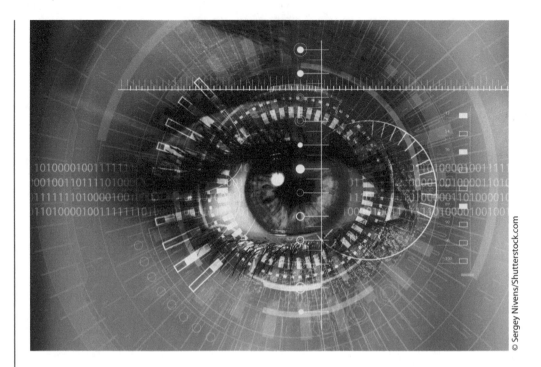

© Sergey Nivens/Shutterstock.com

on the situation and if the parties involved do not understand that there are different cultural rules in play. Another interesting aspect of gaze is how we use this (or not) to create "psychological distance." For example, think about a time when you were in a very crowded place. Sometimes this context can create a situation in which you are forced to look people directly in the eyes. One strategy that you might use is to purposefully look away from those in your immediate vicinity. Doing so creates a sense of a more culturally appropriate personal space. Erving Goffman (1967) labeled this phenomenon "civil inattention." Essentially we are actively not paying attention to others in order to maintain our own sense of personal space as well as maintaining other's privacy. Notice here how we are using one nonverbal channel (gaze) to influence another nonverbal channel (proxemics).

Gaze also plays a key role in relationship development and the communication of attraction. Burriss (2017) points to research that demonstrates that the pupils of our eyes dilate (i.e., get larger) when we are aroused. The arousal that causes pupil dilation can occur when we are in the presence of someone we find attractive. On top of that, people tend to find dilated pupils more attractive as well. Another interesting study showed that our eye behavior changes if our goal with another person is to communicate either love or lust (Bolmont, Cacioppo, & Cacioppo, 2014). In other words, we use distinct visual patterns if we are trying to communicate love versus sexual desire or lust. There is a good amount of research on gaze and communication, and I would invite you to dive into this fascinating world of nonverbal communication.

Chronemics

Chronemics refers to our use of time in communication. From our experiences, we know that different people treat time in different ways. You probably know someone (it could even be you) that just can't seem to be anywhere on time. Other people may always be punctual in whatever they are doing in life. This becomes important from a communication standpoint, when we consider different contexts in which being late or being punctual means something. Take, for example, a job interview. In many U.S. American contexts, being late for a job interview (regardless of the reason) has a

CHRONEMICS

our use of time in communication.

negative meaning. Likewise, being on time to a party may communicate something slightly negative as well. In the sections on culture, we will discuss different cultural approaches to time as being either monochronic or polychronic (Hall, Covarrubias, & Kirschbaum, 2018). We present this here to simply suggest that our use of time is potentially deeply meaningful.

Silence

Silence as an aspect of communication is profoundly important. Consider the different ways that you use silence to communicate. Everything from remaining silent to show respect, to a moment of silence to mark a memorial, to giving someone the "cold shoulder" is a way to use silence for communicative purposes. The use of silence as communication and its role in the creation of meaning is more pronounced once we investigate the different ways that silence is used across cultural systems. Linguistic anthropologist Keith Basso published a piece in 1970 describing how silence was used among the Western Apache of Arizona. The Western Apache, according to Basso, use silence in markedly different ways than many English speakers in the United States. In his piece, he describes six situations which call for silence. These include the following: (1) when meeting strangers, (2) when courting, (3) when children come home, (4) when getting cussed out, (5) when being with those who are sad, and (6) when being with those for whom they sing. When in these situations, many Western Apache will remain silent. He found this interesting, because some of these situations for him would call for talk. For example, when meeting strangers, many English speakers will engage in talk in order to "get to know the other person." Likewise, when courting, many people understand that going on dates as a way to initiate romantic relationships requires talking. These are both situations that would call for silence among the Western Apache. If we were to look across each of these situations, we would see that they all share something in common. Each of these situations is a case in which the other individual is a stranger. Another way to say this is that each of these situations is one in which the other people are socially distant. At least for some Western Apache, when encountering socially distant others, the cultural rule is to remain silent. This pattern has also been described for other indigenous communities in North America. For example, Scollon and Wong-Scollon (1990) write that among the Dine of Northern Alberta, Canada, and the Northwest Territories, Canada, how this difference in the patterning of silence can sometimes lead to miscommunication that then serves to reinforce negative stereotypes.

CONCLUSION

This has been a brief exploration of the fascinating world of nonverbal communication. It is hard to overstate just how important our nonverbal communication behaviors are when it comes to interacting with others. In this section we covered some characteristics of nonverbal communication along with some general functions of nonverbal communication. We also covered a wide variety of different channels of nonverbal communication. Everything from clothing to smell to space to time is potentially communicative. It is our hope that you find this discussion interesting and worthy of further exploration. Many universities offer courses in nonverbal communication or at least offer courses in which nonverbal communication plays a significant role. As you move forward in your own study of communication, we invite you to seek out opportunities to explore this complex world of communication behaviors.

Discussion Questions

1. Consider a time when you have received "mixed messages" between verbal communication and nonverbal communication. What happened? Which behavior was more believable? Why?

2. Select one of the channels of nonverbal communication. Consider a time when you encountered an interesting use of this channel. What types of assumptions did you make about the person engaging in this behavior? What are some of your beliefs about the appropriateness of this behavior? What are some ways you might improve on the performance of these nonverbal behaviors?

3. All of these nonverbal communication behaviors are guided by cultural rules. Some of them, however, have such widely held beliefs about the appropriate use of them that there are laws that guide our usage. Which ones have laws associated with appropriate use? Under what conditions are violations of nonverbal communication rules considered so severe that there are legal penalties associated with them?

4. Given that facial expressions have been shown to be universal, do you believe that all emotions are universal? If so, why? If not, why not?

References

Altman, I. (1975). *The environment and social behavior.* Monterey, CA: Brooks/Cole.

Baker, A. (2014, Dec.). It's beginning to smell a lot like Christmas: The neuroscience of nostalgia. *Scientific American.* Retrieved from https://blogs.scientificamerican.com/frontiers-for-young-minds/it-s-beginning-to-smell-a-lot-like-christmas-the-neuroscience-of-our-nostalgia/

Basso, K. (1990). To give up on words: Silence among the Western Apache. In D. Carbaugh (Ed.), *Cultural Communication and Intercultural Contact.* Mahwah, NJ: Lawrence Erlbaum Associates, Inc. Publishers.

Bolmont, M., Cacioppo, J. T., & Cacioppo, S. (2014). Love is in the gaze: An eye-tracking study of love and sexual desire. *Pyschological Science, 25*(9), 1748–1756.

Burgoon, J. K., Guerrero, L. K., & Floyd, K. (2010). *Nonverbal communication.* Boston, MA: Allyn and Bacon.

Burriss, R. (2017, Nov). Why the eyes are so central to human attraction. *Psychology Today.* Retrieved from https://www.psychologytoday.com/us/blog/attraction-evolved/201711/why-the-eyes-are-so-central-human-attraction

Cappella, J. N. (1993). The facial feedback hypothesis in human interaction: Review and speculation. *Journal of Language and Social Psychology, 12,* 13–29.

Devito, J. (2014). *Essentials of human communication* (8th ed.). Boston, MA: Pearson.

Ekman, P., & Friesen, W. V. (1969). The repertoire of nonverbal behavior: Categories, origins, usages, and coding. *Semiotica, 1,* 49–98.

Ekman, P., & Friesen, W. V. (1975). *Unmasking the face: A field guide to recognizing emotions from facial clues.* Englewood Cliffs, NJ: Prentice-Hall.

Ekman, P., & Friesen, W. V. (1987). Universals and cultural differences in the judgments of facial expressions of emotion. *Journal of Personality and Social Psychology, 53,* 712–717.

Goffman, E. (1967). *Interaction ritual: Essays on face-to-face behavior.* New York: Harper Collins.

Hall, E. (1959). *The silent language.* Garden City, NY: Doubleday.

Hall, E. (1966). *The hidden dimension.* Garden City, NY: Doubleday.

Hall, B. J., Covarrubias, P., & Kirschbaum, K. A. (2018). *Among cultures: The challenge of communication.* New York: Routledge.

Heslin, R., & Alper, T. (1983). Touch: A bonding gesture. In J. M. Wiemann & R. P. Harrison (Eds.), *Nonverbal interaction.* Beverly Hills, CA: Sage Publications.

Knapp, M. L., & Hall, J. A. (1992). *Nonverbal communication in human interaction.* Fort Worth, TX: Holt, Rinehart, and Winston, Inc.

Matsumoto, D., & Kudoh, T. (1993). American-Japanese cultural differences in attributions of personality based on smiles. *Journal of Nonverbal Behavior, 17,* 231–243.

Scollon, R., & Wong-Scollon, S. (1990). Athabaskan-English inter-ethnic communication. In D. Carbaugh (Ed.), *Cultural communication and intercultural contact.* Mahwah, NJ: Lawrence Erlbaum Associates, Inc. Publishers.

Communication and Ethics

Greg G. Armfield

Objectives

- ▶ Define ethics, morality, virtue.
- ▶ Examine organizational moral codes.
- ▶ Compare and contrast the most common ethical theories.
- ▶ Evaluate the eight principles identified in Principle Based Ethics.

Communication is highly integrated and strongly connected with ethical principles. Regardless if you are engaging in public speaking or an interpersonal exchange, ethical issues will inherently be at play. A broadly agreed upon definition of **ethics** is a systematic study of decisions or personal choices regarding what is right and/or wrong and good or bad (Johannesen, 2002). Ethics is closely aligned with morality.

Morality is argued to be culturally influenced standards of right/wrong, good/bad (Johannesen, 2002) and is a function of influencing a broader application of behavior (Bayley, 2011). This influential process can include the attempt to influence large groups of people. For example, to understand ethics and the application of morality on college campuses one might look toward college campuses that are *dry*, no alcohol sold on campus, or even college campuses that have become smoke-free zones. Both decisions, made typically without student input and at a higher level of administration, are applications of broader moral codes, which are designed to discourage students' consumption of both legal and illegal drugs on campus.

The third part of this equation is **virtue**, or the thought process and behavior guided by a set of moral standards (Bayley, 2011). Virtue is typically shown through behavior. One becomes aware of the ethical standards set by a group, a culture, or an organization and applies those behaviors (morality). By striving to live by a set of moral standards, one becomes a virtuous person. A virtuous person, in turn, *behaves* in an ethical manner and is guided by a set of moral guidelines for all actions and interactions.

While there exists a strong connection between ethics, morality, and virtue, the difference can be revealed when a communicator is forced to make an ethical decision. For example, humans in general tend to believe in a **moral code** or set of rules. These codes or agreed upon rules are individually held and influenced by

ETHICS

a systematic study of decisions or personal choices regarding what is right and/or wrong and good or bad.

MORALITY

culturally influenced standards of right/wrong, good/bad.

VIRTUE

the thought process and behavior guided by a set of moral standards.

MORAL CODE

a set of rules.

your culture and upbringing. The belief that it is not good to lie might be an example of an agreed upon moral belief. Therefore, you would believe it is not good to lie, or it is wrong to lie. Consider the following:

> There is a knock on your door. Your roommate says, "if it's my ex-boyfriend, say I'm not here." You answer the door and it's her ex-boyfriend. Do you lie? Do you let him in?

This is the ethical decision you are left with. If you tell him she is not home, you are lying!

Broader ethical decisions are often not driven by your morality, especially if there is a perception that no harm will be done. However, the truly virtuous individual would never lie; regardless of the harm that may or may not be caused to others.

How often do you engage in ethical decisions that may or may not become a gray area with regard to your individual set of morals or moral code? Ethical decisions provide a lot of gray area in our daily lives and our daily communication. Morals are not always black-and-white. The behavioral decision is far more difficult. Undeniably, it is harder to always live by a moral code and do the right thing.

Does a little white lie hurt anyone? In this section we will review a few organizational ethical codes, discuss some of the most common ethical approaches, and review the concepts of Principle Based Ethics.

Ethical decisions and issues exist when any communicator engages in goal driven communication. The link

© Kwok Design/Shutterstock.com

between ethics and communication has always existed, but research on the two date as far back as the fourth and sixth century B.C., as documented in writings by Aristotle and Confucius (Tubbs, 2010).

The movement for business ethics, however, did not gain momentum until the 1960s when organizations began establishing codes of conduct and values statements (Business Ethics, 2018). In the 1970s, human rights issues of employee treatment became more prominent, more business schools and ethics scholars took a heightened interest in the study of ethical practices, and the U.S. Congress passed the Foreign Corrupt Practices Act in 1977.

By the 1980s the U.S. was suffering from the Savings and Loan scandals, deceptive advertising, and continued use of bribes, illegal contract practices, and unethical business practices (e.g., Sears Automotive and Beech-Nut) became more publicized by media outlets. In partial response to many of these issues the U.S. Code of Ethics for Government Services was introduced. General Dynamics was the first to establishe an ethics office and some companies created ombudsman positions (Business Ethics, 2018). The 1980s also ushered in a new climate of corporate responsibility and liability with the Johnson & Johnson Tylenol tampering incident (Benoit & Lindsey, 1987).

The 1990s came with the growth of more international businesses. Employee/human rights, child labor, and unsafe work conditions continued to be an ethical

issue for some organizations along with increased corporate liability, which was primarily brought on by increased legal action toward tobacco companies and the 1996 Delaware Supreme Court ruling that organizational board members could be held legally and personally liable for lack of oversight with respect to organizational ethics (Demetriou & Olmon, 2007).

With the turn of the century came economic growth and financial failures, primarily due to lacking banking regulations and the extension of ill-conceived loans by mortgage companies. Enron collapsed revealing massive ethical and legal failures. Unrelated to Enron, the negotiation of ethical standards inside of many organizations became challenging with the increasing global business climate and growth of multicultural organizations (Business Ethics, 2018). In 2002 the Sarbanes-Oxley Act mandated stronger ethical safeguards on businesses. An increasingly stronger culture of corporate responsibility and integrity in the U.S. was met with stronger federal sentencing guidelines for ethical misconduct. Furthermore, the U.S. Department of Justice required prosecutors to consider corporate ethics and compliance programs when filing charges against corrupt organizations (Business Ethics).

Today, organizational ethical issues surround the use of big data, consumer privacy, and social media. Common standards of ethical practices continue to be at tension with an increasing loss of personal privacy. Some organizations continue to struggle identifying common standards and values in an increasingly diverse workplace. Furthermore, publicly traded organizations are legally mandated to have a code of conduct, which clarifies the organizations mission, vision, and principles (Why Have, 2018).

Ethical codes of conduct and organizational values statements are important guiding principles for organizational decision-making. All organizations should be guided by their stated mission and vision. Take, for example, Facebook's mission, "to give people the power to build community and bring the world closer together. People use Facebook to stay connected with friends and family, to discover what's going on in the world, and to share and express what matters to them" (Our Mission, 2018). Missions are used as a guiding principle for why the company exists. If Facebook considers a new product or service, one of the primary considerations should be does it "build community," bring people closer, or connect people (Our Mission, 2018, para. 1)?

Organizational codes of ethics work the same way an organization's mission and vision function. An organization's moral code or code of conduct outlines the ethical principles a company stands for and guides the organizational and individual decision-making processes, while influencing behaviors within the organization (Code of Conduct, 2018). Considering this, please see Facebook's Code of Conduct and Mission Statement at the links in the margin.

Code of Conduct (2018). Facebook. Retrieved from https://investor. fb.com/corporate-governance/ code-of-conduct/ default.aspx

Our Mssion (2018). Facebook. Retrieved from https://newsroom. fb.com/company-info/

Employees of Facebook, Inc., or any of its affiliates or subsidiaries, ("Facebook") and others performing work for Facebook or on its behalf, collectively referred to in this code as "Facebook Personnel," are expected to act lawfully, honestly, ethically, and *in the best interests of the company* [emphasis added] while performing duties on behalf of Facebook. . . . Persons who are unsure whether their conduct or the conduct of other Facebook Personnel complies with this code should contact their manager, another Facebook manager, Human Resources, or the Legal Department. This code applies to all Facebook Personnel, including members of the board of directors (in connection with their work for Facebook), officers, and employees of Facebook, Inc. and its corporate affiliates, as well as contingent workers (e.g., agency workers, contractors and consultants) and others working on Facebook's behalf. This code is subject to change and may be amended, supplemented or superseded by one or more separate policies.

If any part of this code conflicts with local laws or regulations, only the sections of this code permitted by applicable laws and regulations will apply. Any policies that are specifically applicable to your jurisdiction will take precedence to the extent they conflict with this code. (Code of Conduct, 2018, para. 1 & 2).

How much guidance does this code give you as an employee? Essentially the code, in far more words, tells Facebook employees to be honest, ethical, and to not break laws (Code of Conduct, 2018, para. 1). Furthermore, if an organizational employee is not being honest, ethical, or is in violation of a local law or regulation, then that employee should abide by the local regulations or law(s) (Code of Conduct, para. 2). Frankly, this does not provide much direction or guidance to Facebook employees. Most individuals' personal ethics, morality, or virtues would discourage them to not break a law!

Let's look at a company that might provide a little more guidance with respect to an organizational code of ethics. The Coca-Cola Company, is a multinational company, much like Facebook. Please see Coca-Cola's Code of Business Conduct in the margin.

© Rose Carson/
Shutterstock.com

Code of Business
Conduct (2016).
The Coca-Cola
company.
Retrieved from
https://www.coca-
colacompany.
com/content/
dam/journey/
us/en/private/
fileassets/pdf/
our-company/
2016-COBC-US-
Final.pdf

"Act with integrity, Around the Globe" (Code of Business, 2016, para. 1). They develop this further with, "Act with integrity. Be honest. Follow the law. Comply with the code. Be accountable" (Code of Business, para. 2). Comparing the two codes, Coca-Cola and Facebook, one can easily observe that Coca-Cola's code is more clear and specific, even though it is shorter. Furthermore, Facebook advocates employees to do what is best for Facebook (Code of Conduct, 2018, para. 1), whereas Coca-Cola takes a higher moral stance asking employees to "do what is right, for ourselves and for The Coca-Cola Company" (Code of Business, para. 6). Later adding that Coca-Cola employees have responsibilities not only to the Company, but "to each other, and to customers, suppliers, consumers, and governments" (Code of Business, para. 6).

If you are an organizational employee and asked to look toward an organizational code, or moral code, to make organizational decisions, which code makes it easier for you to make that decision? You can clearly see Coca-Cola provides far more direction for an employee to make an ethical choice when compared to Facebook's code. Facebook's ethical code is very vague, especially with regard to rule breaking or following laws. Furthermore, Facebook is very ambiguous with regard to what does the organization really stand for. If all employees are charged to act in the company's best interest, what laws or ethical codes might such an organization ask employees to break or violate?

Philosophically speaking, compare your desire to work for an organization that asks you to act in its best interest to an organization that asks you to act with integrity. Which would you rather work for? Coca-Cola asks for you to be honest and act with integrity. Now that we understand organizational and business moral codes, let's look at a broad system of ethics that can be applied to organizations and business alike. As you consider each of the standards of principle based ethics below, apply these ethical standards to the two codes of ethics presented above.

PRINCIPLE BASED ETHICS

Many organizations adopt a set of ethical standards to guide organizational decisions. Several business leaders have done the same. One such person is Bill Daniels, an entrepreneur and businessperson, who believed being ethical was so important he funded a self-named foundation to support an ethical education initiative at the primary and university level (Bill Daniels Condensed, 2018; Grants, 2018).

Daniels, "A man of strong values and principles, lived his life according to" ethical principles, whether making business or personal decisions (Bill Daniels' Values, 2018, para. 1). Daniels' believed his ethical principles were the dominant force behind his success. Based on Daniels strong and deeply held principled belief system, the concept of Principle Based Ethics was created as a framework for personal and organizational decision-making and introduced through the Daniels Fund Collegiate Program (Daniels Fund Ethics, 2018). In coordination with the Daniels Fund Board of Directors and partner Universities (see www. danielsfund.org/Ethics/Collegiate.asp), which are primarily located in the Mountain West, the following eight guiding principles were established: Integrity, Trust, Accountability, Transparency, Fairness, Respect, Rule of Law, and Viability (Daniels Fund Ethics, 2016). These principles form a philosophical foundation for the basis of business and personal ethics.

Integrity is the value of being honest and acting honestly in all situations (Daniels Fund Ethics, 2016). You might have seen a meme on social media that states "integrity is doing the right thing, even when/if no one is watching." Northouse (2019) explains integrity as taking responsibility for a person's actions and argues leaders who have integrity inspire others. In short, integrity is keeping your word. If you say you will do it, you do it, and you stand behind what you say and do.

Trust can be difficult to conceptualize at times. The Daniels Fund argues that leaders should "build trust in all stakeholder relationships" (Daniels Fund Ethics, 2016, para. 2). For me, trust is to rely on or count on a person. To do what you say you will do. To think of trust in a different way, when you go out to your vehicle in the morning you have a level of trust that it will start and get you safely to your destination. Growing up in the Midwest, a cold, snowy winter night would always bring some level of concern, or reduce the level of trust, that my vehicle would start. Long, cold nights test the level of reliability most people have in a car battery. Similar to trust is trustworthiness, which is typically defined as being honest and reliable; having a positive reputation and the courage to always do the right thing (Northouse, 2018).

INTEGRITY

the value of being honest and acting honestly in all situations.

TRUST

to rely on or count on a person.

ACCOUNTABILITY

to be responsible for one's actions and decisions.

Accountability is to be responsible for one's actions and decisions. The Daniels Fund argues accountability is to "accept responsibility for all decisions" (Daniels Fund Ethics, 2016, para. 3). However, oftentimes accountability can be seen as the obligation an ethical individual has to accept responsibility not only for decisions, but for one's actions and behaviors. This definition expands the idea of accountability to include being responsible and holding oneself, and others, accountable for actions at all times; regardless of the situation or circumstance. In other words, regardless of someone's mental state, such as being under the influence of a legal or illegal substance, that person should be held responsible for their actions and behaviors.

TRANSPARENCY

maintaining open and truthful communication with all stakeholders, or persons, at all times.

Transparency is a state of clarity. A photographer sees the negative of an image as a state of transparency when projecting an image or shining light through the negative. With respect to communication, transparency is maintaining open and truthful communication with all stakeholders, or persons, at all times (Daniels Fund Ethics, 2016).

FAIRNESS

engage in fair competition and create equitable and just relationship[s].

Fairness is typically marked by impartiality and honesty. The Daniels Fund advocates for organizations and individuals to "engage in fair competition and create equitable and just relationship[s]" (Daniels Fund Ethics, 2016, para. 5). Fair competition typically will involve conforming to a prior set of established rules, and playing by those stated rules. Northouse (2018) states that fairness implies a strict "adherence to a balanced standard of justice without relevance to one's own feelings or indications" (p. 277). Taking this set of rules or standards to a different level is to engage in an honest competition based on those rules. Regardless of feelings or whether a competitor (organization or team) is also engaging in fair play, one should always engage in fair competition.

RESPECT

honor the rights, freedoms, views, and property of others.

Respect is to "honor the rights, freedoms, views, and property of others" (Daniels Fund Ethics, 2016, para. 6). Northouse (2018) argues there is "no ethical duty to hold people in high esteem, we should treat everyone with respect" (p. 277). Signs of respect are to be considerate of others and use good manners both communicatively and in your actions (Northouse). You do not have to share the same values as others, but you can be considerate of the values and beliefs of others; even if they are different from yours. Respecting others also means to care and show concern for them and work out any disagreements that need to be addressed. All while never considering yourself or your organization more important than anyone or anything else.

Rule of Law is to "comply with the spirit and intent of laws and regulations" (Daniels Fund Ethics, 2016, para. 7). This principle is one that is not commonly found in leadership literature, but one that is very important to organizational competition and business ethics. At the beginning of the section we looked at the published code of ethics by two organizations. Both organizations' code of ethics refers to following the law and legal precedents as part of the ethical principles. However, one organization gave more direction, before simply stating not to break laws. When engaged in competition, whether it be business or personal, regulations and laws should always be adhered to.

Viability is the ability to grow, develop, and sustain organizational development. The Daniels Fund states viability is to "create long-term value for all relevant stakeholders" (Daniels Fund Ethics, 2016, para. 8). In short, viability is the ability to survive, regardless of circumstances or situations. Similar to Rule of Law, leadership scholarship rarely speaks to viability, but some managerial and organization text speak to the idea that organizations should have some level of financial performance (profits) that allow a business to meet its financial commitments or pay off its debts. The goal of ethical viability is to make a profit that allows organizations to sustain financial security and properly reward employees for their efforts.

This framework of principle based ethics provides a foundation for individuals to begin their own set of principles. Framed by the ethical theories discussed in this section, I encourage you to begin a personal journey of framing what values and ethical principles you want to frame in your life. In other words, use this section to reflect on what you as an individual stand for. What values are most important to you? When we discuss organizational communication later in this text look deeper into the ethical principles of the organizations that you would like to work for. Do they align with your ethical principles? Where are the gaps? Does the organization want you to do or act in a way that is not consistent with your core values? All of these questions should be considered before you consider employment with an organization.

Some of the major ethical approaches have developed over time. Keep in mind these approaches are individually based, not organizational or group. Remember, as stated earlier, organizations do not hold morals or values. Morals, values, virtues, and ethics are all individually held. That said, an organization's moral code is put in place to influence an employee's decision-making. The next section will review some of the major ethical approaches. Consider which ethical approach makes the most sense? Which ethical approach is most consistent with your morals? Which ethical approach is most consistent with the virtues you hold? Which ethical approach provides the best plan of action when considering the example at the beginning of the section?

ETHICAL APPROACHES

The first two approaches focus on individual level traits and inner motives, which arguably function to shape a morally fit person. Is the desire to tell the truth in all circumstances (reflecting on the example above) truly a virtue?

RULE OF LAW

comply with the spirit and intent of laws and regulations.

VIABILITY

create long-term value for all relevant stakeholders.

THE DOCTRINE OF THE MEAN

the morally unfit are attracted to extremes and virtue is found in moderation.

Aristotle (384 to 322 B.C.): The Doctrine of the Mean

Several philosophers of the Eastern and Greek tradition have written on ethics in terms of character, as opposed to behavior (covered later in this section). Aristotle derived his focus on character specifically from morality and virtue. Later in history we find morality and virtue referenced in the Sermon on the Mount, "blessed are the pure in heart" (Mathew 5:8, New Revised Standard Version). However, Aristotle and Confucius found moral absolutes troublesome and sought to find an ethical balance between two extremes.

Aristotle admired moderation so much that it became his practicing theory of virtue. He believed that the morally unfit were attracted to extremes and that virtue was found in moderation. He explained this by describing virtue as the middle path between two extremes: the vice of excess and the vice of deficiency (Johannesen, 2002). He called this the Doctrine of the Mean (not a mathematical mean) now called the Golden Mean by many (See Johannesen). Johannesen explains this with the example of generosity. Generosity is defined as the mean between stinginess and wastefulness (Johannesen, p. 4).

Consider two examples. Politicians can become known for reading political polls and telling voters more of what the people would like to hear versus what they actually believe in. Bill Clinton was pretty masterful at following the mean of political polls, especially after he was elected President. Prior to Clinton, Presidential Candidate Walter Mondale was witnessed to tell three differing audiences that their group concerns (civil rights, quality of education, and union rights) were at the "very core of [his] being" (as cited in Johannesen, 2002, p. 4). It goes without saying that Mondale had maintained a very wide *core* of political concerns. Perhaps a more accurate analysis of Mondale's rhetoric is that he was applying Aristotle's belief in the Doctrine of the Mean with regard to his core political beliefs. Of course it should be noted that Mondale's desire for the public to vote for him might have superseded his desire to practice an ethical philosophy.

In summary, Aristotle believed a wise person was one who avoided extremes and practiced moderation. Moderation, Aristotle argued, is where virtue was found and that the person who walks the middle path (the Golden Mean) was indeed an ethical and virtuos person (Johannesen, 2002). However, one might question how virtuous sensuality might be—the golden mean between frigidity and lustfulness—if one becomes overly preoccupied with their indulgence or appetite in something, where is virtue found?

If we return to our example of lying for your roommate presented at the beginning of the section, the extremes you are presented with are lie or tell the whole truth. Aristotle would side with stating truthful statements and not some made-up mean between the two (Johannesen, 2002). What would that look like?

Martin Buber (1878 to 1965): Dialogic Ethics

Buber's ethical approach was to focus on the relationship goals between two parties (individuals), not the middle ground or a moral code as Aristotle believed. Buber focuses on relationships between people and believed true dialogue, as opposed to monologue, between persons is the essence of ethics. The heart of Buber's dialogic view is human communication. Buber argues the fundamental fact of human existence is, what he refers to as, "man with man" or simply a person communicating with another person. Through communication, or human dialogue, a person develops the self, which is their personality and knowledge (Johannesen, 2002). In essence Buber believes that dialogue with other humans develops our sense of who we are (our self) and who we are becoming (our person). This human development process can only

occur in the "between" through dialogue (communication) in relationships with other humans (Johannesen, 2002, p. 56).

The essential or primary movement in dialogue is "turning toward, outgoing to, and reaching for the other" or "experiencing the other side" (Johannesen, 2002, p. 57). This is similar to the expression walk a mile in my shoes. Buber believes that a person does not relinquish their convictions or change their opinions, but strives to understand those of others, while avoiding imposing their own views on others. If this occurs, only then can "genuine dialogue between humans of divergent beliefs" occur (Johannesen, p. 57).

Buber argues that six movements or guidelines must be engaged in by all individuals if true dialogue and understanding is to occur between parties are:

1. Authenticity: Not seeming to be an "other" playing a role, but authentically engaging in dialogue and interacting with each other.
2. Inclusion: You do not have to give up your stance, beliefs, or convictions in order to understand another person's perspective or stance.
3. Confirmation: Do not just tolerate the other person, affirm their importance and engage in dialogue with the person authentically.
4. Presentness: Be fully engaged and involved in dialogue with other people.
5. Spirit of Mutual Equality: Diminish or set aside any unequal status/power status or accomplishments so that equality and dialogue can occur.
6. Supportive Climate: Encourage the other person to communicate and/or help in facilitating communication between the two. If it helps, an outside facilitator can help the dialogue and help maintain equality.

Maintaining these six rules or guidelines will encourage true dialogue between parties.

If genuine dialogue does not, or for some reason cannot, occur the fate of humankind might very well be at stake (Johannesen, 2002). While this is a very weighty and forceful claim, consider the lack of communicative dialogue that occurs between two individuals of divergent opinions. Whether it be politics, religion, and so forth, without dialogue and understanding of viewpoints between two individuals of divergent viewpoints, little understanding will occur between the two.

DIALOGIC ETHICS

a person does not relinquish their convictions or change their opinions, but strives to understand those of others, while avoiding imposing their own views on others.

Buber may have reached too far calling for ethical extremes that casual relationships are not able to develop. Consider the driver with road rage caught in a traffic jam. Is dialogue possible with a raging or angry individual? Unlikely at best. What about our example at the beginning of the section? Is it really beneficial to have dialogue with your roommate's ex-boyfriend? Furthermore, if you and your roommate are close, you may very well have insight into why the breakup occurred. There may very well not be a rational reason to explore or encourage dialogue between the two. The next two theories explore the consequences of behavior. Again, consider the example at the beginning of the section. Can a lie do good or prevent harm?

UTILITARIANISM

the greatest good for the greatest number.

John Stuart Mill (1806 to 1873): Utilitarianism

Mill placed value not in morality or values, but on the consequences of one's actions. He rationalized that an act was good or bad depending on the outcome of the action, not on moral intentions (Tubbs, 2010, p. 193). Focusing on the greatest good for the greatest number, Mill's foundation of utilitarianism is the greatest happiness principle: "Actions are right in proportion as they tend to promote happiness, wrong as they tend to produce the reverse of happiness" (Mill, 1968, p. 249). In short do the greatest good for the greatest number.

© Everett Historical/Shutterstock.com

Mill's focus on happiness, or the greatest good, was to look at pleasure as happiness and unhappiness as pain or the lack of pleasure. But his focus on pleasure was not personal pleasure. It was happiness that leads not to simple pleasures, a treat or drink, but to quality. In short, pleasure for Mills was a broad spectrum of happiness that could be applied to masses, including intellectual pleasures (Tubbs, 2010).

Historically, utilitarianism sought social and political reform for the masses. For example, providing healthcare for everyone. This approach has been criticized as healthcare companies, or the government, could lower costs by reducing benefits for individuals that might be predisposed to have early heart disease or suffer from cancer or diabetes. Again, the greater good, lowering insurance costs, could be achieved by charging those in smaller minority groups more, therefore achieving lower rates for the greatest number of people (Beauchamp, Bowie, & Arnold, 2009; Tubbs, 2010). This example provides just a few issues with applying utilitarianism broadly. However, this principle can easily be widely applied.

What is wrong with a little white lie, or simply bending the truth? Take a look at our example. Does anyone get hurt if you simply tell your roommate's ex-boyfriend she is not there? Well, what if he wanted to apologize? One could argue he gets hurt. But if only one person gets hurt are you acting for the greatest good for the masses? You are really only acting for the greater good for one or two people; you and your roommate. However, one could argue the greater good for the greater number might be just you and your roommate when only considering the three individuals involved.

© nuvolanevicata/Shutterstock.com

As you can see, the application of utilitarianism gets very complicated when applied to both macro and micro situations. The ethical standard of caring for all, or at least a greater good for everyone, has always had an important and permanent place in ethical discussions. You can read more about utilitarianism with respect to health communication in Unit 5, Section 3.

Epicurus (341 to 271 B.C.): Ethical Egoism

ETHICAL EGOISM

everyone should promote their own self-interest and live the good life.

Epicurus also focused on action as outcome, but Epicurus was far more self-centered than Mill. Epicurus historically lived during a similar time period of Aristotle, long before Mill, and was not focused on the greater good for the greatest number, but the greater good for oneself. Considered an ethical egoist, Epicurus believed everyone should promote their own self-interest and live the good life. The good life, as defined by Epicurus, is getting pleasure: "I spit on the noble and its idle admirers when it contains no element of pleasure" (Rist, 1972, p. 124). Epicurus advocated for the enjoyment of all pleasures stating, "no pleasure is in itself evil, but the things that produce certain pleasures entail annoyances many times greater than the pleasures themselves" (Rist, 1972, p. 124). Taking Epicurus at his word, he would have included the ethical acceptance of lying when arguing "no pleasure is in itself evil" (Rist, 1972, p. 124).

Many would argue there are numerous morality issues with the ideal or value of self-interest first; especially when compared to Mill's more wholistic approach of greater good for the greatest number. One could argue it is OK for them to kill people as long as killing people

A selfish man with a crown on his head positions himself as a person who is more important than the rest of the crowd.

brings pleasure. Serial killers and terrorists could arguably be justified and morally centered under this ethical lens.

Consider the counterargument of the pleasure principle. If doing what you want is OK at all times, including immoral and illegal activity, how would that person's life compare to Mother Teresa or Pope Francis? One could argue the egoism principle has little to no ethical value at all given it could support immoral (some would even argue unethical) activities. However, the ethical egoist would argue that Mother Teresa did not lead an ethical life by serving others unless she derived pleasure from her service. Only if Mother Teresa, or any other person, takes pleasure in helping and/or serving others can they lead an ethical life. If Mother Teresa did not take pleasure from serving others, then she was not leading an ethical life and she should stop. Whereas the last group of theories focused on the consequences of an act, the last two principles focus solely on morality as law.

CATEGORICAL IMPERATIVE

belief that there are no exceptions to ethical rules and all moral codes should be considered universal laws.

Immanuel Kant (1724 to 1804): Categorical Imperative

Kant believed people had an ingrained conscience, an engrained moral will and moral reason, and that all individuals possess a deep-rooted internal sense of right and wrong (Johannesen, 2002). Based on this belief, Kant rationalized that all acts could be deemed as right or wrong regardless of the outcome or the reason for taking action. This absolutist view connotes Kant's belief that there were no exceptions to ethical rules and all moral codes should be considered universal laws. Kant (1964) maintained, "Truthfulness in statements which cannot be avoided is the formal duty of an individual to everyone, however great may be the disadvantage accruing to himself or another" (p. 346). In maintaining his belief in universal laws Kant (1959) argued one should "act only according to that maxim by which you can . . . that it

should become a universal law" (p. 39). Furthermore Kant claimed one should "always act so that you treat humanity, whether in your own person or in another, as an end, and never merely as a means [treated as things]" (Johannessen, p. 43). Treating people differently from things shows that a person should be treated with respect, counter to a Machiavellian perspective, and shown dignity.

This ethical belief system in absolute universal laws (categorical) that dictated an individual's obligation to act (universal) regardless of the situation became the categorical imperative. Kant has argued the categorical imperative has no exceptions; thus making behaviors in certain situations unacceptable (Tubbs, 2010). For Kant, truth telling is sacred. There is no circumstance where lying would be acceptable, because a lie, regardless of situation or need, would harm a person. Furthermore, if there is no direct harm to a person there would be harm to humankind because a person who lies is undermining the nature of law (Tubbs, 2010).

Returning to our example at the beginning of the section, Kant's categorical imperative provides a moral guide that is absolute and without exception. It dictates that you cannot lie when you answer the door. If the ex-boyfriend asks if your roommate is home, you must tell the truth. Otherwise one person will be harmed. And, the perceived harm to anyone that is done by telling the truth is not a concern. When a person lies (even a little white lie) Kant would retort; what if everyone lies? What would happen if a promise was not kept? That said, one might ask; what if you promised to lie? In Kant's view, you have a solemn duty to humankind to tell the truth, regardless of your duty to friends, groups, or organizations. Kant argues that the potential exists that promises could never be kept, therefore, creating a slippery slope of the world disintegrating and the potential for anarchy. Kant is clear, lying is wrong regardless of rationale.

John Rawls (1921 to 2002): Justice and the Veil of Ignorance

John Rawls is one of the few influential U.S. American modern era ethical philosophers who is widely cited. Rawls' (1971) argues for justice as fairness as opposed to Kant's laws or Mill's utilitarianism (Johannesen, 2002). Justice, according to Rawls, does not depend on intuition to determine what is right, but fair procedures where a society can establish a set of ethical principles. These ethical principles will then serve to free oneself, and humanity, of the bias and self-interests based on social positions and education (Tubbs, 2010, p. 194). In order to accomplish this, Rawls argues that one should place themselves behind a veil of ignorance (Tubbs, p. 194). Behind this veil of ignorance we will not be biased by our place in society. Rawls' (1971) argues, "no one is in a position to tailor principles to" their advantage (p. 139). However, differences in status, power, wealth, and intelligence give privileged members of society an unequal advantage and more clout when certain moral ground rules of society are hammered out. Unless we place ourselves behind the veil of ignorance, those privileged members of society will use their position as an advantage.

In order to discover ethical rules that promote freedom for everyone, Rawls (1971) created the illusion of an ethical discussion held before we enter the world. Rawls presumes everyone can be positioned behind the veil of ignorance by agreeing on binding rules of behavior before they have any idea what societal position they will occupy. In doing so, Rawls defines an ethical system that is accepting and inclusive for everyone. Behind this veil of ignorance, rational people can create rules of justice that protect everyone. In short, if you don't know what societal position you will occupy, you cannot take a position that is self-serving to your own social position.

JUSTICE AND THE VEIL OF IGNORANCE

if you don't know what societal position you will occupy, you cannot take a position that is self-serving to your own social position.

Turning to our example again at the beginning of the section, ethical rules have not been agreed upon prior to the knock on the door. Perhaps a modified version of interactional rules might have been agreed upon by the roommates prior to the ex-boyfriend knocking on the door. Even if this had happened, Rawls would consider lying to the ex-boyfriend a violation of justice and the roommates would have positioned themselves in a higher social role, violating the rules of justice.

In a utopian society, this ethical theory would be perfect. However, given that humans do not agree upon a set of ethical rules prior to birth, Rawls might be asking for an impossible task for all of society to look at ethical decisions behind his "veil of ignorance." That said, Rawls does propose an interesting principle to explore societal justice and fairness. He provides the greatest benefits to the least advantaged and presents a framing of what many of these rules could look like if society were to exist behind this "veil of ignorance."

By now you may have grown weary of ethical principles. It has been my experience that students may have one of three responses to this content. The first is apathy. Unfortunately, even if you choose to show no interest or concern for ethics, you are still affected or engaged in ethics on a daily basis. If you are not aware of ethical principles, ultimately you will be driven by emotional and potentially erratic choices. Not by moral or ethical choices and decisions. Worse, you might be simply driven by your ego alone or even become a narcissist.

A second reaction is to cherry-pick from ethical approaches. In doing so, you will likely be predisposed to choose a theory or approach that best suits your immediate needs. For example, you could take an egotistical view when it suits your needs, but at other times choose to be an absolutist, like Kant, when asked to lie. Or, if you just need to tell a little white lie decide Aristotle was correct and the golden mean dictates that little white lies are acceptable.

The final approach is to select one theory or approach and balance your life choices based on the ethical framework you believe is best. By adapting a set of ethical principles, it will guide you through the hard times in life and when you are faced with a hard decision, you already have a framework in place to provide direction when you are facing a tough choice or decision.

© stoatphoto/Shutterstock.com

Discussion Questions

1. Define each of the following and be able to provide a short (1–2 sentences) explanation of each: ethics, morality, virtue.

2. Be able to briefly summarize each theory and provide an argument pro and con supporting or criticizing each theory.

3. Be able to briefly (1–2 sentences) explain in your own words the eight principles of Principle Based Ethics.

4. Consider what your own Moral Code or Ethical Code would say. Try writing one and getting feedback from peers and/or relatives.

References

Bayley, B. (2011). *Ethics, morality, and virtue: A foundation for modern training.* Retrieved from https://www.correstoinsone.come/corrections-training/articles/3225913-Ethics-morality-and-virtue-A-foundation-for-modern-training/

Beauchamp, T., Bowie, N., & Arnold, D. (2009). *Ethical theory and business* (8th ed.). Upper Saddle River, NJ: Prentice-Hall.

Benoit, W. L., & Lindsey, J. J. (1987). Argument strategies: Antidote to Tylenol's poisoned image. *Journal of the American Forensic Association, 23*, 136–146.

Bill Daniels Condensed Biography. (2018). Daniels Fund. Retrieved from http://www.danielsfund.org/About-Us/Bill-Daniels.asp

Bill Daniels' Values. (2018). Daniels Fund. Retrieved from http://www.danielsfund.org/About-Us/Bills-Values.asp

Business Ethics and Compliance Timeline. (2018). *Ethics & Compliance Initiative.* Retrieved from https://www.ethics.org/resources/free-toolkit/ethics-timeline/

Code of Business Conduct. (2016). The Coca-Cola Company. Retrieved from https://www.coca-colacompany.com/content/dam/journey/us/en/private/fileassets/pdf/our-company/2016-COBC-US-Final.pdf

Code of Conduct. (2018). Facebook. Retrieved from https://investor.fb.com/corporate-governance/code-of-conduct/default.aspx

Daniels Fund Ethics Initiative Overview. (2018). Daniels Fund. Retrieved from http://www.danielsfund.org/Ethics/

Daniels Fund Ethics Initiative Principles. (2016). Daniels Fund. Retrieved from http://www.danielsfund.org/_Assets/files/Ethics-Initiative/Daniels_Fund_Ethics_Initiative_Principles.pdf

Demetriou, A. J., & Olmon, J. T. (2007). Stone v. Ritter: The Delaware Supreme Court affirms the Caremark Standard for corporate compliance programs. *ABA Health eSource, 3*(6). Retrieved from https://www.americanbar.org/newsletter/publications/aba_health_esource_home/Volume3_06_demetriou.html

Grants. (2018). Daniels Fund. Retrieved from http://www.danielsfund.org/Grants/NewMexico.asp

Johannesen, R. L. (2002). *Ethics in human communication.* Waveland: Long Grove, IL.

Kant, I. (1959). *Foundations of the metaphysics of morals* (L. W. Black, Trans.) (2nd ed.). Indianapolis, IN: Pearson.

Kant, I. (1964). On a supposed right to lie from altruistic motives. *Critique of Practical Reason and Other Writings in Moral Philosophy* (L. W. Beck, Trans. & Ed.). Chicago, IL: University of Chicago.

Mill, J. S. (1968). *Selected writings of John Stuart Mill* (Maurice Cowling, Ed.). New York, NY: New American Library.

Northouse, P. G. (2018). *Introduction to leadership: Concepts and practice* (4th ed.). Los Angeles, CA: Sage.

Northouse, P. G. (2019). *Leadership: Theory and practice* (8th ed.). Los Angeles, CA: Sage.

Our Mission. (2018). Facebook. Retrieved from https://newsroom.fb.com/company-info/

Rawls, J. (1971). *A theory of justice.* Cambridge, MA: Harvard University Press.

Rist, M. (1972). *Epicurus: An introduction.* Cambridge, Eng.: Cambridge University.

Tubbs, S. (2010). *Human communication: Principles and contexts* (12th ed.). New York, NY: McGraw-Hill.

Why Have a Code of Conduct. (2018). Ethics & Compliance Initiative. Retrieved from https://www.ethics.org/resources/free-toolkit/code-of-conduct/

Culture and Communication

Eric L. Morgan

Objectives

- ► Explain the various reasons for the importance of studying communication and culture.
- ► Be able to define a symbolic definition of culture.
- ► Define enculturation and be able to apply concepts to personal experience.
- ► Identify sources of enculturation.

Culture. This term seems to be everywhere. We encounter the word "culture" on the news, in classes, in conversations, in newspapers, magazines, books, on the radio, reading blogs, and so forth. In many cases, people use the word as some sort of explanation. For example, one might claim that the reason a company suffered losses was because of "culture." Or perhaps, a certain team lost because of a "bad culture." Other times, one might hear people claim that they do certain things because it is their "culture." But what is culture? Why are so many people interested in understanding this concept? What good does it do us? These next sections will explore this concept and its relationship to the study of human communication. Before diving into a definition of culture for this first unit, I will first discuss some of the reasons why it is important to study cultural and intercultural communication. Along the way, I hope you will come to find the study and consideration of culture as fascinating as I do.

REASONS TO STUDY CULTURE

The world, as you probably know, is filled with all sorts of different people. It probably comes as little surprise that humans differ in the way they approach the world. People speak different languages, eat different foods, worship differently, and basically lead vastly different lives. Each of these areas of difference are a part of people's cultural systems. All of these differences create a diverse society. The fact that the world is culturally diverse is enough for many people to take an interest, but that fact alone is not the only reason we should be interested in the study of culture.

Consider how the world has changed in your lifetime alone. There have been enormous advances in both communication and transportation technologies (Martin & Nakayama, 2013). While it is true that many of you taking this class have never known a world without the Internet or cell phones (Nief & McBride, 2013), the pace of technological development remains extraordinary. I often invite students to consider what life would be like without a mobile device. This thought is almost always met with horror and consternation. With the increased access given to us through these technologies, we now live in a world where we can communicate with people from different parts of the world and different cultures instantly. One example that comes to mind is the relationships that I maintain with colleagues and friends in Finland, Egypt, Italy, and the Canadian Arctic. These relationships are now mostly maintained via communication technologies that have not existed for very long. Developments in transportation technologies have also increased rapidly over the course of the past few decades. Our ability to travel to other places within the space of days or hours is a relatively recent phenomenon. Did you know that it was only in 1959 when jet service was introduced into the aviation industry, thereby making flying much more accessible to large numbers of people (Petzinger, 1995)?

In fact, here in Southern New Mexico, we now have a commercial spaceport. The purpose of the Spaceport is to "enable affordable, efficient, and effective space access

... for everyone" (Spaceport America, 2012, ¶1). Because of these advances in technology, we often hear that the world is getting "smaller." One effect of this is that people from vastly different cultures now find it easier than ever before to interact with one another. Studying cultural and intercultural communication will help us in these interactions.

Although our ability to access diverse places in the world has increased dramatically, this is not the only reason to be concerned with issues of culture. You do not

© Mascha Tace/Shutterstock.com

even need to leave your place of residence to encounter other people who are culturally different. In fact, just by being in this class and a student at a university, you are confronted with cultural difference on a constant basis. As you are well aware, every 10 years the U.S. government takes a census. This is done for a number of reasons, including the apportionment of congressional seats as well as generating valuable data to determine how federal dollars should be spent.

One of the things the government measures is diversity of ethnic and racial groups. One indication from the 2010 Census was an estimation that more than half of all births in the United States would be classified as a minority (ESRI, 2012). Furthermore, all regions in the United States increased in diversity (ESRI). These data show convincingly that one need not even leave his or her home to encounter opportunities to engage in intercultural communication.

Intercultural scholars Judith Martin and Thomas Nakayama (2013) write that there are at least six different reasons why students in American universities should study intercultural communication. They call these reasons "imperatives" suggesting that we should not just be concerned with intercultural communication, but that it is an urgent necessity (Martin & Nakayama, p. 4). Aside from the technological and changing demographic imperative discussed previously, they also discuss an economic imperative, a peace imperative, a self-awareness imperative, and an ethical imperative. The economies of different nations are becoming increasingly interdependent on one another (a phenomenon known as globalization), which leads to potentially increased contact. Without an understanding of different cultural systems, this contact can potentially lead to global conflicts. Thus, the economic and peace imperatives are increasingly important. The self-awareness imperative suggests that studying intercultural communication can also be rewarding in the sense that we can grow in our understandings of ourselves. Personally, I have realized much about myself after traveling abroad and believe that these experiences have greatly enriched my life. Finally, the ethical imperative teaches us that through a careful study of cultural and intercultural communication we will be better able to resolve the inevitable ethical conflicts that arise whenever humans interact.

Martin and Nakayama (2013) list these six imperatives as reasons for studying intercultural communication; however, there are other reasons as well. Hall (2005) argues that through the study of cultural and intercultural communication, one is more likely to develop rewarding and fulfilling relationships. There are as many reasons for studying intercultural communication as there are those who study it. As you read through this section, I invite you to consider the ways that understanding different cultures can enrich your life. The remainder of this section will provide some background information that will help as you begin this journey.

DEFINING CULTURE

As mentioned, our society seems to use the term culture a lot. This leads us to ask what culture actually is. You may be surprised to learn that there are many different definitions of culture. In 1952, anthropologists Kroeber and Kluckhohn attempted to catalogue all the different definitions of culture in order to provide some clarity on the concept. They cited 150 different definitions. One would assume that a work of this scope would be sufficient for moving us forward. This assumption, however, is incorrect. Scholars from numerous disciplines continue to debate the concept to this day. In 2006, for example, Baldwin, Faulkner, Hecht, and Lindsley published an edited text that tries, yet again, to provide some clarity on the concept of culture. Their discussion highlights the strengths and weaknesses of many different definitions of culture. While it can be fun to explore these differences in depth, for our purposes, a specific definition of culture grounded in communication will be used.

One way to begin to approach the understanding of culture in the field of communication is by exploring how it is used by communication scholars. Essentially, there are three approaches that people take when treating culture in the study of communication. First, culture can be understood as a set of characteristics that particular groups share. These characteristics often include traditions, habits, foods, clothes, and ways of acting. When treated this way, culture can be associated with a particular group. It can also be understood as a variable that correlates with other variables such as demographic characteristics like ethnicity, age, or sex (Hall, 2005; Merrigan & Huston, 2015; Oetzel, 2009). A second popular approach to the study of communication defines culture as a "site of struggle" (Oetzel, 2009). This approach uses culture as a way to explain how different groups relate to each other in terms of power. In other words, we may try to understand how communication processes serve to marginalize certain groups and create systems of oppression (e.g., Gramsci, 1971). A third approach to the study of culture looks at culture as a system of meaning. This perspective sees culture as a way to describe how people make sense of the world (Carbaugh, 1988; Geertz, 1973; Philipsen, 1992). It is this last approach that forms the foundation for the definition we will use.

There are quite a few variations of discursive or communication-based definitions of culture. Perhaps the most succinct is David Schneider's (1976) view that culture is a "system of symbols and meanings" (p. 198). Bradford Hall (2005) similarly defines culture as an "historically shared system of symbolic resources, through which we make our world meaningful" (p. 4). A more detailed definition, and the one that we will operate with throughout the remainder of this section is that **culture** *is a complex system of symbolic resources, worldviews, values, and norms for the appropriate enactment of behavior.* This is a multifaceted definition, but one that allows us the best opportunity to explore the richness of culture. In order to better understand this definition, I'll discuss the different aspects.

CULTURE

a complex system of symbolic resources, worldviews, values, and norms for the appropriate enactment of behavior.

Symbols

Symbolic resources represent the "stuff" of culture in this discursive perspective (Carbaugh, 1990; Geertz, 1973; Hall, 2005; Hymes, 1972; Morgan, 2002; Philipsen, 1992). Symbolic resources are what people use to make sense of the world, as Hall reminds us. In order to understand symbolic resources, we first should understand what symbols are. **Symbols**, very simply, are anything that stands for something else (Hall). Flags are good examples. A flag is normally a piece of cloth with a design of some sort on it. This cloth, however, represents something. Sometimes they represent nations, sometimes states or provinces, sometimes cities, sometimes organizations, and sometimes military units. The point is that the cloth represents something else. Words are also symbols. Whenever we use a word to refer to something, that word is symbolically representing something else. More specifically, the word is representing a thought or idea. In this way, symbols are meaningful. In fact, symbols are "infinitely rich in significance" (Colapietro, 1993, p. 191).

SYMBOLS

anything that stands for something else.

This brings us to two important characteristics of symbols; arbitrariness and conventionality (Hall, 2005). A commonly heard description of symbols is that they are arbitrary in their meanings. This means that there is not really any natural reason why a symbol needs to represent what it does. For example, there is no real reason why the particular design of the U.S. flag has to represent the nation-state of the United States of America. Rather, people throughout the world have generally agreed that it does. A good way to demonstrate the arbitrariness of symbols is to look at different languages. The Merriam-Webster Online Dictionary (2013) defines a table as a "piece of furniture consisting of a smooth flat slab fixed on legs." In Spanish, this same piece of furniture is labeled "mesa." Neither label is more correct than the other. In

© Peter Hermes Furian/Shutterstock.com

fact, there is nothing about the words themselves that must mean a slab fixed on legs. Rather, people who speak these languages generally agree that they do. This notion of general agreement is referred to as conventionality. Conventionality means that a relatively large group of people agree that a certain symbol will refer to a thought concept. Oftentimes, these concepts are real objects in the world, but not always. For instance, because we have these symbols, we are able to refer to more abstract entities like freedom, liberty, or spirit. Because symbols are conventional, they tend to be relatively stable within groups. You can't just go about making up new symbols for things in the world and have anyone understand you.

Symbolic Resources

A resource is anything that people use. One example of a natural resource is water. People throughout the world need to use water in order to survive. Because of this, people have created societal institutions to ensure the availability of water and its distribution. Another example of a resource is oil. Oil is used to create energy to power vehicles, heat homes in many parts of the world, and create plastic, among many other things. Because of its many uses, oil is highly valued as a resource. Perhaps a more important resource, however, are symbolic resources. People use symbols to refer to objects, to express emotions, to create and maintain groups, and generally to make the world around us meaningful. Without symbols, we could not coordinate our actions to use any other type of resource, like oil. In other words, we have to be able to refer to oil, and generally share the same conception of what it is, if we want to be able to drill for it, refine it, transport it to your local gas station, and pump the gas into your vehicle.

Differences in the systems of symbolic resources lead to differences in cultural groups. Different people use different symbols to do different things. Idioms serve as a good example. In spoken American English, it is common to hear "Hey, what's up?" as a greeting. Speakers of this language know that this question is not really a request to inform the speaker of what is above her or him; rather, they understand that it is a greeting. Oftentimes, speakers of different languages in the United States for the first time become confused by the use of this symbolic resource. These international visitors might mistake the greeting for an actual question, thus causing some confusion. In this case, there is simply a difference in understanding how these symbolic resources are to be used. The same American who says, "What's up?" may be confused if confronted with the Korean phrase, "odgaseyo." Literally, translated, this means, "Where are you going?" It functions the same way as saying "How are you?" or "What's going on?" in English (Hall, 2005). The expectation is not that the person being asked tell the speaker where she or he is going, but rather to engage in a greeting. Our use of these symbolic resources in a meaningful way is taught to us, an idea we'll explore next.

CULTURE IS LEARNED (HISTORICALLY SHARED)

ENCULTURATION

the process of learning one's native cultural system.

The process of learning one's own cultural system is known as **enculturation**. In fact, it is a process in which the systems of symbolic resources and the meanings they represent are passed on from generation to generation and within communities. In this way culture is shared, but how is it that we share culture? One way that culture is shared is through families. As children grow up, they are taught the system that allows them to appropriately communicate. This includes learning the language as well as the rules for appropriate use of language and the rules for understanding what certain symbolic resources mean.

Many children learn this from their parents and other extended family members. I'm fortunate to have two nieces. Over the years, I have watched and engaged in the instruction of appropriate language and communication use for my nieces. I'm always fascinated by how quickly they learn words. This learning process, at least for the variety of English that my family members and I are teaching, consists of pointing out objects in certain contexts and then saying the word. We also correct their use of language when words are mispronounced or used inappropriately. In doing so, we are teaching the children the meaning of certain symbolic resources.

© Lara Cold/Shutterstock.com

Another source of cultural learning comes from our peers. In the United States, many children are exposed to schooling at increasingly young ages. Throughout our educational lives, we learn from others in similar positions. For example, you may have learned how to play schoolyard games from your friends at school. You also learn how to appropriately (and sometimes inappropriately) act with others of a similar age. Our peer groups exert enormous pressure on us to conform to particular ways of being and acting. Everything from how to talk, to how we dress, to the music we listen to, and the activities we engage in is influenced by our peers. When asked, students frequently report that their preferences for popular culture artifacts like music, movies, or fashion are mostly influenced by their peer group.

Yet another source of cultural learning is from other societal members who may not be peers. An example is perhaps the best way to explain this concept. I grew up in the southwestern United States. When I was in my mid-20s I moved to New England. I had been to big cities before, but I had never had to negotiate one on a daily basis until I moved there. One of the things I learned was how to ride the subway system in Boston, known as the "T." I learned this by watching others. From observing, I knew that I had to purchase a token (the T no longer uses tokens, so I would probably need to relearn everything), quickly move through the turnstile, and wait patiently for a train. While on the train, I learned the rules guiding where and how to sit and even how to look at people. Not looking at people seemed to be a crucial aspect of appropriately riding the subway, especially when it was crowded. No one ever explicitly told me these rules. Rather, I learned them from the members of society who were more experienced at riding the subway.

An important source of cultural knowledge is the media. The influence of the media on people's behavior is a well-researched topic. Perhaps the most comprehensive program of study is the work done by George Gerbner and his colleagues (see Morgan & Shanahan, 1996, for a comprehensive review). This program of study is broadly known as the Cultural Indicators Project. Scholars in this tradition work hard to determine the effects that media, particularly television, has on people. One theory that these scholars have developed is cultivation analysis. The basic argument of this theory is that the media cultivates particular attitudes, which lead to a shared way of perceiving the world (Littlejohn & Foss, 2011). For instance, they have found that heavy viewers of television tend to see the world as a violent and gloomy place because of all the violence on television. This belief can be so strong that people will believe that the world is a more violent place than it actually is. This is known as the "mean world syndrome" (Signorelli, 1990).

The point here is that the media provides us with an understanding of the cultural worlds in which we live. Try watching your favorite television program while thinking about the cultural messages that are being communicated. You may be surprised at the types of understandings you have because of this. Because media is such a powerful source of cultural knowledge and enculturation, many advocacy groups monitor the representation of various communities in the media. Organizations like the Media Education Foundation help to educate media consumers about the possible influences of media (both negative and positive).

This brief section introduces you to the concept of culture. In this section, the goal was to establish the link between the study of culture and communication as well as to discuss some aspects of enculturation. In the next section, we will explore the various ways that culture is expressed.

Discussion Questions

1. What are some other benefits to studying and engaging in intercultural communication not discussed in the section?

2. What might be a few drawbacks to studying and engaging in intercultural communication?

3. How does thinking about culture as a meaning system differ from other ways that culture is used in your interactions with others?

References

Baldwin, J. R., Faulkner, S. L., Hecht, M. L., & Lindsley, S. L. (Eds.). (2006). *LEA's communication series. Redefining culture: Perspectives across the disciplines.* Mahwah, NJ, US: Lawrence Erlbaum Associates, Inc. Publishers.

Carbaugh, D. (1988). Comments on culture in communication inquiry. *Communication Reports, 1,* 38–41.

Carbaugh, D. (Ed.) (1990). *Cultural communication and intercultural contact.* Mahwah, NJ: Lawrence Erlbaum Associates, Inc. Publishers.

Colapietro, V. M. (1993). *Glossary of semiotics.* New York: Paragon House.

ESRI. (2012). Diversity index statement 2012. Retrieved from http://www.esri.com/library/whitepapers/pdfs/diversity-index-methodology.pdf

Geertz, C. (1973). *The interpretation of cultures.* New York: Basic Books.

Gramsci, A. (1971). *Selections from the prison notebooks* (Q. Hoare & G. N. Smith, Trans.). New York: International Publishers.

Hall, B. J. (2005). *Among cultures: The challenge of communication.* Belmont, CA: Thompson Wadworth.

Hymes, D. (1972). Models of the interaction of language and social life. In J. Gumperz & D. Hymes (Eds.), *Directions in sociolinguistics: The ethnography of communication.* New York: Holt, Rinehart, and Winston.

Kroeber, A., & Kluckhohn, C. (1952). *Culture: A critical review of concepts and definitions.* Cambridge, MA: Harvard University Press.

Littlejohn, S. W., & Foss, K. A. (2011). *Theories of human communication* (10th ed.). Long Grove, IL: Waveland Press, Inc.

Martin, J. N., & Nakayama, T. K. (2013). *Intercultural communication in contexts* (6th ed.). New York: McGraw-Hill.

Merriam-Webster. (2013, April). Definition of table. Merriam-Webster Online. Retrieved from http://www.merriam-webster.com/dictionary/table

Merrigan, G., & Huston, C. L. (2015). *Communication research methods.* New York: Oxford University Press.

Morgan, E. (2002). *Communicating environment: Cultural discourses of place in the Pioneer Valley of Western Massachusetts.* Doctoral Dissertation. (University of Massachusetts, Amherst). Dissertation Abstracts International, 63, 1A.

Morgan, M., & Shanahan, J. (1996). Two decades of cultivation research: An appraisal and a meta-analysis. In B. Burleson (Ed.), *Communication Yearbook, 20.* Thousand Oaks, CA: Sage Publication.

Nief, R., & McBride, T. (2013). Beloit mindset list 2016 [Video file]. Retrieved from http://sofo.mediasite.com/Mediasite/Play/5a4306b5820a411fb6a7dfb4551380ce1d

Oetzel, J. (2009). *Intercultural communication: A layered approach.* New York: Pearson.

Petzinger, T. (1995). *Hard landing: The epic contest for power and profits that plunged the airlines into chaos.* New York: Times Business.

Philipsen, G. (1992). *Speaking culturally: Explorations in social communication.* Albany, NY: State University of New York Press.

Schneider, D. (1976). Notes toward a theory of culture. In K. H. Basso & H. A. Selby (Eds.), *Meaning in anthropology.* Albuquerque, NM: University of New Mexico Press.

Signorelli, N. (1990). Television's mean and dangerous world: A continuation of the cultural indicators perspective. In N. Signorielli & M. Morgan (Eds.), *Cultivation analysis: New directions in media effects research.* Newbury Park: Sage Publications.

Spaceport America. (2012). Spaceport America: Your invitation to space. Retrieved from http://spaceportamerica.com/

Section 7

Expressions of Culture and Communication

Eric L. Morgan

Objectives

▶ Understand the importance of narrative in the communication of culture.
▶ Recognize and analyze ritual as a form of cultural communication.
▶ Characterize and describe worldviews, values, and norms.

The previous section discussed some of the sources of cultural knowledge and learning. Even if you travel to a different country as an adult, you will likely turn to peers, other societal members, the media, and sometimes family for cultural understanding. This section discusses how cultural knowledge is communicated to us more specifically through narratives and rituals.

EXPRESSIONS OF CULTURE

Narratives

The stories we tell each other are vitally important as a means for the transmission of culture (Fisher, 1987; Hall, Covarrubias, & Kirschbaum, 2018). These stories are referred to as narratives. A narrative, according to Hall (2005), is a retelling of events from a specific point of view. We tell narratives to one another all the time. As children, we are often told narratives that are important to our families.

Perhaps it was the story of how your family came to live where they do, or perhaps it was a story about your crazy uncle who got into trouble. Regardless, these narratives teach us about culture. We also learn culture through broad narratives that many people share. Stories like fairy tales and legends communicate important cultural messages. In short, narratives are an important aspect of our daily communicative lives.

NARRATIVE

a story. A retelling of events from a particular viewpoint.

They are particularly important because they function to do at least four things.

Hall (2005) outlines four functions of narrative. The first function of narrative is that they provide us information about our place in the world relative to society and other people. In this way, narratives help us shape our identities. Second, narratives tell about how the world works in both general terms and in particular contexts. Third, narratives tell us how to act in the world. Finally, narratives tell us how to evaluate the world around us in terms of good and bad, right and wrong. The following example of my own story may shed some light on how narratives operate.

> Throughout my childhood, I was told the story of how my mother's side of the family came to live in New Mexico. My grandfather was one of 11 children who grew up in Alabama on a farm.

> When he was 14, my great-grandparents lost the farm and ended up traveling to Arkansas. At a very young age, my grandfather struck out on his own trying to find work as a farm laborer. His situation was made all the more difficult because of the Great Depression. Anyway, he met and married my grandmother in Arkansas and they sought to make a living in California. By this time, World War II had broken out, and there was word that work could be had for ship laborers in San Francisco. They journeyed to the Bay area, and my grandfather worked in the shipyards. He was too old to join the military by this time, but he was still in need of a job. After the war, one of his brothers was hired on as a miner in Carlsbad, NM. My grandfather packed up the family and moved to Carlsbad in hopes of finding work. They arrived, but due to an injury sustained in the shipyards, my grandfather was unable to work the mines. He was a carpenter by trade, so they journeyed north to Artesia, where he remained working as a carpenter for many years.

What types of lessons might I learn from this story? Well, first, it tells me about who my family is and by extension who I am and where I fit in society. The family was not wealthy, which meant that they had to travel in order to find work to survive (place in the world and how to act in the world). Second, the narrative teaches me that the world, at least at that time, required people to sacrifice for the war effort and labor in any way they could. I also learned that work could be hard to find (how the world works). Third, the story teaches me to work hard and eventually life will become more comfortable (how to act in the world). Finally, the story teaches me that working hard and continually striving to be better is a good thing (how to evaluate the world). I could relate any number of stories by way of example, but doing this exercise yourself can be quite illuminating from a cultural perspective.

Rituals

Culture is performed constantly. Every action we perform is influenced in some way by culture. Oftentimes, these actions are structured and performed repeatedly. When this occurs, we are dealing with rituals. A ritual, according to Hall (2005), is a sequence of events that functions to "celebrate" an important cultural value or aspect. Rituals are important to understand because they remind us what our cultural systems value. Charles Frake (1990) writes about an interesting ritual that he analyzed when he worked with the Subanun in Zambrano Province in the Philippines. He recounts that the structure of drinking is an important ritual that allows the group to resolve disputes and reaffirm their sense of community. The drinking ritual occurs when drinking *gasi*. Gasi is a rice-fermented beverage that is drunk from a jar with a straw. Apparently, according to Frake, the liquid packs quite a punch if one drinks a lot of it. Anyway, after the invitation to drink occurs, there will be a series of rounds in which people drink from the same jar one after the other. Over the course of the drinking ritual, there is a structured way of communicating. First, the invitation is provided and permission is granted to drink. During the initial rounds, the people involved engage in small talk. In later rounds, group disputes are brought up, discussed, and resolved. Finally, the drinking ritual concludes with a number of competitions. Frake notes that this is a general order, but that these elements will be present in all drinking rituals. This is far different than the "drinking" rituals found on college campuses throughout the United States, as you might imagine. Considering this example, what do you think is being "celebrated through this ritual"? One analysis might suggest that for the Subanun, this drinking ritual pays homage to a particular form of interaction that accomplishes the work of living together in community. As such, the ritual celebrates a sense of being Subanun. There are many such rituals across cultures that celebrate community involvement.

Another good example of ritual was outlined by Tamar Katriel (1990) who writes about "griping" among some Israelis. According to Katriel, groups of Israelis will gather on Friday evenings and discuss the Situation. (Note: Situation is capitalized here because it refers to the situation in which everyday Israeli citizens find themselves by virtue of living in Israel.) The discussion takes on the character of griping and is only conducted with other Israelis. If one finds him- or herself with close friends, then they will begin griping about specific situations and move to more general situations. With acquaintances, precisely the opposite occurs. The structure of the ritual sees people engaging in turns at griping where one person will begin and everyone in the group will then take a turn at griping. What is being reinforced here is a sense of community that is unique to Israelis. As with narratives, we could go on all day about different rituals from different cultures; however, it will be more meaningful if you analyze one of your own rituals as with the narratives discussed.

WORLDVIEWS, VALUES, AND NORMS

Now that we discussed some ways that culture is communicated, let's turn our attention to some other aspects of culture. Recall the definition of culture used in this class. It is a complex system of symbolic resources, worldviews, values, and norms for the appropriate enactment of behavior. The following discussion will explain what is meant by worldviews, values, and norms. An extended example from my research in the Canadian Arctic will follow in order to illustrate how these differ cross-culturally.

Worldviews

A worldview is a deeply felt assumption or basic premise about the way the world is (Hall, 2005). People differ in their orientations to the world at fundamental levels. Where some people will orient to the world as perhaps an evil place, others may orient to the world as a fundamentally good place. This diversity is often hard to grasp, because we tend never to question our assumptions about the world. The world simply is the way it is for many people.

Investigating differences in worldviews has been the hallmark of most cultural research. Cultural researchers are interested in documenting the variation in

WORLDVIEW

deeply felt assumption about the nature of the world.

humanity's take on the world. Hall, Covarrubias, et al. (2018) discuss at least eight different worldview dimensions that can be used to analyze the diversity of cultural groups. Each of these worldview dimensions describes the answer to some fundamental question. The worldview dimensions and their questions, along with some other clarifying questions, are summarized in the following table (note that the basic questions in the table are Hall et al.'s, while the clarifying questions are my interpretation).

Cultural groups will normally share a general sense of the answers to these questions. The system of meaning for each cultural group organizes the answers to these fundamental questions. The result is a cultural worldview. For instance, many U.S. Americans hold to the following worldviews. They fundamentally believe that people are individuals who should work hard to achieve their position in society. This is possible because all people are fundamentally equal. Nature is seen as something that should be mastered in order to best serve the needs of society. Language is a primary tool for exchanging information, and is, therefore, the primary way that meaning is

Table **1.1**

Worldview Dimension	Basic Question	Clarifying Question
Identity is grounded in… Individualism–Collectivism	Who Am I?	Am I an individual first (individualism), or am I a member of a group first (collectivism)?
Social position gained through… Ascription–Achievement	How do people gain their position in society?	Are people given their position in society (ascription), or do people have to work for their position (achievement)?
Society as… Egalitarian–Hierarchical	How is society organized?	Is society assumed to be comprised of equals (egalitarian), or are there basic differences between types of people (hierarchical)?
People are basically… Good–Evil	What is the basic nature of humans?	Are people believed to be basically good, or are people believed to be basically evil?
People's relationship to environment is one of… Mastery–Adaptation	How do people orient to the natural environment?	Do people shape their environment to meet their needs (mastery), or do people adapt to the environment and live according to its rhythms and patterns (adaptation)?
Language is conceived as… Information–Social Lubricant	What is the fundamental purpose of language?	Is language primarily a tool for providing information, or is language used primarily for facilitating relationships among people (social lubricant)?
Meaning can be considered… High Context–Low Context	Where does meaning lie?	Does meaning come mostly from the contexts in which people find themselves (i.e., is meaning highly contextual)? Or is meaning found primarily in the explicit, verbal message (low context)?
People orient to time as…. Polychronic–Monochronic	What is time?	Do people see time as progressing in a linear fashion with things happening one after the other (monochronic), or does time flow in a more circular fashion with multiple things occurring simultaneously (polychronic)?

shared. Time is normally conceived of as linear, and events and tasks are normally accomplished one after the other, thus pointing to a more monochronic orientation.

Another way to think about these fundamental assumptions that organize communities is with the idea of cultural premises (Carbaugh, 1996, 2005, 2007; Fitch, 1996; Morgan, 2002; Scollo, 2011). Just as with a worldview, a cultural premise can be seen as a deeply felt assumption about the way the world works. In general, scholars discuss five basic premises, which include personhood, emotion, acting, relating, and dwelling. Personhood refers to fundamental assumptions about what a person is. This would encompass both the individualism–collectivism dimension and the good–evil dimension highlighted in the table. The cultural premise of emotion describes the different ways that people experience emotion. The cultural premise of acting describes the culturally viable ways that people can act in the world. Relating refers to the cultural premise of how relationships between people are accomplished. Finally, the cultural premise of dwelling describes the different ways people inhabit the earth.

Each perspective on worldview is useful for describing and understanding the diversity of humanity. People across the globe are members of cultures that fundamentally differ in the ways these premises and dimensions are patterned. It is important to realize that because worldviews and cultural premises are assumptions, they are rarely, if ever, questioned by members of cultural groups. In fact, these assumptions form a lens through which cultural members see the world. This lens is particular to a cultural system. When confronted with a different lens, many people can sometimes feel threatened and therefore judge alternative lenses as inferior. This is a phenomenon known as ethnocentrism. **Ethnocentrism** literally means understanding one's own group as the "center." This can sometimes lead to members of cultural groups believing that their group is superior to other cultural groups. This belief in the superiority of one's own group defines prejudice and can lead to the discrimination of others who operate with a different cultural lens on the world. It is impossible to escape ethnocentrism, but we can be vigilant in suspending our judgments of right and wrong, better and worse, when it comes to interacting with others from different cultures. This is particularly true when it comes to ethically interacting with others who may differ in terms of values.

ETHNOCENTRISM

the belief that one's cultural framework is superior to all others.

Values

A value is a belief about how the world should be (Hall, 2005). Values differ from worldviews in that these are often discussed among people, sometimes debated, and held up as ideals to which people should aspire. Values arise from worldview assumptions or cultural premises. A value can sometimes be related to worldviews in seemingly contradictory ways; however, from a cultural standpoint, worldviews and values will always be consistent. Take the worldview topic of good and evil, for example. Many people believe the world is a bad place filled with bad people. Because of that, people should value honesty in order to make the world a better place. People within the same cultural system can disagree as to specific values; however, it is unlikely that people within the same cultural system will hold vastly different worldview assumptions about the world.

Norms

A norm is a behavior. It isn't just any behavior though, it is a typical behavior that conforms to, and therefore reinforces, a sense of appropriateness (Carbaugh, 1990; Schneider, 1976). I'm sure you've noticed that people act in patterned ways. It would be an odd sight indeed to see a complete stranger come into class completely nude and start yelling. In fact, I would bet that you have never seen this occur. This is because such behavior would not make cultural sense. There would certainly be culturally patterned ways that we make sense of such an act, but the behavior itself is outside the norms of culture. In fact, we would likely determine that such a person was unfit to continue to live a normal life and probably put them away in an institution. As a rule, we tend not to act in random ways or in ways that others around us wouldn't understand. This is because our behaviors are culturally grounded in notions of appropriateness. Every time we engage in a behavior, we do so in such a way that reinforces our cultural system. If a behavior does not make sense, then a lot of "work" goes into finding out how we can make sense of the behavior.

An Arctic Interlude

One way we can really start to see just how different cultures are and how certain behaviors are made sense of differently is to travel abroad. During my travels and study in Arctic Canada, I routinely acted in ways that did not make cultural sense to the people living there. This was simply because I did not know enough of the cultural system of symbolic resources, worldviews, values, and norms in order to act in a culturally appropriate way. Several incidences come to mind that highlight how these aspects of culture operate. What follows is a brief account of how I came to learn about ways of living in the Arctic.

I had arrived in the town of Iqaluit, Nunavut, Canada, full of excitement and wonder about the place I would be living for a while. It was my first time "north of 60" (north of 60 degrees N latitude), and I was ready to live the life of an arctic adventurer. I was planning to spend some time in Iqaluit talking to people and researching how the establishment of the territory of Nunavut was impacting the cultural ways of life of people who lived there. During those days, I made a number of friends both Inuit and non-Inuit. One evening I was sitting with some Inuit friends learning how to carve soapstone. The conversation turned to what I would be doing the next week and I causally said, "I'm going out on the land." When I said this, the gentleman who asked me the question paused in his sanding of the stone, looked at me quizzically, and muttered, "Huh?. eeeeeee huh. OK." The other folks around looked at each other and smiled. I knew I had said something that didn't quite make sense. This came as a bit of a surprise to me because I had heard a lot of people say the phrase "on the land." I assumed that the phrase was just the way to refer to camping or backpacking, which was the activity I was going to do. I had even seen the phrase in the newspaper! We went back to sanding our soapstone in silence. I was confused because I really wanted to share my excitement about my upcoming trek with these folks, but they seemed profoundly uninterested. Finally, one of the men looked up at me and said, "You have a gun?" "Nah." I replied. He shrugged his shoulders and said, "You want, you can take mine." I shrugged, and with furrowed brow, replied, "Nah. I think I'm good." There were general shrugs all around.

The next day I was having lunch with another Inuk friend of mine. She asked what I was doing over the next couple of weeks. Still not knowing much, I replied with, "I'm heading out on the land." She looked at me with a startled expression and said, "huh?" I repeated that I was going "out on the land" thinking that perhaps she hadn't heard me the first time. While I was expecting the next question to be, "Where are you going?", I was surprised when she replied with, "Uh. OK . . . (long pause). . . you taking a gun?" You can imagine my surprise when she said this. I replied that I did not have a gun and that some other folks asked me the same question. She shrugged as if she expected that response and said, "You want to take mine?" This came as a total surprise, but I was trying to be nonchalant, as an insider would, and simply replied, "Nah. I think it will be too heavy." She shook her head slightly and said that I should call immediately upon my return in a couple weeks or she would call the RCMP (Royal Canadian Mounted Police) to come find me. We finished our lunch, and I wandered off confused by the entire exchange. I knew by this time that I was clearly saying something wrong, but I wasn't clear yet that it was the phrase "on the land." Things became a bit clearer a few days later.

One evening, I was sitting outside watching the sun low in the sky light up the bay and the clouds with a variety of colors. Two Inuit acquaintances were walking by and stopped to ask how I was. One didn't speak a word of English, while the other one enjoyed chatting and translating into Inuktitut. My skills with Inuktitut were not such that I could carry on much of a conversation, so I was especially happy that this person was here. Inevitably, they asked what I was going to do over the weekend. I replied that I was flying up to Qikiqtarjuaq and walking to Pangnirtung, a town 180 kilometers south. Notice that I did not say "on the land." I figured that I could ask about that phrase but hadn't gotten around to it yet. I knew

that my acquaintance who was translating was from Qikiqtarjuaq and had made that same journey a number of times in her youth. She seemed pleased and asked, "Do you have a husky dog?" This was not a question I expected. I half expected her to ask if I had a gun, but certainly not a dog. I told her that I did not have a dog (or a gun for that matter). She shrugged and said, "I have my brother. . . . he's up there . . . you want . . . you can take a husky dog . . . he has some."

What do you think was going on? I asked myself this question repeatedly. While I knew that these were a friendly and hospitable people, their offers just seemed to be too generous. I found out that one reason for the offer of both guns and dogs was to protect against *nanuq*. Otherwise known as *ursa maritimus*, or the polar bear. Going out "on the land" without a gun for protection or a dog for warning was, quite simply, crazy in

the minds of my friends. A more profound explanation, however, lies in the worldviews, values, and norms that shape Inuit life. To illustrate, I will briefly contrast my cultural orientation with that of many Inuit.

I grew up in Santa Fe, New Mexico. My family lived in a small house on the south side of town. We had two cars, a grocery store down the street, and when I was about 10, a new shopping mall was built about a mile down the road. While in town, I lived like everyone else. I wouldn't think twice about getting in my car to drive a couple blocks to buy a candy bar. I never thought twice about the effort it took to keep lights on or to provide heat in the winter. In short, my life was one that had all the modern conveniences associated with life in a developed nation. Growing up, my father would take me fishing or camping on weekends to the mountains around Santa Fe. It was here that I learned to love wilderness. I cherished my time in the mountains and worked to acquire camping and backpacking gear so I could spend more time in the mountains. For me, the mountains were a place to escape from the pace of everyday life in town. They were a place of awe-inspiring tranquility and a place to recharge. I knew that the mountains could be a harsh environment, but that only added to their beauty and reinforced their separation from life in an urban environment. This was how I learned to dwell in, or inhabit, the land around me. The urban environment was the place to engage in "important" activities like working and school while the non-urban environment was the place to go for recreation. This patterning of place represents a cultural worldview premise. It is also one that is fairly widespread throughout some of the world.

In the Arctic, spending time with nature in the way just described does occur, but there is also a different way to dwell. There is, in short, a different cultural premise surrounding dwelling. The Arctic environment is brutally harsh, especially in the winter. Depending on how far north one is, one will experience 24 hours of sunlight in the summer and 24 hours of darkness in the winter. Because the land, when it isn't covered in snow and ice, remains frozen (tundra), no agricultural crops can be cultivated on a wide scale. This means that the indigenous people, the Inuit, have had to adapt to life in this environment. They have done so successfully for over 4,000 years. Traditionally, the Inuit were (and some still are) a nomadic people. They would move from hunting camp to hunting camp depending on the changing conditions of the environment around them. They would hunt seal, caribou, walrus, whale, and the occasional polar bear. They would fish for Arctic Char. In the brief late summer, they would gather berries before the snows came again. Today, in Nunavut (which means "our land" in Inuktitut), more and more Inuit are moving into permanent communities like Iqaluit ("place of many fish"), Qikiqtarjuaq ("Big Island"), or Pangnirtung ("Place of Bull Caribou").

Given this brief description of the Inuit in the Arctic, it is possible to figure out why I kept speaking in ways that didn't make cultural sense. First, when someone says "on the land," she or he is using a symbolic resource that means that someone is going to live off the land, including hunting and fishing. There is a sense that this life is closer to the traditional Inuit way of living. When I kept saying it, my friends and acquaintances were surprised that I would do such a thing. First off, I'm not Inuit, which meant to them that I would need to live with a group of Inuit on the land in order to learn the appropriate behaviors. Second, I believe they doubted my capabilities in being able to live on the land in a traditional sense. It was well known there that

I was a newcomer interested in learning about Inuit ways of life. However, I hadn't been there long enough to gain the appropriate skills necessary to be self-sufficient. I wasn't even taking a gun, which meant that either I was going to scrounge for my food or I wasn't really going "out on the land." In short, when I used this symbolic resource, I was invoking a cultural worldview about dwelling and its associated value of self-sufficiency, which my friends knew was highly unlikely. Thus, the confusion. Eventually, I made it through my backpacking trip with my close friend and had to come home to the United States. While there, though, I learned many powerful lessons about what it means to live in an environment radically different from one I'm used to and was able to begin the process of cultural adaptation.

CONCLUSION

In this brief section, we explored some various ways that culture is expressed. There are certainly more ways that this occurs, and (as with all discussions in this book) I would invite you to explore further. Here we learned about the importance of narratives and rituals and how they play important roles in teaching us about culture. We also covered what I sometimes refer to as the "stuff" of culture. Worldviews, values, and norms are concepts that help us describe and understand various cultural systems. In the next section, we will briefly cover what happens when we expose ourselves to different cultural spaces.

Discussion Questions

1. How would you respond to the questions associated with Hall's worldview dimensions?

2. Think of a family story. What are the cultural lessons learned from that story?

3. Describe a cultural ritual in which you engage regularly. After the description, discuss what is being celebrated through the performance of this ritual.

References

Carbaugh, D. (Ed.). (1990). *Cultural communication and intercultural contact.* Mahwah, NJ: Lawrence Erlbaum Associates, Inc. Publishers.

Carbaugh, D. (1996). *Situating selves: The communication of social identities in American scenes.* Albany, NY: SUNY Press.

Carbaugh, D. (2005). *Cultures in conversation.* Mahwah, NJ: Lawrence Erlbaum Associates, Inc. Publishers.

Carbaugh, D.(2007). Cultural discourse analysis: Communication practices and intercultural encounters. *Journal of Intercultural Communication Research, 36*(3), 167–182.

Fitch, K. (1996). *Speaking relationally: Culture, communication, and interpersonal connection.* New York: Guilford Press.

Fisher, W. R. (1987). *Human communication as a narration: Toward a philosophy of reason, value, and action.* Columbia, SC: University of South Carolina Press.

Frake, C. O. (1990). How to ask for a drink in Subanun. In P. P. Gigioli (Ed.), *Language and social context.* New York: Penguin Books.

Hall, B. J. (2005). *Among cultures: The challenge of communication.* Belmont, CA: Thompson Wadworth.

Hall, B. J., Covarrubias, P., & Kirschbaum, K. A. (2018). *Among cultures: The challenge of communication.* New York: Routledge.

Katriel, T. (1990). 'Griping' as a verbal ritual in some Israeli discourse. In D. Carbaugh (Ed.), *Cultural communication and intercultural contact* (pp. 99–117). Mahwah, NJ: Lawrence Erlbaum Associates, Inc. Publishers.

Morgan, E. (2002). *Communicating environment: Cultural discourses of place in the Pioneer Valley of Western Massachusetts.* Doctoral Dissertation. (University of Massachusetts, Amherst). Dissertation Abstracts International, 63, 1A.

Schneider, D. (1976). Notes toward a theory of culture. In K. H. Basso & H. A. Selby (Eds.), *Meaning in anthropology.* Albuquerque, NM: University of New Mexico Press.

Scollo, M. (2011). Cultural approaches to discourse analysis: A theoretical and methodological conversation with special focus on Donal Carbaugh's cultural discourse theory. *Journal of Multicultural Discourses, 6*(1), 1–32.

Cross-Cultural Adaptation

Eric L. Morgan

Objectives

- ▶ Describe the process of acculturation.
- ▶ Apply aspects of one model of acculturation to one's life.
- ▶ Characterize and describe some principles for intercultural communication.

LEARNING DIFFERENT CULTURAL SYSTEMS

We've covered a lot of ground in these sections on culture up to this point. Now, we should consider what might happen if you decide to travel to a different culture. In order to begin, I'll remind us of one term and introduce another, enculturation and acculturation. Enculturation is the process of learning one's dominant cultural system. As a U.S. American, I learned a cultural system that many other U.S. Americans learned. My Inuit friends, likewise, learned a cultural system that other Inuit have learned. It's important to realize that we learn culture and are not born into it. One could take a child, for example, an Inuk child, born in Iqaluit and raise that child in the Outback of Australia and the child will be enculturated into the dominant cultural system in Australia. **Acculturation**, on the other hand, is the process of learning another cultural system. If we were to travel abroad or immigrate to a different country, we would have to go through this process. More specifically, Hall (2005) defines acculturation as the "process of becoming communicatively competent in a culture we have not been raised in" (p. 270). Here, Hall is using the notion of **interpersonal communication competence**, which requires that the person communicating do so in both *effective* and *appropriate* ways (Spitzberg & Cupach, 1984). In order to adjust to a different cultural system, we need to learn both the communication skills to be effective (i.e., language and nonverbal communication) as well as to recognize what is appropriate.

One scholar of acculturation, Kalvero Oberg (1960), found that people sometimes had difficulty when they traveled to different cultures. He called this phenomenon **culture shock.** Culture shock can also be understood as "acculturative stress" or the psychological and physical stress associated with adjusting to a different cultural system. Culture shock occurs when people feel discouraged and disoriented when in a new culture (Hall, 2005). This discouragement and disappointment arises

ACCULTURATION

the process of learning a different cultural system. Becoming communicatively competent in a different cultural system.

INTERPERSONAL COMMUNICATION COMPETENCE

communicating in effective and appropriate ways.

CULTURE SHOCK

feeling disoriented and discouraged in a different cultural system because one's expectations are continually unmet.

when our expectations are not met. Recall that culture provides us with a framework for making sense of the world. Whenever we encounter a different culture, we are, in fact, encountering a different framework, and things just don't make sense. Over time, these feelings can build up and lead to frustration. Part of being able to cope with culture shock is understanding that cross-cultural adjustment takes time. Oberg sought to explain culture shock and acculturation by providing a relatively simple model. This model is known as the U-curve model, and it traces cross-cultural adaptation through four distinct stages.

The first stage of the U-curve model is the Honeymoon Stage. This is the time when the traveler first arrives and finds everything new and exciting. The sights, the smells, the sounds are all exotic, creating a sense of adventure. During this stage, the traveler may make mistakes, but because everything is so new, these mistakes are quickly forgotten as the traveler moves to the next exciting interaction or event. If a person stays long enough, however, she or he will likely move to the second stage, called the Crisis Stage. Over time, the foreignness of the different cultural framework becomes difficult to cope with on a continual basis. This is the stage where culture shock is most profoundly felt. One thing that often happens to people when they travel in different places is that they get sick. Prolonged exposure to different foods, different microbes in the water, and the fatigue associated with trying to get along in a different culture can all add up to a weakened immune system and lead to illness. As you might imagine, this physical condition can compound culture shock. It is at this point that many travelers unfortunately leave. Sometimes the frustration is so great that the traveler has a hard time seeing how anything could get better, so he or she catches the next plane, train, bus, or car out of town. When people leave during this stage, they are often left with profoundly negative associations concerning the host cultural environment. This is truly unfortunate, because almost inevitably if a person stays long enough, she or he will start to enter the Recovery Stage.

The U-Curve Model

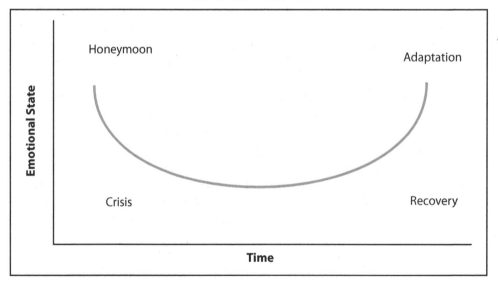

© Kendall Hunt Publishing Company

The Recovery Stage is characterized by a slow realization on the part of the traveler that the host culture isn't so bad after all. It's at this point that the person may begin to be able to use the language with more ease. The traveler may also begin to develop relationships with host cultural members. One interesting thing that tends to happen during this stage is that people start to develop negative attitudes toward their own cultural system. After a bit of time, however, this stage evolves into the next stage known as the Adaptation or Acculturation Stage. At this stage, the traveler has fully adapted to the new cultural system. The person is likely fluent in the local language and is able to get through daily life with relative ease. Attitudes during this stage are more realistic concerning both the host culture and the traveler's own culture with the person recognizing both good and bad aspects. True adaptation is hard to achieve, and some would even argue almost impossible. I believe that with time and effort, people can and do adapt to different cultures.

The U-curve model is useful for sketching various stages of cross-cultural adjustment in broad terms. It is also useful as a sense-making tool. In other words, these stages provide a framework that can help travelers make sense of their acculturation experiences. However, it also has some drawbacks. For instance, it is possible that people who travel can move back and forth between stages. For this reason, other models have been developed that can help shed light on the acculturation process.

One particularly useful model is that of communication researcher Y. Y. Kim. Her Stress-Adaptation-Growth model takes into account the variability of people's experiences as well as the role of communication (Kim & Ruben, 1988). In short, her argument is that traveling cross-culturally will create stress. With stress comes a need to change. Sometimes we change in ways that move us closer to cultural adaptation, and sometimes we change in ways that hinder our growth. Because of this, our acculturation process more closely resembles a series of circles that move back and forth between stress and adaptation until eventually we find ourselves more in the adaptation range than the stress range. Her model is quite complex, but generally speaking the factors that influence either growth or what she calls "hibernation" are the traveler's background, the host cultural environment, and the communication practices involved in the adaptation process. The traveler's background is composed of six variables that may influence one's ability to adapt. These include (1) familiarity with the host culture, (2) a person's reason or motivation for going to a different culture, (3) one's self-image, (4) one's personality in terms of extroversion or introversion or tolerance for ambiguity, (5) one's age, and (6) one's education level. The factors associated with the host cultural environment include such things as the similarity of the culture to one's own culture, the potential to interact with host cultural members, the attitudes toward outsiders and cultural others that members of the host culture share, and the amount of demand for conformity on the traveler by the host culture. Finally, the role of communication is important in terms of the number of contacts the traveler has in a host culture, exposure and ability to understand media, and an ability to engage in supportive communication with a host cultural member.

In my own travels, I have seen the relevance of both the U-curve model and Kim's adaptation model in describing my acculturation. For instance, my first trip to Iqaluit, Nunavut, in the Canadian Arctic was a perfect example of Oberg's U-curve model. I remember being enormously excited when I first got off the plane and noticed the signs written in syllabics (the form of writing Inuktitut) and heard the language being spoken. I was so excited that the fact that the airline accidentally sent my bag to Edmonton didn't even bother me. As it turns out, I had packed my jacket in my bag and ended up walking through a cold Arctic squall with nothing but a t-shirt. I was able to quickly acquire appropriate clothing and set off on my adventure. This was the Honeymoon Stage. It wasn't too long, however, when things began to get frustrating. I was cold all the time, I couldn't understand the language very well, I had twisted my ankle and had a hard time walking, and the person I was supposed to meet had gone out of town for a month. Ah, culture shock. I was discouraged and frustrated, and I really wanted to go home. However, despite my frustrations, I stayed there. I'm really glad I did because it wasn't long until I began to make some friends. These friends were enormously helpful in teaching me the language and instructing me in all manner of cultural activities, including what it meant to live "on the land." I don't believe I ever fully achieved the adaptation stage. I still have a ways to go to become fluent in the language, and I believe I would need to live there for many years before I reached full adaptation. My time there, though, was one of the most rewarding and enriching experiences of my life.

To complete this final section, I want to share some tips and bits of advice that I have collected from others who have gone through some part of the acculturation experience. These tips will hopefully be able to alleviate some of the more difficult portions of culture shock and increase the chances that one will have a productive and empowering experience. First, prepare. While it can be fun to try and navigate new and interesting places with little knowledge, it can also set one up for disaster. The level of preparation can vary widely depending on how much one is comfortable with ambiguity. However, at a minimum, one should at least try to prepare for emergencies. Knowing how to contact a consulate, being familiar with how to treat illness, or even knowing how to access money can be a lifesaver. Second, if at all possible, try to find a cultural mentor. A cultural mentor is someone who is from the place you are visiting that can help you on your journey. This person will probably be able to help you with everyday interactions, like how to go to the grocery store, but will also be able to help you understand when things just don't make sense. Third, take care of yourself. Travel, particularly travel abroad can be very taxing physically, and as we've discussed, mentally. Therefore, it is a particularly good idea to concentrate on eating healthy foods, trying to get enough sleep, and getting exercise. This type of self-care will increase the chances of a positive experience abroad. Finally, get involved. Try your best to get involved with the community, with any organization that you might be connected to, or with friends. This will provide a rich experience and go a long way toward achieving one of the benefits of cross-cultural travel, which is developing lasting and profound friendships. On this last point, I would like to provide one last piece of advice. Please be careful of the amount of time spent on social media while traveling. Our ability to connect with others instantaneously is great and can be very comforting; however, it can also be too much of a distraction. Imagine missing the spectacle of the Tour de France or the Spring Festival (Chinese New Year) in Beijing or Diwali in Mumbai because you were so connected to your phone! There are many more pieces of advice that we could discuss. The point of all of this, however, is to encourage you to step outside of your cultural comfort zone and also to provide you with a set of tools that will help in your experiences.

CONCLUSION

These last three sections have introduced the concept of culture and intercultural communication. While we cover a number of important issues here, the study of culture and intercultural communication is much more complex and fascinating than can be adequately described in the course of a few pages. For that reason, I would encourage you to continue your study of culture in your educational choices and in your daily life. More than that, though, I would strongly encourage you to travel to different cultures. Cross-cultural experiences can be difficult, but they can also be some of the most rewarding and enriching experiences of your life.

Discussion Questions

1. Think of a time you have undergone some sort of transition. After describing this transition, use the U-curve model to explain it. What types of insights did you gain from applying this model?

2. Where would you like to go in the world? Spend some time researching the place. Pay particular attention to the communication aspects of narrative and ritual.

3. Look up a program for studying abroad at your university. If possible, make an appointment with a study abroad advisor to seek opportunities to travel abroad.

References

Hall, B. J. (2005). *Among cultures: The challenge of communication.* Belmont, CA: Thompson Wadworth.

Kim, Y. Y., & Ruben, B. D. (1988). Intercultural transformation: A systems theory. In Y. Y. Kim and W. B. Gudykunst (Eds.), *Theories in intercultural communication.* Thousand Oaks, CA: Sage Publications.

Oberg, K. (1960). Culture shock: Adjustment to new cultural environments. *Practical Anthropology, 7,* 177–182.

Spitzberg, B. H., & Cupach, W. R. (1984). *Interpersonal communication competence.* Beverly Hills, CA: Sage.

Unit

Public Speaking in Action

Eric L. Morgan and Greg G. Armfield

On November 19, 1863, President Abraham Lincoln stood upon the Gettysburg Battlefield and delivered a brief and powerful speech. This speech, commonly known as the Gettysburg Address was a mere 266 words long and lasted just over 2 minutes ("Gettysburg Address," 2019a). Lincoln delivered this speech following a 2-hour presentation by Edward Everett. Interestingly, one of the phrases Lincoln used was that his words would not be remembered when he stated "The world will little note, nor long remember what we say here; while it can never forget what they did here" ("Gettysburg Address," 2019b, para 2). Of course, this address has turned out to be one of the best known, most celebrated, and most remembered pieces of American oratory that exists. This speech also reminds us of the power that oratory has. These few words delivered in a brief amount of time now serve as a stark reminder of the tragic events that forged this nation and of the character of its citizens. We can consider other speeches as well, such as Dr. Martin Luther King, Jr.'s "I Have a Dream" speech, and it becomes clear that public speaking is and can be one of the more powerful forces in any society. Dr. King's speech is, arguably, the most well-known public speech in U.S. American history. Countless articles and reflections have been written about this speech, but one thing remains clear; this speech changed the course of how we understand history. It has become a symbol of a time of great societal change. To this day, this speech delivered over 50 years ago, serves as an inspiration for people all over the world.

Public speaking is everywhere in modern society. From politicians arguing policy positions, to business leaders informing boards and shareholders, to educators explaining processes and patterns, to clergy expounding upon religious doctrine, we find examples of people giving all manner of speeches. Public speaking is not just reserved for an elite few, rather it is also found and practiced in the daily lives of people. Consider a toast delivered at a wedding or a eulogy at a funeral as examples. Regardless of the setting, when we hear public speeches, we enter into a world of potential. This is a world in which words spoken publicly can teach us, move us, and even change our society. Indeed, public speaking can help us to understand a bit more about our own sense of who we are as a people.

This unit will explore the phenomenon of public speaking from a number of different angles. To begin, we will discuss reasons why one might be interested in learning more about public speaking. This will be followed by a more thorough discussion of what public speaking is and can be. Section Two will cover the importance of research when composing a speech as well as provide useful guidance concerning the use of supporting materials. Section Three will present different ways that we can organize a public speech. Here we also provide examples for outlines. Section Four focuses on aspects of delivery. This section will also provide some helpful advice concerning speech anxiety and how to manage that. The final section focuses on how we can be active and ethical listeners when we find ourselves in public speaking situations. Hopefully, this unit will provide you with a set of tools that will allow you to be successful as you encounter public speaking situations in your own life.

Fundamentals of Public Speaking

Eric L. Morgan and Greg G. Armfield

Objectives

► Describe why public speaking is an important skill.
► Explain the purpose of public speech.
► Apply audience analysis techniques.
► Explain the relationship between culture and public speaking.

WHY STUDY PUBLIC SPEAKING

Employment

Public speaking is one of the main reasons why you are currently enrolled in this class. Universities across the country recognize that all students need to be well grounded in the development and assessment of public speech. Beyond these requirements, however, consideration of and practice in public speaking has numerous other benefits as well. One obvious benefit is that proficiency in public speaking can be extraordinarily helpful in one's professional career. To be able to speak with confidence and skill in a variety of professional settings, such as board meetings or professional conventions, can lead to positive outcomes in terms of career advancement. Likewise, employers consistently cite that they are looking for potential employees that have refined oral communication skills.

Competency in technical job skills is important, but being able to effectively communicate those job skills is every bit as important in the eyes of potential employers. Here's just one out of numerous examples. The U.S. Department of State requires entry-level foreign-service officer candidates to go through quite a rigorous selection process. First, potential candidates must pass the Foreign Service Written Exam. If successful, candidates must then pass an all-day oral assessment that rates candidates' abilities on 13 dimensions. You can probably guess already that one of the dimensions is "oral communication." In this instance, the U.S. government requires that its diplomatic face to the world be competent, at least to some extent, in public speaking.

© garetsworkshop/Shutterstock.com

Education

A second benefit to studying public speaking concerns one's general education. As you no doubt know, this course is a general education course. These courses exist because one of the guiding principles of higher education is that in order for one to count as being educated, this individual should have a broad and general knowledge base across a variety of areas. This principle dates back all the way to the Ancient Greeks, where the formal study of rhetoric began. In this classical tradition, understanding oratorical traditions and their impact was a critical portion of a person's education.

It is my passion to become a great public speaker. After talking to a few great speakers they told me that the best place to start would be to pursue my degree in Communication Studies followed up with my master's degree in communication. I have no regrets in doing so. The degree has taken me well beyond my expectations.

—Mike Tellez

Citizenship

A third reason to study public speaking concerns citizenship. What does it mean to be a citizen? What does it mean to be a community member? Answers to these questions are, of course, varied and often debated, but one thing we can see is the prevalence of public speaking within civic discourse. When asked, most people would say that to be a member of a democracy requires, in some measure, participation in the democratic process. Most often this participation takes the form of voting, but certainly public speaking can just as easily be counted as a meaningful act within this form of government. Beginning with the founding of this nation, public speech has been inextricably linked to this process. Consider Patrick Henry's fiery speech to the Second Virginia Convention on March 20, 1775, as just one example of how one speech set the course for a nation. In that speech, Henry was trying to persuade his fellow delegates to adopt a more defensive posture to an increasingly hostile British force. In so doing, he concluded by uttering these famous words, "I know not what course others may take; but as for me, give me liberty or give me death!" (Wirt, 1831). Examples of political speech such as this one abound throughout the course of history. Moments of great political change seem to always coincide with great public speaking.

It is not just the great speeches that we should be concerned with here. We should also recognize the role that public speaking plays within the realm of electoral politics generally. In order to be elected president, one must "go out on the stump" for well over a year. This phrase simply means to go from location to location delivering speeches of all kinds. This process occurs for presidential candidates to congressional candidates to candidates for local office. Certainly if you have designs on political office, public speaking will be a necessity. The more important point here, though, is that simply by being a member of a representative democracy, you will need to understand the role of public speaking. While the previous reason for study concerns political speech as related to citizenship, I want to also advocate a related point concerning citizenship. Have you ever seen or heard something in your community that you want to change? How does this change happen? Certainly, there are petition drives, letter writing campaigns, Internet organizing, and so forth. At some point, though, this movement for change will likely require a public speech. These speeches may be delivered in front of a rally of supporters (or protesters) or in front of government officials. Regardless, once again public speaking finds itself center stage in the daily progress of community life.

I chose communication because I wanted to work in media. As a Latina, I saw myself misrepresented on advertising and television. Communication studies allowed me to challenge and change those narratives, and part of this is through public speaking.

—Eva Videla

These are just a few reasons why we should be concerned with the art and practice of public speaking. There is no doubt that there are many more reasons, too many in fact to produce an exhaustive list. The point here is not to simply recall certain moments, but to argue that public speaking is still a part of the daily fabric of our lives. Therefore, in understanding this unique communication event, we come to understand ourselves better as well. Now that we have a sense of why public speaking is important, we can turn our attention to what it is.

DEFINING PUBLIC SPEAKING

Public speaking can be defined as a communication event in which a speaker addresses a live audience normally without interruption. This definition is rather simple on the surface, but if we look at it more closely with the lessons presented in Unit 1, it becomes rather complex. Prior to that, however, let's consider the first part of the definition. Public speaking moments are **communication events**. A communication event is an event

PUBLIC SPEAKING

a communication event in which a speaker addresses a live audience normally without interruption.

COMMUNICATION EVENT

an event that is defined by rules of communication.

that is defined in terms of rules for communication (Hymes, 1972). For example, the public speaking event begins with communication acts, is made up of communication acts, and concludes with other communication acts. For these acts to make sense, we have certain conventions or "rules" that guide how they are done. Naturally, different people have different sets of rules when it comes to these communication events. In other words, there are cultural rules that define the event. We will consider these in more depth in a later section. For now, though, we need to simply understand that public speaking is a distinct type of event that occurs in specific cultural situations. Consider, for instance, all the different times that you are either a practitioner of or a witness to public speaking in your own life. All of these times made sense because they were patterned by certain normative rules that you came to understand as you learned to be a cultural member. The second part of the definition also requires some consideration, which is that a speaker addresses a live audience. What happens when a speaker addresses an audience? Is it simply one person delivering a string of words to a passive group of people? The answer to this second question is obviously no. In order to better understand this, please recall the transactional model of communication presented in Unit 1. This model conceives of communication as being a simultaneous process of exchange between two parties. One important aspect of this model is that it reminds us that the parties involved in communication are both sending and receiving messages at the same time, both parties are encoding and decoding at the same time. If we apply this to the public speaking situation we quickly realize that public speaking is not just about one person standing up and performing for a non-responsive audience. Rather, it is a dynamic interchange between the speaker and the audience. When one speaks to an audience, that speaker is attending to the reactions of the audience and often adjusting the speech while speaking. In fact, many of the most memorable speeches are those in which the audience is clearly engaged with the speaker and vice versa. Quite simply, this is what public speaking is.

I was a very shy and timid person before I had my first speech class in high school. I was a freshman and I was a little different appearance wise, so I tried not to draw too much attention to myself. That first speech class gave me the opportunity I needed to come out of my shell. I was given the chance to show people that I was not just that girl that looked like a boy but that I had a voice. I had stuff to say that was worth saying . . . It gives students an opportunity to show the world, their peers, their family or their co-workers who they are.

—Crystal Romero

PURPOSES OF PUBLIC SPEECH

When embarking on a public speech, you will most assuredly have a particular purpose in mind. While a speaker is afforded the opportunity to address an audience, in general, there are three different purposes that a public speech can have. These purposes include informing an audience, persuading an audience, and speeches that mark a special occasion and/or entertain an audience. We will treat each in turn. To get a better understanding of what public speaking can be, let's take a look at different types of speeches.

Different Types of Speeches

Informative speaking occurs when an individual wants to teach the audience something. Informative speaking is defined by description, elucidation, and education. Thus, the main goal of informative speaking is **not** to persuade your audience. Within an informative speech, you may have a specific goal in mind. Turner, Lindsey, and Deatrick (2008) suggest that there are three primary goals associated with informative speaking. First, a speaker may wish to communicate new information to an audience. With this goal, the speaker must assume that the audience does not already know about the topic. Thus, the content of the speech may be focused on background information necessary to understand the phenomenon. Second, a speaker may wish to extend what an audience already knows about a topic. Third, a speaker may wish to update old information in light of recent advances. Notice that the distinctions among these three goals are subtle and are based on one's analysis of an audience.

INFORMATIVE SPEAKING

a speech with the primary purpose of information giving, and no persuasive appeals.

Beebe and Beebe (2006) discuss five different types of informative speeches that may be delivered. These different types include (1) speeches about objects, (2) speeches about procedures, (3) speeches about people, (4) speeches about events, or (5) speeches about ideas. Clearly identifying what type of speech will help you, as a speaker, coherently express your ideas to your audience. When constructing a speech, you may also want to consider a number of different strategies for the delivery of main points. Rothwell (2010) outlines five different strategies that may prove helpful. First, a speaker may report on information by delivering brief and concise information. Second, a speaker may explain information by clarifying information about complex issues. Third, a speaker may demonstrate information by acting out a process of some sort. Fourth, a speaker may tell a story about something in order to help illustrate a point in a relatable fashion. Finally, a speaker may compare points in order to better highlight the features or qualities of something.

Persuasive Speaking

A **persuasive speech** is one in which the speaker tries to change the audience in some way. Specifically, persuasive speaking should be focused on changing the audience's beliefs, attitudes, values, and/or behaviors. You will read more about persuasion as a social process later in this text. Those principles will help as you prepare a persuasive speech; however, there are some special points about persuasive speaking specifically that should be addressed. Following the form used for the discussion of informative speaking, we will discuss goals of persuasive speaking, the means of persuasion, and at least one organizational pattern to be considered.

Generally speaking, we can think of persuasive speaking as having one of three goals. These goals are adoption, discontinuance, and prevention. The goal of adoption is evident when the speaker attempts to get the audience to adopt a particular behavior, attitude, or belief. The effort here is to get the audience to *start* doing something. For example, a dietician may deliver a speech with the goal of getting the audience to start eating more fiber. Another example may be a concerned citizen trying to get a city council to adopt a new fitness program for young children. The second goal of discontinuance is the opposite of adoption. This goal is evidenced by a speaker trying to get an audience to stop believing a certain way, to stop holding a particular attitude, or to stop behaving in a certain way. A good example of a massive persuasion effort is the numerous campaigns to get people to stop smoking. Another example of a persuasive speech with the goal of discontinuance would be to try and persuade a group of college students to stop engaging in risky behaviors such as binge drinking. Finally, the goal of prevention is evident when a speaker tries to prevent an audience from engaging in a particular behavior, or holding a particular attitude or belief. Many of you may be familiar with the national D.A.R.E. program. The acronym stands for Drug Abuse Resistance Education ("D.A.R.E.," 2019). This program is geared toward trying to prevent school-aged children from engaging in drug use. A speech trying to prevent students from drinking and driving is another example of deterrence as a goal of persuasive speaking. It is vitally important to recognize that one's goal in persuasive speaking is directly related to one's analysis of the audience. Delivering a discontinuance speech about smoking is useless if the audience is made up of non-smokers, for instance.

Along with the specific goal of a persuasive speech, speakers should also consider the means with which persuasion may be accomplished. This has been a concern of philosophers and scholars for millennia. For example, the Greek philosopher Aristotle was one of the first to outline a systematic discussion of persuasive means. These persuasive means are called **persuasive appeals**. Aristotle discussed three categories of persuasive appeals labeled logos, pathos, and ethos (Rapp, 2010). Logos refers to persuasion through appeals to logic or reasoning. Pathos refers to persuasion through appeals to emotion. Ethos refers to persuasion through credibility. An effective persuasive speech will utilize these appeals throughout the speech.

Appealing to logic in order to persuade can take a number of different forms. Two common types are through induction and deduction. Induction is the reasoning process that draws a conclusion based on evidence from numerous examples. When applied to persuasive speaking, induction may take the form of the speaker outlining several examples and then explicitly drawing a conclusion from these examples. For example, if I wanted to convince a group of hikers to avoid rattlesnakes because they are dangerous, I could tell several stories of how hikers have been bitten by snakes. To conclude, I would then state forcefully something to the effect of, ". . . so it is clear that these examples demonstrate that snakes can be dangerous." Deduction, on the other hand, is a reasoning process in which one draws a conclusion about a specific case from a commonly held belief. In a persuasive speech, the speaker may state a commonly held belief and then state that the audience should judge a specific case based on this belief. For instance, if I wanted to convince a city council to fund a program that would invest in after-school programs for elementary school students, I may state that we all believe that the children are the future of our community; therefore, we should invest in this specific program. There are other types of appeal to logic as well, but these are two common ones.

Appealing to an audience's emotions can be another effective strategy in persuasive speaking. In fact, these appeals are quite important in the persuasive process. Freedman (2017) reminds us that Plato once wrote that "all learning has an emotional base." Ultimately, any emotion is available as a means of persuasion, but overt appeals to emotion should be used with care. For example, appealing to a sense of fear can be quite effective, but only under certain conditions. This will be discussed later in Unit 5, Section 3 on Health Communication. You are likely quite familiar with pathos appeals even if you don't recognize it. Most advertising is grounded in appeals to people's emotions. Advertisers are adept at understanding which emotions will persuade people to purchase certain products.

Appealing to one's credibility as a speaker (ethos) is not just effective, it is critical to the persuasive speaking event. One will be much more persuasive if one is believed to be credible about the topic. Credibility has a number of dimensions, but three easy ones to remember are competence, charisma, and character or trustworthiness (Beebe & Beebe, 2006). When delivering a speech, the speaker needs to come across to the audience as being competent in the area about which they speak. If not, the speaker runs the very real risk of having the audience stop paying attention. It is also helpful if the speaker is seen as charismatic or dynamic when speaking. Keeping an audience engaged through dynamism increases the likelihood that the persuasive message will be memorable. Finally, it is important that an audience believes that the speaker has integrity (character) when speaking. As you might imagine, audiences react poorly if the members believe they are being lied to.

Speeches to Mark a Special Occasion

The previous two sections outlined two common purposes of public speaking. These are the two that often receive the most attention because they are the moments in which a speaker is given time to really develop a number of points. Perhaps the more common purpose of public speaking, though, is neither informative nor persuasive. Rather, these are the speeches that occur when we must mark a special occasion or entertain an audience. Special occasion speaking typically encompasses toasts, award presentations, acceptance speeches, nomination speeches, keynote addresses, commencement addresses, tributes or commemorative addresses, eulogies, and ceremonial speaking. You most likely have been a part of some cultural scene that calls for a ceremonial speech, such as a wedding or a funeral. Moments like these are very important in people's lives and the speeches that are a part of them also take on a special significance.

The final type of speeches we have broadly included in special occasion speakers are speeches to entertain. The most common speech to entertain includes after-dinner speeches. An after-dinner speech is commonly delivered after a celebratory dinner for an organization or individual. Nonprofit organizations will host fundraisers or banquet dinners and invite a person to speak. These speeches that might celebrate an individual or organization are often the most audience centric. However not all after-dinner speeches are "after dinner." Conroy (1989) reported that former first lady Barbara Bush was known to schedule the presentations first and dinner later in the evening. At some point in your life, you will likely be called upon to deliver such a speech. You may even be called upon to do so with relatively little warning. Regardless of the amount of time, remember not to panic. Instead, try to remember the following points:

► The reason you are likely to be asked is because you are uniquely qualified to speak in the situation.
► Speak from the heart.
► Consider the audience.
► Remember that the reason for the speech is to honor someone else.
► Rehearse.

© Jacob Lund/Shutterstock.com

AUDIENCE ANALYSIS

A central theme in all discussions of public speaking should be about the audience. Unfortunately, we too often conceive of the public speaking event as solely being about the speaker. Recall, however, that public speaking is a transactional communication event in which the audience is an active participant. Given this, it is vitally important that we place the audience foremost in our thinking when embarking on the composition of a public speech. Beebe and Beebe (2006) have even written an entire book (and it's a long one too) on an "audience-centered approach" to public speaking. These scholars argue that the audience should be central to **every** aspect of the public speech composition process. So, how do we go about analyzing our audience appropriately for a speech? The answer to this can take a number of forms, so we will simply provide a few suggestions. When analyzing an audience, one should consider the following:

► Demographic composition
► Cultural background

- ▶ Attitudinal orientation
- ▶ Past experiences of the audience

The demographic composition of an audience provides clues as to how an audience may respond to a particular speech. What are demographics? Demographics, or more specifically, demographic data, refer to the characteristics of a particular population. Typically, this is understood in terms of age, income, ethnic origin, gender, and so forth. I should note that these types of characteristics will **never** let us know how any one individual feels about a particular topic. These data can only provide broad clues as to what might be relevant for any particular audience. For example, giving speeches on the latest advances in string theory to a group of elementary schoolchildren may not be received as well as one would hope. Notice that I use the term "may" in this instance. It is vitally important to realize that demographic characteristics are not deterministic. Just because you may be speaking to a group of 18–24-year-old college students, does not mean that each individual will think and act a certain way. Demographic considerations are useful simply to get a broad sense of the audience.

Considering cultural background may lead to a more refined sense of how an audience will respond to a speech. Remember in the discussion of the definition, we noted that public speaking events were guided by cultural rules. One such rule concerns the formality with which one should speak. In many U.S. American contexts, public speaking can take on informal tones in which the speaker engages in witty banter with the audience. There is, at times, an effort made on the part of U.S. American speakers to minimize the power discrepancy between the speaker and the audience. Other cultural systems may require a much more formal approach in order for a public speech to count as effective. Beebe and Beebe (2006) report that in Russia and the Bahamas, public speeches are highly formal events.

Attitudinal orientations are also important considerations. Thinking about what general attitudes an audience may hold toward a particular topic can go a long way in terms of formulating an effective speech. One way to gauge these attitudinal orientations is to ask yourself why an audience has gathered together in the first place. It may well be that audience members share a common outlook on some facet of daily life.

The past experiences of an audience can also play a role in how a speech may be received. As with attitudinal orientation, these experiences may be a reason why people are gathered in an audience in the first place. A speech delivered to a Veterans of Foreign Wars (VFW) chapter will likely take on specific qualities that a speech delivered elsewhere may not have.

These four areas are a useful way to begin an audience analysis, but it is also important to consider the various identities of your audience. While the demographic characteristics discussed above play a role in identity, it does not cover everything. Recall in Unit One, Section Three the discussion of identity and verbal communication. In that section, we discuss how identity is a two-part process of avowal (who one says one is) and ascription (who others say one is). When conducting an audience analysis, consider the ways that audience members may be expressing who they are in terms of the roles they play and their aspirations. Consider also the ways that members may be characterized by others. Doing this can give you insight into ways that you might identify with the audience.

These considerations just scratch the surface of an audience analysis. Each audience analysis will take on a different form with each public presentation. We must also remember Beebe and Beebe's (2006) point that audience consideration should be an ongoing process throughout every aspect of public speaking.

© Rawpixel.com/Shutterstock.com

CULTURE AND PUBLIC SPEAKING

We should take a brief moment to consider the relevance of culture in the public speaking context. We encounter public speeches in different cultural contexts all the time, such as in classrooms, during elections, at meetings, and during religious observances, to name a few. The society we live in is also quite diverse, made up of individuals from many different cultures. Different cultures value and practice public speaking differently. As public speakers, it is important to recognize these cultural differences, not just in terms of what we talk about, but also in terms of how public speaking gets done. It is also important to realize that at every point in the speech production process, culture is influential.

> Communication creates and shapes our reality; if we address this aspect of life we can progress to a better understanding of societal problems and offer informed solutions.
>
> —Gryffin Loya

The influence of culture is profound and is related to how we even come to understand what a public speech is in the first place. Recall in the definition portion of the unit that we discussed how communication rules function to constitute what a public speech is. These rules are essentially cultural communication rules. Cultural rules are those rules that are commonly shared, widely accessible, and deeply meaningful for the participants (Carbaugh, 1988). Thus, when we talk about cultural rules, we are referring to those rules that everyone will likely understand, even though they may not necessarily adhere to them. For example, in many U.S. American contexts, the members will understand that in a public speaking event, the speaker will present information in a sustained manner. She or he will also do so without being interrupted.

Generally speaking, we can think about two different types of cultural rules, which include normative rules and code rules. **Normative rules** are those rules that guide social behavior and interaction (Carbaugh, 1990). Within a particular cultural system, then, public speaking will be guided by certain normative rules. For example, in many U.S. universities, one of the norms taught about public speaking is to maintain consistent eye contact. This, however, is particular to a certain cultural system that sees this as an appropriate behavior. It is also important to consider code rules in this instance. Carbaugh (1990) tells us that **code rules** are those rules that tell cultural members what counts as something meaningful. In other words, people in a culture will share a rule for what counts as a public speaking event.

NORMATIVE RULES

rules that guide social behavior and interaction.

CODE RULES

rules that inform cultural members what counts as meaningful.

Culture and Topic Selection

Delivering a public speech to a culturally diverse audience requires that we pay attention to the different worldviews, attitudes, values, beliefs, and communication practices that may be represented in the audience. We also must recognize that these beliefs, values, and norms will lead to different interpretations by members of a culturally diverse audience. Thus, the audience analysis step for constructing a speech becomes very important. When analyzing an audience from a cultural standpoint, ask yourself the following questions:

- ▶ What cultural groups are represented in my audience?
- ▶ Are there specific beliefs that different cultural group members might hold about my topic?
- ▶ If so, how will this affect my speech?
- ▶ Does my topic challenge or conform to cultural values held by members of my audience?
- ▶ If so, how will this affect my speech?

When you deliver a speech in this course, you will be addressing a culturally diverse audience. Thus, it is important that you be sensitive to different cultural practices. Almost always, a lack of cultural sensitivity has negative effects. For example, making jokes about members of particular cultural groups is not only insensitive; it is also ineffective for public speaking.

Differences in Public Speaking Across Cultures

Norms are an important part of culture. It follows, then, that public speaking will be done differently by different groups. As a competent public speaker and audience member, one needs to recognize this aspect of public address. While the cultural differences in public speaking are too numerous to mention here, here are some general points to consider.

- ▶ Awareness: Being aware that cultures differ in their approaches to public speaking helps us to recognize the potential goals and expectations of the public speaker. Being aware of the different situations in which public speaking is called for in different cultures helps us recognize the appropriateness and effectiveness of the public speech.
- ▶ Listening: A successful public speech greatly depends on the audience. As audience members, listening attentively is a responsibility. When we listen we tend to assign meaning to the multiple messages that we are confronted with, often without thinking about it. Thus, when someone from a different culture is speaking, we need to remember that there will most likely be different nonverbal messages sent during the public speech. For example, norms guiding eye contact (when to use it and what it means) may differ significantly.

In this course, you will be learning a particular set of strategies useful for public speaking in a predominately U.S. American context. Therefore, it is important to realize that the approaches for delivery, topic selection, and speech structure will make the most sense and be most effective in a U.S. American context. A competent speaker, however, must become adaptable to different situations. Realizing that culture greatly influences those situations goes a long way to developing competence in public speaking.

The following sections provide a broad and brief survey of some of the principles of public speaking. It is, by no means, an exhaustive account. As mentioned before, public speaking has a long history of both study and practice. Because of this, there are tons of volumes dedicated to this practice. As you go forward to engage in public speaking, remember to utilize the myriad resources available. Doing so will provide you with a solid footing from which to speak eloquently and confidently. Furthermore, I would invite you to seek opportunities to engage in public speaking. The more you do it, the more comfortable you will be with it. This class will provide some of those opportunities, and I along with the professors and graduate assistants would encourage you to make the most of this time.

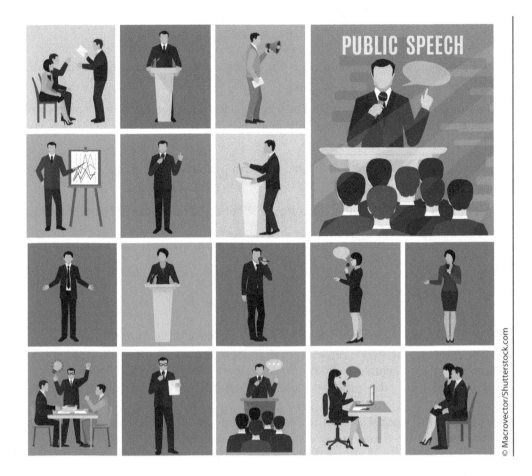

Discussion Questions

1. What were some of the most memorable public speeches you have heard? What made these speeches memorable?

2. In what ways do you think that public speaking can be beneficial to you in your chosen major or career path? Are there opportunities for you to engage in public speaking that will help you develop your skills in this area?

3. Consider an area that you are passionate about. In what ways can you ethically persuade others through public speaking to share your passion?

4. Research public speaking as it occurs in different cultures. What are some of the differences that you found interesting or surprising?

References

Beebe, S. A., & Beebe, S. J. (2006). *Public speaking: An audience centered approach* (6th ed.). Boston, MA: Allyn and Bacon.

Carbaugh, D. (1988). Comments on culture in communication inquiry. *Communication Reports, 1*(1), 38–41.

Carbaugh, D. (1990). *Cultural communication and intercultural contact.* Mahwah, NJ: Lawrence Erlbaum Associates, Inc. Publishers.

Colonial Williamsburg Foundation. (2010). Patrick Henry's 'Give me liberty or give me death' speech: The Colonial Williamsburg Official History Site. Retrieved from https://www.history.org/almanack/life/politics/giveme.cfm

Conroy, S. B. (1989, November 10). State dinners offer speech as first course. *Austin American-Statesman.*

D.A.R.E. America. (2019). *The official D.A.R.E. website.* Retrieved from www.dare.org

Freedman, J. (2017). Emotional WHAT? Defining and history of EQ (2017 update). *Sixseconds: The Emotional Intelligence Network.* Retrieved from https://www.6seconds.org/2017/05/28/emotional-intelligence-definition-history/

Gettysburg Address. (2019a). *Library of Congress.* Retrieved from https://www.loc.gov/exhibits/gettysburg-address/

Gettysburg Address. (2019b). *Library of Congress.* Retrieved from https://www.loc.gov/exhibits/gettysburg-address/ext/trans-nicolay-copy.html

Hymes, D. (1972). Models of the interaction of language and social life. In J. J. Gumperz & D. Hymes (Eds.), *Directions in sociolinguistics: The ethnography of communication.* New York: Basil Blackwell.

Rapp, C. (2010, Febuary 1). "Aristotle's Rhetoric." *The Stanford Encyclopedia of Philosophy.* Edward N. Zalta (Ed.). Retrieved from https://plato.stanford.edu/archives/spr2010/entries/aristotle-rhetoric/

Rothwell, J. D. (2010). *In the company of others: An introduction to communication* (3rd ed.). New York: Oxford University Press.

Turner, M., Lindsey, L. L. M., & Deatrick, L. M. (2008). Public speaking. In E. Morgan & A. E. Lindsey (Eds.), *Principles and practice in human communication: A reader and workbook for COMM 265* (2nd ed.). Dubuque, IA: Kendall Hunt Publishing.

Wirt, W. (1831). *Sketches of the life and character of Patrick Henry.* Gloucester, United Kingdom: Creative Media Partners, LLC.

Section 2

Research and Supporting Material

Greg G. Armfield and Eric L. Morgan

- ▶ Choose the appropriate supporting material for developing a speech.
- ▶ Gather credible research.
- ▶ Critically assess online documents.
- ▶ Demonstrate appropriate source citation.

RESEARCH

As we have demonstrated throughout this section, public speaking is so much more than simply getting up and talking about something you care about. Public speaking takes careful preparation and practice. A key part of that preparation lies in research. Here we refer to research as generating sufficient material to support your claims. As will be demonstrated throughout this section, the competent use of supporting material is absolutely critical to producing an effective public speech.

© Rawpixel.com/Shutterstock.com

SUPPORTING MATERIAL

The use of supporting material will make the difference between a poorly developed speech, an average speech, and a great speech. A great presentation must contain relevant, precise, and current supporting material that will engage the audience. Modern audiences are often skeptical of speakers with whom they are unfamiliar. Even if they are familiar with a speaker, audiences are trained to be critical listeners. As you design your speech, make sure your supporting material fits together with the organizational pattern and structure you have chosen. And, most importantly, your supporting material should reinforce and strengthen your main points so that you enhance your credibility (ethos). When choosing supporting material and evidence, ask yourself if your audience will be skeptical or unconvinced by what you say. Good supporting material should address the "so what?" and "why should I believe you?" questions. Consider the last time a friend failed to persuade you. It is very likely your response was "so what?" or you were not convinced ("why should I believe you?"). In order to continuously reinforce and strengthen your credibility, your supporting material should be convincing and varied. The following will review the major types of supporting material you can rely on to have an impact on your audience.

EXAMPLES

a specific illustration to represent or explain a group of people, ideas, conditions, or experiences.

Examples. Vivid concrete examples have a strong impact on listeners. Without examples and illustrations, concepts can often be shallow and not fully developed. An example is a specific instance (one item, person, or event) that illustrates, represents, or explains a group of people, ideas, conditions, experiences, or the like. Examples can be used to clarify, reinforce, and personalize your ideas. Consider the following example built from the information one can gain from Hank Haney (2012), Tiger Wood's coach from 2004 to 2010, to illustrate clarity, reinforcement, and personalization.

> Many professional athletes practice long hours. Tiger Woods has a long history of practicing in excess of 12 hours a day in his off-season. Haney details Tiger's rigid practice schedule in his book *The Big Miss*. Tiger begins his day at 6:00 a.m. with a workout at home. At 9:00 a.m. he will practice hitting at the driving range for about 2 hours. After lunch Tiger will head back to the driving range for another 2 hours; afterward he will play nine holes then return to the driving range

© Tony Bowler/Shutterstock.com

for another hour or so. Around 6:00 p.m. he will return home and complete a second workout before eating dinner around 7:30 p.m. It's dedication like this to practice and fitness that professional athletes must maintain to be at the top of their game.

Examples come in many forms. Lucas (2004) breaks examples into the following types: brief, extended, and hypothetical. However, the most logical distinction should just be the obvious difference of length between brief and extended examples. Both brief and extended examples can be factual or hypothetical. Extended examples should be used when a long illustration is needed to reinforce an idea or further clarify an argument. Oftentimes a hypothetical example can be very effective as the speaker should set up a realistic scenario and relate it precisely to the audience.

Illustrations. A close relative of examples is illustrations. Illustrations are the most memorable type of supporting material. An illustration is a tale, account, personal experience, or short story. Illustrations also come in brief, extended, or hypothetical forms. These are often considered the same as an **anecdote**, which is a brief and often amusing story. The main distinction is that anecdotes are never extended and anecdotes are amusing, whereas illustrations rarely utilize humor.

Everyone likes a good story. The trick to using illustrations effectively is to directly relate the illustration to the point you are trying to make. Illustrations should also be chosen wisely to ensure the story is relatable and relevant to your audience. If the audience fails to identify with a speaker's supporting material, the impact a speaker is trying to make will be, as they say, lost in translation. For example, one semester a male student decided to reveal he liked to wear women's clothes. He chose to do this by removing layers of clothing during his speech and accounting for his personal experiences. However, this illustration failed to relate to many of the audience members in the classroom, ultimately leading to several of his audience members beginning to believe that the speaker was going to undress in the classroom. The point the student was attempting to make was lost on his audience. However, with more audience analysis, this illustration could have been modified for the audience. Further, this illustration, based on audience analysis could be very impactful given to a different audience.

Analogies, Similes, and Metaphors. An analogy is a way of making a point about one thing by exemplifying its similarities with something else. When making a comparison, analogies increase understanding. An oft-used analogy from the movie *Forrest Gump* demonstrates life is full of many choices, much like a box of chocolates.

ILLUSTRATION

a tale, account, personal experience, or short story.

ANECDOTE

a brief, often amusing story.

ANALOGY

a comparison between two things.

© Rawpixel.com/Shutterstock.com

But an analogy is more of a logical argument than a simple figure of speech. Consider the following:

- Finding a good man is like finding a needle in a haystack.
- That is as useful as rearranging deck chairs on the Titanic.
- Explaining a joke is like dissecting a frog. You understand it better, but the frog dies in the process.
- I am as graceful as a piano falling down a flight of stairs.
- Worrying is similar to a person tapping you on the shoulder all day long.

Analogies, similes and metaphors are closely related, but they are not the same. Because making comparisons are useful for both speaking and writing, all three are considered key literary devices. A simile compares two things using the words "like" or "as" to create a new meaning. These comparisons are direct and typically easy to understand. Some common examples include:

- As sly as a fox
- Crazy like a fox
- As stubborn as a mule
- As blind as a bat (actually bats are not blind!)

A metaphor is a figure of speech used to make a comparison between two seemingly dissimilar items. These comparisons describe one thing in terms of another, but the comparison does not use the words "like" or "as."

- You are the wind beneath my wings.
- He is a diamond in the rough.
- Life is a roller coaster with lots of ups and downs.
- Early to bed, early to rise, makes one healthy, wealthy, and wise.

Analogies, similes, and metaphors are great ways to provide memorable supporting material for your audience.

Testimony. When most people think of testimony they visualize a person testifying in a court of law or perhaps in front of a legislative body (e.g., Congress or Senate). Using testimony as supporting material for your speech consists of quoting or paraphrasing a person with primary firsthand knowledge on a given subject. Three types of testimony can be used as supporting material.

- Expert testimony is testimony from an individual who is a recognized expert in their field.
- Peer testimony is testimony from an ordinary individual or peer with firsthand experience or insight on a specific topic.
- Prestige testimony is testimony from a celebrity and often evidence is based solely on name recognition or status, not from direct knowledge on a specific topic or subject.

While you can conduct your own interview to gather testimony, testimonies can also be located while conducting research for your speech. For example, researching health communication and the positive effects of exercise on the human body would likely result with several examples of testimony on how dieting and exercise can positively affect an individual's health. Regardless of the type of testimony you use in your speech, make sure you

SIMILE

a comparison using like or as.

METAPHOR

a comparison between two seemingly dissimilar things.

TESTIMONY

quoting or paraphrasing a person with firsthand knowledge on a given subject.

Tips

Tips for using testimony in a speech

- Quote or paraphrase accurately.
- Use testimony from qualified sources.
- Use testimony from unbiased sources.
- Identify the people you quote or paraphrase.

supply the name and qualifications of the person's testimony you are using as supporting material.

Statistics. The word statistics can scare some people, but statistics are a simple way to summarize data by providing a way to demonstrate or describe a trend, make comparisons, or show causality and relationships. Take weather for example. Temperature is a simple data point used to give us an indicator as to how to dress for outdoor activities. The meaning assigned the numerical point can vary by region and culture. For example, if you live in the northern part of the United States, cold might mean 20 degrees or lower. Whereas, in the southwest part of the United States many people refer to 60 degrees as cold. Linguistic relativity aside, science has very specific meanings for temperatures measured in Fahrenheit: 212 degrees is the boiling point and 32 degrees is the freezing point for pure water. However, if you have been in the southern part of the United States, I bet you have heard someone proclaim, "it's freezing out there" when the temperature is nowhere near 32 degrees.

Descriptive **statistics** summarize data or information for comparison, are most commonly used in speeches, and simply are summaries of data sets. For example, according to the Hagerty Price Guide Index of American Muscle Cars (2019) the average value of the most sought-after American muscle cars has increased approximately 57% over the last 5 years since 2014. But sometimes data driven information can be misleading.

Looking further into the Hagerty data, one can determine from graphically displayed data, that at least 55% of that 57% value increase happened between 2014 and 2015, and that the value of these vehicles have not fluctuated more than 1 to 2% over the last 3 years. Now, if you were to invest in a muscle car, learning the second part of this analysis is instrumental before making an investment. In short, classic vehicles should be viewed as long-term investments, ones that rarely increase by 50% over 2 years as these vehicles did toward the end of this decade recession. This discussion brings up a few points about how to present data in a presentation, versus print.

When presenting statistics, the most important issue is to verify your chosen statistics are from a reliable and unbiased source. For example, surveying ESPN viewers on who the best athlete in the world is would produce very biased results as the survey only sampled ESPN viewers. To answer this question in an unbiased way, the survey designer would need to ensure the sample process was random, giving an equal chance to every person to answer the question. The most valid surveys are ones that don't rely solely on participants that are predetermined (this is called a convenience sample).

There are two myths that you should be familiar with. The first, numbers never lie and the second, numbers lie. The reality is that neither statement is inherently true or false. The concern with using statistics is that they can easily be manipulated as was documented by Huff (1954). For example, can you tell me what the fastest animal in the world is? Typically, a person would answer a cheetah, or a pronghorn antelope. But, did you know at least three birds are faster than both animals above? (see "10 Fastest Animals," 2014). Now, you could argue that I'm cheating, but factually a peregrine falcon can achieve upward of 200 mph in a dive, and if you were its prey does the fact that it cannot fly as fast as a cheetah or pronghorn antelope really matter at this point?

The issue at hand is really one of representativeness. When searching for statistics as supporting material you should balance, at a minimum, the measures of central tendency (mean, median, and mode), which are most commonly used to describe or summarize a data set in one number. The **mean**, most commonly called the average, is determined by summing all numbers in a data set and dividing by the total number

STATISTICS

summarize data for comparison.

MEAN

the average.

MEDIAN

the middle number.

MODE

number that occurs most frequently.

SKEW

an unequal distribution of numbers in a data set.

of items. The **median** is the middle most number from a set of numbers when ranked from highest to lowest, or vice versa. Another way of thinking about the median is that it is the point that splits a data set in half. The **mode** is the number that occurs most frequently in a set of numbers. Most data sets will be reported with an average (mean) and that's it. For example, if you are shopping for a home or apartment, often websites or realtors will try to describe the community and price a home based on the average home sold in your neighborhood, while attempting to account for more qualitative variables such as curb appeal, landscaping, or modern updates to bathrooms and kitchens. This tends to be an accepted and accurate measurement to value and accurately price a home. However, when home sizes vary in a neighborhood, a more accurate measurement would be price per square foot, given that all the above qualitative variables are accounted for. But, for other data sets, specifically ones that are **skewed** (having an unequal distribution), the median can be more descriptive.

Let's suppose that you have taken an exam in your class and your professor reports that the average test score on the exam was 73%. This is a pretty acceptable percentage for most courses, assuming that the students taking the exam performed well enough to produce a normal distribution of scores; that is the exam scores are not skewed. But, what if the exam scores from your class are skewed and your professor doesn't reveal it. Let's look at two scenarios for negatively and positively skewed distributions and how median and mode play a role in describing a data set.

A data set could be negatively skewed if the class exam was possibly easy, or the students were very well prepared and did well, but a few students might not have attended class and did poorly on the exam. If the results of the exam were mostly A's and B's (scores of 80% and higher) the median (middle number of a distribution) should be used instead of the mean, because a few low scores will influence the mean. This actually holds true for a positively skewed distribution also. The mean of a set of numbers is influenced by a small set of high or low numbers in a data set. In the case of a positively skewed distribution, meaning the exam was possibly hard, or the average student was ill prepared, a small group of students did very well. This would result in the vast majority of students failing or scoring less than 70% and only 10 to 20% of the class scoring an A or B. In both cases the mean is the number that is biased by the skewed data distribution and the median provides a better description of the exam. So why does your professor not report both the median and the mean on your exams? Good question. Unless the exam has a normal distribution, the mean is a biased number, and a student will only know if the exam scores were skewed (unless your professor shows you the visual graph of the distribution of exam scores) if the course professor reports both the mean and median. If a data set is skewed, the median is considered to be representative and more descriptive of the data set.

So, where does the mode play a role? In a perfect world on the perfect exam, the median, mean, and mode would all fall within a percentage or two of each other, thus representing a symmetrical or balanced distribution of scores. In both examples above, the mode could fall anywhere above or below the mean. Let's consider the possibility that your professor gives a pop quiz. The distribution of a five-question pop quiz on 30 to 50 students will not vary much given the low value with only five opportunities and a score possible from zero to five. If the majority of students are prepared they may only miss one question and score four out of five. Four is then the mode, the number occurring most often. One other situation in which reporting the mode in addition to the median and the mean would be useful is in the case of bimodal distribution (a data set having two modes). This is particularly true if both modes are far apart. This situation might arise if a lot of students do well and a lot of students do poorly. The mean, in this case, would provide very little information and even suggest that scores were clustered around the midpoint. To conclude, these measures of central tendency are extraordinarily useful tools in providing information in a speech, provided that the speaker takes the time to explain what these numbers might indicate.

Using Statistics in Your Presentation. Statistics are best used to quantify ideas. Most audiences will be bored with the over usage of statistics, so cite the source of your data and explain your statistics. When discussing statistics, be sure to explain the statistics that you are using and round complicated statistics. For example, there is no reason to state that the total student loan debt is $1,531,800,958,800 ("Student Loan Debt," 2019), when simplifying the number for your audience and stating that student loan debt exceeds 1.53 trillion dollars. This can be further personalized for your audience by stating the average college student in the class of 2019 graduated owing $37,172. You can further simplify and personalize this number by stating the average student graduated in 2017 owing over $37,000. Doing so makes the number simpler and easier to remember for your audience. Another way to personalize your statistics through personalization would be to state that if student loans are not a concern for you, realize that over a quarter of college graduates, or one in four, will graduate owing about $400 a month for 10 years ("Student Loan Debt"). Finally, using visual aids to clarify statistics and demonstrate historic trends will help audience members who are not comfortable or sometimes struggle interpreting statistical data. Bar and line graphs are particularly useful, as are pie charts.

Tips

Tips for using statistics

- ▶ Only cite statistics from reliable sources.
- ▶ Use statistics to quantify your ideas.
- ▶ Round off numbers.
- ▶ Personalize your statistics.
- ▶ Use statistics sparingly.
- ▶ Explain your statistics.
- ▶ Use visual aids to clarify statistical trends.

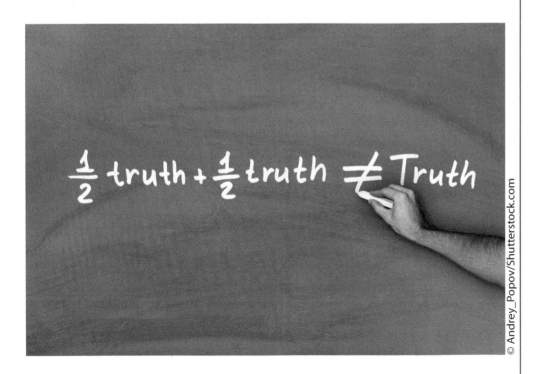

© Andrey_Popov/Shutterstock.com

RESEARCHING

Gathering and Citing Supporting Material. One of the first ways to begin gathering information for a speech is to start with your own personal experiences and knowledge. Much like choosing a topic, starting with your own knowledge and experience allows you to provide personalization for your audience. Your own stories and examples from personal experiences can be rich and vivid. However, personal experience will not count toward your assignment requirement to cite sources and locate additional research on the topic. For this, you will need to conduct primary research, which can include the use of the Internet, but in most cases will require you to locate information not found on a website. So where to begin? We will discuss four primary resources for researching speech topics: library catalogues, librarians, electronic databases, and the Internet.

Begin with your local or university library. The days of card catalogues have long passed, but they have been computerized for your convenience. By logging into your library web page, you can search library holding (books and periodicals), electronic databases (more on these below), and e-book holdings. Because all library catalogues tend to vary, it's worth investing some time exploring your university electronic catalogue so that you can learn how to maximize your time, thus benefiting you throughout your university career.

© Rawpixel.com/Shutterstock.com

Librarians are a great resource and very friendly. I have found that most students are afraid to ask questions in the library or just don't want to bother the librarians when they are working. But, they are there and want to help you. Librarians are experts in their field and are the most experienced and knowledgeable people regarding research methods and the tools the library has to help you complete research. Further, they can even help in tracking down very specific and even scarce sources.

Electronic databases. In addition to a library's electronic catalogue, practically every library subscribes to specialized electronic **periodical** databases. Two of the most popular databases in the communication sciences, and holds the most communication related research journals, are Communication Mass Media Complete and Communication Abstracts. Other disciplines have similar databases that your university likely pays lots of money (your student fees) for you to have access to. In addition to scholarly databases there are more generalized databases that are beneficial for researching a wide variety of topics for speeches:

PERIODICAL

a magazine, newspaper, or scholarly journal.

> ▸ Academic One File is a database of full-text articles from some of the leading peer-reviewed journals on a variety of subjects.
> ▸ Academic Search Complete holds full-text articles from a wide array of scholarly and popular periodicals from a variety of academic disciplines.
> ▸ EBSCO (e-Book Collection) holds full-text articles from several local and national newspapers, magazines, and journals in the sciences, social sciences, humanities, and business fields.
> ▸ Expanded Academic ASAP has citations, abstracts, and full-text articles from a wide selection of academic journals, magazines, and newspapers.

- Lexis-Nexis Academic Universe is a reference for current news, business, legal, and reference information.
- MEDLINE is the United States National Library of Medicine (NLM) life sciences database.
- PsycINFO holds citations and summaries of journal articles, book sections, books, technical reports, and citations to dissertations in the fields of psychology, medicine, psychiatry, nursing, sociology, education, pharmacology, physiology, linguistics, anthropology, business, law, and related disciplines.
- SocINDEX is a comprehensive database from the disciplines of sociology, anthropology, criminology, criminal justice, cultural sociology, demography, economic development, ethnic and racial studies, gender studies, marriage and family, politics, religion, rural sociology, social psychology, social structure, social work, sociological theory, sociology of education, substance abuse, urban studies, violence, welfare, and other related disciplines.
- Web of Science holds journals, conference proceedings, book contents focused on the sciences, social sciences, humanities, and arts.
- WorldCat is the most comprehensive bibliography with 40 million bibliographic records in 400 languages.

These are just some of the major or most popular databases for conducting research that can assist you in preparing your speech. Your library will have access to a wide variety of general and subject specific databases. Knowing how to use these databases will benefit you throughout your college career.

The Internet provides a variety of sources. A large number of national newspapers (www.usatoday.com, www.washingtonpost.com, and www.nytimes.com), weekly news magazines (www.newsweek.com and www.time.com), news services (www.cnn.com, www.npr.org, and www.ap.org), as well as local and regional newspapers and television stations' websites can provide valuable information for research topics as well as keep you up-to-date on local news. Statistical data can also be a valuable knowledge source. Pew Research Center (www.pewresearch.org) is a nonprofit bipartisan organization that collects survey data on social issues, public opinion, and demographic trends impacting the United States and the world. The United States Census Bureau (www.census.gov) is part of the U.S. Department of Commerce and publishes data about the United States economy and its citizens. Crime reports about the United States are published by the Federal Bureau of Investigation (FBI). The Uniform Crime Report and others can be found at https://www.fbi.gov/services/cjis/ucr/publications. While there are thousands of reputable websites, we have provided these as a starting point for you. Keep in mind Web addresses are dynamic and they will change over time. We hope the ones we have discussed above can help you get a start on your research.

There is one other Internet-based resource that is certainly worthy of discussion, Google Scholar. Google Scholar is a good place to help identify foundational studies and scholarship that have been heavily cited over time as well as some new research that can help advance scholarly inquiry. Further, Google Scholar does a good job of locating relevant research on your topic search from other disciplines. For example, I research Sports Communication and

Mass Media. Searching in Google Scholar on the topic of Fantasy Sports will not only bring up articles from Communication and Media (those that I could easily find in Communication and Mass Media Complete) but it will also identify important articles that deserve my attention from the disciplines of Sociology, Business, Management, and even Psychology. All articles that I clearly would not have found by searching only in my discipline-specific databases. As you go about gathering the sources you will include in your speech, remember the importance of establishing your ethos (credibility) during your presentation.

The final issue with regard to research that we will cover is evaluating and citing sources properly to avoid plagiarism. One way to ensure your sources are credible is to evaluate them based on a set of criteria. Meriam Library at California State University, Chico created the CRAAP Test for evaluating information. Each of the evaluative criteria may be more or less important depending on your situation ("Evaluating Information," 2010). CRAAP is an acronym that stands for the evaluative criteria of currency, relevance, authority, accuracy, and purpose. The reader should attempt to judge **currency** or timeliness of the information by asking the following questions:

- ► When was the information published or posted?
- ► Has the information been revised or updated?
- ► Is the information current or out-of-date for your topic?
- ► Are the links functional? ("Evaluating Information," 2010, para.2).

The second evaluative criterion of **relevance** attempts to judge the importance of the information in relation to your informational needs:

- ► Does the information relate to your topic or answer your question?
- ► Who is the intended audience?
- ► Is the information at an appropriate level (i.e., not too elementary or advanced for your needs)?
- ► Have you looked at a variety of sources before determining this is one you will use?
- ► Would you be comfortable using this source for a research paper? ("Evaluating Information," 2010, para. 3).

The third evaluative criterion is **authority** and explores the source of the information:

- ► Who is the author/publisher/source/sponsor?
- ► Are the author's credentials or organizational affiliations given?
- ► What are the author's credentials or organizational affiliations given?
- ► What are the author's qualifications to write on the topic? Can they be verified?
- ► Is there contact information, such as a publisher or e-mail address?
- ► Does the URL reveal anything about the author or source? ("Evaluating Information," para. 4).

The fourth evaluative criterion judges the **accuracy**, reliability, truthfulness, and correctness of the content by asking:

- ► Where does the information come from?
- ► Is the information supported by evidence?
- ► Has the information been reviewed or refereed?
- ► Can you verify any of the information in another source or from personal knowledge?

▸ Does the language or tone seem biased and free of emotion? ("Evaluating Information," para. 5).

▸ Are there spelling, grammar, or other typographical errors?

The fifth and final evaluative criterion, **purpose,** asks the reason the information exists:

▸ What is the purpose of the information? to inform? teach? sell? entertain? persuade?

▸ Do the authors/sponsors make their intentions or purpose clear?

▸ Is the information fact? opinion? propaganda?

▸ Follow the money. Who stands to gain from this?

▸ Does the point of view appear objective and impartial?

▸ Are there political, ideological, cultural, religious, institutional, or personal biases?

▸ What clues does the format give to the purpose, audience, quality? ("Evaluating Information," para. 6).

While the importance of the five criteria of the CRAAP evaluation technique may alter in importance, the questions allow audiences to evaluate the information provided. Furthermore, many websites can be categorized by the domain registration. Probably the most common, .com, is reserved for commercial registrations and typically signifies a for-profit endeavor. A second type, .net, was to be reserved for network technologies, such as Internet service providers, but this was never fully enforced. .net is likely the second most common domain extension. A third extension, .org, was reserved primarily for nonprofit organizations, but this also has not been well enforced. Additional extensions include .edu for educational institutions; .mil which was reserved for United States military branches; .tv for television and multimedia organizations; and .gov for government (typically U.S. government entities including townships, cities, states, and federal agencies). Regardless of the source that you need to evaluate, the application of the above criterion will give you guidance on whether or not the information you have discovered should be considered as credible.

Regardless of the type of information or where you located your supporting material, you will need to properly document and orally cite the research. Clearly documenting the sources you used, were informed by, or even inspired by to prepare your assignments is necessary in order to rightfully give credit to all of the works you used in preparing your own speeches and writings. Effective documentation of sources includes three aspects. First, documentation in the reference section of your paper or outline; second, in-text (for an outline or essay) citation; and third, oral citation in the delivery of your speech. When orally citing sources, you should state three of the following: the author, date of publication (or update for online sources), the title, or the source (journal, magazine, or Internet site). With the exception of books, it is best to provide the title of an article along with the author and date. For a book, only the author and title are needed, unless the book has had several editions (like textbooks).

Irrespective of the sources you draw upon for your research, your final product will be far superior if you start your research and writing early, draft outlines for revisions, and document all of your research by keeping a preliminary bibliography. Learning proper research skills early during your college career will become very beneficial, as well as taking thorough notes while researching for your speech.

Discussion Questions

1. What type of supporting material do you think will make your speech more memorable? Why?

2. What types of supporting material have you witnessed speakers use in a memorable way?

3. What are other places or ways that you can gather supporting material for your speech?

4. How can you present statistics in a memorable way?

5. How can you explain statistics and relate statistics to your audience?

References

10 Fastest Animals On Earth. (2014, April 6). Retrieved from https://www.conservationinstitute.org/10-fastest-animals-on-earth/

Evaluating information—Applying the CRAAP test. (2010). Meriam Library, California State University, Chico. Retrieved from https://www.csuchico.edu/lins/handouts/eval_websites.pdf

Hagerty Price Guide Index of American Muscle Cars. (2019, January). *Hagerty Muscle Cars: Index of 1960s American muscle cars.* Retrieved from https://www.hagerty.com/apps/valuationtools/market-trends/collector-indexes/Muscle_Cars

Haney, H. (2012). *The big miss: My years coaching Tiger Woods.* New York, NY: Three Rivers Press.

Huff, D. (1954). *How to lie with statistics.* New York, NY: Norton.

Lucas, S. E. (2004). *The art of public speaking* (8th ed.). New York: McGraw-Hill.

Student Loan Debt. (2019). A current picture of student loan borrowing and repayment in the United States. Retrieved from https://www.cometfi.com/student-loan-debt-statistics

Composing, Organizing, and Outlining

Greg G. Armfield and Eric L. Morgan

Objectives

► Compare and contrast organizational patterns.
► Apply the appropriate organizational pattern for your speech topic.
► Compose a properly structured and organized speech.
► Construct an effective outline.

ORGANIZATIONAL PATTERNS

Regardless of the goal, type, or even the specific strategies, one of the most important decisions you will make while writing your speech, or any manuscript for that matter, is the organization of your content. Thompson (1960) took a well-organized speech and rearranged all the points. He then had the same presenter deliver the original speech and scrambled speech to two randomly selected audiences. After the presentation the audience was given a test. It should not surprise you that the audience who listened to the well-organized speech performed much better on the exam. A few years later Sharp and McClung (1966) conducted a similar experiment, only they surveyed the audience to determine the effect of organization on speaker ethos. Again, you should not be shocked to learn that the well-organized speaker was judged as significantly more trustworthy, competent, and credible. All informative speeches should be guided by a well thought out overarching organizational pattern. While there may be variations, here are several of the most common organizational patterns (Beebe & Beebe, 2006).

Informational Organizational Patterns

Cause-Effect Organization. The **causal** organizational pattern sees main points arranged by outlining causes and their effects or vice versa. This pattern is particularly useful for structuring a speech about a process or even historical events. Using causal pattern, the speaker organizes the first main point as the causes of an event and the second main point as the effects of said event. Depending on your topic you may choose to reverse the pattern which would obviously result in presenting

CAUSE AND EFFECT

focuses on the causes of an issue and its effects, or vice versa.

the effects followed by the causes. Because of the versatility of this organizational pattern it can be utilized for informative or persuasive speeches. We will discuss other persuasive patterns later in this section.

© Terdsak L/Shutterstock.com

CHRONOLOGICAL

organized in a time sequence.

PROBLEM AND SOLUTION

focus on the problem and then the solution to an issue.

SPATIAL

organized by location or position.

© Arthimedes/Shutterstock.com

Chronological Organization. Using this pattern, the speaker organizes her or his main points according to how they are related in time. Speeches about historical events or processes are often best served by this organizational pattern. For example, a speech about the history of public speaking could be organized in terms of different eras. Speeches that describe processes can also be usefully organized chronologically. For instance, in describing the process of photosynthesis, a speaker may choose to organize the main points according to what happens first, second, third, and so forth. Other examples include the development of the Olympic Games or the sequence of events that led to a significant historical event.

Problem and Solution. This organizational pattern is useful when the speaker presents a problem and then outlines the solutions to the problem. While this is often used in persuasive speaking, it can be useful in informative speaking as well. A problem can be anything that invokes a response of some sort. This is what Bitzer (1968) called an exigence. An exigence exists when there is a problem in the world that can be addressed through human action. Bitzer argued that, in these cases, an exigence will call for persuasion; however, a useful informative speech could be designed to outline the problems and provide the range of solutions available for response.

Spatial Organization. This pattern organizes main points according to how objects or topics are related to one another in space. This pattern is especially useful when talking about a particular place and its various features. For example, if one wanted to deliver a speech about state parks in New Mexico, the speaker could organize the speech in terms of those that are located in the northwestern portion of the state, the northeastern portion, the southwestern, and the southeastern portion. Another example might be a speech delivered by a university campus official giving a tour to prospective students. This person could structure his or her points according to the layout of the campus.

Topical or Categorical Organization. The last informative organization pattern we will discuss is to organize the main points in the body of your speech topically or in terms of types. This type of organizational pattern is the most common and useful if the speech is delineating different types of objects, processes, or phenomena. In doing so, the result from categorizing or dividing your speech into topics and subtopics is a series of statements that then become a main point (topic) or subpoint (subtopics) in your speech. For example, a speech about different types of categories of animal species or types of programs offered at a university would lend itself nicely to this type of organizational pattern.

TOPICAL

organized by logical or natural divisions of a subject into parts or subtopics according to the speaker's preference.

Choosing the proper organizational pattern for your presentation will lead to a coherent speech that will more likely be memorable for the audience. Further, consider how a speech will change given the type of organizational pattern used. For example, let's say that you wanted to deliver a speech on the Thirty-Years War fought throughout continental Europe in the early 1600s. If you were to choose a topical pattern, that may lead you to focus on the various battles that made up the war such as the Battle of Breitenfeld, the Battle of the Alte Veste, or the Battle of Prague. The problem here, though, is that the Thirty-Years War was a really long war with a lot of battles. If you were to choose a chronological pattern, that would lead you to tell the story of the war as it played out over the first half of the 17th century. A spatial pattern would allow you to explain the war in terms of where it was fought and by whom. Finally, a cause-effect pattern would lead you to focus on the myriad causes of that tragic time. Hopefully, it is clear how an organizational pattern is important for structuring a coherent speech.

Before moving on to discuss persuasive speaking, we would offer this word of warning. Over the years, we have watched countless speeches delivered by students. One common error is that students will think of a topic and come up with the first three things that come to mind and use those as their main points. The problem lies in that often these things belong to different organizational patterns. This can often lead to rambling speeches that exceed the time limit, or it leads to confusion on the part of the audience because each topic cannot be explained in the appropriate depth. A much better solution is to choose a topic, and then focus on a single organizational pattern.

Persuasive Organizational Patterns

Effective organization is crucial when one is attempting to persuade. While there is no one best way to organize a speech, the organization of a persuasive speech undoubtedly has a major effect on your persuasive success. The first persuasive pattern, cause and effect, can be very useful and was previously discussed. Problem and solution can also be used as either an informative or persuasive organizational pattern. Below we will discuss three prominent organizational patterns designed for persuasive speaking.

Logical Reasons. Very similar to topical organization, this pattern, as you might assume, categorizes the reasons your audience should support

© REDPIXEL.PL/Shutterstock.com

your position, purchase your product, and so forth. This approach provides a simple and straightforward pattern to present the speaker's reasoning. The first main point should be your second strongest reason, the second point should be your weakest reason (or subsequent weaker reasons if more than three main points), and your last main point should be your best or strongest argument.

Comparative Advantages Order. If you already have buy-in from your audience that the issues you are speaking on are a problem and exist, rather than droning on about the problem you can devote each main point of your presentation to addressing why one solution (yours) is better than the alternatives. In doing this, you rationalize advantages of your solution to the audience. For example, you could compare the advantages of purchasing a PC over a MAC or an iPad versus a Surface.

Monroe's Motivated Sequence. In the 1930s, Alan Monroe developed a strategy for public speaking that has seen some success (Monroe & Ehninger, 1969). This organizational pattern is now commonly known as Monroe's Motivated Sequence. It organizes a persuasive speech in terms of the following five steps: (1) attention step, (2) need step, (3) satisfaction step, (4) visualization step, and (5) a call to action.

The first task of any persuasive speech, according to this model, is to gain the audience's attention. This step is critically important as it sets the tone for your overall persuasive goal. We'll discuss ways to capture the audience's attention a bit later, but for now, it should be stated that any attempt to gain the audience's attention should be relevant to the overall speech.

The second step of the model, need, is your first main point in the body of your speech. Having previously gained the attention of your audience, you should now focus on the problem at hand and the need to support change. Focus on why something needs to change. This should be done clearly and the speaker should focus on illustrating the need for change with strong supporting material (statistics, examples, testimony) and link the supporting material closely to the audience's values and interests (Lucas, 2004). Any persuasive speech should be focused on some sort of social need or exigence.

The third step, satisfaction, requires the speaker to state what will satisfy both the need and the audience's sense of what is required. This is where you establish your plan and solution to address the need described above. Develop this main point by explaining how your solution will work. While you don't have to go into in-depth details at this stage, you do need to provide enough detail so that your listeners have a clear understanding of how the problem(s) you outlined will be solved.

The fourth step of visualization should intensify the audience's desire to help you solve the problem. In this step you should give the audience a sense of what it is if your solution were or were not implemented. Visualization actually can take two forms, positive and negative. Positive visualization requires the speaker to paint a picture of the beneficial state of the world if the proposal is accepted. Negative visualization occurs when the speaker explains the negative consequences that will result if the proposed solution is not accepted. Or, you can present both positive and negative visualizations. The problem will be solved if your plan is implemented, but the world is going to be much worse if your plan is not implemented (Beebe & Beebe, 2006).

Finally, a persuasive speech should always end with a strong call to action. Once the audience is convinced that your policy is good and beneficial you must have a call to action in order to get your audience to act. State exactly what you want your audience to do. Explain what action they should take or what they should implement in order to effect change. For example, you can provide an e-mail address they can write to or a petition to sign. You could start a petition on change.org and provide the Web address for them to sign your petition. However, sometimes signing a petition is not enough. Consider organizing a march, encourage your audience to donate financially to causes, or tell them who to vote for in the Student Body President race. In short, outline and tell your audience the specific action you want them to take.

Using these steps is one of the best ways to organize an effective persuasive public policy speech. The advantage of this formula is that it is straightforward and detailed, more so than problem–solution for example. Monroe's sequence follows a logical process of human thought and directs the speaker to follow a step-by-step process that will lead an audience to take a desired action (Lucas, 2004). The fact that it is so widely used lends validity to its applicability and success.

COMPOSING YOUR SPEECH

Up to this point, we've considered different types of speeches as well as different purposes for public speaking. Each of these areas gives us general clues about broad organizational patterns. These patterns are a requirement, but they still don't tell us what specifically should be included in a speech. In this section, we will briefly consider some components of all public speeches as well as some strategies for effective composition. A good rule of thumb guiding some of these ideas is to both start strongly and finish strongly.

THE SPEECHMAKING PROCESS

The first step is choosing your topic. Earlier in the previous section we discussed some of the cultural aspects of speaking and **topic** choice. In keeping your audience in mind, first and foremost, consider subjects that you already have knowledge of or would like to learn more about. Begin by brainstorming or listing several ideas. Two primary approaches to brainstorming are to conduct a listing activity or cluster. To create a list, begin with broad categories such as hobbies, activities, cultural celebrations, and social concerns. Spend 5 minutes focusing on each broad category and list as many subjects as come to mind.

TOPIC

the subject of your speech.

© g-stockstudio/Shutterstock.com

Clustering works in a similar fashion, but the categories tend to be more specific. Examples might be people, places, processes, concepts, things, events, problems, and so forth; spend some time listing what comes to mind for each category. Regardless of the approach, the next step is to narrow down from your potential list. For example, you might decide you want to focus on outdoor activities. In that category you might have biking, hiking, and climbing. Get narrow (or specific); think local bike paths or trails, maintenance on bikes, local hiking trails, places to climb (both indoor and outdoor). As you get narrower you will be able focus on a speech that can be accomplished in a typical 3 to 5 or even 6 to 8-minute classroom assignment.

While choosing your topic can be a relatively quick decision, take time to narrow your topic for the given time limit of your speaking occasion. Broad topics like persuading an audience to quit smoking or informing about Biology will have little to no effect on an audience because you will not be able to go into depth about these topics. Narrowing your topic so that you can go into depth will have a greater impression on your audience. For a persuasive speech consider persuading your audience to purchase or carry a reusable water bottle, or to start the day with one plastic bottle and refill it throughout the day to reduce society's impact on plastic consumption and the environment. Or, inform your audience about the purpose or behaviors of animals or insects.

Determining your purpose. After you have chosen your topic, it is time to determine your purpose. As you will recall from Section One of this unit, there are three primary purposes of public speaking (informative, persuasive, and special occasion). Similarly, the purpose of your speech will be one that is to inform, to persuade, or to entertain, with the latter being the least popular. Based on the examples above, you would write your **specific purpose** as follows:

SPECIFIC PURPOSE

state precisely what you want to accomplish in your speech in a single infinitive phrase.

- ▶ To inform my audience about the new indoor climbing wall at the campus REC center.
- ▶ To inform my audience about the new mountain bike trail outside of town.
- ▶ To persuade my audience to explore the new bike path that was completed downtown.
- ▶ To entertain my audience with the story of when I restored my 1963 Schwinn Sting-Ray.

Note the language used. The design of your speech should follow the concepts of understanding the **general purpose** (to inform, to persuade, or to entertain) along with the reminder that public speaking is an audience-centered performance. You should never say your specific purpose in your speech, the specific purpose is for planning and organizing your speech. We will address how to start your speech in the section below entitled "A Strong Start."

GENERAL PURPOSE

the broad goal of your speech.

Tips

When writing a specific purpose Lucas (2004) suggests the following guidelines:

- ▶ It should be a complete sentence.
- ▶ It should not be written as a question.
- ▶ It should avoid figurative language.
- ▶ It should only have one distinct idea.
- ▶ It should be clear and explicit, not vague or general.

Expressing your thesis. Now that you have determined the topic and purpose of your presentation, you are ready to write your **thesis**. The distinction between a specific purpose and thesis is the specific purpose is a goal or what you want to accomplish by delivering your speech. The thesis is what you expect to say and what you want your audience to do or learn. When composing your thesis consider the goal and purpose of your speech. In other words, if the audience remembers only one thing from your speech, what would you want that to be? That is likely the thesis of your speech. The thesis should summarize your speech and be expressed as a simple declarative statement.

Questions to ask about your specific purpose (Lucas, 2004):

► Does it meet the assignment?
► Can it be accomplished in the allotted time?
► Is it relevant to my audience?
► Is it too trivial or technical for my audience?

THESIS

a one-sentence statement that sums up or encapsulates your speech.

© GaudiLab/Shutterstock.com

Guidelines for writing your thesis (Lucas, 2004):

► Make sure the thesis is not too general or vague.
► State the thesis as a complete sentence.
► State the thesis as a statement, not a question.
► Avoid figurative language.

Consider the previous topic example of mountain biking for putting all four (topic, general purpose, specific purpose, and thesis statement) together.

Topic:	New mountain bike trail
General Purpose:	To inform
Specific Purpose:	To inform my audience about the new mountain bike trail outside of town
Thesis:	The new mountain bike trail "Canyon Springs" in the Organ Mountains is scenic but challenging

From this we can see that if you use topical organization the following three main points can be discussed:

A.   First, I will elucidate the scenery along the trail.
B.   Second, I will elucidate the challenges the trail presents.
C.   Last, I will elucidate some advice for riding the trail.

The same topic, organized in a spatial order, could be framed as:

A.   The first stage of the trail is rather flat and perfect for novice riders.
B.   The second stage of the trail is predominantly uphill and requires advanced riding techniques.
C.   The last stage of the trail is predominately downhill and has 180-degree cutbacks requiring very advanced riding skills.

As you can see, once you have determined your thesis the next step is to start building your speech and choose a logical organizational pattern for the speech topic. Next, we will address how to develop and support the main points of your presentation.

The Body

Developing the main points of your speech is the next logical step, as you just read. Consider the main points of your speech the highlights of your presentation. They should be precisely phrased, carefully worded, and arranged strategically based on one of the organizational patterns previously discussed. One way to accomplish these three goals is to follow the tips we have highlighted here.

▶   Keep each main point separate.
▶   Use the same pattern of wording for all main points.
▶   Balance the amount of time devoted to each main point.

When choosing an organizational pattern that best suits your speech, consider the following. First, look at your thesis. Are there any logical divisions or steps? For many speeches there will be a logical division. Take for example the topics: the major accomplishments of Barry Sanders, or the major benefits of a laptop computer. Both topics can easily break into equal sections. Second, can you support your thesis? If you have personal experiences you can rely on your own experiences to create examples and illustrations along with other forms of supporting material from your research. Last, are there any reasons your thesis is true? If your thesis places a value judgment (something is good or bad), you should focus on the reasons why your thesis is true. For example, to argue that Barry Sanders is the best NFL running back to play the game, would clearly need to examine values that would make Sanders the best, when compared to other great running backs who have played the game. Each of those values would become truths you would argue, and thus each truth will be the main points of your speech.

The body of your speech should be developed to the extent that 75 to 85% of your speech should be spent discussing the main points and supporting material. Speeches should have between two and five main points; unless they are impromptu. That said, the majority of speeches will have only two or three main points. If you have more than five main points you have not provided enough depth for each point and you will certainly go over the time limit for typical classroom speeches that average under 10 minutes. But even more important, your main points will not be the highlight of your speech. If a speaker tries to make too many points during a limited time period the audience will get confused and the speaker will have a very limited impact on their audience.

TRANSITIONS

The last item that we need to discuss with regard to speech composition is the glue that holds the three main sections (introduction, body, and conclusion) together. Without proper overviews, signposts, and summary statements, even the simplest information can be confusing. If audience members lack the ideas necessary to make sense out of the specific facts that are given, they are likely to have difficulty following the speech. Thus, they will retain less information. Consider the following:

> The procedure is actually quite simple. First, you arrange things into different groups depending on their makeup. Of course, one pile may be sufficient depending on how much there is to do. If you have to go somewhere else due to lack of facilities that is the next step. Otherwise, you are pretty well set. It is important not to overdo things. That is, it is better to do too few things at once than too many. In the short run this may not seem important, but complications can arise quite easily. A mistake can be expensive as well. At first the whole procedure will seem complicated. However, soon it will become just another facet of life. It is difficult to foresee any end to the necessity for this task in the immediate future, but then one never can tell. After the procedure is complete, one arranges the materials into different groups again and distributes them to their appropriate places. Eventually they will be used and the whole cycle will have to be repeated. But, that's life!

Can you figure out what process is being described? It's Laundry.

The above paragraph would be much easier to identify if it included transitions and signposts. The necessity for transitions in public discourse is intensified given that when you read the above paragraph you could pause and take as much time as needed to decipher what was being communicated. An audience for a speech or presentation is not given that luxury.

Transitions are phrases that indicate a speaker is shifting the conversation. In other words, transitions signify a speaker is finished with one thought or idea and is moving to the conversation in a different direction. Signposts are also used for engaging the audience and leading through a series of important key ideas. Signposts tend to be a word or two whereas transitions are phrases or sentences. Signposts function much like road signs, or signposts, in that they alert audiences to an important point. For example, if you are listing the steps to smoking a brisket, using a series of signposts would help the audience follow all the steps. Similarly, if you are explaining how to change the oil in a vehicle, the presentation could be presented with two main points and a summary transition that moves from the first to second main point like so:

> Now that we have discussed how to remove the old oil from your motor, let's discuss how to complete the job by filling the engine with the appropriate fresh motor oil.

TRANSITIONS

signify a shift between two ideas in a speech.

SIGNPOST

a word signifying an important point of movement in a speech.

SUMMARY TRANSITION

Summarizes one main point and previews the next main point.

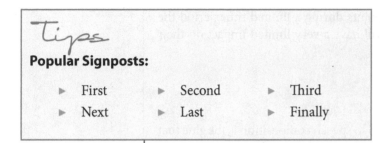

Popular Signposts:

- ▶ First
- ▶ Next
- ▶ Second
- ▶ Last
- ▶ Third
- ▶ Finally

Obviously, there are several steps in removing oil, locating and removing the oil filter, locating and removing the drain plug, and so forth. Those steps should be highlighted with signposts to keep the audience's attention and track the chronological process of changing the motor oil in a vehicle. Finally, transitions or signposts should be used to distinguish the introduction from the body of a speech and the conclusion.

A STRONG START

All speeches must begin. How they begin is entirely up to the speaker, and it is the duty of the speaker to capture the attention of the audience. This is done with what is normally called an attention-getter. There are a number of different types of attention-getters or hooks that are commonly and effectively used, including narratives, quotes, declarations, and questions. We'll visit each one in terms of advantages and disadvantages.

Narratives

NARRATIVE

a story.

A **narrative** is a story. The advantages of telling narratives to begin a speech include being able to set the stage for upcoming points for the audience. Stories are also easily relatable for the audience and thus can help keep the audience engaged. You can use a story from personal experience or find a story to share from your background research. Furthermore, starting off with a story can provide a useful organizing theme that can last all the way to the conclusion of the speech. A disadvantage to the use of narratives is that they can take up a lot of time. Likewise, they should be relevant to the speech, and not simply offered for the sake of telling a story.

Quotes

QUOTE

reproducing original words from another source. Representing testimony from another.

Quoting notable figures can be another useful way to start a speech. One advantage is that, depending on the person being quoted, one can develop a sense of ethos for the speech. Quotable people are normally credible people, and this can help establish your own credibility as a speaker. As with narratives, quotes can also provide a grounding point which can be returned to in the conclusion. Two requirements for the use of quotes are that they need to be relevant to the topic as well as easily understandable. There are times, for instance, when the words of some notable person have become meaningful to us individually given certain contexts. It is possible, at times, to forget that not everyone shares that same context, and so the meaning of the quote may be muted for the listeners.

Representatives

REPRESENTATIVE

any statement that is presented as being true or as "representing" the world. Common examples are shocking statistics, startling statements, or personal references.

A **representative** is any statement that a speaker presents as true (Searle, 1990). Quite commonly, speakers will use a shocking statistic, startling statement, or personal reference to engage an audience. This can be useful as long as the source is credible.

© HitToon/Shutterstock.com

One way to introduce incredible threats to one's credibility is to cite non-credible sources.

Questions

By far, the most common attention-getting strategy I've seen used over the years is the rhetorical question. Just because this is the most common strategy does not make it the best strategy. In fact, it can become trite and cliché, which is probably the biggest drawback to the use of the rhetorical question. Another drawback is that it is often delivered as a statement and thus fails to engage the audience as intended. One advantage of the question is that, if delivered properly, it can actually serve to get the audience engaged through interaction.

These are four common strategies for attention-getting devices. In each case, the speaker should try to consider the best way to orient the audience to the topic at hand. One last thing about attention-getting devices. Only under very specific circumstances should one start by introducing him- or herself. In some cases, another person will introduce you and, in most cases, you will be known to the audience. At this point, an introduction is merely redundant and could actually be understood by the audience as condescending. However, if you are addressing an audience that does not know you, an introduction would be appropriate. Addressing a city council or other government board is a good example. However, beginning a classroom speech with your name is a horrible strategy and should never be used. Finally, under no circumstances should you apologize for speaking.

After you have used a hook to gain the attention of your audience, the next part of the speech introduction is to include a coherent thesis statement and preview of the rest of the speech. A thesis statement should be clear and concise and allow the audience to easily recall what the speech will be about. Next you need to establish your credibility on the topic. Modern audiences are skeptical and you should identify with the audience by establishing your expertise on the topic or issue you are addressing early. Simple ways to establish your credibility include explaining why the topic is important to you, why you are speaking on the topic, or simply citing research or expert sources on the topic. Likewise, the introduction should include a preview of each main point of the speech. This will help the audience follow along throughout the duration of the speech. The only other optional, or additional steps, you should consider are the definitions of unfamiliar terms or to provide any needed historical or background information. Keep in mind the entire introduction should only be 10 to 15% of your entire speech.

These four components (an attention-getter, a thesis statement, a credibility statement, and a preview of each main point) are vitally important for an effective introduction. If careful attention is paid to these components, then three things should occur. First, the audience will have a clear idea of what the speaking situation will be about. Second, the audience will be able to relate to the topic. Finally, you, as a speaker, will have successfully established your credibility.

A STRONG FINISH

As with introductions, conclusions to speeches are essential to an effective public speech. While conclusions will vary according to speech purpose, they should include at least two components. First, an effective conclusion should provide a summary of the main points. Scholars of public speech will often say that good speakers will tell the audience what they will tell them (preview), they will then tell them (body of the speech), and then they will tell them what they told them (summary). The summary helps remind the audience in both form and content what the main points are. This significantly increases the chances that an audience member will remember the speech. The second component of an effective conclusion is a clincher. The most successful strategy for composing an effective clincher is to relate it directly back to the attention-getter. For example, if you began with a quote, you can provide the quote again and show how it helps us to understand the main points of the speech.

In a persuasive speech, the conclusion should also include a call to action. This is an explicit statement that lets the audience know what exactly you want them to do. Calls to action are most effective under two conditions. First, they should be specific. The more specific a call to action is, the more likely an audience will be to engage in it. In this sense, changes in specific actions are better than vague calls to change attitudes. Second, calls to action should be reasonable. Asking for massive amounts of change within the context of a single speech simply invites the audience to find reasons not to do it. Asking for reasonable, even small, amounts of change will structure the range of potential responses from an audience, and, thus increase the likelihood that they will engage in the change.

As with introductions, there are a couple of things to avoid when delivering an effective conclusion. Keep in mind the entire conclusion should only be 5 to 10% of your entire speech. First, once you begin to conclude your speech, try not to introduce new information. We've all been in situations in which the speaker has mentioned that she or he will conclude, just to go on to present all sorts of new information. When this happens, the audience begins to focus on the ending of the speech and not the new information. If the information is important enough, then one should include it in the body of the speech. Second, make sure to conclude the speech. Don't simply stop speaking or say something trite like, "that's it."

OUTLINING YOUR SPEECH

OUTLINE

the process of getting your thoughts in order.

Outlining is the process of getting all of your thoughts into order. It is the written plan that provides structure to your presentation through the uses of symbols, spacing (indentation), and content (as discussed above) that shows how important each piece of material is to your audience. The previous section discussed the process of conducting research and developing your supporting material. This section discusses how to put everything together to make the best argument, for persuasive speaking, and to best make an impression on your audience. Once you have decided, roughly, what your thesis is and identified an organizational pattern, the process of outlining, or getting your thoughts in order, should begin.

Why Outline?

An outline sets forth, in plain view, the structure of a speaker's thoughts. In doing so, the outline helps a speaker:

1. Verify your thought patterns are suitable, orderly, and consistent.
2. Ensure your supporting material (subpoints) is logically related, but subordinate to, your main points.
3. Confirm your supporting material is of a kind, quantity, and quality that will:
   a. Sustain your main points.
   b. Develop your subject as fully and completely as you wish.
   c. Influence your audience as much as possible in the way you want.
4. Organize their thoughts and remember the main points, sequence, and development of the presentation (including multimedia transitions).
5. Ensure the audience will comprehend the speech and retain what they learned.

Proper organization requires the author to follow a systematic process that includes six outlining standards.

Begin With Specific Purpose and Thesis

The specific purpose should be stated at the top of the outline, underneath your title and name. Including the specific purpose on your outline makes it easy for you to refer back and assess how closely you have followed your initial purpose as you constructed your outline. If you have not accomplished your initial goal well, you will need to revise your specific purpose or your outline to ensure they are still aligned.

As with the specific purpose, you should also begin with your thesis. I'm a BIG proponent of stating your thesis, but never begin your speech with your thesis (see discussion on strong start). Your thesis should be stated relatively soon after you begin your speech with your attention device, established audience relevance, or the reason your audience should be interested in your topic, and you have also established your credibility. This will place your thesis at about the fourth main point in the introduction and stated before you preview your main points (see sample outline on next page). Other teachers will prefer a different order of the elements of the introduction. I advise you to verify this with your teacher.

Basic Outline Format

Title of Speech
by Jane or Joe Student

Specific Purpose: To inform my audience about how great this class is.

Introduction
I.   Attention-getting opening/create interest
II. Reason audience is interested in speech
II. Establish your credibility
IV. Thesis statement/what do you want them to do as a result of your speech?
    A. Main point one
    B. Main point two
    C. Main point three

[Transition or signpost to body of speech]

Body
I.   Main point one
    A. First level supporting material
        1. Second level supporting material
        2. More second level supporting material
    B. Additional first level supporting material

[Transition to main point two: summarize main point one and preview main point two]

II. Main point two
    A. First level supporting material
    B. Additional first level supporting material
        1. Second level supporting material
        2. More second level supporting material

[Transition to main point three: summarize main point one and two, preview main point three]

III. Main point three
    A. First level supporting material
    B. Additional first level supporting material
    C. More supporting material

[Transition or signpost to conclusion]

Conclusion
I.   Summarize the presentation's main points
    A. Restate main point one
    B. Restate main point two
    C. Restate main point three
II. Closing statement (action statement in a persuasive speech), refer to introduction.

References
(should be cited using APA Style)

Label all Sections of the Outline

There are four major sections on any outline that should be properly labeled (see sample outline). Three of the sections align to our previous discussion on organizing your speech. The introduction includes the attention devise, gaining the audience's interest in your topic, establishing your credibility, thesis, and preview of main points. The second major section is the body of the speech, which consists of two to five main points. The third major section is the conclusion which only consists of reviewing your main points and closing your speech. The fourth and final section is a listing of all your references. References should be listed alphabetically (not numbered) and follow the formatting guidance of your instructor. Typically, in-text references and reference lists will adhere to APA or MLA standards.

Symbols and Indentation

A consistent set of symbols should be used to represent proper subordination for all main points, subpoints, sub-subpoints, sub-sub-subpoints, and so on. Main points are the most important and should be developed to a minimum of two subpoints on shorter speeches. The longer the speech the more each main point should be developed. Main points are identified by roman numerals (I, II, III, etc.). Subpoints represent the second level and are identified by capital letters (A, B, C, etc.). Sub-subpoints represent the third level and are identified by Arabi numerals (1, 2, 3, etc.). Sub-sub-subpoints represent the fourth level and are identified by lowercase letters (a, b, c, etc.). If needed the next level is sub-sub-sub-subpoints and identified by small roman numerals (i, ii, iii, iv, etc.). This can continue, but for the purpose of most classroom speech outlines will rarely need to be developed beyond the sub-sub-subpoint level.

I. Main Point: Represented by Roman Numerals (use capital I)
    A. Subpoint: Represented by Capital Letters
        1. Sub-subpoint: Represented by Arabic Numerals
           a. Sub-sub-subpoint: Represented by lowercase letters

In addition to consistency of symbols, you need to have a consistent and patterned indentation (as represented above) that is constantly followed for each main point, subpoint, and so forth, throughout the outline regardless of the section. In other words, the main points for the introduction should be on the same plane as the main points in the body of the speech and the conclusion. The same holds true for subpoints and so forth. The guideline for indentation is similar to symbols in that the greater the importance of the item, the closer it should be placed to the left-hand margin. If a statement takes up more than one line, the second line should be indented exactly as the beginning of the item (see sample outlines on the following pages).

Tips

Consistent Set of Symbols

I. Roman numerals (use capital I)
    A. Capital letters
        1. Arabic numerals
           a. Small letters
              i. Small roman numerals (lower case i)

Consider the following statements that you might have jotted down for a speech with the specific purpose: To persuade my audience to lift weights regularly; and a thesis of: You can improve your health and appearance in just 3 hours a week by lifting weights. Determine which statement is the main point, which statements are sub-points, and which statements are supporting material or sub-subpoints.

Lifting weights helps you deal with stress.
Lifting weights strengthens your heart.
Lifting weights will improve your health.
This allows more blood (oxygen) to be pumped.
Lifting weights gives you more energy.

The third statement ("lifting weights will improve your health") is the main point as it is the broadest. Lifting weights to improve your health is one of the primary issues your speech should address, given the Specific Purpose and Thesis. What two statements would support the main point? The first and the fifth. Both support the main idea and are subordinate to the main point. The final two statements (second and fourth) support, and are subordinate to, the subpoint of "lifting weights gives you more energy." Arranged properly, the main point would be outlined as follows.

I.   Lifting weights will improve your health.
    A.   Lifting weights helps you deal with stress.
    B.   Lifting weights gives you more energy.
        1.   Lifting weights strengthens your heart.
        2.   This allows more blood (oxygen) to be pumped.

The idea behind subordination and outlining is one of structure. If you think about the structure in organizations (see Unit 4, Section 1), the most important point or thought is farthest to the right, much like the persona at the top of an organizational chart. Each person one rank below the CEO or President of an organization is like the next most important point in a speech and should be one level to the left. As information or organizational positions become lower on the organizational chart, on the outline they would be spaced further to the left. And, so on and so forth. It would look something like this.

I.   CEO or President
    A.   Vice-President of Marketing
        1.   Public Relations Manager
        2.   Advertising Manager
            a.   Media Buyer
            b.   Copy Writer
    B.   Vice-President of Sales
        1.   Eastern Sales Manager
            a.   Northeast Sales Manger
                i.   District One Salesperson
                ii. District Two Salesperson
                iii. District Three Salesperson

       b. Southeast Sales Manager
          i.   District Four Salesperson
          ii. District Five Salesperson
          iii. District Six Salesperson
  2. Western Sales Manager
       a. Northeast Sales Manager
          i.   District Seven Salesperson
          ii. District Eight Salesperson
          iii. District Nine Salesperson
       b. Northwest Sales Manager
          i.   District Ten Salesperson
          ii. District Eleven Salesperson
          iii. District Twelve Salesperson

As you can see every point or person has a place on the outline. However, not everything that you will say in your speech has to be outlined.

Writing Main Points and Subpoints

There are three guidelines for writing main points and subpoints. First, they should be stated as complete sentences. **Keyword** outlines only give a vague idea to the speaker or reader of the content. Keyword outlines can also be rushed and completed with very little thought or preparation. Full sentences allow the writer and viewer to logically organize as well as check for sound reasoning, subordination, and progression of content.

In addition to using complete sentences on main points and subpoints, the outline should not contain more than two sentences per symbol on the outline. Second, there should only be one sentence per symbol. Writing more than one sentence per symbol can confuse the relationship between the statements and the point can become unclear. With the exception of the attention device or closing device, you rarely, if ever, need more than one sentence per symbol. Third, all statements under a main point should be directly related to the main point under which it appears.

KEYWORD

words or phrases that define the content.

Transitions

Transitions help your audience follow your presentation. Oftentimes the audience will be distracted or simply get lost in your speech. **Transitions** keep the audience on track and are an instrumental part of the outline. However, they are not represented by any symbols. Transitions are needed between each main point, and between the major segments of the speech: introduction to body and body to conclusion. They can be labeled or simply inserted in the outline or placed within parenthesis.

TRANSITION

a word or phrase that indicates when a speaker has finished one thought and is moving on to another.

References or Sources Cited

You should always include a bibliography or alphabetical list of sources cited. Typically labeled as bibliography or references, you will list all research materials that you used for quotations and paraphrases. Everything, with the exception of personal communication, that you orally cite in your speech should be listed in the section. Common citation styles used are APA and MLA, but regardless of the style your instructor asks you to adhere to, make sure you accurately list all material.

THE SPEAKER'S OUTLINE

The speaker's outline is a modified version of the preparation outline discussed above, but with special notes and additional material for delivering your speech. For example, in the text of your outline you may not have typed out all of the source information. Your speaker's outline would include the information needed for a full oral citation. Second, you want to provide delivery cues for yourself. As you practice your speech you will notice that you might have a tendency to speak too fast in certain sections, so you would want to write "slow down" to remind yourself to pace your speech. Additional notes would include reminders to make eye contact or pause after impactful statements. Quite often I will also shorten statements on my outline to keywords or add keywords or phrases to prompt me on what I need to speak on. For example, if you are going to tell a short story about swimming, all you really need on a speaker's outline is "swimming story" or "tell story about swimming." Typically, your speaker's outline should have tips for delivery cues such as slowing down, speeding up, speaking louder, or making eye contact.

A final note on speaking from note cards or outlines. Most instructors will not have a preference on speaking from note cards or from an outline. The best advice is to speak using the notes that you are most comfortable with. If you choose to speak off of note cards, you can transfer your speaker's outline and print your cards or simply print on half sheets. Most speakers who use note cards prefer larger cards such as 5x7 or cards no smaller than 4×6. Regardless of whether you choose full size paper outlines or transfer to smaller cards, number your notes in case you get them out of order, print in a larger than normal font (I prefer 14- or 16-point font), and have white space.

The following is an outline of a speech by Madelyn Stoltze using Topical Organization.

Green Hot Chile Peppers

by Madelyn Stoltze

Specific Purpose: To inform my audience about the history of New Mexico and Hatch Green Chile.

Introduction:
I.   Red or Green?: This is the famous question asked when ordering a traditional New Mexican dish at a restaurant.
II. New Mexico is known around the world for its Hatch Green Chile.
III. Green Chile is an important part of New Mexico's culture, heritage, and tradition.
   A. First, I will discuss the rich history of chile production in Hatch, New Mexico.
   B. Next, I will discuss the unique process of the chile harvest.
   C. Last, I will share with you the sense of pride chile brings to the people of New Mexico.

[Let's begin with the history of chile production in Hatch.]

Body
I.   Hatch, New Mexico, is the Chile Capital of the world.
   A. In 1954 Dencil and Mary Gillis began farming in the Hatch Valley, which is known for producing chile with a unique flavor.
   B. Hatch, New Mexico, is commonly known as the Chile Capital of the World (Gillis Farms, 2016).
      1. According to USA Today Travel, Hatch is featured as one of USA Today's America's famous food capitals (Huguelet, 2015).
      2. Each year, over 30,000 people visit Hatch to attend the annual Hatch Chile Festival (New Mexico Tourism Department, 2019).

[Now that I have told you about the history of Hatch, NM, I want to tell you about growing chiles.]

II. Hatch wouldn't be the Chile Capital of the World without the hardworking hands of the farmers.
   A. For years New Mexico's green chile crops have been hand-harvested, a practice that guarantees minimal damage and preserves the high quality the state's iconic crop has enjoyed for decades (Smith, 2015).
   B. Many New Mexican farm workers are committed to picking the perfect chiles. "Jesus Soto, who has been hand-picking chile most of his adult life, says careful selection of the chile is required to insure which chiles are ripe for harvest and which need to remain on the plant for ripening" (Hawkes, 2015, p. 17).
   C. Hatch is proud to have never experienced a crop failure! (Hatch Chile Festival, 2016)
[Now that we have discussed the history and process, I want to discuss the heritage of chile farming.]

III. From the hardworking hands of the farmers, Hatch green chile has become the pride of New Mexico.
   A. New Mexico green chile is a valued commodity and source of pride for the state's agricultural industry (Smith, 2015).

B. While I've highlighted the value and production of Hatch green chile, the red chiles of New Mexico also symbolize pride throughout the state.
   1. For example, chile ristras are strung pods of dried red chiles that are commonly displayed near doors and windows throughout New Mexico.
   2. They are said to bring health and good luck ("Albuquerque Convention," 2016).

[To conclude]

Conclusion
I. Green chile is more than just a food, it's an important part of New Mexico culture.
   A. First, I covered the history of chile in Hatch, New Mexico.
   B. I then covered the importance of harvest season.
   C. Finally, I discussed the sense of pride chile brings to New Mexico.
II. Whether it's red or green, consider yourself fortunate to be a part of New Mexico culture.

References
Albuquerque Convention & Visitor Bureau. (2016). Retrieved from: http://www.visitalbuquerque.org/albuquerque/culture-heritage/holiday-traditions/ristras/

Gillis Farms. (2016). *Our Story*. Retrieved from: http://www.gillisfarms.com/our-story/

Hatch Chile Festival. (2016). *Hatch Chile Festival*. Retrieved from http://www.hatchchilefest.com/

Hawkes, L. (2015). Mechanical chile harvester being tested in New Mexico. *Southwest Farm Press*, *42*(18), 16–17.

Huguelet, C. (2015, August 30). America's famous food capitals. *USA Today*. Retrieved from: http://experience.usatoday.com/food-and-wine/story/best-of-food-and wine/food/2015/08/30/american-food-capitals/71278088/

New Mexico Tourism Department. (2019). As summer cools down, the Village of Hatch, New Mexico heats up. Retrieved from https://www.newmexico.org/places-to-go/regions-cities/southwest/hatch/

Smith, R. (2015). Mechanical harvester shows promise for New Mexico green chile production. *Southwest Farm Press*, *42*(22), 5–6.

The following is an outline of a speech by Madelyn Stoltze using Logical Reasons Organizational Pattern.

Let's Get Moving

by Madelyn Stoltze

Specific Purpose: To persuade my audience that integrating daily exercise into their life will improve their health and well-being.

Introduction
I.   How many of you exercise at least 30 minutes a day?
II. Understanding the positive impact physical activity has on the body is important for both the active and inactive person to know, as it affects your overall health.
III. According to Harvard Men's Health Watch, the fraction of Americans who say they meet national guidelines for exercise has remained at a stable 25%, but objective measurements suggest that the actual percentage of adults who get enough exercise is close to 5% ("Harvard Men's," 2012.)
IV. Integrating daily exercise into your life will significantly improve your health and well-being.
   A. There is a need to incorporate exercise into our daily routine in order to maintain a healthy lifestyle and reduce obesity rates.
   B. Exercising daily has a positive impact on our overall health.
   C. Daily exercise is simple, and can start with just 30 minutes a day.

[Let's begin.]

Body
I.   Many Americans are not active on a daily basis.
   A. Research that supports the need: In fact, ABC News (2011) reports 30% of people in the South alone do not get any physical exercise.
   B. This lack of exercise is evident when looking at obesity rates in the U.S. According to the Center for Disease Control and Prevention (2015), more than 78.6 million U.S. adults are obese.

[It is clear that something must be done to decrease this obesity rate and improve our overall health.]

II. Through exercise and physical activity these health concerns can be reduced.
   A. According to the Mayo Clinic (2016) the number one benefit of regular physical activity is weight control.
   B. Exercise also combats health conditions and diseases such as type 2 diabetes, depression, and high blood pressure (Mayo Clinic, 2016).
   C. Additionally, exercise can positively affect your overall sense of well-being by releasing endorphin chemicals to the bloodstream (Keiley, 2006).
   D. Exercising can also lead to weight loss and improved fitness (Cerdá et al., 2016).
   E. "The benefits of exercise in reducing body fat and metabolic risk profiles can be achieved by performing in obese adolescents" (Monteiro et al., 2015, p.1).

[The benefits of daily exercise can greatly influence your life. Let's take a look at how you can join the movement.]

III. Improving your life is simple—take just 30 minutes from your day to focus on your health.
  A. The American Heart Association defines physical activity as anything that makes you move your body and burn calories ("American Heart," 2015).
  B. Start with walking: A walking program is flexible and yields high success rates because it is easy for people to stick with ("American Heart," 2015).

[To conclude]

Conclusion
I. It's time for you to take action and engage in daily exercise.
  A. It is clear that there is a need for change based on the lack of people engaging in exercise.
  B. The benefits of physical activity have the potential to increase your overall health and well-being.
  C. All that is needed to improve yourself is 30 minutes a day of physical activity.
II. Only you have the ability to take control of your body. Make a change, take responsibility, and better yourself by exercising just 30 minutes a day.

References
ABC News. (2011, February 16). New CDC report says many Americans get no exercise. Retrieved from http://abcnews.go.com/Health/cdc-report-americans-exercise/story?id=12932072

American Heart Association. (2015, August 17). *American Heart Association recommendations for physical activity in adults*. Retrieved from http://www.heart.org/HEARTORG/HealthyLiving/PhysicalActivity/FitnessBasics/American-Heart-Association-Recommendations-for-Physical-Activity-in Adults_UCM_307976_Article.jsp#.VwuwS4-cGUk

Center for Disease Control and Prevention. (2015, September 15). *Division of Nutrition, Physical Activity, and Obesity: Adult obesity facts*. Retrieved from http://www.cdc.gov/obesity/data/adult.html

Cerdá, B., Pérez, M., Pérez-Santiago, J. D., Tornero-Aguilera, J. F., González-Soltero, R., Larrosa, M., & De Filippo, C. (2016). Gut microbiota modification: Another piece in the puzzle of the benefits of physical exercise in health? *Frontiers In Physiology, 7*, 1–11. doi:10.3389/fphys.2016.00051

Harvard Men's Health Watch. (2012). *Obesity in America: What's driving the epidemic?* Retrieved from http://www.health.harvard.edu/staying-healthy/obesity-in-america-whats-driving-the-epidemic

Keiley, L. (2006, June/July). *Mother Earth News: The secret life to stress relief*. Retrieved from http://www.motherearthnews.com/natural-health/anxiety-and-stress-zmaz06jjzraw.aspx

Mayo Clinic. (2016). *Exercise: 7 benefits to regular physical activity*. Retrieved from http://www.mayoclinic.org/healthy-lifestyle/fitness/in-depth/exercise/art-20048389

Monteiro, P. A., Chen, K. Y., Lira, F. S., Cicotti Saraiva, B. T., Mello Antunes, B. M., Campos, E. Z., & Freitas Jr, I. F. (2015). Concurrent and aerobic exercise training promote similar benefits in body composition and metabolic profiles in obese adolescents. *Lipids In Health & Disease, 14*, 1–9. doi:10.1186/s12944-015-0152

The following is an outline of a speech by Kendra Jacobs using Monroe's Motivated Sequence.

Life (Saving) Changes

by Kendra Jacobs

Specific Purpose: To persuade my audience to support a presumed consent organ donation policy in the United States.

Introduction
I. Look around the room. The number of people you see is how many people die each day in the United States from not receiving a life-saving organ transplant.
II. Although, hopefully none of us will need an organ transplant, the need for a new organ is often unexpected, and can happen to anyone. We can help ensure people who do need life-saving transplants do not spend the rest of their lives on the waiting list.
III. Loved ones have been affected by the current organ donation shortage, which prompted me to conduct extensive research on a better system that could be implemented.
IV. Today, I am going to persuade you to support an opt-out organ donation policy.
    A. There is a devastating organ donation shortage in the United States.
    B. Adopting a presumed consent policy would decrease the organ shortage.
    C. Saving lives is possible, and starts with one decision.

[Let's get started by taking a look at the current organ donation situation in the United States.]

Body
I. The organ donation shortage in the United States must be addressed.
    A. More than 160,000 people are on the organ transplant waiting list, and an average of 20 people die every day because they do not receive a transplant ("Organ Donation Statistics," n.d.).
    B. The current opt-in policy assumes individuals do not wish to be organ donors unless explicit consent is given through registering as a donor.
    C. Many people do not take the necessary steps to register as organ donors, despite almost all being in favor of it.
        1. 95% of adults in the United States are in favor of organ donation ("Organ Donation Statistics," n.d.).
        2. Yet, barely half are registered as organ donors ("Organ Donation Statistics," n.d.).

[Now that I have explained why change is needed, let's discuss a solution to this crisis.]

II. Incorporating an opt-out, or presumed consent, system will drastically decrease the organ shortage.
    A. Under this system, every individual would be considered a consenting organ donor unless they take the necessary steps to be removed and become a non-donor.
    B. A presumed consent system simply changes the default option for donation registration.
        1. An opt-out policy would remove the burden of responsibility from those who wish to be donors, while still allowing the freedom of choice.
        2. Approximately 75% of individuals around the world support a presumed consent policy (Abadie & Gay, 2006).

[It is clear a presumed consent policy would help satisfy the shortage, so let's look at how this small change could make a life-saving difference.]

III. Implementing a presumed consent policy is truly a matter of life and death.
   A. According to Abadie and Gay (2006), countries with presumed consent organ policies have higher organ donation rates than countries with opt-in policies.
      1. There are often donation rates greater than 90% in countries which hold opt-out policies, which is six times greater than countries with opt-in systems that have measly 15% donation rates (Davidai, Gilovich, & Ross, 2012).
      2. Countries, including France, Italy, Spain, and Wales, among others have adopted opt-out organ donation systems and experienced donation leaps of up to 25% (Leins, 2016).
   B. Continuing to follow an opt-in organ donation system means continuing to fail ill people who are helplessly waiting for a miracle.
      1. For every 80 people who receive a life-saving transplant each day, the number of people in this room die from not receiving one (McIntosh, 2014).
   C. Do your part to save lives.
      1. Opt-out bills are being introduced around the country, including in states such as Texas, Connecticut, Colorado, and Pennsylvania (Samuel, 2017), and will soon find their way to New Mexico.
      2. Support presumed consent legislation, and encourage your family and friends to, as well.

[In conclusion]

Conclusion
I. Today, I hope to have persuaded you to support a presumed consent organ donation system.
   A. There is a devastating shortage of organ donations in the United States.
   B. Adopting a presumed consent policy would decrease the organ shortage.
   C. Saving lives is possible, and starts with one decision.
II. Be a hero. Register as an organ donor by visiting organdonor.gov and support presumed consent legislation, which could give the gift of life to up to eight individuals.

References

Abadie, A., & Gay, S. (2006). The impact of presumed consent legislation on cadaveric organ donation: A cross-country study. *Journal of Health Economics, 25*(4), 599–620.

Davidai, S., Gilovich, T., & Ross, L. (2012). The meaning of default options for potential organ donors. *Proceedings of the National Academy of Sciences, 109*(38), 15201–15205.

Leins, C. (2016). Should the government decide if you're an organ donor? Retrieved from https://www.usnews.com/news/articles/2016-02-12/presumed-consent-and-americas-organ-donor-shortage

McIntosh, J. (2014). Organ donation: Is an opt-in or opt-out system better? Retrieved from https://www.medicalnewstoday.com/articles/282905.php

Organ Donation Statistics. (n.d.). Retrieved from https://www.organdonor.gov/statistics-stories/statistics.html

Samuel, L. (2017). To solve organ shortage, states consider 'opt-out' organ donation laws. Retrieved from https://www.statnews.com/2017/07/06/opt-solution-organ-shortage/

Discussion Questions

1. Discuss which organizational pattern would be best given your topic choice.

2. What are the structural differences between an informative and persuasive speech?

3. Why is outlining important to speech making and giving?

References

Beebe, S. A., & Beebe, S. J. (2006). *Public speaking: An audience centered approach* (6th ed.). Boston, MA: Allyn and Bacon.

Bitzer, L. (1968). The rhetorical situation. *Philosophy and Rhetoric, 25*(1), 1–14.

Lucas, S. E. (2004). *The art of public speaking* (8th ed.). New York: McGraw-Hill.

Monroe, A. H., & Ehninger, D. (1969). *Principles of speech communication* (6th ed.). Glenview, IL: Scott, Foresman, & Company.

Searle, J. (1990). A classification of illocutionary acts. In D. Carbaugh (Ed.), *Cultural communication and intercultural contact.* Mahwah, NJ: Lawrence Erlbaum Associates, Inc. Publishers.

Sharp, H. Jr., & McClung, T. (1966). Effects of organization on the speaker's ethos. *Speech Monographs, 33,* 182–183.

Thompson, E. C. (1960). An experimental investigation of the relative effectiveness of organizational structure in oral communication. *Southern Speech Journal, 26,* 59–69.

Section 4

Delivery and Apprehension

Eric L. Morgan and Greg G. Armfield

Objectives

► Become familiar with different types of delivery styles.
► Be able to identify and put into practice aspects of effective delivery.
► Define communication apprehension.
► Apply strategies for managing communication apprehension to personal experience.

DELIVERY

I had a friend in college that would memorize comedians' jokes, even a full comedy routine by a comedian, and retell them. While he was a funny person, and could tell a good joke, he was never as funny as the original comedian. To put it another way, there is an old comedy routine by Richard Pryor (you can Google it, it's on YouTube) about little kids lying to their parents. I could do a similar routine talking about all the funny ways my kids have tried to lie or cover up accidents. But, ultimately, I will never be as funny as Pryor.

Actors and comedians are skilled at the use of delivery. For most people even with years of practice, their timing, pacing, gestures, facial expressions, and vocalics will never reach the level of expertise as professionals. However, with that understood, good delivery will improve any speech. This section will review the basic delivery methods used today as well as techniques to improve your presentational delivery.

© l i g h t p o e t/Shutterstock.com

DELIVERY METHODS

Generally speaking there are four different types of speeches that are normally delivered. These include the following: manuscript speeches, memorized speeches, impromptu speeches, and extemporaneous speeches (Beebe & Beebe, 2006).

Manuscript Speaking

Manuscript speaking occurs when the speaker reads a speech from a printed manuscript. Manuscript speaking requires the speaker to write out the speech word-for-word. These kinds of speeches can be useful in two cases. The first case is if the words themselves are vitally important. It's hard to say just where this threshold of importance lies, but there are certainly cases when, as a speaker, you will want to focus very closely on the form and content of the speech. One example may be when one addresses an audience with the media present. Because this speech will be broadcast to a large, heterogeneous audience that is not present, the words themselves will have a different status than when uttered in the transactional space of a live audience. The second example is if the speaker's position in society is such that every word uttered will be scrutinized. A good example of a speaker who routinely uses a manuscript speech because of both reasons is the President of the United States. While writing out a speech word-for-word may seem like a good idea, it may be inappropriate in quite a few cases. Three drawbacks in particular come to mind when discussing manuscript speeches. The first is that we do not speak like we write. Writing is a much more formal process of communication than speaking. Typically, when we speak, we do so in phrases and sentence fragments often changing the content and form to meet the needs of our speaking partners. The second drawback is directly related to the first. If the speech is written out, there is little room for the speaker to engage and respond to the audience. The event shifts from public speaking to public reading. Finally, one drawback is much more practical in nature. What would occur if the manuscript somehow got lost or put out of order? This may cause quite a bit of anxiety for the speaker, which in turn, could cause anxiety for the audience, which will cause more anxiety for the speaker, and so on. It's a vicious cycle.

© michelmond/Shutterstock.com

Memorized Speaking

A memorized speech is one in which the speaker attempts to memorize the entire speech for delivery. This obviously would require the speaker to write out the speech prior to delivery, so it is closely related to the manuscript speech. Instead of the shift from public speaking to public reading, the event now becomes a monologue. This is more the province of acting than public speaking. However, there is at least one benefit to a memorized speech. According to Beebe and Beebe (2006), a memorized speech might allow for the speaker to focus on the audience the entire time. Being able to do this effectively would, of course, take enormous amounts of effort. It's why good actors are good. They are able to naturally deliver memorized texts.

Perhaps the biggest drawback to memorized speaking can best be relayed through a story. I had been invited to speak on a panel in honor of my mentor and friend. Because this was a celebration of a lifetime of work, many people were in attendance. I was quite nervous going in because I wanted to properly honor someone who has been incredibly influential in my life. In order to stem some of these nerves, I tried to memorize large sections of my presentation. On the day of the event, my time to present came all too quickly. I began to speak and things were going quite well. It seemed that the audience was engaged and paying attention. About halfway through, a person whom I had not seen for many years walked in the door. This took me completely by surprise, and I simply forgot what I was saying. All of a sudden, the audience got that "uh-oh" look on their faces as I sat trying to remember what I was saying and where to go. I awkwardly shifted through my notes and finally was able to continue. That one moment stays with me to this day.

Impromptu Speaking

Impromptu speaking is a situation in which a speaker is required to speak without much, if any, preparation. This type of speaking off the cuff can be common for students who are called on to speak in class. Practicing impromptu speaking can help one develop skills in oral presentation as well as help alleviate some public speaking apprehension. The biggest drawback is obviously a lack of preparation and resources to engage the situation as one might want. However, impromptu speaking can also lead to a heartfelt speech (Beebe & Beebe, 2006). Impromptu speaking situations will arise every now and then. Quite often they will arise in your professional life

© Pressmaster/Shutterstock.com

when a co-worker asks you for an update on a project, or someone asks you what you are working on. When faced with these situations, try not to panic. Another useful strategy is to take a few seconds and think of two or three points that you would like to share before you begin speaking. Even this little bit of preparation can go a long way toward an effective impromptu speech.

Extemporaneous Speaking

Extemporaneous speaking is the type of speaking that we have focused on in this unit. It is also the type of speaking that your instructors will likely be teaching you. An extemporaneous speech is one that is well prepared, practiced, and delivered with the aid of notes. It is not a speech that has been memorized or written out beforehand. This last point is essential in understanding what you will likely be required to do in a public speaking class. The only drawback to extemporaneous speaking is that it requires time and effort to be able to speak skillfully (Beebe & Beebe, 2006). The benefits, however, are well worth the effort it takes to engage in this type of speaking. So, now that we know what public speaking is and what some of the different forms it can take are, we can turn our attention to delivery skills.

DELIVERY SKILLS

There are many books that have been written about the delivery of public speeches. Within these texts, there are likewise many useful tips students of public oratory may employ to deliver effective speeches. However, after decades of teaching public speaking, we have come to believe strongly in a single piece of advice more than others when it comes to the delivery of public speeches. Simply, this piece of advice is to *try to create something with your audience.* Every single piece of advice for what to do and what not to do when delivering a public speech centers around this idea as public speaking is an audience-centered activity. The things you should do are those things that engage the audience. The things you shouldn't do are those things that create a divide between you and the audience. That said, it will still be useful to think about a couple of different strategies for effective speaking delivery.

Vocal Enthusiasm

We use the term "vocal enthusiasm" as a broad term that encompasses all aspects of vocal delivery. These aspects are sometimes referred to as prosody or paralanguage (Rothwell, 2010), and include such things as rate of speech, tone of voice, volume, pitch, effective use of pauses, and so forth. When delivering a public speech, it is important to pay attention to these vocalic cues. Clearly, one would not want to speak too quickly or too slowly. In both cases, the audience may start to focus on the delivery of the speech more than the content of the speech. In my experience, people are sometimes quite shocked at how quickly they speak when in front of an audience. Perhaps it is due to nervousness or just general excitement, but speaking too quickly makes it difficult for the audience to follow the speech. One's tone of voice can also impact the reception of a speech. In spoken English, we tend to use quite a bit of inflection in order to cue our listeners into how what we are saying should be understood. For example, I may indicate that I am surprised by raising my voice and speaking a bit louder. In a public speaking situation, try to vary your tone of voice. A monotone delivery (in English at least) is, more often than not, understood as boring. What follows are some basic tips for using vocal enthusiasm:

- ▶ Speak up! Do not mumble.
- ▶ Be enthusiastic but keep a steady and somewhat varied pace.
- ▶ Likewise, do not speak too fast.
- ▶ Furthermore, if you speak too slow, or in a monotone, listeners will get bored listening to you.

▸ Use the correct pronunciation. If you are unsure how to pronunce a word, use the audio tool available in the online dictionaries.

Gestural Enthusiasm

As with vocal enthusiasm, using appropriate gestures helps you, as a speaker, keep the audience engaged. Generally speaking, you want to use gestures that accomplish the goal of creating something with your audience while avoiding those gestures that create distance between you and the audience. Over the years, we have come across quite a few different speakers who were beginning to develop gestural habits that were distracting. These ranged anywhere from using no gestures at all, putting their hands in their pockets, to going completely over the top by flailing their hands during the delivery. Just as one does not want to be stiff and mechanical in one's delivery, one should also avoid overly bombastic delivery. What follows are some basic tips for using gestural enthusiasm:

▸ Stand comfortably and erect with your feet shoulder-width apart. **Do not sit!**
▸ Movement, even subtle ones, will help reduce your tension and is useful for transitions. You must move around, but not so much (think pacing back and forth) to distract your audience.
▸ Don't slouch over or lean on a lectern, wall, table, and so forth. Avoid swaying back and forth, side to side, pacing back and forth, or standing at attention like a statue.
▸ Avoid random gestures or habits of self-grooming (e.g., playing with your hair, pencils, pens, or notes; rubbing your face or a body part, etc.). If you have practiced and are comfortable with your material, the gestures will come naturally with practice.

Eye Contact

One of the key aspects to effective public speaking delivery in this society is to maintain consistent eye contact with as much of the audience as possible. Maintaining this eye contact once again helps you to engage the audience and keep them interested. A lack of eye contact likewise will create distance between you and the audience. Beebe and Beebe (2006) note that if one maintains less than 50% eye contact with the audience, then the speaker will be seen by the audience as less believable, less trustworthy, less friendly, less informed, and more dishonest than those speakers that maintain consistent eye contact. Certainly, the amount of eye contact will vary by culture, but, in general, in North America, maintaining consistent eye contact with the entire audience is important.

In the past, you may have heard that one way to relieve some of the apprehension you may be feeling when speaking is to look over the heads of your audience. Do not do this. It is one of the more distracting things a speaker might do, and it violates the rule of co-creation with the audience. Also, try to vary your eye contact with all members of the audience not just a select few. Staring down a few select members of the audience is creepy. What follows are some basic tips for using eye contact:

► Never read the first part of your introduction (attention device, credibility, and thesis) or the conclusion. Look at your audience in the eyes when you begin and end the speech. **Engage the audience.**

► You need to make eye contact with the audience in order to gauge the response (feedback) of the audience while you speak.

► Look for people who are friendly and supportive or seem interested in your topic, but don't ignore the rest of your audience.

► Try not to read directly from your notes, especially for long periods of time. Pause briefly in an effective way (not long) to glance at your notes and begin talking. As you are speaking, practice thinking ahead in your speech and glancing at your notes to verify the next part of your speech. This is especially effective when you are stating your summary transitions.

Facial Expressions

Your facial expressions should be congruent with your material. When you are happy, smile. If you are speaking about something sad or serious you should have more muted facial expressions. Earlier we discussed enthusiasm. You must show interest in your topic. If you are not interested in your topic, why should your audience be? Show enthusiasm, conviction, and excitement for the topic you have chosen.

Humor

Using humor in your speech and during your presentation can help enormously with audience identification. However, we suggest you follow some of these basic guidelines:

► Brevity: Keep it short, on point, and simple; think anecdotes. Do not waste time with long drawn out stories or examples that are only tangentially related to your topic. Short, concise humor is more effective.

► Relevance: Humor usage should be appropriate for the topic and the speaking situation. Don't use humor just because you think you are funny, or for the sake of telling a joke. Humor needs to be appropriate for the speaker, if you are not comfortable using humor do not use humor, as well as the situation.

Practice, Practice, Practice

These areas are just a brief discussion of the many different facets of delivery. Once again, the important thing to remember is that the speaker should strive to create something with her or his audience that is authentic. This requires engaging in behaviors that keep your audience involved with you and your topic while avoiding those behaviors that create distance between you and the audience. It would take many pages of text to list all the different types of behaviors that can be distracting, and trying to focus on each one individually would be a futile task. The solution lies in understanding the broad principles of delivery and doing one other critical thing . . . practice, Practice, PRACTICE!

In public speaking, practice is essential. It is only through practice that one will develop that natural looking delivery that is the hallmark of good public speakers. Practice requires time and effort, which makes the actual speech composition process pretty rigorous. Practicing one's speech should also be done in as formal a manner as possible. Once you have a working speech composed with notes, presentation aids, and so forth, set aside enough time to go through the entire speech. Practice in full voice with appropriate pacing and gestures. If you have the opportunity, try to practice your speech in the place that you will be delivering your presentation. As you practice, time yourself so you know where you may alter the speech if time constraints become an issue. One piece of advice that we've found useful is to practice your speech in front of family or friends. Doing this can feel very awkward, which turns out to be a good thing. The public speaking situation is not one that we engage in every day. Therefore, it is itself an awkward situation. By placing yourself outside your comfort zone, at least in terms of the communication scene, you will get a feel for what it is like to deliver your speech when things are "not normal." One last point: going over the speech in your head and practicing mentally is very useful and helpful, but it is not as beneficial as practicing aloud with visual aids in front of an audience.

COMMUNICATION APPREHENSION

Communication Apprehension or Communication Anxiety (CA) occurs for most people who deliver a public speech. It is a normal bodily response to anxiety by producing and releasing extra adrenaline. Commonly called stage fright, normal people experience this, especially when faced with public speaking or a situation in which the performance is important and the outcome is uncertain. CA can result in three different types of responses (Fujishin, 2006). These include physical, emotional, and psychological responses. Some physical symptoms of CA include dryness of the mouth, shaking of the hands, increased heart rate and/or respiration rate, creaking or quavering of the voice, perspiration, sweaty hands/palms, and blushing. These symptoms can occur long before the day of the speech, as just thinking about speaking in front of an audience can bring on anxiety, and continue the day of the speech persisting throughout the duration of the speech. Emotional responses to CA include feeling overwhelmed, loss of control, fear, extreme nervousness, and even sometimes shame and anger (Fujishin). Psychological responses include loss of memory and even lowered self-esteem. While all of these things can occur, CA can be overcome and even your fear and anxiety can be channeled into positive outcomes! The last portion of this section will list some of the major causes of communication apprehension and then we will close with suggestions from two scholars along with insight that we have gleaned from close to 50 years of combined experience teaching and speaking in front of large audiences.

Major Causes of Communication Apprehension

1. An intense desire to be successful.
2. An approach/avoidance conflict within the self. In other words, you want to speak because it makes you feel and look important, but you also want to be done with it as soon as possible.
3. A feeling of inadequacy or possibly a poor self-image or lacking confidence about yourself as a speaker.
4. A distortion of the speech situation. In other words, speakers might tend to exaggerate the bad things that happen or even judge their performance too harshly.

Suggestions for Controlling and Reducing Communication Apprehension

Randy Fujishin (2006) provides a number of extremely helpful suggestions for controlling CA. They include the following:

- ▶ Realize that it is normal and natural to be nervous in these situations.
- ▶ Remember the audience plays a very important role in the communication process.
- ▶ Recognize that you probably appear much more relaxed than you feel.
- ▶ Speak on issues that are important and meaningful to you.

- ► Concentrate on the main point of the speech, not so much on the exact wording.
- ► Visualize being successful.
- ► Do something to relieve tension associated with CA.
- ► Understand that the audience is on your side!
- ► Recognize that experience matters. The more you do public speaking, the less you will experience anxiety.

Practice is one of the most critical components to reducing CA. Osborne and Osborne (1997) share the following tips:

- ► Try to practice in a space in which you will be delivering your speech. Also practice in "full voice."
- ► Practice using a formal outline first, then moving to note cards or a keyword outline.
- ► While practicing, consider your nonverbal gestures.
- ► Time your practice for your speech and use the feedback to revise your speech.
- ► Practice until you feel comfortable.
- ► Practice in front of friends and family, and make changes based on their feedback.

Practice, practice, practice is by far the most common advice given, and the best way to overcome CA. In addition to all the tips discussed, we would like to close with some advice to implement immediately prior to speaking. Get comfortable. Approach the podium confidently and take a few seconds to organize your notes. Read through your introduction and breathe deeply to calm your nerves and reduce your heart rate. Set your feet comfortably about shoulder-width apart. Look at your audience and begin with your attention device while maintaining direct eye contact with a variety of your audience members. After a good start, your anxiety will begin to lower and you will become more comfortable.

© metamorworks/Shutterstock.com

Discussion Questions

1. Make a list of the five most effective public speakers you can think of. Thinking about his or her delivery, what made that person such an effective public speaker?

2. Provide an example of one or two poor public speaking performances you have witnessed. What aspects of delivery were a problem for these performances?

3. Using the concepts from the chapter, consider ways that you might improve your own public speaking delivery.

4. Write about a time when you have experienced communication apprehension (public speaking anxiety). What did you do at the time to manage this? Now that you have read this unit, what will you do in the future to manage communication apprehension?

References

Beebe, S. A., & Beebe, S. J. (2006). *Public speaking: An audience centered approach* (6th ed.). Boston, MA: Allyn and Bacon.

Fujishin, R. (2006). *The natural speaker* (5th ed.). Boston: Allyn and Bacon.

Osborne, M., & Osborne, S. (1997). *Public speaking* (4th ed.). Boston: Houghton Mifflin Company.

Rothwell, J. D. (2010). *In the company of others: An introduction to communication* (3rd ed.). New York: Oxford University Press.

Listening

Eric L. Morgan

Objectives

- ► Understand the dimensions of active listening.
- ► Recognize different types of distractions to active listening.
- ► Understand and apply strategies to overcome distractions to active listening.

One of the key themes throughout this unit has been that public speaking is not simply about the speaker delivering a presentation. Just as communication is a transactional process, in which meaning is co-created among all participants, public speaking is a co-creation of meaning between speaker and audience. Therefore, the audience has responsibilities just as the speaker does in participating in the communicative event. These responsibilities revolve around active listening. Active listening occurs when participants in a communication event consciously and actively attend to the entire situation (O'Hair, Stewart, & Rubenstein, 2008). In order to better understand active listening, it may be useful to contrast hearing and listening. **Hearing** refers to the physiological capability of humans to perceive sound. If one has the ability to hear sound, then one cannot help but to perceive sound (Beebe, Beebe, & Ivy, 2004). It is an unconscious and automatic response to aural stimuli. Many humans have this capability, but what we do with these auditory stimuli moves us into the realm of active listening. **Listening**, as opposed to hearing, is a conscious and purposeful act of attending to a message. When we engage in active listening, we purposefully orient to the speaker in as full a manner as possible. This means not just listening to the words, but attending to all the environmental cues as well. Doing this is easier said than done, so to speak, as there are quite a few typical listening distractions.

HEARING

the physiological ability of humans to perceive sound.

LISTENING

the conscious and purposeful act of attending to a message.

© fizkes/Shutterstock.com

O'Hair et al. (2008) discuss a number of listening distractions that are useful in understanding how we can become better listeners. External listening distractions are those that come from the environment itself. It is impossible to predict when these will occur, but as a speaker and a listener you can take steps to minimize their impact. As a listener, strive to place yourself in a position to best be engaged with the speaker. As a speaker, try to address the distraction for the audience as quickly as possible. External distractions can even serve as useful moments in which the speaker and the audience can come together around an external situation and thus create a memorable public speaking situation. For example, I was giving a presentation at a professional meeting a few years ago, and in the middle of it, a work crew arrived to begin construction just outside the door. While this was distracting, it also served as a way for me to connect with the audience to work together to overcome the distraction. Internal distractions are those that come from the listener. These were discussed as psychological and physiological noise in Section One of the previous unit. As a listener, try to anticipate internal distractions and deal with them prior to the speech. For example, try to deal with hunger, tiredness, and restroom needs prior to the speech.

External and internal distractions are not the only barriers to active listening. O'Hair et al. (2008) also note that listeners can have a tendency toward **scriptwriting** and defensiveness as well. Scriptwriting occurs when the listener assumes that he or she already knows what the speaker is going to say and starts to "write a script" of the speech. This is common not only in public speaking, but in conversation as well. **Defensiveness** occurs when listeners believe the speaker will say something with which they will disagree. Because of this, the listener is listening for "attacks" or other possibly hostile or negative statements. We do this in order to defend our sense of self, or our argument, or some other aspect of the appropriate way we see the world. The problem is the speaker may or may not have actually said this. Defensiveness is a difficult distraction to overcome, and, as a listener, one has a responsibility to allow the speaker an opportunity to express his or her position prior to judgment.

These are just a few distractions that can impact active listening. Recognizing these can help one to become a more active listener, but there are a number of other strategies to employ as well. The first strategy is to understand your listening style. A **listening style** is a tendency that we have when it comes to listening. Have you ever noticed that you may listen for certain things more than other things? For example, you may be a person who really wants the speaker to get to the point, or you might be someone who listens to another with a focus on that person's motivations or feelings. These point to different listening styles. We should emphasize here, however, that these styles are oftentimes associated with particular contexts. There are four common listening styles identified by Weaver, Watson, & Barker (1996). These include person-oriented listening, content-oriented listening, action-oriented listening, and time-oriented listening. Person-oriented listening occurs when a person typically listens to another with a focus on the other person's thoughts, feelings, and motivations. Content-oriented listening occurs when a person listens for the development

SCRIPTWRITING

a distracting process in which a listener anticipates what a speaker will say instead of actually listening to what is being said.

DEFENSIVENESS

a distracting process in which the listener believes the speaker might be hostile toward his or her position, and thus listens in order to defend one's postion.

LISTENING STYLE

a tendency to listen in particular ways.

of a particular point. The focus here is on how well the speaker is supporting and elaborating arguments. Action-oriented listening sees the individual listening solely for what actions the speaker would like the listener to do. The listening effort is not about empathy or elaboration, but rather about "what do I need to do after hearing this speech." Finally, time-oriented listeners are concerned primarily with the amount of time invested in the public speaking situation. Obviously we can engage different styles at different times, but we also tend to do one or the other more frequently. What style do you typically use?

Another strategy is to set your listening goals (O'Hair et al., 2008). When setting listening goals, ask yourself the following questions:

- ▶ What do you want to get out of a speech?
- ▶ How should you evaluate what you heard?
- ▶ How will you keep yourself focused on the speech?
- ▶ What will you do to ensure you got as much out of the speech as you wanted?

These questions applied to each speaker will help keep you actively listening and also help keep the distractions away. When listening, it is also a good idea to train yourself to work with the content in specific ways. Doing so will increase your ability to recall information in the future, and will also allow you to better engage other's points. This strategy can be summarized as the "3 RE's." First, when listening, try to *repeat* what the speaker is saying. Simply saying something again can help solidify the main points in your mind. Second, try to *re-sort* the information presented. In other words, try organizing the main points in a way differently than the speaker did and in such a way that makes more sense to you. Finally, try to *rephrase* the main points. If you are able to rephrase what someone else has said, it indicates that you have access to the information in a unique fashion as opposed to simply being able to regurgitate content.

Listening is a skill just as speaking is a skill. As such, when we are involved in public speaking situations, we need to take every opportunity to increase our listening effectiveness. Listening is considerably more than simply hearing sound. It requires focused effort and is indeed a responsibility of an audience member. Next time you find yourself drifting off in a presentation setting, try some of the strategies suggested here. They will help you to be actually present in a situation.

Discussion Questions

1. Do you find it hard to pay attention to others sometimes? In these situations, can you identify the aspects that you find distracting? Are these consistent with the concepts presented in this unit? Describe why or why not.

2. Provide an example of a time when you have engaged in scriptwriting or defensiveness when listening. How could you better engage in active listening in these situations?

3. What is your listening style?

References

Beebe, S. A., Beebe, S. J., & Ivy, D. K. (2004). *Communication: Principles for a lifetime* (2nd ed.). Boston, MA: Pearson.

O'Hair, D., Stewart, R., & Rubenstein, H. (2008). Listening. In E. Morgan & A. E. Lindsey (Eds.), *Principles and practice in human communication: A reader and workbook for COMM 265* (2nd ed.). Dubuque, IA: Kendall Hunt Publishing.

Weaver, J. B., Watson, K. W., & Barker, L. L. (1996). Individual differences in listening styles: Do you hear what I hear? *Personality and Individual Differences, 20*(3), 381–387.

THREE

Unit

Interpersonal Communication in Action

Eric L. Morgan and Greg G. Armfield

WHAT IS INTERPERSONAL COMMUNICATION?

Communication between a customer and a salesperson, a doctor and a patient, a mother and a daughter, two partners who are in a fight, two partners who are in love, two friends talking on a park bench who join in conversation with a third friend who stops by and sits down, an e-mail from a soldier to his girlfriend. All these scenarios are examples of interpersonal communication. Scholar Brant Burleson (2010) defines **interpersonal communication** as "a complex, situated social process in which people who have established a communicative relationship exchange messages in an effort to generate shared meanings and accomplish social goals" (p. 151). Burleson (2010) further explains that people form a communicative relationship when "the recipient recognizes the source's intention to convey an internal state, and the source recognizes the recipient's intention to interpret" (p. 152).

Burleson's definition of interpersonal communication has several implications. First, Burleson's definition is different than traditional definitions in that it does not limit interpersonal communication to that which occurs in a face-to-face relationship or a dyadic context where only two people are present. For example, interpersonal communication still occurs over e-mail and phone, and even the presence of other people does not halt interpersonal communication. Second, interpersonal communication is not always effective. In other words, communicators do not always have shared understanding about the intentions and interpretations of messages. This is what makes the study of interpersonal communication so fascinating. Interpersonal scholars are often interested in studying relationships, not because the communication is so good and harmonious but rather to gain an understanding of a problematic issue in a relationship. To learn more about these problems,

INTERPERSONAL COMMUNICATION

social process in which people who have established a communicative relationship exchange messages in an effort to generate shared meanings and accomplish social goals.

scholars can focus their study on certain communication episodes such as conflicts, support messages, influence attempts, or expressions of affection. Third, to be in a communicative relationship does not require that one is in a close, intimate relationship. Interpersonal communication can include the study of public, short-term relationships where the interactants do not know each other well (e.g., a grocery clerk and a customer). However, interpersonal scholars have devoted extraordinary time to studying how people communicate in close, intimate relationships given that such relationships impact our well-being so deeply.

The goal of this chapter is to explore interpersonal communication scholarship in just one type of relationship—the development and maintenance of romantic relationships. Anthropologists and evolutionary psychologists argue that humans have a fundamental need for social connection and are compelled to form romantic pair bonds (Fisher, 1992; Schmitt, 2008). The first part of the unit examines partner attributes and preferences that influence the kinds of people we seek out for romantic relationships, followed by an analysis of the communication that occurs in relationship development. Even though people are drawn toward romantic relationships and have high hopes for maintaining them, 50% of all first marriages end in divorce or separation within the first 20 years (Bramlett & Mosher, 2001; Kreider, 2005), and an even greater percentage of dating relationships dissolve. Divorce, or the dissolution of any romantic relationship, can be one of the most serious stressors a person will face in a lifetime, with the potential to strain one's mental and physical health (Segrin & Flora, 2011). The latter part of the chapter considers how people communicate in an attempt to maintain their romantic relationships, with a focus on behaviors that promote relationship well-being.

Relationship Initiation and Development

By Jeanne Flora

Objectives

- ▶ Define interpersonal communication.
- ▶ Examine individual and contextual factors that influence the initiation and development of romantic relationships.
- ▶ Explore how communication in romantic relationships changes as relationships develop.

INDIVIDUAL AND CONTEXTUAL FACTORS

Individual and contextual factors together influence ideas about romantic relationships and how to communicate in them. Individual factors include considerations such as a person's *romantic beliefs, age,* and *past relationship* or *family experiences.* For example, teenagers tend to have more idealized views of romantic relationships (e.g., they are more likely to believe in love at first sight or that love can overcome all problems) as compared to adults over 20 (Knox, Schacht, & Zusman, 1999). As people get older, they also pay less attention to physical features in their choice of partners, such as whether the partner is "trendy" or "seductive," and focus more on "communal characteristics" like sensitivity, intelligence, and conventionality (Wood & Brumbaugh, 2009). Further, the average age of people when they first marry has risen dramatically in the last several decades. In 1956, the average age at first marriage was 22.5 years for men and 20.1 years for women in the United States. Comparable averages in 2011 were 28.6 for men and 26.7 for women (U.S. Census Bureau, 2013). People are not delaying romantic relationships; they are just delaying getting married, with many opting instead to cohabit (i.e., live together) as a prelude to marriage or an alternative to marriage. Besides age, past relationship experiences influence readiness for a romantic relationship. When past romantic relationships have a sense of closure or people can see clear reasons why the relationship failed, they have an easier time entering a new relationship (Merolla, Weber, Myers, & Booth-Butterfield, 2004). Even past or present family relationships are influential because they often serve as a training school for how to interact in intimate relationships. For example, adolescents who have a "reliable alliance" with their parents are more likely to experience adult romantic relationships characterized by happiness, friendship, trust, and acceptance (Seiffge-Krenke, Shulman, & Klessinger, 2001).

Contextual factors refer to sociocultural forces that impact romantic relationships, for example: *media and societal messages about romantic relationships* as well as *proximity to available partners.* The media presents both explicit and implicit messages about how to conduct romantic relationships. For instance, nearly every issue of *Cosmopolitan,* and other magazines of the same genre, provides explicit advice on topics such as how to communicate better or how to have better sex. Films and television shows also present messages about romantic relationships, sometimes portraying romantic relationships with realism, but often depicting such relationships as "trivialized, sexualized, oversimplified, and stereotyped in order to offer audiences tantalizing, humorous, satirical, or short-term glimpses of dating life" (Segrin & Flora, 2005, p. 104). Although many people interpret dating reality shows as fictional comedies or fairytales, others, and in particular children, can be seduced by the implicit messages in such shows that emphasize superficial and sex-related qualities over important social-psychological qualities (Hestroni, 2000). Media messages, along with other family and societal messages and models, shape people's views about romantic relationships. Relationship scholar Steven Duck argues that "we do not think about such cultural underpinnings of our own relationships . . . because they are hidden parts of the cultural ideology to which we all unwittingly subscribe" (1998, p. 5). What prompts us to consider our own relational ideology, besides taking a course like this, is meeting someone who has a different ideology than our own. For example, relational ideologies may differ regarding whether marriages should be arranged or initiated by individual choice, whether men and women have fluid or set gender roles, how to deal with conflict, whether having children is an expectation or not, or whether a good relationship rests on passion and emotional fulfillment and/ or the ability to support dependents and uphold religious and family tradition. Even dating partners who think they come from similar backgrounds often realize that they have critically different ideas about how to run a relationship, in part because no two people come from the same family system.

Arguably, the number one contextual factor that affects one's ability to find a partner is proximity. In other words, if one is to develop a romantic relationship with a person, he or she must have the opportunity to come into contact with that person. In addition, the opportunity for repeated interactions (e.g., seeing a person regularly at work or in a class) allows one to size up a person over time. Through repeated exposure and interaction, one may even grow to view a person as a potential partner, even if one only viewed the person as a friend or colleague at first. My own grandparents grew up on farms in a small community in Ohio. My grandmother lived a few farms away from my grandfather growing up, which allowed them the physical proximity to meet each other and come into repeated contact. Today, people can access travel and technological advances that allow them to come into contact with many more people and even to maintain long-distance relationships. Indeed, a quarter to half of all university students' dating relationships are estimated to be long-distance relationships (Cameron & Ross, 2007; Maguire, 2007). In addition, online dating sites make it possible for people to meet many more potential partners than in prior times. Around 25% of single people in the United States report using an online dating service (Miley, 2009). Online dating appears to be just as common if not more so among single people approaching middle age and old age. Traditional-age university students are already in close physical proximity to a lot of other single adults, but some middle and older adults, who have other life factors that limit their exposure to potential mates, might find appeal in an online service that can increase their proximity to others—even if it is only online proximity. Thus, it seems as if people have so many more choices of potential partners now as compared to past times. Yet, as we will explore in the next section, people often have very specific preferences that they desire in a partner, and they must be able to communicate with that partner in such a way as to develop a successful relationship. In other words, just being around a lot of people does not necessarily lead to a relationship. Sometimes the loneliest people are those who are around a lot of people but are not able to develop an emotional connection with any of them.

PARTNER ATTRIBUTES AND MATCHING

According to the U.S. Census Bureau (2011), there were 112,806,642 people between the ages of 18–44 in the United States in 2010. This may seem like a lot of potential mates, but some are already taken; some are too old or young; some you will never meet; and some may not like you even if you like them! Plus, most people have some standards and preferences when it comes to partner attributes. This section explores what people say they prefer in a mate, keeping in mind that people do not always act on their preferences.

Buss, Shackelford, Kirkpatrick, and Larson (2001) conducted a longitudinal analysis of people's stated preferences for a mate at different time periods between 1939 and 1996 in different regions of the United States. The findings from their analysis are fascinating because they show how **mate preferences** can transform with time. Buss et al. found that over the course of their analysis people gradually devalued mate qualities such as chastity or a woman's ability to cook and keep house. These qualities used to be very highly valued and still are by some, but it's a shrinking number. Also, both men and women reported *increased* preferences for a physically attractive partner and a partner who has good financial prospects. Thus, looks matter more now than in the past as does a partner's ability to make money—a noted change for women who

MATE PREFERENCES

what qualities people say they are looking for in a mate.

© Pand P Studio/Shutterstock.com

were faced with a different set of expectations in prior times. It was not until 1967 that preferences for a mate with whom one shared (1) love and (2) mutual attraction entered as the top two mate preferences, and these two preferences have remained at the top of the list across more recent time periods (Buss et al.). Why is it that physical attractiveness has become an increasingly valued mate quality—and is that good? One reason might be that people simply come into contact, primarily through media, with so many more images of physically attractive people now as compared to the past. Perhaps this tricks the brain into thinking that there are so many more physically beautiful people available or exposes people to more images of a collective ideal that they could try to attain. For sure, the diet, fashion, cosmetic, and cosmetic surgery industries are happy to take people's money in exchange for helping them attain this collective image. However, it is not as if physical appearance never mattered in the past. One of human beings' best senses is their sense of sight. How someone looks is a primary means by which we recognize and distinguish people, as compared to dogs, for example, who recognize people by their smell. While there may be some merit to the adage that "beauty is in the eye of the beholder," there is actually considerable consensus across individuals and, to some extent, across cultures about what makes for a physically attractive person (Segrin & Flora, 2011). Body and facial symmetry as well as indicators of good physical health and youthfulness appear to be universal qualities of physical attractiveness. These qualities are also noted by biologists for their connection to reproduction and survival (Kowner, 2001). Even though men do not bear children, the survival of children is boosted by men's ability to contribute to their care and resources, which often depends on good health (unless one can trade other resources in exchange for good looks—like lots of money). Yet even if appearances may attract people's attention, Riggio, Widaman, Tucker, and Salinas (1991) assert that attractiveness is a "multifaceted" concept. Beyond how someone looks in a still photo, dynamic expressions and communication abilities can make people become much more attractive over time in the eye of the beholder. Thus, if given the chance, an average-looking person with excellent relational and communication skills may have the edge after all when compared to a good-looking person who lacks such skills.

What about another old adage? Do similarities attract? There is evidence that, more so than chance, people tend to be drawn to others with whom they are similar on certain social and psychological characteristics. This tendency is termed **assortative mating**. For example, people tend to match up with others who have similar levels of education or socioeconomic status. It is not as if most people explicitly say, "I want to find someone who has a similar family income and also has a BA degree from a public university." Instead, "society is organized so that people of similar class are more likely to come into contact with each other" (Segrin & Flora, 2011, p. 96). New Mexico State University (NMSU) students tend to meet other NMSU students. Harvard students tend to meet other Harvard students. There is also some evidence for assortative mating for physical attractiveness (i.e., people of a similar level of attractiveness matching up), age (i.e., people of a similar age matching up), race (although the tendency to match on race is decreasing), and even for some social-psychological traits like gender role preferences (e.g., pairing with someone with whom you share traditional or egalitarian views) (Houts, Robins, & Huston, 1996). Interestingly, there is little evidence that people choose partners based on similar communication styles; however, if people end up with a partner who has similar values for expressing affection (Burleson, Kunkel, & Birch, 1994) or similar approaches to dealing with conflict (Gottman, 1994), they report more relationship satisfaction. Finally, people are more inclined to like others who like them. This phenomenon is known as **reciprocal liking** (Trenholm & Jensen, 2013). It is flattering for people to learn that someone likes them—so much so

ASSORTATIVE MATING

occurs when people are drawn to others with whom they are similar on certain social and psychological characteristics.

RECIPROCAL LIKING

suggests that people are more inclined to like others who like them.

that it may prompt them to consider a romantic relationship with that person even if they only ever considered the other a friend.

Partner Interaction

How do partners communicate in romantic relationships? The following section describes work by scholars who have attempted to provide examples of communication that is typical at various stages in romantic relationship development. The relationship stages are useful for discussion, but it is imperative to understand that real-life relationships do not necessarily progress through linear stages. That is, people engage in relationships at different rates, skip stages, or even go backward. In real-life relationships, there can be upturns, downturns, stagnation, or even chaos in relationship commitment and communication. Events that spark an upturn in commitment in one relationship could trigger a downturn or chaos in another. Think, for example, about how people might respond differently to relational events like the following: a big fight, sharing with a partner that you are pregnant, sharing with a partner that you will be deployed or got accepted to graduate school. With these complicating factors in mind, following are relational stages and representative scripts, as originally described by Knapp (1978, 1984), along with additional descriptions of the behaviors common to each stage, as described by Welch and Rubin (2002).

Initiating Stage

Typically first, this stage is about catching another's attention, presenting oneself as intriguing, and initiating communication. In this stage, communication is highly scripted. People use scripted lines for greeting and acknowledging people, such as "Hey" or "Good to meet you" or "Hi, I'm Alicia." Flirting is a hallmark of this stage. Moore (1998, 2002) identified typical nonverbal behaviors—such as a glance, smile, touch, hair flip or toss, or a laugh—used to flirt and attract attention. The nonverbal behaviors often precede the verbal lines. Sometimes all it takes is looking at another person or hearing the first line out of his or her mouth to know that there is no potential for a relationship. But if the initiation sparks intrigue, then the avenue for interaction has been opened.

Experimenting Stage

A stage that commonly follows initiation is experimenting. This stage is about getting to know the other, often through self-disclosure. For many people, this occurs in gradual ways, as described by a common theory of relationship development: Altman and Taylor's (1973) Social Penetration Theory. The theory uses the analogy of peeling an onion to describe how people self-disclose and get to know each other gradually, first by peeling off the outer layers and, not until later, penetrating the inner core. The experimenting stage is about getting to know the "outer layer." It can be prompted by scripted small talk characterized by questions and statements about one's interests, hobbies, and background. It sounds like: "Where are you from?" "Do you like to ski?" "I play volleyball." "What is your major?" The questions are superficial at first. This small talk is important because it gives partners a chance to explore each other without risking the disclosure of significant information, especially when it is unclear how a partner will respond. Knapp explains that most relationships do not progress beyond this stage (Knapp & Vangelisti, 2005). Something in the process gives one or both persons pause, and the relationship settles at the status of friendship or dissipates to something less. Finding out that a person is *not* a potential romantic partner is highly informative. Before moving to the next stage, it is important to point out that in some cases people skip the experimenting stage at first. For example, they may become physically intimate and then later feel they want to get to know each other. However, the experimenting stage is critical for most couples and is characterized by a type of communication in which committed partners still engage as they realize that part of maintaining intimacy is staying updated on a partner's likes, dislikes, feelings, and events of the day.

Intensifying Stage

Couples who respond positively to the experimenting begin to intensify their interactions. They do so by self-disclosing more personal information and values, expressing emotional and physical affection for one another, spending more time together, and expressing their own commitment and liking for one another. Romantic relationships are voluntary, and confirmation that the partner is similarly committed is important. The talk in this stage may sound like: "I'm really scared of. . . .", "I've got some stress in my family now because of. . . .", "My faith is really important to me because. . . .", "I really like you", "I think I love you, too." The nonverbal behaviors include increased physical intimacy, more mutual gaze and postural matching, more forward lean, as well as more shared space and things. Some relationships halt at the intensifying stage for a variety of reasons. Perhaps all the increased closeness makes one realize that this is not the right partner for them or the time for a serious relationship. The increased closeness can lead to conflict.

Integrating Stage

Continued integration leads partners to think of themselves as a couple. They begin to refer to themselves as "we," plan their schedules around each other, get invited to places together given others' view them as a couple, and in some cases begin to fuse their interests, social networks, and even wear things (e.g., a gift) or display objects (e.g., pictures) that remind themselves and others of their relationships. Nonverbally, they express tie-signs (i.e., public behaviors, like holding hands, that display the relationship to others). Their physical intimacy also increases. But again, all the togetherness can lead to problems. Thus, this is also a time when partners often experience their first big fight. Solomon and Knobloch (2004) assert that the move from casual dating to serious involvement can be marked by relational turbulence. The turbulence results from *relational uncertainties* and *relational interference* (Solomon & Knobloch). Partners may question, "Is my partner as committed as I am to the relationship?" "Is my partner being faithful to me?" "Is this really the right person for me for the future?" Serious relationships also interfere with one's independence, and partners may disagree about how to coordinate their schedules and plans, how to integrate friend and family networks, and whether their life goals are compatible in the future. Some couples draw closer as they deal with uncertainties and find a comfortable level of interdependence. Some never figure a way to commit their lives to one another even though they felt passionate about the partner for a period of time. In these negotiations, some partners learn how to argue constructively—a crucial ability for the future of the relationship. Others discover conflictive issues that will get in the way of a future relationship or, more importantly, discover that they or their partner lack the problem-solving and perspective-taking skills to deal with conflict effectively. Why should partners pay so much attention to how they deal with conflict in a dating relationship? Because it often predicts how they will deal with conflict if they proceed to marriage or a committed partnership (Segrin & Flora, 2011). What is unfortunate is that so many people proceed into marriage or have a child together in spite of serious relationship problems, relationship violence, and negative ways of dealing with conflict. The reality is that most of these problems do not get better with marriage or with having a baby together.

Bonding

The bonding stage is marked by the decision to publically formalize one's union, perhaps through engagement, marriage, or a commitment ceremony. Most of these public ceremonies are culturally based and serve to garner social and legal support for the relationship as well as stand as a relational, moral, and legal contract between the partners. Bonded relationships are more difficult to exit but also more supported by social and legal networks. People progress into formal relationship commitments in different ways. Some date for a short time; some for years. Some enter with strong, realistic knowledge of their partner's strengths and weaknesses; some enter with fairytale dreams. Huston, Caughlin, Houts, Smith, and George (2001) model the different ways people progress into marriage. The *disillusionment model* explains that some people progress into marriage with unrealistically high expectations for a perfect relationship. After working to manage these impressions of a trouble-free relationship, partners soon become disillusioned with the work it takes to keep the relationship going. They then become dissatisfied with the marriage when the positive illusions are replaced with reality. An alternative to the disillusionment model is the *enduring dynamics model.* This model posits that other partners progress into marriage well aware of each other's strengths and weaknesses. They carry the patterns of interaction, both good and bad ones, established during courtship into marriage. A third model, the *emergent distress model,* describes that some people enter into marriage fairly satisfied with the relationship, but negative interactions and destructive conflict behaviors begin to emerge and erode satisfaction.

This section defined interpersonal communication and explored processes of interpersonal communication in the context of developing romantic relationships. We began by addressing questions like "What do people say they are looking for in a mate?" "How do contextual factors influence processes of mate selection?" and "What makes for partner compatibility?" A primary focus of this section examined "How do people communicate in dating relationships?" Although no romantic relationship is the same, we reviewed common stages of romantic relationship development and communication that is characteristic of each stage. In the section to come, we move beyond romantic relationship initiation to explore how people communicate to maintain the relationships they have developed.

Discussion Questions

1. How might the following factors influence a person's readiness to be in a romantic relationship or success in a relationship?
   - ▶ romantic beliefs
   - ▶ age
   - ▶ past relationship or family experiences
   - ▶ media and societal messages about romantic relationships
   - ▶ proximity to available partners

2. How have individual preferences for mate qualities (e.g., physical attractiveness) changed or remained stable over time?

3. Consider how communication and interaction may change depending on a couple's relational stage: initiating, experimenting, intensifying, integrating, and bonding.

References

Altman, I., & Taylor, D. A. (1973). *Social penetration: The development of interpersonal relationships.* New York: Holt, Rinehart & Winston.

Bramlett, M. D., & Mosher, W. D. (2001). First marriage dissolution, divorce, and remarriage: United States. *Advance Data from Vital and Health Statistics No. 323.* Hyattsville, MD: National Center for Health Statistics.

Burleson, B. R. (2010). The nature of interpersonal communication. In C. R. Berger, M. E. Roloff, & D. R. Ewoldsen (Eds.), *The handbook of communication sciences* (2nd ed., pp. 145–164). Thousand Oaks, CA: Sage.

Burleson, B. R., Kunkel, A., & Birch, J. D. (1994). Thoughts about talk in romantic relationships: Similarity makes for attraction (and happiness, too). *Communication Quarterly, 42,* 259–273.

Buss, D. M., Shackelford, T. K., Kirkpatrick, L. A., & Larsen, J. (2001). A half-century of mate preferences: The cultural evolution of values. *Journal of Marriage and the Family, 63,* 491–503.

Cameron, J. J., & Ross, M. (2007). In times of uncertainty: Predicting the survival of long-distance relationships. *The Journal of Social Psychology, 147*(6), 581–606.

Duck, S. (1998). *Human relationships* (3rd ed.). Thousand Oaks, CA: Sage.

Fisher, H. E. (1992). *Anatomy of love: A natural history of mating, marriage, and why we stray.* New York: Fawcett Columbine.

Gottman, J. M. (1994). *What predicts divorce: The relationship between marital processes and marital outcomes.* Hillsdale, NJ: Lawrence Erlbaum Associates, Inc. Publishers.

Hetsroni, A. (2000). Choosing a mate in television dating games: The influence of setting, culture, and gender. *Sex Roles, 42,* 83–106.

Houts, R. M., Robins, E., & Huston, T. L. (1996). Compatibility and the development of premarital relationships. *Journal of Marriage and the Family, 58,* 7–20.

Huston, T. L., Caughlin, J. P., Houts, R. M., Smith, S. E., & George, L. J. (2001). The connubial crucible: Newlywed years as predictors of marital delight, distress, and divorce. *Journal of Personality and Social Psychology, 80,* 237–252.

Knapp, M. L. (1978). *Social intercourse: From greeting to goodbye.* Boston, MA: Allyn & Bacon.

Knapp, M. L. (1984). *Interpersonal communication and human relationships.* Boston, MA: Allyn and Bacon.

Knapp, M. L., & Vangelisti, A. L. (2005). Interpersonal communication and human relationships (5th ed.). Boston, MA: Allyn & Bacon.

Knox, D., Schacht, C., & Zusman, M. E. (1999). Love relationships among college students. *College Student Journal, 42,* 1015–1022.

Kowner, R. (2001). Psychological perspective on human developmental stability and fluctuating asymmetry: Sources, applications and implication. *British Journal of Psychology, 92,* 447–469.

Kreider, R. M. (2005). *Number, timing, and duration of marriages and divorces: 2001.* Current Population Reports (pp. 70–97). Washington, DC: U.S. Census Bureau.

Maguire, K. C. (2007). "Will it ever end?": A (re)examination of uncertainty in college student long-distance dating relationships. *Communication Quarterly, 55*(4), 415–432.

Merolla, A. J., Weber, K. D., Myers, S. A., & Booth-Butterfield, M. (2004). The impact of past dating relationship solidarity on commitment, satisfaction, and investment in current relationships. *Communication Quarterly, 52*(3), 251–264.

Miley, M. (2009). Dating sites still attracting users. Advertising. *Age, 80*(8), 8.

Moore, M. M. (1998). Nonverbal courtship patterns in women: Rejection signaling—an empirical investigation. *Semiotica, 3,* 205–215.

Moore, M. M. (2002). Courtship communication and perception. *Perceptual and motor skills, 94,* 97–105.

Riggio, R. E., Widaman, K. F., Tucker, J. S., & Salinas, C. (1991). Beauty is more than skin deep: Components of attractiveness. *Basic and Applied Social Psychology, 12,* 423–439.

Schmitt, D. P. (2008). An evolutionary perspective on mate choice and relationship initiation. In S. Sprecher, A. Wenzel, & J. Harvey (Eds.) *Handbook of Relationship Initiation* (pp. 55–74). New York, NY: Psychology Press.

Segrin, C., & Flora, J. (2005). Family communication. Mahwah: NJ: Lawrence Erlbaum Associates, Inc. Publishers.

Segrin, C., & Flora, J. (2011). Family communication (2nd ed.). New York: Routledge.

Seiffge-Krenke, I., Shulman, S., & Klessinger, N. (2001). Adolescent precursors of romantic relationships in young adulthood. *Journal of Social and Personal Relationships, 18,* 327–345.

Solomon, D. H., & Knobloch, L. K. (2004). A model of relational turbulence: The role of intimacy, relational uncertainty, and interference from partners in appraisals of irritations. *Journal of Social and Personal Relationships, 21,* 795–796.

Trenholm, S., & Jensen, A. (2013). Interpersonal communication (6th ed.). New York: Oxford.

U.S. Census Bureau. (2011, May). *Age and sex composition: 2010* (C2010BR-03). Retrieved from http://www.census.gov/prod/cen2010/briefs/c2010br-03.pdf

U.S. Census Bureau. (2013, February). *2009–2011 American Community Survey.* Retrieved from http://factfinder2.census.gov/faces/tableservices/jsf/pages/productview.xhtml?pid=ACS_11_3YR_B12007&prodType=table.

Welch, S. A., & Rubin, R. B. (2002). Development of relationship stage measures. *Communication Quarterly, 50,* 24–40.

Wood, D., & Brumbaugh, C. C. (2009). Using revealed mate preferences to evaluate market force and differential preference explanation for mate selection. *Journal of Personality & Social Psychology, 96*(6), 1226–1244.

Relationship Maintenance

by Jeanne Flora

Objectives

- ► Explore how people maintain romantic relationships by:
  - ► communicating intimacy
  - ► communicating positive affect
  - ► constructively managing conflict
- ► Explore typologies of successful couple types, including their similarities and differences.
- ► Explore dialectical tensions that play a role in maintaining romantic relationships.

How is it possible for couples to capitalize on and maintain any good feelings they have about their partner and relationship? Maintaining a romantic relationship over time is arguably more challenging than initiating a relationship. Destructive conflict and hurtful behaviors seem to come too easily. For this reason, much of the scholarly research on communication in romantic relationships has been devoted to studying negative interactions and conflict. Indeed, there is a whole section in this book devoted to interpersonal conflict management. Although there is very good reason to study destructive forms of conflict and negative relational processes, creating a good relationship depends on more than simply avoiding negative behaviors (Segrin, 2006). For example, Huston, Caughlin, Houts, Smith, and George (2001) found that above and beyond the influence of conflict, declines in positive affect during the early years of marriage predict a greater risk for divorce. People desperately need good information about the kinds of behaviors and perceptions that can help maintain their relationships. The remaining part of the section summarizes just some of that information.

THE RELATIONSHIP BANK ACCOUNT

Howard Markman (1984) first introduced a model of relationship maintenance that compared the interactions in a romantic relationship to a bank account. According to the model, partners do well to keep a positive balance in their relationship bank account. They do so by making more deposits than withdrawals to the relationship. My colleague and I summarize deposits and withdrawals as follows: "Making a deposit requires expressing positive relational behaviors (e.g., affection, intimacy, compliments, agreements). Withdrawals result from negative relational behaviors (e.g., put-downs, criticisms, defensiveness)" (Segrin & Flora, 2014). What becomes challenging in relationships is that negative interactions and behaviors carry a lot of weight. One negative comment can linger and cancel out several positive interactions. Premier relationship scholar John Gottman (1994) describes that the relationships of stable, satisfied couples are characterized by at least five times as many positive behaviors as negative behaviors, even when they are dealing with conflict or discussing difficult topics. When discussing nonconflictual topics, the ratio of positive to negative behaviors may even be as high as 10:1. Partners nurture a culture of positivity whereby the positivity outweighs the negativity.

How do partners nurture this positive culture? As I write this section, it is almost Valentine's Day. Many couples will spend a lot of money on an extravagant dinner or fancy gifts. But those Valentine's Day expressions will do little to fix a relationship that is full of negativity and distrust on a daily basis. Although some relationship maintenance behaviors are strategically planned behaviors, many of the most important relationship maintenance behaviors are small, ordinary, spontaneous, and even mundane behaviors that are offered to one's partner on a daily basis. Either way, Segrin and Flora (2011) describe that "the idea behind relationship maintenance is for couples to care for their relationship in a preemptive way, rather than waiting until the health of the [relationship] has deteriorated" (p. 119).

A TYPOLOGY OF RELATIONSHIP MAINTENANCE BEHAVIORS

Several prominent researchers have developed lists or typologies of relationship maintenance behaviors. This section presents one such typology, originally developed by communication scholars Daniel Canary and Laura Stafford (1992), and then later refined by the work of Stafford and colleagues. The typology was first developed through inductive techniques, whereby Canary and Stafford asked partners to report what they do to maintain their romantic relationships. The researchers then catalogued these behaviors, understanding that their list was not exhaustive, but that it portrayed some of the common ways partners say they maintain their relationship. Based on this early work, Stafford created a 7-factor measure of relationship maintenance behaviors in 2011. The seven factors, or relationship behaviors, included the following, as described by Segrin and Flora (2014):

> (1) *positivity* (i.e., acting upbeat, cheerful, optimistic, or having a global positive demeanor); (2) *understanding* (i.e., expressing understanding rather than judgment, and offering forgiveness or an apology); (3) *self-disclosure* (i.e., self-disclosing general feelings and fears and encouraging the partner to share thoughts and feelings); (4) *assurances* (i.e., showing and telling a partner how much s/he means and talking about a future together); (5) *tasks* (i.e., helping with household tasks and other responsibilities that face the couple); (6) *networks* (i.e., relying on a joint family and/or friend network for activities and aid); and a final type of self-disclosure that Stafford found to be *negatively* related to relational quality, (7) *relational talk* (i.e., discussing the quality and state of the relationship).

© Pushish Images/Shutterstock.com

Stafford's (2011) recent work shows that not all forms of self-disclosure (e.g., compare relational talk with self-disclosure) function to maintain relationships. Relational talk is a type of self-disclosure partners use to discuss relational problems and evaluate the relationship. For many couples, the outcome of this kind of talk may be more negative than positive.

Key Themes From Research on Relationship Maintenance

The relationship maintenance behaviors that partners report using are congruent with many of the behaviors that scholars have observed satisfied couples using during interactions, as well as with much of the theoretical work regarding how to maintain a relationship. The space remaining summarizes just some of this work.

Fostering Intimacy: Feeling Understood, Validated, and Cared For

Reis and Patrick (1996) describe that **intimacy** is an *interactive* process. Some people think that self-disclosure is what leads to intimacy. While it appears that satisfied couples do spend more time self-disclosing their feelings, likes, dislikes, and even just discussing events of the day (Vangelisti & Banski, 1993), intimacy is about more than just self-disclosure and self-expression. Imagine if you had a partner whom you felt never really listened to you or responded to all your self-expressions with criticism, defensiveness, or contempt. Reis and Patrick clarify that intimacy develops over time when people *respond* to their partners' self-expressions in a way that makes their partners feel understood, validated, and cared for. Put simply, careful partner responsiveness is the hallmark of intimacy. Gottman explains that romantic partners constantly make bids for attention, affection, love, support, or acknowledgment. This is what Gottman terms the emotional bidding process (Gottman & DeClaire, 2001). Some bids are subtle, like a glance, touch on the back, a sigh, a laugh, opening a door,

INTIMACY

emotional intimacy develops when people respond to their partners making them feel understood, validated, and cared for.

pointing out something of shared interest. Other bids are more explicit and direct, like a kiss or saying "Let's go have coffee" or "Let's catch up." Either way, Gottman and DeClaire define an *emotional bid* as a gesture that says "I want to be connected to you" (2001, p. 4). When people make bids for attention, their partners have a choice in how to respond. They can ignore the bid, for example, by not responding as if they did not hear. This is what Gottman and DeClaire (2001) term *turning away* from a bid. Or they could *turn against* a bid, which they describe as worse yet because the partners criticize or mock the bid for attention. Think for a moment about how it feels to have your bid for connection ignored (e.g., your partner continues texting and doesn't even look up to acknowledge you) or criticized (e.g., your partner says, "That's a stupid idea"). The response that builds intimacy is to *turn toward* the bid by responding with affirmation, support, or at least attention and acknowledgment. Sometimes a simple nod or "Mmm" is enough to make a partner feel understood, validated, and cared for. My colleague and I found that regardless of whether wives were expressing complaints or compliments during an interaction, if their husbands gazed at them more while listening, their marital well-being was higher (Flora & Segrin, 2000). It may have been that the husbands' gaze communicated "I'm taking the time to be attentive to you." Even a seemingly small nonverbal gesture can let people know that their partner values them enough to take the time to turn toward them.

Positive Affectivity: Optimism, Adaptive Coping, and Personal Expansion

Positive affectivity is related to higher marital satisfaction (Gordon & Baucom, 2009). As described by Gordon and Baucom, positive affectivity involves three factors: optimism, adaptive coping skills, and personal expansion. Having a general sense of *optimism*, or a positive outlook about the partner and the relationship, is beneficial. The idea is not to have an unrealistic optimism that ignores severe relational problems, but instead to not "sweat the small stuff," as McNulty, O'Mara, and Karney (2008, p. 631) say. In addition to having a general sense of optimism, *expressing* that optimism about the partner and relationship is critical. After years of observing couples interact in research studies, Gottman noticed that satisfied couples spent more time expressing their fondness and admiration for one another (Gottman & Silver, 1999). There are both direct ways (e.g., complimenting your partner or telling them you love them) and indirect ways to do this. Responding to a partner's disclosure of positive events and feelings is another way to capitalize on positivity. The research of Gable, Gonzaga, and Strachman (2006) reveals that couples tend to have higher relational well-being when partners respond to one another's disclosures of good events by showing enthusiasm, pride, and validation of the partner's strengths. For example, when one person says, "I got the job," the partner responds saying, "That's great! You deserve it!" It's not much fun to come home with exciting news and be met with a partner who can only find the negative in the situation or who cannot seem to find the time to recognize what a big deal it is.

The second component to positive affectivity is *adaptive coping skills,* whereby people help their partners to positively reframe stressors, cope with problems, and boost esteem. For example, sometimes people provide social support for their partners regarding problems outside the relationship (e.g., the partner had a stressful day at work, got in a fight with a friend, is sick, or got turned town for a job). In such circumstances, there are lots of ways a partner could try to offer support, such as giving advice, providing information, providing tangible assistance (i.e., doing something to help), attempting to boost a partner's self-esteem, or communicating understanding and emotional support. All of these strategies can have their merits, depending on the situation, but it is also easy to see how some of these strategies could be interpreted negatively. For example, sometimes people do not want advice or information about what they should have done to prevent getting sick—they just want someone to comfort and care for them. Sometimes people do not want tangible assistance because, for instance, when a partner swoops in and proofreads their paper for a class it may make them feel like they were inadequate in their abilities. Indeed, in their research on support giving among married couples, Brock and Lawrence (2009) found that husbands who get more informational support from their wives and wives who get more informational and tangible support from their husbands tend to be less satisfied with the relationship. Brock and Lawrence's findings should not be interpreted to suggest that these kinds of support are universally negative. Sometimes they are great, but they have their limits and must be delivered with the right spirit and skill. Esteem support (i.e., bolstering a partner's self-worth) and emotional support (i.e., communicating concern, care, and warmth) are most consistently linked to relational satisfaction—in fact, the more the better when it comes to esteem support (Brock & Lawrence).

The third component to positive affectivity is *personal expansion*. People often talk about the desire to "keep their relationship alive," "not get stuck in a rut," or to "still find meaning in the relationship." What do they really mean? Several researchers have explored what might be behind these statements. For example, the married couples in Reissman, Aron, and Bergen's (1993) research reported higher marital satisfaction to the extent that they participated in joint activities that were "exciting" and "self-expanding" versus "boring" or simply "pleasant." Of course, it is not just the activity itself that promotes the relational satisfaction, but the interaction that occurs during the activity (Flora & Segrin, 1998). Partners may plan what they think will be an exciting activity together, but they fight the whole time. Have you ever seen a couple at Disneyland—what is supposed to be the "Happiest Place on Earth"—ironically look like they are anything but happy because they cannot get along? Personal expansion is about enjoying one's time, gaining new perspective, and finding new meaning or rediscovering meaning in one's relationship. Gottman (1999) encourages couples to continually find ways to create shared meaning, whether it be through a shared goal or activity, a way to reaffirm the relationship through a vacation or anniversary celebration, or shared rituals that couples look forward to.

Constructively Managing Conflict

There is a whole section on conflict management in this book, and there could be a whole section alone on all the destructive ways that partners interact with each other. Still, it seems imperative to mention that managing conflict effectively is one of the primary ways that couples maintain their relationship. Instead of focusing on what *not* to do in conflict, this section takes a very brief look at what to do in order to approach conflict in a way that maintains and strengthens the relationship. For a more in-depth discussion of these approaches, see Segrin and Flora (2019).

(1) *Initiate Conflict in Gentle Ways* Gottman (1999) can be credited with suggesting that partners should bring up conflicts in a soft or gentle manner, instead of in a manner that he terms harsh start-up. If someone attacks you briskly and harshly, the natural response is to defend yourself and your behavior (e.g., "I did not do that"), even if you were in the wrong. One of my favorite analogies that Gottman uses is as follows: he suggests dealing with conflict as if you were casually kicking around a soccer ball (Gottman, 2008). One partner says gently, "So here's what I'm thinking about last night . . . what do you think?" The other partner tosses back, "I kind of see what you mean . . . it's hard though because. . . ." There is no name-calling, character

attack, or blaming. Sometimes it even helps to think of small changes, like changing the pronouns one uses when bringing up conflict. Mitnick, Heyman, Malik, and Slep (2009) studied what difference it made if married partners brought up conflicts and change requests by using "You" (e.g., "You should . . .") versus "We" (e.g., "We should . . ."). Even this small difference of using "We" led to change requests that were met with less resistance, especially for wives.

(2) *De-escalate Negativity* Partners benefit from avoiding behaviors like defensiveness, contempt, sarcasm, verbal aggression (i.e., attacking a partner's character), and mindreading (e.g., "You always think. . . .") (Gottman, 1994, 1999; Infante, Chandler, & Rudd, 1989). These behaviors do nothing to facilitate productive conversation, and they only trigger increased heart rates, or emotional flooding, and the likelihood that partners will respond in kind. Some of these behaviors, like verbal aggression, are also risk factors for physical violence (Infante et al.). When people are **emotionally flooded**, they feel overwhelmed with negative feelings and their heart rate increases dramatically. As a result, they want to escape the situation and escape what they feel are unprovoked, harsh attacks from their partner. Their options are to flee the situation, either by physically exiting or mentally stonewalling (i.e., ignoring the partner), or they can find a way to soothe the negative affect and calm their heart rate. Technically, **soothing** involves taking a break or even introducing neutral or positive affect for a moment to give spouses time to calm themselves and change perspective. Soothing can be anything that allows partners a chance to calm their heart rates. Many therapists teach methods of self-soothing that include techniques like taking a break from the conflict and then coming back to it or cognitively reframing their thoughts. Just as partners can be the ones to inflict flooding, they can also be the ones to soothe their own partner. Some partners interject positive affect or even humor at a moment when things get very heated as a way of toning down the negativity. They may say for example, "Look at us . . . this is silly . . . I know I love you . . . so let's just take a moment and try this again."

(3) *Use Good Problem-Solving Skills* Many of the conflicts that couples face can be approached using some of the useful skills discussed in the conflict management section of this book. High on the list for relationship researchers are skills like *compromise, patience, cooperation, focusing on the problem at hand,* and *apologizing.* Yet, when people are in the midst of their own conflicts, they are often reluctant to use these constructive approaches, even if they know how to perform them. Consider apologies, for example. People rarely offer them; although, when genuinely offered, apologies are highly effective. The ability to repair conflict seems to separate couples who have strong relational well-being from those who do not (Gottman, 1999). In turn, couples who are more committed to each other are more motivated to repair their conflicts (Brandau-Brown & Ragsdale, 2008).

(4) *The Respect Approach* Not all problems can be easily solved. Gottman (1999) describes that some problems are "perpetual problems." These are problems that are deeply rooted in tendencies that are not easily changed, like different personality traits, different views of religion, parenting, money, or other important values. These are problems that are not going away. Alternatively, they are issues that keep coming up again and again in a relationship. Unfortunately, many partners become emotionally flooded each time these issues come up. Or they shut down and offer the silent treatment, a strategy that has been found to be very ineffective (Dunleavy, Goodboy,

EMOTIONALLY FLOODED

feeling overwhelmed with negative feelings.

SOOTHING

introducing neutral or positive affect.

Booth-Butterfield, Sidelinger, & Banfield, 2009). Unless one is prepared to dissolve the relationship (which sometimes is the best strategy), Gottman and Silver (1999) suggest forgetting about completely solving these problems and instead finding ways "to cope with them, to avoid situations that worsen them, and to develop strategies and routines that help us deal with them" (Gottman & Silver, 1999 p. 131). The more people can nurture a mutual respect for their partner and the relationship, the more motivated they may be to do this. Thus, the end goal may not be eliminating the differences but dealing with them.

Couple Types

At about this point in any book chapter on relational communication, readers often begin to question general recommendations for relationships, because all relationships and people are different, right? Not the same thing works for everyone, right? The answer is yes, to some extent. Relationship success is grounded in a concept termed **equifinality**. Equifinality asserts that there is often more than one way to achieve the same end goal (Bochner & Eisenberg, 1987). In other words, there is not a rigid prescription for what to do to have a good relationship, but rather, a variety of paths toward achieving that end.

> **EQUIFINALITY**
>
> asserts that there is more than one way to achieve the same end goal.

In 1994, Gottman introduced a typology of marital couple types. The typology describes three types of couples, each reasonably capable of sustaining high levels of marital satisfaction. The three functional couple types differ in conflict interaction, namely in the way they exert influence, resolve conflict, and communicate about emotions. The three couple types are termed Volatile, Validating, and Conflict-avoiding couples (Gottman, 1994). What is similar about the interaction of the three functional couple types is that they each maintain a climate rich in positivity, even during conflict interactions. They do so by regulating their interactions to maintain at least a 5:1 ratio of positive interactional behaviors to negative ones. Gottman (1994) describes a fourth, dysfunctional, couple type, the *Hostile* couple type, which suffers from non-regulated interactions characterized by as much or more negativity as positivity. In addition to more *frequent* negative interactions, the *form* of the negativity expressed by Hostile couples is more severe in intensity. Hostile couples are experts at critical personal attacks, contempt, defensiveness, and stonewalling, and the result is that they become overwhelmed or emotionally flooded by the negativity. Hostile couples have a knack for those communication behaviors that are especially injurious to their relationship. Among the three functional couple types, positive expressions soothe some of the negative emotional flooding, but hostile couples have so little positivity that they cannot stop the negative "emotional inertia" (Madhyastha, Hamaker, & Gottman, 2011).

The three functional couple types can be distinguished as follows. **Volatile** couples are the most emotionally expressive, in displays of both positive and negative emotion (Gottman, 1994). Put simply, the spouses are passionate in their interactions. They feel it is important to deal with differences openly and honor individual expression. They may fight a lot, but they also express a lot of positive expressions such as relational affirmations, affection, and humor. Plus, they make up easily. They maintain a 5:1 ratio of positive to negative behaviors, even though, for example, they may achieve this at a rate of 25:5. In other words, they may have five times as many fights as another functional couple type, but they also have five times the positivity. **Validating** couples exhibit moderate levels of emotional expression (Gottman, 1994). They take a careful approach to conflict, bringing up issues only when necessary. When they deal with conflict, they show great concern for timing and positive conflict strategies.

> **VOLATILE**
>
> couples are the most emotionally expressive, in displays of both positive and negative emotion.

> **VALIDATING**
>
> couples exhibit moderate levels of emotional expression.

CONFLICT-AVOIDING

couples are characterized by low levels of emotional expression.

They highly value togetherness, companionship, cooperation, and respect for the partner's opinion. **Conflict-avoiding** couples are characterized by low levels of emotional expression (Gottman, 1994). Their preference is to avoid or minimize conflict. Conflict-avoiding couples focus on accepting their partners as they are and compromising. They turn their attention toward areas of agreement in the relationship. Many conflict-avoiding spouses may have the skills to deal with conflict in other open, direct, and expressive ways. However, they would rather use tactics such as compromising and "agreeing to disagree" because their priority is in promoting solidarity, similarities, and partner needs (Gottman, 1994).

The Volatile, Validating, and Conflict-avoiding couple types all have significantly higher marital quality than the Hostile couple type (Gottman, 1994; Holman & Jarvis, 2003), and they have been observed to have more stable marriages over a 4-year time span (Gottman, 1993). Of the three functional couple types, Holman and Jarvis (2003) found Validating couples to have slightly higher marital quality, followed in order by Conflict-avoiding and then Volatile couples, but differences were not great. Further, Gottman (1994) expresses concern about marital quality when partners in a marriage are "mismatched" (e.g., a Volatile spouse with a Conflict-avoiding partner). The term *mismatch* foretells Gottman's contention that these spouses are not well-suited for one another and that their marital quality will be compromised as they struggle to overcome disagreements about when and how to exert influence, resolve conflict, and communicate about emotions.

Dialectical Tensions

DIALECTICAL PERSPECTIVE

sympathizes with the idea that contradictions are inherent in relationships and that opposing forces must be managed in relationships.

Just as couples can be distinguished by their different, yet functional, interaction patterns, other researchers have expanded on the idea that relationships, and the feelings and behaviors that people have in those relationships, are not static. Relationships are characterized by changing feelings and events, as put forth in an approach called the dialectical perspective. The **dialectical perspective** (Baxter & Montgomery, 1996) sympathizes with the idea that contradictions are inherent in relationships and that opposing forces must be managed in relationships. The dialectical perspective describes these opposing forces as dialectical tensions. Examples of a few of the common tensions include autonomy versus connectedness, openness versus protection, and novelty versus predictability (Baxter, 1990).

The *autonomy/connectedness* tension points at how couples must strike a balance between wanting to share time, space, conversation, and joint activities, but also have needs for separate space, other relationships, and individual interests. When people get busy with work or school, they commonly talk about how much they are looking forward to a vacation or weekend with their partner. But after spending a certain amount of time together, the very same people might be heard saying, "I'm ready for some 'Me-time'" or "We need a break from each other." The *openness/ protection* dialectic reveals questions couples have about how much to protect certain information and how much to share. Are certain topics off-limits? How much information is necessary and useful to share? For example, is it important to talk about past relationships? Is it important to debrief the events and feelings of the day together? The *novelty/ predictability* tension explains how couples sometimes desire change and new adventures, but other times they want the comfort of stable routines that they know. This tension often surfaces as couples plan their free time and as they plan their futures together (e.g., whether to take a job in another state or country).

The dialectical perspective is less about the tensions people have in their own mind and more about the struggles between people in a relationship and how partners manage those struggles together. Indeed, there are a variety of strategies that couples can use to deal with their tensions. Some are more dysfunctional, like ignoring the tensions, and others are more functional, like compromising or considering what approach is appropriate for the activity and time.

CONCLUSION

This section opened by addressing the question "What communication behaviors help to maintain romantic relationships?" Specifically, we explored communicative strategies for maintaining intimacy, expressing positive affect, constructively managing conflict, and dealing with common dialectical tensions. We also addressed the question "Is it possible for people to have different, yet similarly effective, ways of maintaining their relationships?" People often find the area of interpersonal communication to be a personally practical area of inquiry. Reading this unit on interpersonal communication may have sparked other questions you have about personal relationships, including "What specific communication processes lead to the decline of romantic relationships?" To answer this or other fascinating questions about interpersonal relationships, you may be interested in taking a class in interpersonal or family communication in the future.

1. Consider the key themes from research on relationship maintenance and provide examples from your own life.

2. Consider the techniques for constructively managing conflict and provide examples from your own life.

3. Which dialectical tensions have you experienced in your own close relationships?

4. How are Gottman's couple types similar and different?

Baxter, L. A. (1990). Dialectical contradictions in relationship development. *Journal of Social and Personal Relationships, 7,* 69–88.

Baxter, L. A., & Montgomery, B. M. (1996). *Relating: Dialogues and dialectics.* New York: Guilford Press.

Bochner, A. P., & Eisenberg, E. M. (1987). Family process: Systems perspectives. In C. R. Berger & S. H. Chaffe (Eds.), *Handbook of communication science* (pp. 540–563). Beverly Hills, CA: Sage.

Brandau-Brown, F. E., & Ragsdale, D. (2008). Personal, moral, and structural commitment and the repair of marital relationships. *Southern Communication Journal, 73*(1), 68–83.

Brock, R. L., & Lawrence, E. (2009). Too much of a good thing: Underprovision versus overprovision of partner support. *Journal of Family Psychology, 23*(2), 181–192.

Canary, D. J., & Stafford, L. (1992). Relational maintenance strategies and equity in marriage. *Communication Monographs, 59,* 243–267.

Dunleavy, K. N., Goodboy, A. K., Booth-Butterfield, M., Sidelinger, R. J., & Banfield, S. (2009). Repairing hurtful messages in marital relationships. *Communication Quarterly, 57*(1), 67–84.

Flora J., & Segrin, C. (1998). Joint leisure time in friend and romantic relationships: The role of activity type, social skills, and positivity. *Journal of Social and Personal Relationships, 15,* 711–718.

Flora, J., & Segrin, C. (2000). Affect and behavioral involvement in spousal complaints and compliments. *Journal of Family Psychology, 14,* 641–657.

Gable, S. L., Gonzaga, G. C., & Strachman, A. (2006). Will you be there for me when things go right? Supportive responses to positive event disclosures. *Journal of Personality and Social Psychology, 91*(5), 904–917.

Gordon, C. L., & Baucom, D. H. (2009). Examining the individual within marriage: Personal strengths and relationship satisfaction. *Personal Relationships, 16,* 421–435.

Gottman, J. M. (1993). The roles of conflict engagement, escalation, and avoidance in marital interaction: A longitudinal view of five types of couples. *Journal of Consulting and Clinical Psychology, 61,* 6–15.

Gottman, J. M. (1994). *What predicts divorce: The relationship between marital processes and marital outcomes.* Hillsdale, NJ: Lawrence Erlbaum Associates, Inc. Publishers.

Gottman, J. M. (1999). *The marriage clinic: A scientifically based marital therapy.* New York: W.W. Norton.

Gottman, J. M. (2008). *Making marriage work* [DVD]. Available from The Gottman Institute, Inc. Retrieved from http://www.gottman.com

Gottman, J. M., & DeClaire, J. (2001). *The relationship cure.* New York: Crown.

Gottman, J. M., & Silver, N. (1999). *The seven principles for making marriage work.* New York: Crown.

Holman, T. B., & Jarvis, M. O. (2003). Hostile, volatile, avoiding, and validating couple-conflict types: An investigation of Gottman's couple-conflict types. *Personal Relationships, 10,* 267–282.

Huston, T. L., Caughlin, J. P., Houts, R. M., Smith, S. E., & George, L. J. (2001). The connubial crucible: Newlywed years as predictors of marital delight, distress, and divorce. *Journal of Personality and Social Psychology, 80,* 237–252.

Infante, D. A., Chandler, T. A., & Rudd, J. E. (1989). Test of an argumentative skill deficiency model of interspousal violence. *Communication Monographs, 56,* 163–177.

Madhyastha, T. M., Hamaker, E. L., & Gottman, J. M. (2011). Investigating spousal influence using moment-to-moment affect data from marital conflict. *Journal of Family Psychology, 25,* 292–300.

Markman, H. J. (1984). The longitudinal study of couples' interactions: Implications for understanding and predicting the development of marital distress. In K. Hahlweg & N. S. Jacobson (Eds.), *Marital interaction: Analysis and modification* (pp. 253–281). New York: Guilford.

McNulty, J. K., O'Mara, E. M., & Karney, B. R. (2008). Benevolent cognitions as a strategy of relationship maintenance: "Don't sweat the small stuff " . . . . but it is not all small stuff. *Journal of Personality and Social Psychology, 94,* 631–646.

Mitnick, D. M., Heyman, R. E., Malik, J., & Slep, A. M. S. (2009). The differential association between change request qualities and resistance, problem resolution, and relationship satisfaction. *Journal of Family Psychology, 23*(4), 464–473.

Reis, H. T., & Patrick, B. C. (1996). Attachment and intimacy: Component processes. In E. T. Higgins & A. W. Kruglanski (Eds.), *Social psychology: Handbook of basic principles* (pp. 523–563). New York: Guilford Press.

Reissman, C., Aron, A., & Bergen, M. R. (1993). Shared activities and marital satisfaction: Casual direction and self-expansion versus boredom. *Journal of Social and Personal Relationships, 10,* 243–254.

Segrin, C. (2006). Family interactions and well-being: Integrative perspectives. *Journal of Family Communication, 6,* 3–21.

Segrin, C., & Flora, J. (2011). Family communication (2nd ed.). New York: Routledge.

Segrin, C., & Flora, J. (2014). Marriage. In P. J. Schultz and P. Cobley (Series Eds.) & C. R. Berger (Vol. Ed.), *Handbooks of communication science: Vol. 6. Interpersonal communication* (pp. 443–466). Berlin: De Gruyter Mouton.

Stafford, L. (2011). Measuring relationship maintenance behaviors: Critique and development of the revised relationship maintenance behavior scale. *Journal of Social and Personal Relationships, 28,* 278–303.

Vangelisti, A. L., & Banski, M. A. (1993). Couples' debriefing conversations: The impact of gender, occupation, and demographic characteristics. *Family Relations, 42,* 149–157.

Technology and Interpersonal Relationships

By Danielle Halliwell

Objectives

- ▶ Define technologically mediated communication.
- ▶ Describe the seven features of communication media.
- ▶ Explain media multiplexity theory and the symbolic value of media.
- ▶ Compare and contrast the five relationship functions of digital media.
- ▶ Evaluate technology's impact on relationships.

I still remember the <u>first</u> text message I ever received. It was in January of 2005, shortly after I had upgraded to Verizon's new LG VX8000 flip phone. As I was drifting to sleep one night, my phone started buzzing from my nightstand and a little envelope icon popped up on the outside display screen. I assumed it was an alert from Verizon and flipped open my phone without much thought. However, instead of an automated warning about data usage flashing across the screen, I was greeted with a mysterious, one-word message: "Hello?"

Confused and slightly scared, I ran across the hall to my roommate's bedroom. "Ashley! What do you think this is?" I waved my phone in front of her face so she could see the eerie notification. She started laughing and said, "I sent you that message, silly." A co-worker had introduced her to the SMS (short message service) feature on her phone and she wanted to test whether my device also had text messaging abilities. My fear quickly turned into curiosity. "Wait here!" I instructed. "I'm going to try sending you one." I thought it would be weird to message her from the same room, so I raced back to my bedroom and closed the door.

Phone in hand, I sat on my bed and typed a response to Ashley's message: "Yes?" Almost immediately after I hit the *send* button, I heard her phone beep from across the hall. "Got it!" she yelled, rushing into my room to prove that my message appeared on her phone. We spent the next hour texting each other, experimenting with different messaging features, and eventually figuring out how to send a picture message. Once the excitement wore off, we concluded that the SMS function was good for goofing around and not much else. My initial thought was that perhaps text messaging would catch on with the more tech-savvy crowd, but it certainly was not something I anticipated using often—if at all.

To say I was wrong about the future of text messaging is putting it lightly. I had no way of knowing that the method of communication Ashley and I used to exchange those tentative, one-word messages would spark a monumental transformation in how people connect with others. By the end of 2007, the average mobile phone user in the U.S. sent and received more text messages each month than phone calls (Reardon, 2008), and more recent trends show that text messaging is the most frequently used form of communication among Americans under the age of 50 (Newport, 2014; Smith, 2016). Of course, texting is by far not the only way we use technology to communicate on a daily basis. Due to advances in digital technologies such as smartphones and tablets, as well as the continued growth and popularity of social networking, online apps, and virtual communities, there are now more ways to interact with others than ever before.

Although new technologies allow for increased closeness and connectedness in our relationships, they can also create an illusion of intimacy and lead to superficial ties (Baym, 2015; Turkle, 2015). With this in mind, the goal of this section is to shed light on the complex role technology plays in interpersonal relationships. I begin by defining key terms and features related to mediated communication. The next section explores how integrating multiple forms of digital media into our lives influences our personal relationships, which is followed by a review of the specific relational functions of digital media. Finally, I conclude the section by considering the ways technology can both help and harm our connections with others. By thinking more critically about your own use of digital communication devices, you can better understand how they might be strengthening or hindering the important relationships in your life.

DEFINING TECHNOLOGICALLY MEDIATED COMMUNICATION

Since the invention of the World Wide Web in 1990, communication and media scholars have sought to understand the ways in which Internet technologies have changed the nature of human interaction and impacted the process of relating. Much of the early research in this area focused on identifying the differences between face-to-face communication and *computer mediated communication* (CMC), which was originally defined as any text-based electronic communication sent from one person's computer to another's (Walther, 1992). Today, the meaning of CMC has been extended to include any communication facilitated through computer or Internet technology, and the term is still widely used to refer to mediated interactions of all kinds. Over the years, numerous other labels have also emerged to reflect the growth of digital media and new modes of communication (e.g., information and communication technology, mobile technology, digital communication, mediated interaction, etc.).

Although there is no agreed-upon name for describing communication via digital media and technologies, researchers typically treat the above terms as synonyms and use them interchangeably in their research. Likewise, this section will draw on

© Rocketclips, Inc./Shutterstock.com

a variety of terms in order to best represent the dynamic and ever-changing modes of communication in the digital age. For a simple definition to begin the discussion, I join other scholars who employ the term **technologically mediated communication** (TMC) because it clearly encompasses the full range of available media and digital technologies (see Bevan, 2017; Caughlin & Sharabi, 2013). TMC, then, refers to any communication that is facilitated through digital media, mobile technology, or other technology-assisted devices or platforms. From this perspective, *communication* is broadly viewed as any type of human interaction such as voice calls, video-chats, and text-based messages (including the sharing of images, photographs, and emoticons). Therefore, texting a friend a meme without a written message is considered a technologically-mediated interaction. You are also engaging in TMC when you like, favorite, or retweet your friends' content on social media. In short, TMC accounts for both the earliest (e.g., e-mail) and the latest (e.g., SnapChat stories) ways of communicating with others through technology.

TECHNOLOGICALLY MEDIATED COMMUNICATION

any form of communication that is facilitated through digital media, mobile technology, or other technology-assisted devices or platforms.

Features of Communication Media

With such an immense variety of digital media available, it can be difficult to pinpoint how, exactly, technology influences personal relationships. As Baym (2015) argued, understanding the effects of technology on our relational lives requires that we avoid treating "media" as a one-size-fits-all idea and instead recognize the important ways media and communication technologies differ from one another. She identified seven concepts that draw attention to the variation among different digital media, as well as the similarities and differences between TMC and face-to-face interaction. Table 3.1 outlines these core features of communication media discussed by Baym: interactivity, temporal structure, social cues, storage, replicability, reach, and mobility.

$\mathcal{T}able$ **3.1**

Features of Communication Media

Characteristic of Communication Media	Description of Characteristic
Interactivity	The extent to which a medium allows individuals to interact with others. Social media sites, for example, offer numerous tools for interactivity among members. Mobile phones are designed for social interaction, but are also used for non-interactive activities such as browsing the Internet, navigation, and online shopping. Thus, the interactivity of a given communication technology is best understood as a continuum that varies based on how people use it.
Temporal Structure	The duration of time that passes between messages when using a specific medium. *Synchronous* communication media (e.g., face-to-face conversations, phone calls, instant messaging) allow for messages to be exchanged in real time. *Asynchronous* communication media (e.g., e-mail, online support groups) have time delays between messages. The convenience of digital media enables asynchronous communication to become synchronous, such as when you and a friend send text messages back and forth in real time.
Social Cues	The medium's ability to give access to verbal and nonverbal cues that provide information about context and help people interpret the meaning of a message. In general, digital media provide fewer social cues than face-to-face interactions. However, communication technologies such as FaceTime and Skype give communicators access to a rich array of cues including facial expressions, body language, and tone of voice. Additionally, in text-based media, the use of emoticons and punctuation can convey information about the sender's intention and mood.
Storage	A medium's potential to store or save messages. Whereas communication that occurs face-to-face or over a phone call typically vanishes in the moment, most messages (both written and audio) sent via digital media are automatically saved. Many devices and websites create a permanent record of messages unless they are deleted by a user.
Replicability	A medium's capability to store and make copies of—or replicate—a message. Most asynchronous media allow users to save messages, retrieve them at a later date, and replicate (or edit) them before re-posting online or re-sending to others. For example, many people edit and re-post previous status updates and comments on social media. Likewise, if I receive an e-mail about a subject or an issue that I have addressed in a prior e-mail, I often replicate and/or edit the old message and then send it to the new recipient.
Reach	The size of the audience that a medium can reach. Communication that occurs face-to-face typically only reaches the people in the same physical space. Groups can interact via text messaging, phone calls, and video conferences, but various constraints (e.g., physical space, media capabilities, etc.) often limit how many people can join the group. Social media and other online forums, on the other hand, allow individuals to quickly and easily spread messages to a greater number of people and across greater distances than ever before.
Mobility	The medium's ability to enable users to communicate with others from any location. Most face-to-face interactions require people to be in a specific location and remain stationary; although they can change locations by walking or other forms of travel, they must stay together if they want to continue their conversation. Desktop computers and landline telephones allow individuals to interact with others in different geographic locations, but they are tied to wherever the device is located. Newer media—such as laptops, tablets, and mobile phones—have revolutionized interpersonal communication by enabling people to communicate with one another at any time and from any location.

THE MULTIMODALITY OF PERSONAL RELATIONSHIPS

On the television series *Parks and Recreation,* Tom Haverford (played by Aziz Ansari) is known for his obsession with technology and social media. At one point, he admits to having 26 different online dating profiles in an effort to expand his pool of potential romantic partners. In another episode, he crashes into a fire hydrant while live-tweeting his drive to work, and a judge sentences him to a week without screens or technology of any kind. This punishment proves to be very difficult for Tom, who typically starts off each day by "hitting up Facebook, Twitter, Tumblr, and Instagram" and occasionally LinkedIn "for the professional shorties." His daily digital media habits also include checking out Reddit, chatting with others through instant messaging services, finding creative ways to use emojis in his text messages, and recording a podcast with his best friend. Clearly, Tom relies heavily on technology to share his experiences with others and fulfill his need for social connection.

Although Tom's screen addiction is purposefully exaggerated throughout the series, the way he engages with multiple forms of media from sunrise to sunset has become a norm of modern life. For example, research shows that nearly 80% of American mobile phone users ages 18–44 check their phone within the first 15 minutes of waking up; among 18–24-year-olds, the percentage rises to 89% ("Always Connected," 2013). When people first open their phones in the morning, the most common activities they take part in are checking e-mail, scrolling through social media, and sending and receiving text messages ("Always Connected"; "Smartphone Statistics," 2017). Therefore, it is not unusual for individuals to interact with family and friends on various platforms before they even get out of bed.

Just as people tend to start their day by checking their phones, over 50% report that the last time they use their device each day is right before they go to bed and 13% report that they do not disconnect until they fall asleep ("Always Connected," 2013). This means that many smartphone users are connecting and sharing with members of their social networks from the time they wake up in the morning until they fall asleep at night. Further, people conduct these interactions with family members, friends, and acquaintances through many different media and devices, often simultaneously (Baym, 2015; Ledbetter, 2015). Having access to countless technologies that enable people to communicate around-the-clock and across distances has greatly altered the landscape of interpersonal relationships. With new modes of communication emerging almost constantly, conducting daily interactions often involves a great deal of choice. How do we decide whether to text, e-mail, call, comment, share, tweet, like, or snap? In what situations and with whom do we prefer to communicate face-to-face? Two ideas that help explain how we choose which media to employ in our personal relationships are *media multiplexity* and *symbolic value.*

Media Multiplexity

When I was in middle school during the late 1990s, there were two ways I interacted with my friends: in person or over the (landline) phone. Over the summer before my freshman year, my best friend and I stayed in touch during the weeks we could not get together by exchanging handwritten letters in the mail. I started to use e-mail and AOL Instant Messenger with a few friends by the end of high school, but most of my interactions still took place in person or over the phone. Today, my 18-year-old niece stays in constant contact with her friends throughout the day using a variety of methods: face-to-face conversations, text messaging, FaceTime, SnapChat, Instagram, and Facebook (to name a few).

**MEDIA
MULTIPLEXITY
THEORY**

a theory based on
the assumptions that
relational partners
communicate
through more than
one medium, and that
partners with stronger
ties use more media
than those with
weaker ties.

The contrast between the way I maintained friendships in my teens and the way my niece does now shows that technology has made our lives increasingly *multimodal*; that is, we use multiple types of media to build and sustain our personal relationships. In recent years, **Media Multiplexity Theory** (MMT; Haythornthwaite, 2005; Ledbetter, 2015) has emerged as a useful framework for studying the multimodality that characterizes contemporary relational experiences. Haythornthwaite coined the term "media multiplexity" after observing that relationship partners communicate through more than one medium (i.e., mediated and/or face-to-face methods of communication), and that the variety of media they employ says something about the nature of their bond. Based on this idea, MMT's primary goal is to "explain how and why the strength of an interpersonal bond is associated with the number of media used to maintain the relationship" (Ledbetter, 2015, p. 363). In particular, the theory rests on the assumption that partners with a stronger bond use a greater number of media to interact than those with weaker ties. Why do we tend to use more types of media in our closest relationships? Ledbetter asserts that exchanging information and support through multiple media is often necessary to sustain the intimacy expected of our "strong ties" (e.g., close friendships, long-term romantic relationships, family bonds, etc.), whereas very little interaction is required to maintain a "weak tie" with a casual acquaintance.

The premise of MMT becomes more apparent if you consider how you use media in your own relationships. For example, the strong bond you have with your closest friend is likely sustained through multiple types of media. In a typical week, the two of you might exchange numerous text messages, share pictures and videos via SnapChat, "like" or "retweet" one another's social media posts, compete in an online game, catch up over FaceTime, and then hang out in person when you go home for the weekend. On the other hand, maintaining ties with an acquaintance—such as your chemistry partner from last semester—does not require so many different channels. In fact, you may only say "hi" when you pass each other on campus and occasionally "like" his or her pictures on Facebook. However, suppose you and your former chemistry partner gradually started texting regularly, commenting on one another's social media posts, and eating lunch together a couple times a week. Adding new media to your relationship over time increases the likelihood that it will develop into a strong tie; likewise, subtracting communication channels used in a close bond can cause the tie to become weaker (Ledbetter, 2015).

An important takeaway regarding MMT is that individuals do not assign methods of communication to their various relationships at random. Rather, they choose to use multiple media to maintain their bonds with some people and not with others based on their goals for the relationship and the strength of the tie. If our goal is to sustain a close bond or strengthen a weak tie, we will strive to increase our methods of communication. When we are not interested in being more than casual friends or acquaintances, or if we become less invested in maintaining a strong tie, we will not make the effort to interact via multiple channels. We now understand how the number of media employed in a relationship, or *media multiplexity*, influences the strength of our relational ties. Next, we will consider how relational partners assign symbolic value to specific types of media.

Symbolic Value of Media

As people discover and engage with digital technologies, they form ideas about which occasions, relationships, and messages call for which media (Baym, 2015). By developing expectations regarding how and when a certain digital technology should (or should not) be used, individuals assign their own meaning and significance—or **symbolic value**—to the communication medium. Gershon (2010) argued that these beliefs people develop about a particular medium influence how a message is perceived and, as a result, the medium "becomes part of what is being communicated" (p. 3). In other words, the decision to use one medium instead of another often carries meaning on its own and can reveal important information about the relationship and/or the person sending the message (Gershon, 2010; Madianou & Miller, 2012). Additionally, if the method of communication does not seem fitting for the message, it can undermine or otherwise distract from what was said (Gershon). For instance, given that private, person-to-person media (e.g., phone calls, private messaging, etc.) are generally associated with strong ties (Haythornthwaite, 2005), it may be upsetting if a close friend only wishes us "Happy Birthday" on social media and does not call or send a personal text message. Based on our beliefs about what medium a good friend should use to send a birthday message, we might worry that we did something wrong or start to question whether the friendship is as close as we thought. As a result, the content of the friend's birthday post takes a backseat to the meaning we derive from his or her medium of choice.

In many ways, the rapid growth in communication technologies has introduced a new responsibility for individuals to carefully consider their media choices in personal relationships (Madianou & Miller, 2012). Not every family member, friend, or romantic partner is going to share our beliefs about the media we use, which creates the potential for conflicts and misunderstandings. As Baym (2015) observed, "It is no longer enough to send the right message, we must also do it through the right medium" (p. 159). A former student named "Tess" once told me that one of her best friends from high school was upset with her for a few weeks and she had no idea why. After some probing, the friend revealed that it hurt her feelings when Tess disclosed that she had a new boyfriend in a group text message with three of their other friends instead of telling her individually. Although Tess thought using a group message to share important news with her closest high school friends showed that she wanted to maintain a strong connection with all of them, her friend viewed it as a sign that they were drifting apart. According to media scholars, relational partners can minimize these types of issues by taking each other's beliefs about media into account when they interact (Baym; Groshen, 2010). In mediated exchanges, interpreting a message correctly often depends on understanding the symbolic value each person attaches to the medium.

RELATIONAL FUNCTIONS OF DIGITAL MEDIA

The fact that relationship pairs make use of multiple forms of media and digital technologies to communicate has been well-established. As such, it is necessary to understand what purposes digital media serve in personal relationships. Although research indicates that people engage in mediated interactions for a variety of reasons, digital media appear to facilitate five main relational functions: (1) relationship presentation, (2) relationship initiation, (3) relationship maintenance, (4) relationship dissolution, and (5) relationship reconnection (see Baym, 2015; Bryant, Marmo, & Ramirez, 2011; Chambers, 2013).

Relationship Presentation

Many digital technologies enable, and even encourage, people to manage and display their relationships in public spaces (Tong & Walther, 2011). Many bloggers, for example,

SYMBOLIC VALUE

the beliefs people develop about a particular medium, such as when and how it should be used; these beliefs influence how a message delivered through that medium is perceived.

focus on family relationships in their entries and use the platform to create a portrait of their relational experiences for a mediated audience (Child & Petronio, 2011). Social network sites (SNSs), which allow users to maintain personal relationships and share aspects of their lives in an online environment, are also well-suited for "publicly displaying connectedness" (Chambers, 2013, p. 4). On Facebook, romantic partners can publicly disclose their relationship online by linking their profiles with the appropriate status (e.g., *In a Relationship, Engaged, In a Domestic Partnership*, etc.), referred to as making the union "Facebook Official" (Fox, Warber, & Makstaller, 2013). Media scholars have also pointed out that SNSs are the first mechanism that allow for the public declaration of friendships (Baym, 2015; Chambers). Unlike the social and legal recognition given to married partners and family ties, there were no means of publicly formalizing friendships prior to the creation of social media (Baym).

Overall, SNSs and other new media technologies provide family members, friends, and romantic partners with the option to publicly display their connections and disclose aspects of their relationship to others online. Even relational exchanges conducted through private, person-to-person media—such as text messaging and e-mail—can become public if they are shared on social media, a blog, or any other Web page.

Relationship Initiation

Relationship initiation via digital media occurs when people who were previously unknown to each other meet online or through some other mediated context and start to explore a friendship or romantic relationship. Most relationships that start online do not develop into a meaningful, off-line bond. In general, people who meet on the Internet tend to maintain weak ties through mediated channels or fall out of touch altogether (Baym, 2015). However, recent data indicate that more and more online friends eventually meet in person and become members of one another's off-line circles. In 2000, Americans reported having an average of 0.7 off-line, face-to-face

© Georgejmclittle/Shutterstock.com

relationships with people they had met online; by 2016, the number had risen to six (Cole, 2017). Many of these online friendships are formed based on shared interests, with people meeting on SNSs or online groups dedicated to specific hobbies or topics (Baym & Ledbetter, 2009; Bryant et al., 2011). Additionally, some individuals may add weak ties (e.g., a friend of a friend) on social media so that they can learn more about them and possibly initiate a relationship (Bryant et al.).

Perhaps the most common way people develop new relationships over the Internet is through online dating websites and apps. Attitudes about Internet dating have become more positive in recent years, with 59% of Americans agreeing it is a good way to meet potential romantic partners (Smith, 2016). The growing acceptance of online dating practices, combined with the emergence of mobile dating apps, has sparked an increase in the popularity of these services. A survey conducted by the Pew Research Center indicated the percentage of 18–24-year-olds who reported using online dating services nearly tripled from 10% in 2013 to 27% in 2015; for 55–64-year-olds, usage doubled from 6% to 12% during the same time period (Smith).

As searching for a romantic partner online becomes more and more commonplace, it is important to explore which factors cause some online dating relationships to succeed and others to fail. Deception is often cited as one of the main reasons some Internet romances do not work out (Couch, Liamputtong, & Pitts, 2012; Vandeweerd, Myers, Coulter, Yalcin, & Corvin, 2016). One study found that, in addition to fake photographs, online daters encounter people who lie about their age, marital status, careers, whether they have children, and relationship intentions (Couch et al.). Along with explicit acts of deception, people may exaggerate positive elements and downplay or omit negative information in order to create a more desirable impression on their online dating profiles (Wotipka & High, 2016). Thus, because digital technologies allow individuals to edit their communication and be selective in how they present themselves, people who meet online often develop a more favorable view of one another than if they had met in person (Baym, 2015; Walther, 1996). Baym argued the "idealization" that occurs early in online relationships can cause people to develop unrealistic expectations about the other person or the relationship, leading to disappointment when they meet face-to-face. Accordingly, after their first face-to-face date, many people report that their online dating partner's behavior and attractiveness did not live up to their expectations (Ramirez & Wang, 2008; Sharabi & Caughlin, 2017).

Not surprisingly, honesty appears to be essential to the development of positive and successful online dating relationships. For example, Wotipka and High (2016) found people develop more positive impressions about online dating profiles that have high *warranting* value, meaning they contain information that cannot be easily manipulated or falsified (e.g., links to blogs and external websites, specific height, multiple photographs, etc.). Participants also viewed profiles that contained fewer embellishments more favorably than those in which the profile owner bragged about his or her appearance and accomplishments. Overall, people indicated they were more likely to contact the profile owners who seemed honest and trustworthy (Wotipka & High). In addition to establishing trust, research also shows effective communication plays an important role in online dating success. In a recent study, Sharabi and Caughlin (2017) discovered individuals who engaged in frequent communication with their online dating partner prior to meeting in person experienced less disappointment and were more likely to want to continue the relationship than individuals who reported low levels of communication. As the authors speculated, high quality interactions may help online daters validate their impressions and build a solid foundation for their relationships before meeting face-to-face.

Relational Maintenance

Digital media and new technologies are predominantly used to maintain existing off-line relationships. Although the seven relational maintenance behaviors discussed earlier in Section 2 of this unit (e.g., positivity, understanding, self-disclosure, assurances, tasks, networks, and relational talk) were developed based on face-to-face interactions, communication researchers have demonstrated that people also perform these behaviors to sustain ties in mediated contexts (Ledbetter, 2010; Rabby, 2007). Texting a family member "I love you" is an *assurance* of how much they mean to you; sending a friend a funny picture through SnapChat to wish her good luck on a test helps maintain *positivity* in the relationship. Many relational partners also use digital technologies to conduct important conversations such as sharing feelings (self-disclosure) and apologizing or expressing forgiveness (understanding).

Among the various digital media available, social network sites (SNSs) are especially useful for maintaining and strengthening personal relationships. One of the main reasons people are drawn to SNSs is that they enable users to easily keep in touch with old friends and other people they might not get to see very often in person (Bryant et al., 2011). Another helpful way SNSs promote relational maintenance is by alerting people to both exciting and difficult events in their friends' lives, which gives them an opportunity to offer well wishes or provide support (Bryant et al.). Facebook and other social media platforms also encourage people to perform relationship maintenance signals, such as commenting on or "liking" content on a friend's page (Ellison, Vitak, Gray, & Lampe, 2014; Tong & Walther, 2011). According to Ellison and colleagues (2014), these signals serve as "visible traces" that "indicate one has seen and attended to any individual piece of content on the site" (p. 858). A few years ago, I went to dinner with some friends from graduate school and one of them spent the entire meal scrolling through her phone and randomly clicking content on the screen—while still maintaining decent eye contact with the group. Someone finally asked what she was doing, and she replied that she was catching up on "liking" and "favoriting" all of her close friends' social media content from the week. She did not even read most of the posts; viewing her friends' information was not as important as leaving a "visible trace" of her support.

Although SNSs help us sustain strong ties with close friends, most of the relationships maintained through these sites consist of weak ties who rarely, if ever, interact (Baron, 2008; Baym, 2015). Research on Facebook "friendships" indicates most users only exchange messages with a small percentage of people in their network, and many only consider about one third of their Facebook connections to be "real" friends (see Baym). The hundreds of "friends" and connections the average SNS user has is far greater than the number of close friends one could realistically maintain; thus, many people use social media sites primarily to gain access to and manage a broad network of weak, nonclose ties (Rozzell et al., 2014; Steinfield, Ellison, & Lampe, 2008). This does not mean SNSs are not a helpful and fun tool for enhancing ties with our closest friends. If you got rid of your social media accounts, though, you would still maintain contact with the friends and family in your inner circle through text messaging, phone calls, face-to-face conversations, and various other media that you likely already use in those relationships. However, without access to SNSs, you may lose touch with an acquaintance from high school and you likely would never know what your former roommate's cousin's ex-boyfriend is up to again.

Mobile devices appear to be the most widely used communication technology for the regular maintenance of strong ties (Pettegrew & Day, 2015). In particular, the convenience of phone calls and text messaging allow relational partners to coordinate

© GoodStudio/Shutterstock.com

daily actions and communicate quickly and easily at any time, thus keeping strongly tied pairs even more connected (Baym, 2015). Mobile phones, as well as other forms of digital media, play a particularly important role in maintaining closeness in long-distance relationships or while partners are physically separated (Pettegrew & Day; Tong & Walther, 2011). According to Tong and Walther, interacting via digital technologies can create a feeling of being "present" with a relational partner; in other words, viewing a status update on social media or receiving an e-mail may make us feel intimately connected to the other person. Tong and Walther also assert that digital media provide a way for people in relationships to share mundane activities and experiences with one another, helping them keep up with daily happenings while apart. For my dissertation, I interviewed sibling pairs about their communication behaviors after the older sibling left home for college, and many said that exchanging quick text messages about their activities and viewing one another's social media posts allowed them to maintain a sense of day-to-day closeness without having to talk every day. One sibling stated that seeing her sister's updates on social media gave her "talking points" for the next time they spoke, which led to meaningful conversations that "never happened" when they lived together. Clearly, Internet technologies are a vital means of maintaining all types of relationships, providing both proximate and distant partners with new ways to interact and accomplish relational goals.

Relational Dissolution

Using digital media to conduct the difficult task of ending a relationship is a relatively common, yet debatable, practice (Baym, 2015; Gershon, 2010). When Gershon asked college students to describe a "bad break up," most told stories about being dumped online or via digital technologies, which she refers to as *mediated breakups* (p. 1). Nearly all of the young adults she spoke with agreed that breaking up with someone over text message or on social media was inappropriate and disrespectful. Ending a relationship through text was considered too informal and sometimes confusing because it contradicted how the couple had used the medium in the past. Because many dating partners use text messaging for joking, flirting, and other lighthearted exchanges, a person might not take a "we should break up" text seriously. In terms of social media, students in Gershon's study described experiences where former girlfriends or boyfriends posted status updates indicating that they were happy about being single or removed the "in the relationship" status before they had agreed to go public with their split. They felt these acts were rude and hurtful because it was like a public announcement to everyone that their ex did not care about them or their relationship, and put their breakup even more on display.

The public nature of breakups on social media can make it more difficult to adjust to the separation. Couples who are "Facebook Official" or otherwise publicize their relationships often worry about how their friends will react to the news (Gershon, 2010). People may attempt to signal the breakup quietly by concealing their relationship status rather than marking "single" (Gershon; LeFebvre, Blackburn, & Brody, 2015) but other clues likely remain. I have learned of several divorces on social media after noticing female friends replace their marital name with their maiden name. After one acquaintance returned to her maiden name on her profile a few years ago, a relative of her ex-husband commented on her page that it was "about time you stopped ruining my family's name." Although incidents like that are extreme and relatively rare, it does illustrate that publicly terminating a relationship can be stressful and challenging. For instance, individuals must also figure out how to manage lingering visible ties to their ex-partner such as photographs, comments and exchanged messages, and statuses (Fox, Osborn, & Warber, 2014; LeFebvre et al., 2015). Whereas some choose to avoid social media or deactivate their accounts, others conduct what LeFebvre et al. call a "relational cleansing" by changing their relationship status, untagging or deleting pictures, and removing wall posts.

One of the most difficult decisions social media users face following a breakup is whether to delete their ex from their network. Participants in one study expressed that deleting a former romantic partner from their account is not considered socially acceptable; therefore, many people will stay connected with their exes on social media even if it impedes recovery. Individuals who have access to their former partner's social media profile are more likely to engage in maladaptive behaviors like ruminating about the breakup and stalking their ex's page (Gershon, 2010; Tran & Joormann, 2014). The ability and temptation to view everything going on in an ex's life—as well as the difficulty of "cleansing" every detail about the relationship from one's profile—can create a barrier to achieving closure or a sense of finality about the breakup (LeFebvre et al, 2015). Digital technologies, then, have the potential to create a written, virtual record of relationships that is difficult to completely erase.

Relational Reconnection

The growth of digital media and communication technologies has also created avenues for relational reconnection, defined as "a process that encompasses both the re-initiation of a relationship as well as its continued maintenance after initial contact" (Ramirez & Bryant, 2014, p. 2). In 2010, nearly half of online adults reported they had searched the Internet for information about someone they lost touch with, and 40% stated they had been contacted by a person from their past (Madden & Smith, 2010). An emerging body of research shows SNSs are ideal for conducting relational reconnection attempts because they have many tools that make it easy to find and initiate contact with prior relational partners (Bryant et al., 2011; Ramirez, Sumner, & Spinda, 2015). On Facebook, for example, users can locate long-lost friends by conducting a search for their name, viewing the profiles of members in their network to see if anyone they know is in contact with them, and examine the "people you may know" list (Bryant et al.). Thus, SNSs allow people to covertly seek out and gather information about someone from their past to determine if initiating a reconnection is worthwhile (Ramirez et al., 2015).

TECHNOLOGY'S IMPACT ON RELATIONSHIPS: GOOD OR BAD?

One of the most debated issues of the 21st century concerns whether the use of technology and digital media has a positive or negative impact on our personal relationships. From the optimistic point of view, digital technologies are believed to create new opportunities for building and strengthening ties. However, we are also quick to blame them for our communication failures and the decline of "true" intimacy. Though some people may strongly believe that one side of the debate is the "correct" perspective, the truth is—as I am sure many of you know—technology has the potential to both help and hurt our bonds with friends, family members, and significant others. In the end, the mere existence of media and devices does not impact our relationships as much as how and when we use those devices, the care and thought we put into our mediated messages, and the way we conduct ourselves in face-to-face interactions.

Given that we generally have a say regarding how technology factors into our relational experiences, it is important to understand the ways our media habits might be strengthening or hindering our connections. In the following sections, I review some of the positive and negative effects commonly attributed to technology use in interpersonal relationships.

Ways Technology Can Help Relationships

In contrast with the perception that technology dilutes the strength and quality of our personal connections, many people believe their relationships have been positively impacted by media use. The findings from a 2016 survey of American Internet users revealed that 73% of 18–34-year-olds, 64% of 35–54-year-olds, and 48% of people 55 and older consider the Internet "important" or "very important" for their social relationships (Cole, 2017). Another survey found that the majority (74%) of adult Internet users who believe that technology has impacted their romantic relationships view the impact as positive, with many indicating that they felt closer to their partner because of their mediated exchanges online or through text message (Lenhart & Duggan, 2014).

The notion that communication technologies can help relational partners develop and maintain a strong connection is supported by an extensive body of research (Baym, 2015; Chambers, 2013; Hsieh & Tseng, 2017). This appears to be especially true for many long-distance relationships, whether between family members, friends, or romantic partners (Tong & Walther, 2011). In particular, communicating via digital media enables geographically separated pairs to create a sense of co-presence and contributes to experiences of relational satisfaction, positivity, and openness (Maguire & Connaughton, 2011; Tong & Walther). Further, as Madianou and Miller (2012) emphasize, webcams and video chat services have made it more possible than ever before to develop and maintain relationships across distances. For example, their research examining media use among family members separated by migration revealed that many grandparents use webcams to interact and play with their toddler-age grandchildren, which helps the young children learn who they are and form a much closer bond with them than a phone call would allow. Similarly, when my daughter was born 6 months ago, my dad decided it was time to learn how to use Skype. After 6 months of video chatting with him every other week, she now recognizes her grandpa and smiles at him when he appears on the screen. The fact that my daughter can interact face-to-face with my parents and establish a meaningful bond with them from 1,500 miles away highlights the immense value of technology for friends and loved ones who live apart.

A related benefit of new media and digital technologies is that they can help people maintain important friendships that may not otherwise survive distance. Traditionally, friendship has been considered a "fragile" relationship that depends on frequent face-to-face interaction and, therefore, is prone to dissolution if friends become geographically separated (Fehr, 1999). However, due to the availability and convenience of digital technologies, scholars now argue that friendships are better described as "flexible" to represent how friends adapt to distance and enact new ways of maintaining closeness (see Johnson & Becker, 2011, for a review). Although some friendships are not meant to last a lifetime, the ability to stay connected to the friends who mean the most to us can be a blessing. Research consistently shows that maintaining quality friendships throughout adulthood positively impacts life satisfaction and well-being (Chopik, 2017; Huxhold, Miche, & Schüz, 2013), and that poor relationships with close friends is linked to detrimental health outcomes (Pietromonaco, Uchino, & Dunkel Schetter, 2013). In this sense, using digital media and devices for relational maintenance has the potential to improve not only the strength of our personal relationships, but also the quality of our lives.

Ways Technology Can Hurt Relationships

The widespread, daily use of digital technologies also has the potential to hinder interpersonal communication and relational intimacy. A prevalent concern—what Baym (2015) calls the "dystopian" view of technology—is that TMC and the devices themselves will replace face-to-face interaction, creating a culture of anti-social individuals. Indeed, many young adults prefer text messaging over communicating in person and purposefully avoid off-line conversations with others (Pettegrew & Day, 2015; Turkle, 2015). Accordingly, Turkle argues that a sustained reliance on technology to the detriment of face-to-face conversations is concerning because it deprives us of opportunities to be fully present and attentive, to express ourselves and be heard, and to experience the intimate and emotional nature of human interaction. She further describes how smartphones and other digital media have negatively impacted interpersonal communication and the quality of relationships:

> …technology is implicated in an assault on empathy. We have learned that even a silent phone inhibits conversations that matter. The very sight of a phone on the landscape leaves us feeling less connected to each other, less invested in each other (Turkle, p. 4).

Thus, although technology can be a powerful tool of connection, the way we have integrated digital devices into our lives often disrupts important relational moments and keeps us from engaging in meaningful face-to-face interactions necessary for personal fulfillment and relationship growth. With more than one fourth (26%) of American adults reporting they go online "almost constantly" throughout the day (Perrin & Jiang, 2018), it has become increasingly common for friends and family

© Rawpixel.com/Shutterstock.com

members to only give one another their partial attention when they are together, thereby making conversations rushed and fragmented (Turkle).

By 2012, the tendency for individuals to divide their attention between their phones and the people around them had become so routine that the Macquarie Dictionary called upon linguistic experts to give this problematic smartphone behavior a name. This resulted in the birth of the term **phubbing** (a combination of the words "phone" and "snubbing"), which describes the act of ignoring someone in a social setting by paying attention to one's cell phone instead (Seppala, 2017). Not surprisingly, phubbing and other mobile phone issues in the context of personal relationships have been shown to negatively impact relational satisfaction, trust between partners, perceptions of empathy, and individual well-being (Przybylski & Weinstein, 2013; Roberts & David, 2016). Turkle's (2015) research also shows that most young adults are aware that phubbing causes problems in their relationships and often wish their friends paid more attention during interactions, yet they also frequently "phub" others themselves.

What drives people to interact with their smartphones instead of their friends and family members in front of them? A recent study by Chotpitayasunondh and Douglas (2016) revealed that Internet addiction, fear of missing out, and low self-control are common triggers for excessive smartphone use and phubbing behaviors. The researchers also found participants who frequently experienced both sides of phubbing (i.e., phubbing others and being phubbed by others) were more likely to perceive the behavior as normative. Thus, by phubbing the people in our lives and allowing them to phub us, we reinforce the belief that it is socially acceptable and continue to let our smartphones keep us from connecting with others face-to-face (Turkle, 2015).

When I cover phubbing in class, many students express that using their phone in the presence of others is necessary (and thus socially acceptable) because their family or friends would worry if they did not respond to a message right away. While it is important to reply to someone who is truly concerned, I always play devil's advocate and ask students if they receive so many messages from people who are worried about them that it requires prolonged phubbing to respond. Often, they confess that responding to messages to let others know they are safe is only one of many reasons they focus on their phones while hanging out with friends. Further, the idea that we need to immediately respond when others contact us highlights another issue: that

PHUBBING

the act of ignoring someone in a social setting by paying attention to one's cell phone instead.

our access to technology makes us constantly "on call" in our relationships (Turkle, 2015). Because our smartphones are always within our grasp, others expect that we can be reached at any time and we often feel obligated to provide a prompt response (Baym, 2015). Given these expectations for constant contact, managing our relationships via multiple media can be a stressful and overwhelming enterprise.

CONCLUSION

Advances in technology have profoundly changed the landscape of our relational lives. Just as digital media and devices can provide a means of forming and maintaining meaningful bonds, they can also create a barrier to intimacy and provide a false sense of connection. Although research examining the role of technology in personal relationships has grown considerably in recent years, scholars are still trying to make sense of what these changes mean for our friendships, romantic relationships, and family ties. Thus, as we navigate these exciting and uncertain times, we must choose our methods of communication wisely and take great care in how we interact with others in mediated spaces.

Discussion Questions

1. Consider the different types of media that you use to maintain your relationships. Which relationship(s) do you use the most media to maintain, and which relationships do you use the fewest? Is Media Multiplexity Theory's main assumption (that partners with a stronger bond use more media to maintain their relationships than those with a weaker bond) true for you?

2. How do you decide which media are best to use for each of your relationships? How does the symbolic value you assign to certain media influence these decisions?

3. How, if at all, does your use of technology function to "publicize" your relationships?

4. Is it appropriate to break up with a romantic partner through a text message? Why or why not?

5. Discuss the pros and cons of using digital technologies to maintain personal relationships. In what ways has technology positively and negatively impacted your relationships?

6. Do you believe that phubbing has become a socially acceptable behavior? Why or why not?

Always connected: How smartphones and social keep us engaged. (2013). *International Data Corporation.* Retrieved from https://www.nu.nl/files/IDC-Facebook%20Always%20Connected%20%281%29.pdf

Baron, N. S. (2008). *Always on: Language in an online and mobile world.* Oxford: Oxford University Press.

Baym, N. (2015). *Personal connections in the digital age* (2nd ed.). Cambridge: Polity Press.

Baym, N. K., & Ledbetter, A. (2009). Tunes that bind? Predicting friendship strength in a music-based social network. *Information, Communication & Society, 12*(3), 408–427. doi:10.1080/13691180802635430

Bevan, J. L. (2017). Romantic jealousy in face-to-face and technologically-mediated interactions: A communicative interdependence perspective. *Western Journal of Communication, 81*(4), 466–482. doi:10.1080/10570314.2017.1283048

Bryant, E. M., Marmo, J., & Ramirez, A. (2011). A functional approach to social networking sites. In K. B. Wright & L. M. Webb (Eds.), *Computer-mediated communication in personal relationships* (pp. 3–20). New York: Peter Lang Publishing.

Caughlin, J. P., & Sharabi, L. L. (2013). A communicative interdependence perspective of close relationships: The connections between mediated and unmediated interactions matter. *Journal of Communication, 63*(5), 873–893. doi:10.1111/jcom.12046

Chambers, D. (2013). *Social media and personal relationships: Online intimacies and networked friendship.* London: Palgrave Macmillan.

Child, J. T., & Petronio, S. (2011). Unpacking the paradoxes of privacy in CMC relationships: The challenges of blogging and relational communication on the internet. *Computer-mediated communication in personal relationships.* In K. B. Wright & L. M. Webb (Eds.), *Computer-mediated communication in personal relationships* (pp. 21–40). New York: Peter Lang Publishing.

Chopik, W. J. (2017). Associations among relational values, support, health, and well-being across the adult lifespan. *Personal relationships, 24*(2), 408–422. doi:10.1111/pere.12187

Chotpitayasunondh, V., & Douglas, K. M. (2016). How "phubbing" becomes the norm: The antecedents and consequences of snubbing via smartphone. *Computers in Human Behavior, 63,* 9–18. doi:10.1016/j.chb.2016.05.018

Cole, J. (2017). *Surveying the digital future.* UCLA Center for Communication Policy. Retrieved from http://www.digitalcenter.org/wp-content/uploads/2013/10/2017-Digital-Future-Report.pdf

Couch, D., Liamputtong, P., & Pitts, M. (2012). What are the real and perceived risks and dangers of online dating? Perspectives from online daters: Health risks in the media. *Health, Risk & Society, 14*(7–8), 697–714. doi:10.1080/13698575.2012.720964

Ellison, N. B., Vitak, J., Gray, R., & Lampe, C. (2014). Cultivating social resources on social network sites: Facebook relationship maintenance behaviors and their role in social capital processes. *Journal of Computer-Mediated Communication, 19*(4), 855–870. doi:10.1111/jcc4.12078

Fehr, B. (1999). Stability and commitment in friendships. In J. M. Adams & W. H. Jones (Eds.), *Handbook of interpersonal commitment and relationship stability* (pp. 239–256). New York: Kluwer/Plenum.

Fox, J., Osborn, J. L., & Warber, K. M. (2014). Relational dialectics and social networking sites: The role of Facebook in romantic relationship escalation, maintenance, conflict, and dissolution. *Computers in Human Behavior, 35,* 527–534. doi:10.1016/j.chb.2014.02.031

Fox, J., Warber, K. M., & Makstaller, D. C. (2013). The role of Facebook in romantic relationship development: An exploration of Knapp's relational stage model. *Journal of Social and Personal Relationships, 30*(6), 771–794. doi:10.1177/0265407512468370

Gershon, I. (2010). *The breakup 2.0: Disconnecting over new media.* Ithaca, NY: Cornell University Press.

Haythornthwaite, C. (2005). Social networks and Internet connectivity effects. *Information, Community & Society, 8*(2), 125–147. doi:10.1080/13691180500146185

Hsieh, S. H., & Tseng, T. H. (2017). Playfulness in mobile instant messaging: Examining the influence of emoticons and text messaging on social interaction. *Computers in Human Behavior, 69,* 405–414. doi:10.1016/j.chb.2016.12.052

Huxhold, O., Miche, M., & Schüz, B. (2013). Benefits of having friends in older ages: Differential effects of informal social activities on well-being in middle-aged and older adults. *Journals of Gerontology Series B: Psychological Sciences and Social Sciences, 69*(3), 366–375. doi:10.1093/geronb/gbt029

Johnson, A. J., & Becker, J. A. (2011). CMC and the conceptualization of "friendship": How friendships have changed with the advent of new methods of interpersonal communication. In K. B. Wright & L. M. Webb (Eds.), *Computer-mediated communication in personal relationships* (pp. 3–20). New York: Peter Lang Publishing.

Ledbetter, A. M. (2010). Assessing the measurement invariance of relational maintenance behavior when face-to-face and online. *Communication Research Reports, 27*(1), 30–37. doi:10.1080/08824090903526620

Ledbetter, A. M. (2015). Media multiplexity theory: Technology use and interpersonal tie strength. In D. O. Braithwaite & P. Schrodt (Eds.), *Engaging theories in interpersonal communication: Multiple perspectives* (2nd ed., pp. 363–375). Thousand Oaks, CA: Sage.

LeFebvre, L., Blackburn, K., & Brody, N. (2015). Navigating romantic relationships on Facebook: Extending the relationship dissolution model to social networking environments. *Journal of Social and Personal Relationships, 32*(1), 78–98. doi:10.1177/0265407514524848

Lenhart, A., & Duggan, M. (2014). *Couples, the internet, and social media.* Pew Research Center. Retrieved from http://www.pewinternet.org/2014/02/11/couples-the-internet-and-social-media/

Madden, M., & Smith, A. (2010). *Searching, following, friending: How users monitor other people's digital footprints online.* Pew Research Center. Retrieved from http://www.pewinternet.org/2010/05/26/part-3-searching-following-and-friending-how-users-monitor-other-peoples-digital-footprints-online/

Madianou, M., & Miller, D. (2012). Polymedia: Towards a new theory of digital media in interpersonal communication. *International Journal of Cultural Studies, 16*(2), 169–187. doi:10.1177/1367877912452486

Maguire, K., & Connaughton, S. L. (2011). A cross-contextual examination of technologically mediated communication and presence in long distance relationships. In K. B. Wright & L. M. Webb (Eds.), *Computer-mediated communication in personal relationships* (pp. 244–265). New York: Peter Lang Publishing.

Newport, F. (2014). *The new era of communication among Americans.* Gallup. Retrieved from https://news.gallup.com/poll/179288/new-era-communication-americans.aspx

Perrin, A., & Jiang, J. (2018). *About a quarter of U.S. adults say they are 'almost constantly' online.* Pew Research Center. Retrieved from http://www.pewresearch.org/fact-tank/2018/03/14/about-a-quarter-of-americans-report-going-online-almost-constantly/

Pettegrew, L. S., & Day, C. (2015). Smartphones and mediated relationships: The changing face of relational communication. *Review of Communication, 15*(2), 122–139. doi:10.1080/15358593.2015.1044018

Pietromonaco, P. R., Uchino, B., & Dunkel Schetter, C. (2013). Close relationship processes and health: Implications of attachment theory for health and disease. *Health Psychology, 32*(5), 499–513. doi:10.1037/a0029349

Przybylski, A. K., & Weinstein, N. (2013). Can you connect with me now? How the presence of mobile communication technology influences face-to-face conversation quality. *Journal of Social and Personal Relationships, 30*(3), 237–246. doi:10.1177/0265407512453827

Rabby, M. K. (2007). Relational maintenance and the influence of commitment in online and off-line relationships. *Communication Studies, 58*(3), 315–337. doi:10.1080/10510970701518405

Ramirez Jr., A., & Bryant, E. M. (2014). Relational reconnection on social network sites: An examination of relationship persistence and modality switching. *Communication Reports, 27*(1), 1–12. doi:10.1080/08934215.2013.851725

Ramirez Jr., A., & Wang, Z. (2008). When online meets off-line: An expectancy violations theory perspective on modality switching. *Journal of Communication, 58*(1), 20–39. doi:10.1111/j.1460-2466.2007.00372.x

Ramirez Jr., A., Sumner, E. M., & Spinda, J. (2015). The relational reconnection function of social network sites. *New Media & Society, 19*(6), 807–825. doi:10.1177/1461444815614199

Reardon, M. (2008, September 23). Text messaging explodes in America. *CBS News.* Retrieved from https://www.cbsnews.com/news/text-messaging-explodes-in-america/

Roberts, J. A., & David, M. E. (2016). My life has become a major distraction from my cell phone: Partner phubbing and relationship satisfaction among romantic partners. *Computers in Human Behavior, 54*, 134–141. doi:10.1016/j.chb.2015.07.058

Rozzell, B., Piercy, C. W., Carr, C. T., King, S., Lane, B. L., Tornes, M., ... & Wright, K. B. (2014). Notification pending: Online social support from close and nonclose relational ties via Facebook. *Computers in Human Behavior, 38*, 272–280. doi:10.1016/j.chb.2014.06.006

Seppala, E. (2017, March 23). *Are you 'phubbing' right now? What it is and why science says it's bad for your relationships.* *The Washington Post.* Retrieved from https://www.washingtonpost.com/news/inspired-life/wp/2017/10/13/are-you-phubbing-right-now-what-it-is-and-why-science-says-its-bad-for-your-relationships/?noredirect=on&utm_term=.dc1a3ea839c8

Sharabi, L. L., & Caughlin, J. P. (2017). What predicts first date success? A longitudinal study of modality switching in online dating. *Personal Relationships, 24*(2), 370–391. doi:10.1111/pere.12188

Smartphone statistics: For most users, it's a 'round-the-clock' connection. (2017). *ReportLinker.* Retrieved from https://www.reportlinker.com/insight/smartphone-connection.html

Smith, A. (2016). *5 facts about online dating.* Pew Research Center. Retrieved from http://www.pewinternet.org/2016/02/11/15-percent-of-american-adults-have-used-online-dating-sites-or-mobile-dating-apps/

Steinfield, C., Ellison, N. B., & Lampe, C. (2008). Social capital, self-esteem, and use of online social network sites: A longitudinal analysis. *Journal of Applied Developmental Psychology, 29*(6), 434–445. doi:10.1016/j.appdev.2008.07.002

Tong, S., & Walther, J. B. (2011). Relational maintenance and CMC. In K. B. Wright & L. M. Webb (Eds.), *Computer-mediated communication in personal relationships* (pp. 98–118). New York: Peter Lang Publishing.

Tran, T. B., & Joormann, J. (2015). The role of Facebook use in mediating the relation between rumination and adjustment after a relationship breakup. *Computers in Human Behavior, 49,* 56–61. doi:10.1016/j.chb.2015.02.050

Turkle S. (2015). *Reclaiming conversation: The power of talk in a digital age.* New York, NY: Penguin Press.

Vandeweerd, C., Myers, J., Coulter, M., Yalcin, A., & Corvin, J. (2016). Positives and negatives of online dating according to women 50+. *Journal of women & aging, 28*(3), 259–270. doi:10.1080/08952841.2015.113743

Walther, J. B. (1992). Interpersonal effects in computer-mediated interaction: A relational perspective. *Communication Research, 19*(1), 52–90. doi:10.1177/009365092019001003

Walther, J. B. (1996). Computer-mediated communication: Impersonal, interpersonal, and hyperpersonal interaction. *Communication research, 23*(1), 3-43. doi:10.1177/009365096023001001

Wotipka, C. D., & High, A. C. (2016). An idealized self or the real me? Predicting attraction to online dating profiles using selective self-presentation and warranting. *Communication Monographs, 83*(3), 281–302. doi:10.1080/03637751.2016.1198041

Conflict in Relationships

By Jeanne Flora

Objectives

- ▶ Define conflict and describe various approaches to dealing with conflict.
- ▶ Explore family conflict climates and their impact.

Few other communication processes have been the focus of more attention by communication researchers than conflict. All the attention on interpersonal conflict makes sense, given that conflict is such an inevitable and inescapable part of social relationships. As you reflect on conflicts in your relationships right now, some are probably small grievances that you bring up in indirect ways. Other conflicts may be more major disagreements that get played out in verbal confrontations. Even though the way we communicate in conflict may be influenced by some things we are born into (e.g., our personalities, our family, and cultural influences), people can learn a great deal about how to better manage conflict. This section aims to help you identify forms and patterns of interpersonal conflict. Learning about conflict may also help you meta-communicate about it in your own relationships. **Meta-communication** means being able to look back at a communication episode (e.g., conflict), analyze it, and talk about it—an ability that appears to be very useful for dealing with conflict in close relationships (Abigail & Cahn, 2011).

This section defines conflict as a communication process and reviews types of conflict approaches and conflict climates, also acknowledging that conflict patterns in our family-of-origin can influence how we deal with conflict as adults. One important take-home message is that it is not simply conflict per se or even the sheer frequency of conflict that is most damaging to people's mental and physical health. Rather certain destructive *forms* of conflict appear to be the culprit.

META-COMMUNICATION

means being able to look back at a communication episode (e.g., conflict), analyze it, and talk about it; an ability that appears to be very useful for dealing with conflict in a close relationship.

DEFINING CONFLICT

Conflict can be defined as "an expressed struggle between at least two interdependent parties who perceive incompatible goals, scarce resources, and interference from others in achieving their goals" (Wilmot & Hocker, 2010, p. 11). From a communication perspective, conflict is an ongoing communication *process*, even though people often talk about it as a one-time discrete event. For example, people might say "we had a conflict last night," referring to conflict as one specific conversation or struggle. Yet there is often an emotional buildup or chain of trigger events leading up to any one conflictual conversation; just as any one conflict conversation may leave emotional residue and affect the course of future communication in a relationship. Sprey encourages us to study conflict processes in the same way researchers study processes in the natural world. For example, when studying the course of a tornado or the flow of a river, "it makes sense to study its beginning to speculate about its duration and future path" (Sprey, 1999, p. 668). Thus, it is important to examine the roots of interpersonal conflict, to learn more about what people say and do in conflict interactions, as well as the future consequences.

CONFLICT APPROACHES

One way to generally categorize interpersonal conflict approaches is to consider how (1) direct or indirect and (2) competitive or cooperative people are when communicating in conflict (Canary & Lakey, 2006). Table 3.2 provides examples of behaviors associated with four related conflict approaches as described by Abigail and Cahn (2011): indirect competitive, indirect cooperative, direct competitive, direct cooperative.

© all_about_people/Shutterstock.com

Table **3.2**

Conflict Approaches and Behaviors

Indirect and Competitive	Indirect and Cooperative
Conflict Behaviors: Backstabbing, sabotaging, refusal to talk, shutting off discussion, lack of cooperation, lying, denials (this approach is often referred to as passive- aggressive)	**Conflict Behaviors:** Avoiding, accommodating, changing the subject, smoothing, humor (without sarcasm), requests to talk about the conflict later
Direct and Competitive	**Direct and Cooperative**
Conflict Behaviors: Disagreement, rejection, criticism, denying responsibility, hostile questioning, hostile demands, hostile jokes, negative mind reading, threats, physical intimidation	**Conflict Behaviors:** Collaborating, compromising, expressing willingness to change, statements of understanding, accepting responsibility, apology, problem- solving, meta-communication

Table 3.2 is intended to be a useful beginning for understanding interpersonal conflict and the behaviors that stem from each approach. The next question people often ask is which approach to conflict is best. As this section unfolds, it will become evident that conflict is complex. Even still, Canary and Lakey (2006) argue that "if a person had to place a bet, then cooperative behaviors (direct or indirect) are clearly seen as more competent than competitive behaviors" (p. 200). More specifically, Canary and Canary (2015) state that "direct and cooperative messages are most functional most of the time" (p. 181). One reason why cooperative behaviors are perceived as more competent and functional has to do with the concept of face, which is about showing respect for another's identity and self-worth (Ting-Toomey & Takai, 2006). Cooperative behaviors tend to be perceived as more face-honoring. Competitive behaviors tend to be viewed as more face-threatening, with direct/competitive behaviors being threatening in an attacking way and indirect/competitive behaviors being threatening in a more undermining way (Canary & Canary).

Not only are cooperative conflict behaviors viewed by other people as more competent, but the more cooperative conflict behaviors people use in their relationships the more satisfied they are. For example, Leggett, Roberts-Pittman, and Bycek (2012) examined nearly 1,000 married partners looking for what contributed to their feelings of marital satisfaction/dissatisfaction. They found that 39% of the variance in marital satisfaction could be explained by perceptions of cooperation and positive conflict behaviors. Other classic findings by Gottman (1994) describe that even when in conflict, satisfied couples maintain at least a ratio of 5:1 (cooperative:competitive) behaviors. Dissatisfied couples exhibit a ratio closer to 1:1, meaning that each attempt at a cooperative behavior is met with a competitive behavior, and often a hostile one. Although researchers have discovered some general patterns related to constructive and destructive conflict, it is worth keeping in mind that what works best in one situation or relationship may not always be what works in another. For instance, there may be some functional exceptions of competitive behavior, even though habitual expressions of competitive anger are consistently associated with more troubled marriages (Krokoff, 1991). Another complexity to consider is that some conflict behaviors (e.g., avoidance) may lead to different outcomes that are functional considering the intent, context, and seriousness of the issue. Even though relational, contextual, and cultural complexities mean there may not be one "right" way to deal with conflict in all situations, this section aims to highlight approaches to conflict that are generally more successful.

CONFLICT CLIMATES

The idea of a conflict climate refers to "the psychological atmosphere impacting a conflict" (Abigail & Cahn, 2011, p. 103). For example, some conflict climates have a harmful atmosphere, others a nurturing atmosphere. Being aware of a conflict climate may require insider knowledge of a social situation because the climate is often subtly revealed in cultural norms, previous experience, and nonverbal expressions (e.g., tone of voice, facial expression). You probably have a good feel for the conflict climate in your own family, given years of experience as a family member. However, think about how you feel spending time with a friend's or partner's family for the first time, not knowing what is appropriate to say in what may seem in many ways like a new culture to you.

Family communication climates. Recognizing that children are born into very different communication climates, family communication scholars have set out to explore how conflict climates vary among families as well as the effects of those climates on children. Based on early work by McLeod and Chaffee (1972), Fitzpatrick and colleagues identified two communication orientations (i.e., conversation orientation and conformity orientation) that influence family conflict climates (Fitzpatrick & Ritchie, 1994; Koerner & Fitzpatrick, 2004; Ritchie, 1991). Families can range from being low to high on each orientation. The **conversation orientation** refers to "the degree to which members interact frequently, openly share thoughts on any topic, and include others in decisions that involve them (high conversation) as opposed to families that interact less frequently, withhold private thoughts and information, and limit the input to decision making and exchange of ideas (low conversation)" (Flora & Segrin, 2015, p. 93). The **conformity orientation** describes whether families "encourage similar attitudes, beliefs, and values as well as interdependence and obedience to traditional family structure (high conformity) as opposed to families that value individuality in thought and expressions and independence among family members (low conformity)" (Flora & Segrin, 2015, p. 93).

As described in Table 3.3, Koerner and Fitzpatrick (2004) identify four family conflict climates to describe how parents and children deal with conflict based on being high or low in the conversation and conformity orientation.

The effect of family conflict climates on children. How do family conflict climates influence children? For one thing, a higher conversation orientation tends to promote more open communication between parents and children. In the context of social media, young adults who were raised with a higher conversation orientation are more likely to friend their parents on Facebook (Ball, Wanzer, & Servoss, 2013). These young adults may feel comfortable doing so because they are used to having more open conversations with their parents, given they have not felt as much pressure to conform, as compared to children raised with a high conformity orientation. Parents who favor a conversation orientation tend to talk to and influence their children in a particular way, especially when it comes to topics that are potentially taboo or topics

CONVERSATION ORIENTATION

encouraging frequent interaction and openly sharing thoughts.

CONFORMITY ORIENTATION

encouraging similar attitudes, beliefs, and values.

Table **3.3**

Family Conflict Climate Types

Pluralistic families	Consensual families
(High conversation—Low conformity)	(High conversation—High conformity)
▶ Parents and children embrace conflict rather than avoiding it. ▶ Family members are low in their expression of negative feelings, though not necessarily because they are suppressing those feelings. ▶ Family members productively express conflict and negative emotion when it arises, enabling parents and children to manage it. ▶ The ability to manage conflict tends to result in their high expression of positive feelings.	▶ Conflict is perceived as a threat to family harmony. ▶ Parents spend time explaining their positions and involving children in family discussions. ▶ When conflict is necessary, families freely vent their negative feelings but they desire support and agreement from family members for positive closure to the conflict.
Protective families	**Laissez-Faire families**
(Low conversation—High conformity)	(Low conversation—Low conformity)
▶ Conflict is viewed negatively. ▶ There is pressure to agree and get along. ▶ Conflicts are suppressed, although after time parents and children show bursts of negative emotion that are expressed unproductively given they have little experience sharing feelings and concerns with one another.	▶ Family members tend to avoid conflict. ▶ Children are free to act as they wish. ▶ Family members do not desire to be involved in issues and decisions of others.

that involve behavioral choice. For instance, Baxter, Bylund, Imes, and Scheive (2005) examined the way that parents with a pluralistic orientation attempt to influence children about health behaviors (e.g., nutrition, sleep, sun protection, exercise, alcohol, tobacco, and illegal drugs). They found that families with a pluralistic orientation spent time talking about health behaviors and consequences with their children, and even rewarded healthy choices, but did not threaten to punish them with heavy negative sanctions. Instead, they hoped that their children would internalize the healthy behaviors and decide on their own to make good choices, after weighing the pros and cons with them. One positive outcome of this style may be that children learn to think through decisions on their own. Children may also feel less resentment or rebellion. However, parents relinquish some degree of control.

Children raised with a higher conformity orientation are more used to going along with authority figures and less likely to express contradictory opinions. Buckner, Ledbetter, and Bridge (2013) found that employees who had been raised with a high conformity orientation were less likely to voice upward dissent (e.g., express dissatisfaction to a boss) in an organization. There is also evidence that young adults from protective families may have more problems adjusting to college if they resent their parents' strict demands for conformity and feel more guilt over unresolved family issues (Orrego & Rodriguez, 2001). Thus, family conflict climates influence children's communication and behavioral choices even after they depart from home.

Indeed, parents are influential role models for children, although this influence is not necessarily positive. Social learning theory argues that children learn and adopt behaviors through observation (Bandura, 1977, 2001). By observing a parent behaving in a certain way and getting rewarded for it, children are motivated to model the behavior. Many people argue that children learn how to be spouses, parents, or even how to deal with conflict by watching their parents in these roles. One often overlooked way that parents influence children is by exposing them to their own style of dealing with conflict. For example, when exposed to either their mother's or father's use of competitive and distributive conflict tactics (e.g., being aggressive, threatening, manipulative, insulting, or yelling), children use more of these tactics in their own conflict interactions (Taylor & Segrin, 2010). On the flip side, the more children are exposed to cooperative and integrative conflict behaviors (e.g., being understanding, compromising, finding mutually agreeable solutions), the more they use such tactics (see also Flora & Segrin, 2015).

There is also evidence that the conflict styles children learn in their family-of-origin influence how they deal with conflict in their own peer relationships and even in their romantic or marital relationships as adults. Does this mean we will communicate just like our parents? No, but it gives us clues for tendencies toward which we may be prone. For example, adolescents who experience more hostile conflicts with their parents tend to experience more hostile interactions with peers (Allen, Hauser, O'Connor, & Bell, 2002). Similarly, parents who model hostile conflict behaviors in interactions with their adolescents put those adolescents at risk for problems in their own marriages years later.

The idea is that children grow up learning a style of conflict that they carry into interactions in their future relationships. For example, parents who model more verbal aggression (i.e., comments that attack the self-concept of a partner) end up having adult children who either perpetrate more intimate partner violence or are more likely to be the victim of violence (Palazzolo, Roberto, & Babin, 2010). There may be a normalization effect going on, such that children grow up feeling that verbal or physical aggression is a normal way to deal with or experience conflict.

In addition, the findings of a well-designed study by Whitton, Waldinger, Schulz, Allen, Crowell, & Hauser (2008) present one of the most compelling cases for the far-reaching effects of family conflict climates and parental modeling. In the first phase of Whitton et al.'s 17-year longitudinal study, parents and their adolescent children were asked to choose and discuss a difficult topic of conflict in their relationship. This private conversation was videotaped and later analyzed by researchers to assess the degree of positive and negative engagement behaviors. Seventeen years later, the researchers invited the same adolescents, who were now in their early 30s and married, back to the research laboratory along with their spouses. This time the married couples were videotaped while participating in a similar conflict resolution interaction. Those individuals who as adolescents had more hostile conversations with their parents had more negative engagement behaviors with their own spouses 17 years later. Similarly, positive conflict engagement behaviors between adolescents and parents predicted positive engagement behaviors with a spouse 17 years later. Having explored how family conflict patterns affect future adult relationships, the next section focuses more closely on the way we deal with conflict as adults in romantic relationships.

Discussion Questions

1. What are the pros and cons of the conflict approaches in Table 3.2?

2. Is it possible for any of these behaviors to result in either positive or negative outcomes depending on the situation? Or are some of these tactics predominantly positive or negative?

3. Think of examples of these behaviors that you have used or seen.

References

Abigail, R. A., & Cahn, D. D. (2011). *Managing conflict through communication* (4th ed.). Boston: Allyn and Bacon.

Allen, J. P., Hauser, S. T., O'Connor, T. G., & Bell, K. L. (2002). Prediction of peer-rated adult hostility from autonomy struggles in adolescent-family interactions. *Development and Psychopathology, 14,* 123–137. doi:10.1017/S0954579402001074

Ball, H., Wanzer, M. B., & Servoss, T. J. (2013). Parent-child communication on Facebook: Family communication patterns and young adults' decisions to "friend" parents. *Communication Quarterly, 61,* 615–629. doi:10.1080/01463 373.2013.822406

Bandura, A. (1977). *Social learning theory*. Upper Saddle River, NJ: Prentice Hall.

Bandura, A. (2001). Social cognitive theory: An agentive perspective. *Annual Review of Psychology, 52,* 1–26.

Baxter, L. A., Bylund, C. L., Imes, R. S., & Scheive, D. M. (2005). Family communication environments and rule-based social control of adolescents' healthy lifestyle choices. *The Journal of Family Communication, 5(3),* 209–227. doi:10.1207/s15327698jfc0503_3

Buckner, M. M., Ledbetter, A. M., & Bridge, M. C. (2013). Raised to dissent: Family-of-origin family communication patterns as predictors of organizational dissent. *Journal of Family Communication, 13,* 263–279. doi:10.1080/15267431.2013.823433

Canary, D. J., & Canary, H. E. (2015). Conflict in close relationships. In P. J. Schultz and P. Cobley (Series Eds.) & C. R. Berger (Vol. Ed.), *Handbooks of communication science: Vol. 6. Interpersonal communication* (pp. 177–200). Berlin: De Gruyter Mouton.

Canary, D. J., & Lakey, S. G. (2006). Managing conflict in a competent manner: A mindful look at events that matter. In J. G. Oetzel & S. Ting-Toomey (Eds.), *The sage handbook of conflict communication: Integrating theory, research, and practice* (pp. 185–210). Thousand Oaks, CA: Sage.

Fitzpatrick, M. A., & Ritchie, L. D. (1994). Communication schemata within the family: Multiple perspectives on family interaction. *Human Communication Research, 20,* 275–301. doi:10.1111/j.1468-2958.1994.tb00324.x

Flora, J., & Segrin, C. (2015). Family conflict and communication. In L. H. Turner & R. West (Eds.), *The sage handbook of family communication* (pp. 91–106). Thousand Oaks, CA: Sage.

Gottman, J. M. (1994). *What predicts divorce: The relationship between marital processes and marital outcomes*. Hillsdale, NJ: Lawrence Erlbaum Associates, Inc. Publishers.

Koerner, A. F., & Fitzpatrick, M. A. (2004). Communication in intact families. In A. L. Vangelisti (Ed.), *Handbook of family communication* (pp. 177–195). Mahwah, NJ: Lawrence Erlbaum Associates, Inc. Publishers.

Krokoff, L. J. (1991). Communication orientation as a moderator between strong negative affect and marital satisfaction. *Behavioral Assessment, 13,* 51–65.

Leggett, D. G., Roberts-Pittman, B., & Bycek, S. (2012). Cooperation, conflict, and marital satisfaction: Bridging theory, research, and practice. *Journal of Individual Psychology, 68,* 182–199.

McLeod, J. M., & Chaffee, S. H. (1972). The construction of social reality. In J. Tedeschi (Ed.), *The social influence process* (pp. 50–59). Chicago: Aldine-Atherton.

Orrego, V. O., & Rodriguez, J. (2001). Family communication patterns and college adjustment: The effects of communication and conflictual independence on college students. *Journal of Family Communication, 1,* 175–190.

Palazzolo, K. E., Roberto, A. J., & Babin, E. A. (2010). The relationship between parents' verbal aggression and young adult children's intimate partner violence victimization and perpetration. *Health Communication, 25,* 357–364. doi:10.1080/10410231003775180

Ritchie, D. L. (1991). Family communication patterns. *Communication Research, 18,* 548–565.

Sprey, J. (1999). Family dynamics: An essay on conflict and power. In M. B. Sussman, S. K. Steinmetz, & G. W. Peterson (Eds.), *Handbook of marriage and family* (pp. 667–686). New York: Plenum.

Taylor, M., & Segrin, C. (2010). Perceptions of parental gender roles and conflict styles and their association with young adults' relational and psychological well-being. *Communication Research Reports, 27,* 230–242. doi:10.1080/0882409 6.2010.496326

Ting-Toomey, S., & Takai, J. (2006). Explaining intercultural conflict: Promising approaches and future directions. In J. G. Oetzel & S. Ting-Toomey (Eds.), *The sage handbook of conflict communication: Integrating theory, research, and practice* (pp. 691–724). Thousand Oaks, CA: Sage.

Whitton, S. W., Waldinger, R. J., Schulz, M. S., Allen, J. P., Crowell, J. A., & Hauser, S. T. (2008). Prospective associations from family-of-origin interactions to adult marital interactions and relationship adjustment. *Journal of Family Psychology, 22,* 274–286. doi:10.1037/0893-3200.22.2.274

Wilmot, W., & Hocker, J. (2010). *Interpersonal conflict* (8th ed.). New York, NY: McGraw-Hill.

Conflict in Close Relationships

By Jeanne Flora

Objectives

- ▸ Identify destructive forms of conflict that are commonly used in close relationships such as demand withdrawal patterns and destructive expressions of anger and negativity.
- ▸ Explore the effects of interparental conflict on children's well-being.
- ▸ Explore the effects of marital conflict on partners' well-being.

As Flora and Segrin (2015) write: "How a couple handles their conflicts might be one of the best predictors of the eventual success of their relationship" (p. 103). In the last 30 years, researchers have made remarkable progress in specifying which conflict behaviors are especially corrosive for relational outcomes over time, as well as those conflict behaviors that are beneficial. This is important work for several reasons. To begin, it helps dispel the myth that all conflict is bad and instead shows that it is the *form* of conflict that matters most. To give couples themselves, as well as practitioners who counsel them, a better chance at improving their relationships, it is important to understand and recognize the difference between destructive and productive forms of conflict. Earlier in this unit we focused on positive conflict behaviors that help to maintain satisfying relationships. This current section is different in that it presents some of the most destructive forms of conflict in close relationships. I hope you read all sections of this unit closely. As I often say, there is more to a good relationship than merely the absence of negative behaviors. In other words, productive behaviors (e.g., support, positivity, and compromise) that are discussed in Section 1 are essential to the well-being of relationships. But because destructive conflict takes such a devastating toll, it is critical to understand the forms of conflict presented in this section—both so that you can do well on the exams in this class and, perhaps more importantly, so you can use this information toward the success of your own relationships.

THE FOUR HORSEMEN OF THE APOCALYPSE AND THE DEMAND-WITHDRAWAL PATTERN

FOUR HORSEMEN OF THE APOCALYPSE

four conflict behaviors, conceptualized as a behavioral cascade, whereby the first behavior triggers the next, making the process tough to reverse once set in motion.

CRITICISM

the first dysfunctional conflict behavior is criticism. Criticisms add an additional element of blaming or attacking the partner.

DEFENSIVENESS

people attempt to protect their character by avoiding blame and denying responsibility for any wrongdoing.

With colleagues at the University of Washington, John Gottman has spent most of his career studying the marital interaction patterns of thousands of couples. His techniques typically involve observing married couples interact in the laboratory and following up with longitudinal assessments to track changes in marital quality over time. During these observations, Gottman and colleagues identified a series of four destructive marital conflict behaviors that signal a high risk for eventual divorce (Gottman, 1993, 1994). These four behaviors, which he termed the **Four Horsemen of the Apocalypse**, are conceptualized as a behavioral cascade, whereby the first behavior triggers the next, making the process tough to reverse once set in motion.

The first dysfunctional conflict behavior is **criticism**. Although most people in marriages issue complaints from time to time, criticisms are different in that they add an additional element of blaming or attacking the partner. Complaints issue dissatisfaction about an issue, but they do not tend to trigger such a negative reaction from a partner. Indeed, it is fair and perhaps even productive to issue complaints from time to time. For example, a complaint might be stated as, "We have a lot of repairs to do around the house." However when complaints turn into criticisms, they become destructive. For example, the complaint stated earlier easily turns to a criticism when the statement continues, ". . . and you're always so lazy that you never do anything about it." Criticisms are often issued with language such as "you always" or "you never" to blame the partner for some character flaw (Gottman, 1999).

When people are criticized, they feel compelled to defend themselves. This leads to the next step in the behavioral cascade: **defensiveness**. In defensiveness, people attempt to protect their character by avoiding blame and denying responsibility for any wrongdoing. The spouse might say, "I am not lazy." When criticized, people feel they are under attack. This may be one reason why their defensive responses are often delivered with an element of whining, given they feel like the innocent victim

© Syda Productions/Shutterstock.com

(Gottman, 1994). For example, imagine again the "I am not lazy" defense delivered with a whining tone. One problem with defensiveness is that it is difficult to begin to resolve a conflict when one partner is determined not to admit any wrongdoing. Rather than leading to something productive like an apology or compromise, defensive responses may even be coupled with something called cross-complaining. In cross-complaining, the initial complaint/criticism is met with defensiveness and a counter complaint/criticism, such as: "I am not lazy . . . and if you weren't such a princess, you wouldn't expect everything to be perfect." Unfortunately, cross-complaining further draws attention away from the original issue, making it even more difficult to progress toward conflict resolution (Weger, 2001). Now both people are trying to address criticisms and defend themselves.

The third step in the dysfunctional behavioral cascade is **contempt**. Contempt can be any verbal or nonverbal expression that communicates the message that "you are stupid," "you are incompetent," "you just don't get it," or "I am better than you." Gottman and colleagues have observed couples express contempt in the form of hostile humor (e.g., laughing at what they perceive as their partner's stupidity), hostile mockery (e.g., mimicking a complaint or making fun of the partner), sarcasm, or even a nonverbal contempt expression that involves rolling one's eyes or pulling back one corner of the mouth (Gottman, 1994). Contempt is highly corrosive and difficult to recover from because it is such a degrading and seemingly enduring put-down. According to Segrin and Flora (2014), "by the time couples are expressing contempt in their conflicts, irrevocable damage is being done to the relationship" (p. 454).

When spouses stonewall, they shut down. They may pretend they did not even hear the message by exhibiting a blank facial expression or not even making eye contact. Verbally, they either have no response or a dismissive response, such as saying "whatever" as they walk away with no hope or interest in conflict resolution. Spouses have reached a point where they do not even want to acknowledge or listen to each other anymore. At least when spouses are fighting, they show that they still have some interest, passion, or concern in being involved in the relationship. **Stonewalling** indicates that spouses have given up, and this is why it is so predictive of divorce (Gottman, 1993).

The series of behaviors exhibited in the Four Horsemen of the Apocalypse are a more detailed representation of a commonly studied pattern of marital conflict called the **demand-withdrawal pattern** (Caughlin, 2002). In this pattern, one partner brings up a criticism or demand and the other partner withdraws. The demanding partner can come across as nagging or even hostile. When initial demands are ignored, people often elevate the hostility of the demands, in an approach to conflict initiation that Gottman terms "**harsh start-up**" (Gottman, Coan, Carrère, & Swanson, 1998). It becomes a frustrating cycle. On one hand it is easy to see why an ignored partner would try to elevate demands to get a response. However, it is also easy to see why partners would want to further withdraw from demands that are increasingly hostile. The interesting outcome of withdrawal from conflict is that it damages the marital satisfaction of both spouses (Segrin, Hanzal, & Domschke, 2009), not just the spouse being withdrawn from.

CONTEMPT

the third step in the dysfunctional behavioral cascade. Can be any verbal or nonverbal expression that communicates the message that "you are stupid," "you are incompetent," "you just don't get it," or "I am better than you."

STONEWALLING

contempt leads to the fourth and final stage in the cascade: stonewalling. When spouses stonewall, they shut down.

DEMAND-WITHDRAWAL PATTERN

in this pattern, one partner brings up a criticism or demand and the other partner withdraws.

HARSH START-UP

when initial demands are ignored, people often elevate the hostility of the demands, in an approach to conflict initiation that Gottman terms "harsh start-up."

As far as roles, it is an often held stereotype that women demand more (e.g., "the nagging wife") and men withdraw more (e.g., "the man who escapes to his cave"). However, men can be prone to demand and women to withdraw. When women are in the withdrawing role, it appears to be particularly taxing to marital satisfaction and husband's well-being (Siffert & Schwarz, 2010). In addition, people in same-sex relationships act out the demand-withdrawal pattern just as much as people in different-sex relationships, which challenges the stereotype that women are the nagging demanders (Holley, Sturm, & Levenson, 2010).

PERPETUAL PROBLEMS

conflicts that come up again and again, never getting resolved.

Marital interactions defined by frequent episodes of demand-withdrawal may be reflective of unresolved perpetual problems. **Perpetual problems** are conflicts that come up again and again, never getting resolved. Perpetual problems are often rooted in deep-seated disagreements about values, roles, or personality traits. Gottman and Silver (1999) liken perpetual problems to a chronic physical ailment like a "trick knee" or "bad back," because the same conflicts keep coming up again and again. If couples do not ever get to the root of these problems, then they will be constantly dealing with conflicts that stem from them. If these ongoing problems are dealt with using verbal hostility, threats, and aggression, as opposed to compromise, respect for differences, problem-solving, and support/affection, then there is little hope for conflict resolution or marital satisfaction (Caughlin, 2002; Papp, Kouros, & Cummings, 2009).

Anger, Negativity, and Emotional Flooding

Contrary to popular opinion, anger is not entirely a problematic emotion in conflict. On one hand the experience and expression of anger signals that partners are at least invested enough to fight or be involved, unlike spouses who have disengaged from the relationship and moved on emotionally. Further, for some couples, particularly those who tend to avoid conflict, occasional expressions of anger may improve or maintain the long-term health of a relationship (Krokoff, 1991). The idea is that constantly suppressing conflict can harm a marriage, not to mention harm a person's physical health. For example, spouses who constantly self-silence during conflict (i.e., keep their feelings to themselves) are at greater risk for mortality, as compared to spouses who are able to productively express grievances (Harburg, Kaciroti, Gleiberman, Julius, & Schork, 2008).

In many cases, however, the more anger and negativity that is evident in couples' interactions the more relational dissatisfaction they feel. This dissatisfaction is driven by the tendency for people to express anger destructively. Anger expressed with criticism, contempt, and pessimism rarely turns out well, and usually triggers more anger. A hallmark characteristic of dissatisfied couples is a back–and-forth of negative affect reciprocity, whereby one partner's negativity triggers the other person's subsequent negative response.

NEGATIVE AFFECTIVITY

neuroticism, which characterizes people who are more likely to experience hostility and anxiety.

Indeed, some people are more prone to expressing negativity than others. There is a personality trait social scientists term **negative affectivity**, or neuroticism, which characterizes people who are more likely to experience hostility and anxiety. People who are higher in the negativity affectivity trait are more likely to use conflict behaviors like yelling, criticizing, and snapping at the partner (Caughlin, Huston, & Houts, 2000). They are also more likely to perceive their own partners with a negative bias, seeing them as more hostile and less friendly. The behaviors and perceptions that stem from negative affectivity thwart couples' desires to try to engage in mutual problem-solving. As Woszidlo and Segrin (2013) describe, the more partners exhibit negative affectivity, the less mutual problem-solving they enact. Instead they give up trying to talk things out or feel that conversations about their problems never seem to get anywhere.

It probably comes as no surprise that higher levels of negative affectivity lead to lower marital satisfaction, because of the way conflict is handled (Hanzal & Segrin, 2009).

One unfortunate side effect that often stems from expressions of anger and negativity is emotional flooding. **Emotional flooding** refers to an overwhelming feeling of negative affect in response to a partner's behavior. People tend to get emotionally flooded when they feel they have been attacked or criticized by their partner. When people are overcome or "flooded" with negative emotion it remarkably affects their physical functioning, triggering a sudden increase in heart rate and a rush in the secretion of adrenaline. The physical response is often so overwhelming that it compromises people's ability to creatively problem-solve and listen well. As a result, people tend to engage in self-summarizing (i.e., repeating the same complaint over and over again with elevated negative affect), or they withdraw from the conversation because they are so overcome with emotion and do not see a way out (Gottman, 1994). Because the experience of emotional flooding is so aversive, marital quality tends to be low in relationships where at least one of the partners frequently experiences it (Gubbins, Perosa, & Bartle-Haring, 2010).

The material on destructive conflict communication behaviors in this section is important if people want to learn what specific behaviors to avoid. This includes demand-withdrawal patterns like the Four Horsemen of the Apocalypse, as well as destructive expressions of anger and negativity that lead to emotional flooding. Again, it is important to note that the information on productive conflict and relationship building behaviors in Section 2 are also important, so couples know what positive behaviors to adopt as an alternative. Segrin and Flora (2011) summarize the importance of both sides of the positivity/negativity coin this way: "It is easier to tolerate a lack of positivity in marriage than the presence of angry, hostile behaviors from a partner. But eventually those marriages that lack positive interactions between spouses are seen for what little they are worth and terminated" (p. 255).

EMOTIONAL FLOODING

refers to an overwhelming feeling of negative affect in response to a partner's behavior.

EFFECTS OF CONFLICT ON PHYSICAL AND MENTAL HEALTH

The final section explores the consequences of conflict on individuals' physical and mental health. Many people find it surprising that the way they communicate can affect their health and well-being, and even influence the health of those around them. In this section, we examine (1) the effects of interparental conflict on children's well-being and (2) the effects of marital conflict on partners' well-being.

Effects of Interparental Conflict on Child Well-Being

Exposure to severe interparental conflict can be detrimental to children's mental health. Several large-scale longitudinal studies have demonstrated these dramatic effects. For example Hayatbakhsh et al. (2013) followed 3,000 children from birth to age 21, examining the level of conflict in the family and mental health indicators over time. They found that children who were raised in a family with higher levels of conflict also had a greater propensity for experiencing problems like depression, anxiety, aggression, and delinquency. The general idea is that persistent exposure to hostile conflict increases children's feelings of self-blame, threat, negative affect, and hopelessness toward improving their situation (Goeke-Morey, Papp, & Cummings, 2013). These feelings are all implicated in the development of such mental health problems.

© Maximuz Foto/Shutterstock.com

TRIANGULATION

when children get
caught in or pulled
into interparental
conflict.

Arguably one of the most taxing family conflict processes for children's mental health is triangulation. Triangulation occurs when children get caught in or pulled into interparental conflict (Buehler & Welsh, 2009; Fosco & Grych, 2010). This puts the child in an unfair and unwinnable situation. Children find themselves confused by roles and feeling forced into acting as the go-between, the mediator, the informant, or the ally. They feel torn in their loyalties and frustrated because it is difficult to please both parents. Sensing one parent's anger or sadness, children may try to step in as a friend, but then feel that they are betraying the other parent. Some parents even disclose inappropriate information to their children or manipulatively try to twist opinions of the other parent in a negative way. During triangulation, children often hear their parents criticize and demean each other, and they struggle to make sense of the comments. The unfortunate consequence is that triangulation causes many children to feel guilty and blame themselves for their parents' problems. Indeed, some children become a scapegoat when their parents unfairly blame them for their own marital problems. It is not difficult to see why triangulation takes a toll on children's mental health. For example, children triangulated into parental conflict tend to deal with this stress by exhibiting more internalizing behaviors (e.g., problems focused inward like feelings of depression or anxiety) and externalizing behaviors (e.g., problems focused outward like aggression, hyperactivity, or delinquency) (Buehler, Franck, & Cook, 2009; Buehler & Welsh, 2009; Fosco & Grych, 2008).

People are often curious about the effects of divorce on children, and especially the effects on children's well-being. Many are surprised to find it is not divorce per se that is so detrimental to child well-being, but rather constant exposure to interparental conflict that is the culprit. Although the well-being of children overall tends to be slightly lower if they have experienced divorce, for some children, divorce actually lessens the exposure to conflict and triangulation (Amato & Afifi, 2006). In 1991, Amato and Keith collapsed results from numerous large-scale studies on the effects of divorce on children. They found that children from families whose parents were still together, but who exhibited high levels of destructive conflict, scored lower on several measures of child well-being, as compared to children whose parents had divorced, especially if the divorce did not expose them to a great deal of conflict. Amato and Keith's work has been important in identifying destructive conflict as the critical factor in discerning the effects of divorce on children's well-being.

Besides compromising children's mental health, interparental conflict can be detrimental to children's physical health. Even as early as the 1980s and 1990s, researchers began to notice that children who were raised in an environment of high family conflict reported more headaches and stomachaches (Mechanic & Hansell, 1989), more cardiovascular arousal in response to stress tests (Woodall & Matthews, 1989), more subsequent physical illnesses (Lundberg, 1993), and more hyperreactivity (Davies, Sturge-Apple, Cicchetti, & Cummings, 2007). More recently, researchers have explained these physiological effects by a process called allostasis or allostatic load. Allostasis occurs when the nervous system becomes permanently altered as a result of repeatedly or constantly functioning in a state of heightened responsiveness. When people are exposed to short-term stressors, it is functional for the sympathetic arousal system to be activated so that people can respond to a stressor immediately. However, children who are chronically exposed to a stressful environment of high conflict experience a wearing down of their nervous system, given the system is constantly working on high. Allostasis makes children susceptible to a weakened immune system and dysfunction in other physiological systems such as the cardiovascular or gastrointestinal system (Jones, Beach, & Jackson, 2004).

Effects of Marital Conflict on Adult Well-Being

The negative effects of destructive conflict and marital distress on adults' mental and physical health have also been well-documented. Beginning with a focus on mental health, researchers noticed several decades ago that about 50% of women who were in distressed marriages were also depressed (Beach, Jouriles, & O'Leary, 1985). To be sure, there are two sides to this coin. There is evidence that being depressed can lead to marital distress, but being in a distressing marriage can prompt one to become depressed (see Segrin & Flora, 2019). For example, in the demand/withdrawal pattern of conflict, the withdrawer often begins to self-silence, which has been found to promote depression (Whiffen, Foot, & Thompson, 2007).

As with depression, marital distress can lead to feelings of loneliness, an often overlooked mental health issue. Most people think of marriage as a social relationship that protects people from loneliness. When people marry, they typically expect their relationship will be emotionally intimate, supportive, and satisfying. When these expectations are violated, they begin to feel lonely. Indeed, loneliness can be defined as a discrepancy between a person's desired and achieved level of social interaction (Peplau, Russell, & Heim, 1979).

Gottman's (1994) Distance and Isolation model of divorce explains how over time, marital decline can lead to loneliness. The model acknowledges that the process toward divorce can be drawn out over years. It may begin with a period of time marked by severe conflicts that lead to emotional flooding. After so many of these overwhelmingly negative conflict interactions, partners begin to admit to themselves that their marital problems are severe. Feeling like it does no good to try to work things out together, they try to work things out individually and withdraw into separate lives, even though they are still living together. The last stage of the model is loneliness, when partners find themselves living in an empty marriage with no emotional fulfillment—a violation of what they thought marriage would be.

In addition to mental health, the physical health of adults in distressed relationships can be compromised. Partners in marriages with high levels of destructive

ALLOSTASIS
when the nervous system becomes permanently altered as a result of repeatedly or constantly functioning in a state of heightened responsiveness.

marital conflict, especially more negative, hostile, and controlling behaviors, secrete more stress hormones, experience poorer immune and cardiovascular functioning, and have an increased risk for mortality (Robles, Slatcher, Trombello, & McGinn, 2013). In one very striking example, Kiecolt-Glaser, Bane, Glaser, and Malarkey (2003) compared 90 couples in their first year of marriage by measuring their secretion of stress hormones while they discussed a conflict in the laboratory. Following up with the couples 10 years later, they found that the couples who divorced over the course of the study secreted on average 34% higher epinephrine levels (i.e., stress hormone levels) during the conflict discussion in year one. The researchers concluded that the higher level of stress hormones secreted during conflicts in year one predicted future divorce, even if the couples themselves did not foresee that outcome at the time.

Other research indicates the more demand-withdrawal conflict interactions exhibited by partners, the higher their cortisol levels—another indicator of stress (Heffner, Loving, Kiecolt-Glaser, Himawan, Glaser, & Malarkey, 2006). Persistently high stress hormones are problematic because they thwart the immune system (Kiecolt-Glaser, Malarkey, et al., 1993), making it more susceptible to illness, and promote inflammation, which can slow the body's healing process and lead to a variety of other health problems (Kiecolt-Glaser, Gouin, & Hantsoo, 2010). Of particular concern for middle-aged and older-age partners is the fact that high levels of negative conflict interactions increase the stress hormones that are implicated in greater cardiovascular reactivity (e.g., heart rate, blood pressure). The sum of the story is when marriages are supportive and positive, they protect people from some physical health problems; when marriages are distressing and negative they seem to promote certain physical health problems.

CONCLUSION

Destructive conflict takes a toll on people's mental and physical well-being, especially when exposure to that conflict is intensified in their most close relationships. Understanding the consequences of conflict may provide some motivation to learn how to deal with it better. This section aims to help you identify various approaches to conflict and to better understand specific forms of destructive conflict in close relationships. The effects of destructive conflict reach beyond ourselves, as exemplified by research on the effects of interparental conflict and family conflict climates on children. Applying the information learned in this section may help improve your own relationships and well-being, as well as the well-being of those around you. I always tell my own students that some of the people I admire the most in life are those who can recognize a pattern of negative communication they were exposed to in their family of origin and be the one to change that pattern for the positive. I hope this section starts some of you down that path, or at least provides some backing for you to continue the positive conflict behaviors you are already practicing.

Discussion Questions

1. Think of examples of these behaviors that you have used or seen.

2. Which conflict climate most often characterizes your family? Explain how.

3. What effects might these conflict climates have on children?

Amato, P. R., & Afifi, T. D. (2006). Feeling caught between parents: Adult children's relations with parents and subjective well-being. *Journal of Marriage and Family, 68,* 222–235. doi:10.1111/j.1741-3737.2006.00243.x

Amato, P. R., & Keith, B. (1991). Parental divorce and the well-being of children: A meta-analysis. *Psychological Bulletin, 110,* 26–46. doi:10.1037/0033-2909.110.1.26

Beach, S. R. H., Jouriles, E. N., & O'Leary, K. D. (1985). Extramarital sex: Impact on depression and commitment in couples seeking marital therapy. *Journal of Sex and Marital Therapy, 11,* 99–108. doi:10.1080/00926238508406075

Buehler, C., Franck, K. L., & Cook, E. C. (2009). Adolescents' triangulation in marital conflict and peer relations. *Journal of Research on Adolescence, 19,* 669–689. doi:10.1111/j.1532-7795.2009.00616.x

Buehler, C., & Welsh, D. P. (2009). A process model of adolescents' triangulation into parents' marital conflict: The role of emotional reactivity. *Journal of Family Psychology, 23,* 167–180. doi:10.1037/a0014976

Caughlin, J. P. (2002). The demand-withdrawal pattern of communication as a predictor of marital satisfaction over time: Unresolved issues and future directions. *Human Communication Research, 28,* 49–85. doi:10.1093/hcr/28.1.49

Caughlin, J. P., Huston, T. L., & Houts, R. M. (2000). How does personality matter in marriage? An examination of trait anxiety, interpersonal negativity, and marital satisfaction. *Journal of Personality and Social Psychology, 78,* 326–336. doi:10.1037/0022-3514.78.2.326

Davies, P. T., Sturge-Apple, M. L., Cicchetti, D., & Cummings, E. M. (2007). The role of child adrenocortical functioning in pathways between interparental conflict and child maladjustment. *Developmental Psychology, 43,* 918–930. doi:10.1037/0012-1649.43.4.918

Flora, J., & Segrin, C. (2015). Family conflict and communication. In L. H. Turner & R. West (Eds.), *The sage handbook of family communication* (pp. 91–106). Thousand Oaks, CA: Sage.

Fosco, G. M., & Grych, J. H. (2008). Emotional, cognitive, and family systems mediators of children's adjustment to interparental conflict. *Journal of Family Psychology, 22,* 843–854. doi:10.1037/a0013809

Fosco, G. M., & Grych, J. H. (2010). Adolescent triangulation into parental conflicts: Longitudinal implications for appraisals and adolescent-parents relations. *Journal of Marriage and Family, 72,* 254–266. doi:10.1111/j.1741-3737.2010.00697.x

Goeke-Morey, M. C., Papp, L. M., & Cummings, E. M. (2013). Changes in marital conflict and youths' responses across childhood and adolescence: A test of sensitization. *Developmental Psychopathology, 25,* 241–251. doi:10.1017/s0954579412000995

Gottman, J. M. (1993). A theory of marital dissolution and stability. *Journal of Family Psychology, 7,* 57–75. doi:10.1037/0893-3200.7.1.57

Gottman, J. M. (1994). *What predicts divorce: The relationship between marital processes and marital outcomes.* Hillsdale, NJ: Lawrence Erlbaum Associates, Inc. Publishers.

Gottman, J. M. (1999). *The marriage clinic: A scientifically based marital therapy.* New York: W.W. Norton.

Gottman, J. M., Coan, J., Carrère, S., & Swanson, C. (1998). Predicting marital happiness and stability from newlywed interactions. *Journal of Marriage and the Family, 60,* 5–22. doi:10.2307/353438

Gottman, J. M., & Silver, N. (1999). *The seven principles for making marriage work.* New York: Crown.

Gubbins, C. A., Perosa, L. M., & Bartle-Haring, S. (2010). Relationships between married couples' self-differentiation/ individuation and Gottman's model of marital interactions. *Contemporary Family Therapy, 32,* 383–395. doi:10.1007/s10591-010-9132-4

Hanzal, A., & Segrin, C. (2009). The role of conflict resolution styles in mediating the relationship between enduring vulnerabilities and marital quality. *Journal of Family Communication, 9,* 150–169.

Harburg, E., Kaciroti, N., Gleiberman, L., Julius, M., & Schork, M. A. (2008). Marital pair anger-coping types may act as an entity to affect mortality: Preliminary findings from a prospective study (Tecumseh, Michigan, 1971–1988). *Journal of Family Communication, 8,* 44–61. doi:10.1080/15267430701779485

Hayatbakhsh, R., Clavarino, A. M., Williams, G. M., Bor, W., O'Callaghan, M. J., & Najman, J. M. (2013). Family structure, marital discord and offspring's psychopathology in early adulthood: A prospective study. *European Child and Adolescent Psychiatry.* Advance online publication. doi:10.1007/s00787-013-0464-0

Heffner, K. L., Loving, T. J., Kiecolt-Glaser, J. K., Himawan, L. K., Glaser, R., & Malarkey, W. B. (2006). Older spouses' cortisol responses to marital conflict: Associations with demand-withdrawal communication patterns. *Journal of Behavioral Medicine, 29,* 317–325. doi:10.1007/s10865-006-9058-3

Holley, S. R., Sturm, V. E., & Levenson, R. W. (2010). Exploring the basis for gender differences in the demand-withdrawal pattern. *Journal of Homosexuality, 57,* 666–684. doi:10.1080/0091836100371214

Jones, D. J., Beach, S. R. H., & Jackson H. (2004). Family influences on health: A framework to organize research and guide intervention. In A.Vangelisti (Ed.), *Handbook of family communication* (pp. 647–672). Mahwah, NJ: Lawrence Erlbaum Associates, Inc. Publishers.

Kiecolt-Glaser, J. K., Bane, C., Glaser, R., & Malarkey, W. B. (2003). Love, marriage, and divorce: Newlyweds' stress hormones foreshadow relationship changes. *Journal of Consulting and Clinical Psychology, 71,* 176–188. doi:10.1037//0022-006x.71.1.176

Kiecolt-Glaser, J. K., Gouin, J. P., & Hantsoo, L. (2010). Close relationships, inflammation, and health. *Neuroscience and Biobehavioral Reviews, 35,* 33–38. doi:10.1016/j.neubiorev.2009.09.003

Kiecolt-Glaser, J., Malarkey, W. B., Chee, M. A., Newton, T., Cacioppo, J. T., Mao, H. Y., & Glaser, R. (1993). Negative behavior during marital conflict is associated with immunological down-regulation. *Psychosomatic Medicine, 55,* 395–409. doi:10.1097/00006842-1993090000-00001

Krokoff, L. J. (1991). Communication orientation as a moderator between strong negative affect and marital satisfaction. *Behavioral Assessment, 13,* 51–65.

Lundberg, O. (1993). The impact of childhood living conditions on illness and mortality in adulthood. *Social Science Medicine, 8,* 1047–1052. doi:10.1016/0277-9536(93)90122-k

Mechanic, D., & Hansell, S. (1989). Divorce, family conflict, and adolescents' well-being. *Journal of Health and Social Behavior, 30,* 105–116. doi:10.2307/2136913

Papp, L. M., Kouros, C. D., & Cummings, E. M. (2009). Demand-withdraw patterns in marital conflict in the home. *Personal Relationships, 16,* 285–300. doi:10.1111/j.1475-6811.2009.01223.x

Peplau, L. A., Russell, D., & Heim, M. (1979). The experience of loneliness. In I. H. Frieze, D. Bar-Tal, & J. S. Caroll (Eds.), *New approaches to social problems* (pp. 53–78). San Fransisco: Josey-Bass.

Robles, T. F., Slatcher, R. B., Trombello, J. M., & McGinn, M. M. (2013). Marital quality and health: A meta-analytic review. *Psychological Bulletin.* Advance online publication. doi:10.1037/a0031859

Segrin, C., & Flora, J. (2011). Family communication (2nd ed.). New York: Routledge.

Segrin, C., & Flora, J. (2014). Marriage. In P. J. Schultz and P. Cobley (Series Eds.) & C. R. Berger (Vol. Ed.), *Handbooks of communication science: Vol. 6. Interpersonal communication.* (pp. 443–466). Berlin: De Gruyter Mouton.

Segrin, C., Hanzal, A. D., & Domschke, T. J. (2009). Accuracy and bias in newlywed couples' perceptions of conflict styles and their associations with marital satisfaction. *Communication Monographs, 76,* 207–233. doi:10.1080/03637750902828404

Siffert, A., & Schwarz, B. (2010). Spouses' demand and withdrawal during marital conflict in relation to their subjective well-being. *Journal of Social and Personal Relationships, 28,* 262–277. doi:10.1177/0265407510382061

Weger, H. (2001). Pragma-dialectical theory and interpersonal interaction outcomes: Unproductive interpersonal behavior as violations of rules for critical discussion. *Argumentation, 15,* 313–330.

Whiffen, V., Foot, M., & Thompson, J. (2007). Self-silencing mediates the link between marital conflict and depression. *Journal of Social and Personal Relationships, 24,* 993–1006. doi:10.1177/0265407507084813

Woodall, K. L., & Matthews, K. A. (1989). Familial environment associated with type A behaviors and psychophysiological responses to stress in children. *Health Psychology, 8,* 403–426. doi:10.1037/0278-6133.8.4.403

Woszidlo, A., & Segrin, C. (2013). Negative affectivity and educational attainment as predictors of newlyweds' problem solving communication and marital quality. *The Journal of Psychology, 147,* 49–73. doi:10.1080/00223980.2012.6740 69

FOUR Unit

Organizational Communication in Action

Greg G. Armfield

Students often comment about struggling with the concept of organizational communication. The primary reason for this is that college students have very limited organizational experiences and those experiences they have had involve extremely limited interaction with an organization's culture. The typical college student will work a myriad of part-time jobs, many of which are not related to their future career choice. For example, my first paid job that was not for my father's business was washing dishes at a Chinese restaurant. My second job was making shakes and flipping burgers at a fast-food restaurant call Braum's. By the time I was a traditional college student I was working for a retail drug store. Not until I moved into a part-time management role at that drug store was I really engaged with the culture of the organization and understood many of the managerial responsibilities. The typical student that works as a waiter/waitress, stocks shelves, or works fast-food collects a check and is oblivious of the organization's culture. Furthermore, the typical part-time employee is not included in organizational decisions and typically only receives vertical downward communication while participating minimally in vertical upward communication unless they are asking questions or seeking clarification.

However, the reality is, unless you are literally a hermit you are affected by an organization every day of your life. Even if you are self-employed, work by yourself, or are unemployed, you interact with organizations. Did you wake up to an alarm this morning? That device was made by an organization. Did you take a shower? Brush your teeth? Drink a glass of water? The water you used was most likely supplied by your local municipality (an organization). The same goes for the electricity or gas that you used to heat your water. Did you eat? Unless you grow your own food, your meal was the product of a complex system of organizations working together to bring that meal to you. For these reasons, it is important to learn about organizational communication so you are better prepared to assimilate into organizational life.

Organizational Communication Networks

By Greg G. Armfield

TYPES OF ORGANIZATIONS

There are three common types of organizations. The most common is the for-profit organization. For-profit organizations are primarily concerned with making money or net profits. This includes private, employee owned, and publicly traded companies. The second type of organization is nonprofit. A nonprofit organization focuses on providing services or products without the goal of making money or turning a profit. The last type of organization is a not-for-profit organization. This type of organization can sell goods and services at higher rates than are needed for organizational stability (unlike a true nonprofit) without the desire to truly make a profit (unlike a for-profit). All funds that exceed organizational stability (salaries, supplies, property, etc.) in a not-for-profit organization are donated back to a true nonprofit organization (Richmond & McCroskey, 2009).

DEFINING AN ORGANIZATION

While there are numerous definitions of organizations, the following four provide a nice picture of how organizations function very much like an individual in society. First, **legally** an organization is viewed as an artificial person having entity status under the law. The organization, regardless of its size or status, holds the same rights, privileges, and obligations of a person. It is entitled to hold property, remains subject to search and seizure, is privileged to expand business and secure contracts, obligated to pay taxes and to comply with legal judgments and courts (Brummer, 1991). Second, **communicatively** an organization is a social context where symbols are exchanged to create social reality and shared meaning. Communication is a central process in the creation, maintenance, and extension of collective organizational meaning (Seeger, 1997). Third, **socially**, an organization is responsive and responsible to the public. Finally, organizations are **unique** in size and complexity and have a unique culture with its own norms, values, and symbols. All of these definitions simply show organizational communication is a process of creating, exchanging, interpreting (improperly or not), and storing messages inside a system of human relationships and interactions (Jablin, 1990). Note: the central piece of this definition is that communication or specific to this unit, organizational communication, is the process of exchanging symbols. Communication is a simple

LEGAL FUNCTION

an organization is an artificial person.

COMMUNICATIVE FUNCTION

an organization is a social context where symbols are exchanged to create social reality and shared meaning.

SOCIAL FUNCTION

an organization is responsive and responsible to the public.

UNIQUE

Organizations vary in size and complexity and have a unique culture with its own norms, values, and symbols.

AMBIGUITY

uncertainty.

way to describe an organization in the sense that organizations cannot exist without communication. Furthermore, communication is a central part of the organization's existence.

Conrad (1985) identified three instrumental functions that communication performs in organizations: ambiguity, command, and relational. The **ambiguity** management function illustrates that organizations are ripe with uncertainty. An example of the ambiguity that encompasses many organizations is the effect of the economy on public funding. Local school districts nationwide are forced to make budget cuts commonly thought to be based on inaccurate, at best, economic predictions. For example, the state of New Mexico in 2018 had over a billion dollars in surplus money after years of forced budget cuts; all from an unexpected increase in petroleum revenue. Communication is the means by which organizational members make sense and cope with the uncertainty and ambiguity inherit in organizations. Regardless of if that ambiguity is in the form of why budgets are being so deeply cut, or why a mistake could be made resulting in such a large surplus. Through gaining and sharing information, organizational members attempt to add structure, sense, and understand the organizational environment.

COMMAND FUNCTION

coordination and influential function of communication.

RELATIONAL FUNCTION

communication used to develop relationships within organizations.

The **command** function allows organizational members to "issue, receive, interpret, and act on commands" (Conrad, 1985, p. 7). A command in organizational communication typically comes in the form of downward communication via directions or information used to coordinate and influence the outcome of the many interdependent functions of organizational members.

Finally, organizational communication has a **relational function**. Conrad (1985) states organizational members use communication "to create and maintain productive business and personal relationships with other members of the organization" (pp. 7–8). Organizational relationships differ in the set of communication characteristics and challenges from interpersonal relationships (see Unit 3) in that both formal and informal relationships in an organization exist. In most work settings, formal relationships between organizational employees are identified by title and/or role in the organization. For example, department manager, management trainee, assistant manager, associate manager, store manager, divisional manager, regional manager, vice-president, regional or divisional vice-president, senior vice-president, executive vice-president, and so forth; in the academic setting you should be used to being taught by graduate students, instructors, assistant or associate professors, and full professors. However, the organizational structure still looks upward to department heads/chairs and deans. The importance of relational communication skills cannot be overstated.

A recent survey by the Public Forum Institutes listed interpersonal communication skills as the most important skill a job candidate should possess. Interpersonal communication skills were rated as more important than job specific or technical skills. The challenge of developing formal or informal relationships within organizations involves the rules set forth for appropriate communication channels with upward, downward, or horizontal communication networks. Adding to the confusion with organizational communication networks and how one is expected to communicate in an organization is the fact that many organizational communication rules are unwritten and dictated by the unique culture of the organization. Organizational culture will be addressed later in this unit.

COMMUNICATION NETWORKS

There are two major communication networks or patterns of communication that exist in organizations. The two types of networks are formal and informal.

Formal Communication Networks

Formal communication is a system designed by management to dictate who should talk to whom. In small businesses the formal communication network may go unnoticed. However, in larger organizations, formal communication networks can be sophisticated, and employees are expected to follow officially established channels. A common way to think about communication networks is to think of an organizational chart. If you visit the Department of Homeland Security at http://www.dhs.gov/xlibrary/assets/dhs-orgchart.pdf you can see a representation of the primary organizational structure of Homeland Security and follow a link to see a more extensive representation of each unit.

Formal communication consists of both vertical and horizontal communication. Vertical communication consists of upward and downward communication. Traditional upward communication is subordinate to superior and downward communication is traditionally superior to subordinate. Superiors expect upward communication to be timely, positive, and support current policy. Typical upward workplace communication includes project updates, suggestions, and work-related problems or issues. Typical downward workplace communication includes task-related directions, instructions, or tasks/assignments. For techniques to improve upward and downward communication see Table 4.1.

Table **4.1**

Techniques for improving upward communication:
▸ Informal discussions with one or a few employees
▸ Discussions between higher management and first-level supervisors
▸ Attitude surveys
▸ Outside consultants
▸ Suggestion systems/boxes
▸ Internal publications with complaint or question/answer columns

Techniques for improving downward communication:
▸ Small group meetings that value the exchange of information
▸ Company publications
▸ Supervisory meetings between managers and direct subordinates
▸ Mass meetings of employees
▸ Bulletin boards or posters
▸ Public address announcements
▸ Audiovisual presentations including webcasts or podcasts

Horizontal communication is communication among coworkers with different areas of responsibility or departments that are considered to be on the same hierarchical level within the organization. Horizontal communication is designed to coordinate efforts between employees, groups, or divisions. In doing this horizontal communication contributes to organizational efficiency and assists the organization run more efficiently. Goldhaber (2003) identified four functions of horizontal communication:

- ▸ Problem solving—"It typically takes 3 days for the paint shop to paint a car."
- ▸ Task coordination—"If I get the prep work done on the car can you have it painted in 24 hours?"

FORMAL COMMUNICATION

organizational communication that is work-related, regardless of direction (horizontal or vertical).

VERTICAL COMMUNICATION

upward and downward communication inside an organization.

HORIZONTAL COMMUNICATION

communication among subordinates inside an organization.

► Information sharing—"The new OSHA laws will require the business to change the way we paint cars. This will require the paint booth to be closed for 48 hours in order to comply with the new law."

► Conflict resolution—"I've heard that you complained to the owner about my prep work. I would appreciate it if you spoke to me if you're not happy with my work. Can we talk about this?"

Horizontal communication is far more important in an organization whose culture encourages participation.

Informal Communication Networks

INFORMAL COMMUNICATON

communication inside an organization that is not job- or task-oriented, regardless of direction (horizontal or vertical).

Informal communication within organizations is based on career interests, friendships, proximity, or shared personal aspirations (Adler & Elmhorst, 2008). For example, you may share mutual friendships with a coworker or you may attend the same church. Your children may attend the same school or play on the same athletic team. Coworkers may work out at the same gym or carpool. In short, informal communication revolves around a network of close interpersonal relationships that can develop within an organization or even exist prior to organizational workers joining the same organization. In fact, some interpersonal relationships in organizations develop into romantic relationships (Sias & Cahill, 1998).

Four of the most common types of informal communication work to confirm, contradict, expand, and circumvent formal communication (Adler & Elmhorst, 2008). An example of informal communication that confirms formal communication might look like this, "This time they really mean we can't use our e-mail for personal reasons" or "The Internet filters are really tight this time." Second, contradiction includes if your boss sets a deadline and you find out from a senior coworker, "The deadline is Friday, but first thing Monday morning is alright." Senior coworkers are also very useful for expanding on formal communication. For example, if your organization has a casual Friday policy you would want to find out if casual includes jeans or not.

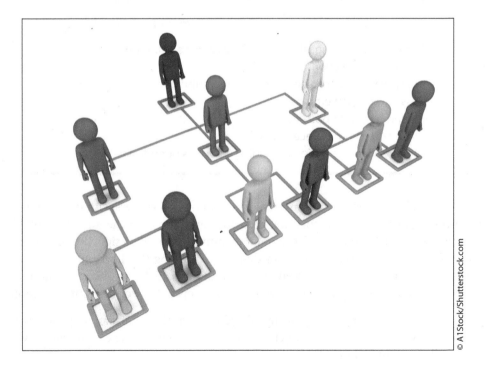

© A1Stock/Shutterstock.com

A coworker might tell you, "Khakis are fine, but no jeans." Finally, informal communication can work to circumvent formal policies or communication. For example, in my previous life I traveled for an organization and had to complete rather precise expense reports. Occasionally I would lose a receipt or other documentation. Since I was always pleasant to the person that approved all the expenses she would help me out if I just showed my credit card statement from the trip. Other examples of this include knowing the right people to expedite purchase orders, paperwork, or reports.

Another function of informal communication consists of what is traditionally called watercooler talk or the grapevine. This type of informal communication is transmitted quickly and works to supplement formal communication as well as the forms of informal information-seeking tactics discussed above. Historically, watercooler talk or information transmitted in this manner was believed to be more gossip than truth. However, studies have shown that information transmitted via the grapevine has proven to be quite accurate even though it contains a mix of business and personal messages (Caudron, 1998). Furthermore, organizations have recognized the grapevine is one aspect of informal communication that allows an organization to function more effectively. In fact, the grapevine has proven to be such an effective communication network, some organizations have tried to encourage informal communication networks by using a management strategy called management by wandering around. This strategy enables managers to engage in informal communication with a variety of employees that they would not regularly talk with. In doing so, management builds informal relationships with a variety of employees at differing levels in the organization. Clampitt (2005) explains, management by wandering around "helps managers learn about employee attitudes, environment, needs, and desires. This, then, helps managers develop an intuitive understanding of their employees' context of interpretation" (p. 38).

Successful organizations encourage informal communication among employees, and successful professionals tend to do the same. Informal communication networks do not operate solely inside the corporate walls. Most cities have professional networks

© wavebreakmedia/Shutterstock.com

that allow professionals and interns within organizations to network with other organizations. Networking is nothing new. Look at your personal network of family, friends, former and current classmates, coworkers, and even those you communicate with on social media. Further, consider the other organizations you are a member of: church, your high school, campus organizations, current and past employers, teachers, students, and even college alumni. The point is that you are already networked with a variety of personal and professional acquaintances. Cultivate those relationships and build on them as you begin to move into your professional life. Personal networks provide numerous benefits to you professionally and personally.

As you expand your personal network, keep in mind these commonly cited tips. First, everyone is a possible network connection, from the person sitting next to you on the airplane to the person standing by you in line at the bookstore, or even your waitress/waiter at the restaurant this weekend. Everyone is a potential contact. Professional and private relationships can be initiated anywhere. I have heard stories where business plans or relationships that led to multimillion-dollar deals or organizations began with a conversation in the airport bar or on an airplane.

Second, treat everyone with respect. How you interact with people that you might perceive as not being instrumental to your career is very telling of your character. Tony Kornheiser, of ESPN fame, would refer to this type of person as a "little." Be nice to the "littles." Quite a few years ago, I was interviewing for a job and I was sitting in the main office waiting for the next person I was scheduled to visit with. They were running a little late so I struck up a conversation with one of the administrative assistants. He was working on a professor's Blackberry (I told you it was a long time ago) that was not synching properly. We talked for a few minutes, then he said to me, "You know, it always amazes me that when candidates come through the interview process how few of them actually talk to one of us in the office." He continued, "last year one of the candidates was very rude to me, and I was really glad when they did not get hired." Detrimental behavior like arrogance can be damaging to a career. Again, every conversation provides a potential networking opportunity, not to mention that treating everyone you meet with respect is just good form.

Third, help others. Don't be a drain on a network by only seeking. I call this type of person a mosquito. All they do is suck blood, or information, from a network. They never pay it forward. Whenever possible, make an effort to assist others and put forth an effort to share information and see that others benefit from their contact with you. Having a reputation of being generous will serve you well in the future.

Fourth, get a mentor. Mentors can come in the form of formal mentors assigned by an organization, or informal mentors that you seek out on your own. Regardless of the formal or informal designation of your mentor, you should seek out multiple mentors for your professional life. A mentor will coach, council, and guide you through your professional life. Relationships with mentors are not a one-time lunch. It is an ongoing relationship. The golden rule of developing a relationship with a mentor is to respect his or her time. Most successful people are very willing to give back. You would be surprised how generous many professionals are with their time, but do not abuse this. If they suggest a reading, an activity, or a conference to attend, follow through with their advice. Also, consider the benefits of keeping a regular meeting time with your mentor.

Fifth, seek out secondary contacts or referrals. One of my most recent interactions with a friend in my network consisted of primarily gathering referrals. I was interested in seeking out information about a professional adventure and knew he had some contacts in that area. While attending a conference, I invited him to lunch and he provided valuable information and, most importantly, additional contacts that I was able to contact for informational interviews. He even bought lunch! So, you cannot beat that.

A final word on mentoring relationships is that these relationships should be kept professional. Do not expect a mentor to do special favors for you or your family. Mentors are there to help you professionally; they are not a therapist and should not be utilized for your personal issues. If you have serious personal issues you should find a professional counselor. The boundaries between your mentor and you should be clear and respected. Remember, any personal insights shared between the two of you should be kept confidential.

The best summary of formal and informal communication networks was presented by Krackhardt and Hanson (1993) who provided the following illustration, "If the formal organization is the skeleton of a company, the informal communication is the central nervous system" (p. 104). Much like the central nervous system, an organization's informal communication network is faster and typically more dependable than the formal communication network (Kanter, 1989).

STRATEGIC COMMUNICATION CHANNEL CHOICE

The task of internal organizational communication remains one of the top priorities of managers in all types of organizations. Dennis and Kinney (1998) reported that more than 50% of a manager's daily tasks involve Face-to-Face (FtF) communication, plus an additional 33% of their time is consumed with other oral and written communication. Given that managers spend over 80% of their time communicating, it is important to discuss proper channel choice with respect to communicating inside organizations.

The **media richness** model, or media richness theory, by Daft and Lengel (1986) is based on the organizational information processing theory by Galbraith (1977). This model of communication exchange focuses on understanding the communication activity and identifying uncertainty reduction techniques employed by organizations to manage ambiguity within a message (Fulk & Boyd, 1991). Accordingly, by understanding the richness and leanness of each communication channel, organizational

MEDIA RICHNESS

the ability to carry multiple cues. The richer a medium, the more cues that can be carried by a medium.

© JKstock/Shutterstock.com

members will be able to make better choices when coordinating activities through information processing. A lean medium is not able to communicate ambiguous information and is perceived as impersonal when compared to a richer medium such as FtF (Dennis & Kinney, 1998). Richness is defined as "the potential information-carrying capacity of data" (Daft & Lengel, 1984). Thus, if a person were able to increase the potential understanding of a message by delivering it with additional nonverbal cues (i.e., gestures, facial expressions, or proxemics) that message would be considered rich. In contrast, a message that has less understanding would be considered lean or low in richness (Daft & Lengel).

Daft, Lengel, and Trevino (1987) furthered the definition of richness to include four aspects to distinguish between rich and lean mediums: (1) Feedback—which allows for questioning. (2) Multiple cues—includes nonverbal actions such as facial expressions, proxemics, and gestures. (3) Language variety—referring to the range of meaning that symbolic language is able to convey. (4) Personal focus—the inclusion of personal feelings and emotions to customize a message. Trevino, Lengel, and Daft added three additional aspects that could influence the way managers select media. These include the ambiguity of the message, the symbolic cues conveyed by the medium itself, and the situational constraints on symbol processing.

The biggest concern with this line of research is that it focuses, overly so, on media usage and not media choice. Media richness scholars have focused on exploring what types of media would be most effective under what conditions. However, they tend not to discuss how managers could use different media more effectively to communicate within an organization. In fact, many of the media richness studies simply report what media or medium a manager uses, or prefers to use; not what medium would be best for each specific communication task.

Russ, Daft, and Lengel (1990) are one of the few researchers who have explored managerial choices and preferences when selecting a medium in relation to the equivocalness of the message. They found there is indeed a relationship between a manager's selection of media and the equivocality of the message. Managers were more likely to select a medium that is richer for messages that are equivocal and a leaner medium for messages that were unequivocal (Russ et al.). The reason media richness is important to future organizational employees is the increased reliance of managers on electronic communication and texting. While FtF communication is the richest, followed by the telephone (see Table 4.2), e-mail use in organizations continue to increase. Yet, due to the beneficial attributes of e-mail: interactivity, asynchronicity, and increasing reliability, this medium may have more appropriate uses when compared to other mediums.

 **4.2**

Media Richness Rankings

▸ Face-to-face, telephone, and written documents (Daft & Lengel, 1984 & 1986).

▸ Face-to-face, telephone, e-mail, and written documents (Trevino et al., 1987).

▸ Face-to-face, telephone, meetings, videos, hard copy text, and electronic mail (Rice, 1993).

▸ Face-to-face, e-mail, telephone, memos, and letters (Sullivan, 1995).

A final note on media choice and using communication networks in organizations consists of studying the culture of the organization and being conscious of individual choices. The culture of several organizations will dictate what and when certain channels will be appropriate for certain messages. For example, I have read stories that Microsoft is so e-mail intensive that some voicemail greetings state, "If you're from Microsoft, please send electronic mail." However, other organizations prefer voicemail. Media richness tells us that a voicemail is richer in quality and more personal because you can decipher tone of voice and fervor. There is a clear link between the culture of technological firms such as Microsoft or Apple and the preference for electronic communication.

In addition, many people have a personal preference. While some prefer the richer qualities of a voice message, others would prefer the perceived simplicity of an e-mail. Personally, I prefer e-mail to voicemail, and FtF when it is appropriate. I will never forget the boss that sent my performance evaluation over e-mail when we were in the same building, on the same floor, and less than 50 yards away from each other in our respective offices. I printed the report, walked down the hall to her office, and had a conversation about my evaluation! Some things need to be performed FtF when at all possible.

Discussion Questions

1. What are the differences between for-profit, nonprofit, and non-for-profit organizations?

2. Consider the type of information (or content) of information that is shared through formal and informal communication networks. How is this information similar or different?

3. Consider the type of information normally shared through the vertical and horizontal channels in an organization. How is this information similar or different?

4. The Media Richness model is quite dated. What, if any, forms of communication is it lacking, and how would those forms rank in perceived richness compared to traditional forms already ranked in Table 4.2?

Adler, R. B., & Elmhorst, J. M. (2008). *Communicating at work: Principles and practices for business and the professions* (9th ed). Boston: McGraw Hill.

Brummer, J. J. (1991). *Corporate responsibility and legitimacy: An interdisciplinary analysis.* New York: Greenwood.

Caudron, S. (1998). They hear it through the grapevine. *Workforce, 77,* 25–27.

Conrad, C. (1985). *Strategic organizational communication.* New York: Holt, Rinehart and Winston.

Clampitt, P. G. (2005). *Communicating for managerial effectiveness* (3rd ed.). Thousand Oaks, CA: Sage.

Daft, R., & Lengel, R. (1984). Information richness: A new approach to managerial information processing and organizational design. In B. Staw & L. Cummings (Eds.), *Research in organizational behaviors* (pp. 191–233). Greenwich, CT: JAI Press.

Daft, R. L., & Lengel, R. H. (1986). Organizational information requirements, media richness and structural design. *Management Science, 32,* 554–571.

Daft, R. L., Lengel, R. H., & Trevino, L. K. (1987). Message equivocality media selection, and manager performance: Implications for information systems. *MIS Quarterly, 11,* 355–366.

Dennis, A. R., & Kinney, S. T. (1998). Testing media richness theory in the new media: The effects of cues, feedback, and task equivocality. *Information Systems Research, 9,* 256–274.

Fulk, J., & Boyd, B. (1991). Emerging theories of communication in organizations. *Journal of Management, 17,* 407–446.

Galbraith, J. (1977). *Organizational Design.* Reading, MA: Addison-Wesley.

Jablin, F. M. (1990). Organizational communication. In G. W. C. G. L. Dahnke (Ed.), *Human communication: Theory and research* (pp. 156–182). Belmont, CA: Wadsworth.

Kanter, R. M. (1989). The new managerial work. *Harvard Business Review, 67,* 85–92.

Krackhardt, D., & Hanson, J. R. (1993). Informal networks: The company behind the chart. *Harvard Business Review, 71,* 104–111.

Richmond, V. P., & McCroskey, J. C. (2009). *Organizational Communication for Survival: Making Work, Work* (4th ed.). Boston: Pearson.

Rice, R. E. (1993). Media appropriateness: Using social presence theory to compare traditional and new organizational media. *Human Communication Research, 19,* 451–484.

Russ, G. S., Daft, R. L., & Lengel, R. H. (1990). Media selection and managerial characteristics in organizational communications. *Management Communication Quarterly, 4,* 151–175.

Seeger, M. W. (1997). *Ethics and organizational communication.* Gresskill, NJ: Hampton Press.

Sias, P. M., & Cahill, D. J. (1998). From coworkers to friends: The development of peer friendships in the workplace. *Western Journal of Communication, 62,* 273–299.

Sullivan, C. B. (1995). Preferences for electronic mail in organizational communication tasks. *The Journal of Business Communication, 32,* 49–64.

Trevino, L., Lengel, R., & Daft, R. (1987). Media symbolism, media richness, and media choices in organizations. *Communication Research, 14,* 553–574.

Organizational Socialization

By Greg G. Armfield

Objectives

- ▶ Analyze the stages of organizational socialization.
- ▶ Compare and contrast the five influences of Vocational Anticipatory Socialization.

When did you first consider what type of career you wanted? What age did you realize people had to work? What age did you seriously consider a career? You know a career that wasn't King, Queen, or superhero? Most kids at some point before preschool realize that many of the adults around them work. It is not like we sneak off and play all day. But, somewhere around later elementary school to middle school adolescents begin to strongly consider different fields and occupations. Even our teachers reinforce this process by assigning career days. I recall my youngest had a career day in kindergarten. As you can imagine the vast majority of his classmates wanted to be police officers, firefighters, doctors, veterinarians, but then there were a few that were a little more focused. So, what are the influencers and influences on adolescents as they make potential career decisions?

For the past quarter century scholars in the field of organizational communication, management, and sociology have actively studied three stages of organizational socialization: anticipatory socialization, organizational entry and assimilation, and organizational disengagement or exit. The two stages of anticipatory socialization are vocational anticipatory socialization (VAS) and organizational anticipatory socialization. Anticipatory socialization is the stage most college students find themselves as they search, explore, and choose a vocation or occupation. VAS explains the process of gathering vocational information, in an intentional and unintentional way, to inform your self-perception and make occupational choices. Jablin (1982, 2001) asserts you develop "a set of expectations and beliefs concerning how we people communicate in particular occupations and work settings" (p. 680) before they join an organization. After a review of VAS, the primary focus of this section, we will briefly discuss organizational anticipatory socialization.

ANTICIPATORY SOCIALIZATION

the conditioning process most children and adolescents get prior to entering an organization or career.

ANTICIPATORY SOCIALIZATION

Anticipatory socialization is the conditioning most children and adolescents get as a preparatory process prior to choosing an occupation or vocation and entering an organization or beginning one's career (Jablin, 2001). This process begins early in your childhood and consists of two parts: vocational anticipatory socialization and organizational anticipatory socialization.

Vocational Anticipatory Socialization. As you matured into adolescents and eventually a young adult you began making cognitive observations and gathering vocational and occupational information in order to compare that information against your own self-concept (Jablin, 2001). In doing so, you began weighing career alternatives and making conscious decisions as to your potential future career directions (Van Maanen, 1975). During this time Jablin and others have discovered five major influences on your vocational or occupational choice. These five influences (family, education, part-time jobs, peers, and mass media) begin long before you join an organization and begin to develop relationships inside an organization (Crites, 1969; Jablin, 1987). Each of the five individual influences of VAS has an important influence on the development of your sense of identity and individuality through social interaction with others (Signorelli, 1993). The following will review the five influences.

Family

Family members, specifically your primary caregivers, tend to serve as one of the most influential on your career choice. "Work and family socialization is a co-constructive process" as parents provide children with opportunities to learn and participate in task-oriented activities within the household setting (Larson, 1983; Medved, Brogan, McClanahan, Morris, & Shepherd, 2006, p. 164).

As early as 4 or 5 years of age, children understand how to respond to work requests and have learned to use justifications and excuses for refusing to perform a task (Dunn, 1988). Children begin gaining knowledge of tasks and work focused around communicating procedures, instructions, or following orders (Goodnow, Bowes, Dawes, & Taylor, 1988). Knowledge developed about work and household chore requests have helped children learn what tasks they should, or can, solicit help to perform and which tasks they should not ask for assistance as they can complete them individually (Goodnow & Warton, 1991). Communication with family members might revolve around the negative or positive aspects of work, such as accomplishments and successes, and these interactions help children shape their perceptions of work (Levine & Hoffner, 2006).

Goodnow (1988) looked at the communicative messages parents use when discussing and performing household chores and tasks. Findings from this and similar studies have shown that the messages used by family members, not just parents, work to value a child's performance of household work and chores (Goodnow & Warton, 1991; Myers, Jahn, Gailliard, & Stoltzfus, 2011). Unfortunately, these studies have focused on two-parent households and it should not be assumed that single-parent households function communicatively in the same fashion. One of the few studies examining single-parent households by Asmussen and Larson (1991) found single mothers are more focused in their interactions with children involving household chores. It has been argued that children raised primarily in single-parent families may hold more control in negotiating household rules as they have also been more involved in household tasks (Barber & Eccles, 1992).

© Monkey Business Images/Shutterstock.com

One of the more obvious communicative socialization processes observed is parents' discussions of their work and career in the household. Piotrkowski and Stark (1987) found a correlation between children's knowledge about their parents' work life and the frequency parents discuss their job and daily activities with their children. Parents would often discuss the day's events and other work news during dinnertime conversation. From these conversations, children learn communication-related work values. In addition, Jahn and Myers (2015) found STEM students who interacted with parents about STEM-related content shaped the child's perception about math and science content as well as STEM occupations in a positive way. Among those STEM students studied, parents and other family members were the most mentioned as having a significant influence on students' career options and aspirations (Myers et al., 2011).

Parents also play a primary role in determining what occupations their children choose. Lindholm, Astin, Sax, and Korn (2002), working with the Higher Education Research Institute's 2001–2002 national faculty survey report approximately one third of professors in higher education claim to have played a major role in persuading their children to pursue a career in academia. Similarly, Gibson and Papa (2000) explored parental influence on blue-collar workers who chose to follow in their fathers' footsteps into a blue-collar organization. Fathers were proud and boisterous about their "hard working" children who had chosen to work in the same blue-collar organization as their fathers (Gibson & Papa, 2000).

Educational Institutions

All educational institutions, including day care centers, have a directive to socialize young people into productive members of society (Brint, Contreras, & Matthews, 2001). From the ages of 6 to 18, children spend the majority of their waking hours in an educational system, and the educational system is typically the first structured social system a child encounters outside of home (Vondracek, Lerner, & Schulenberg, 1986). From the interactions around formalized education, adolescents learn communicative strategies, develop interpersonal relationships, manage those relationships, and communicate with others in a task setting. In addition to the structured rule-based system education provides, adolescents begin to develop tactics for communicating in interpersonal relationships and learn communicative skills for swaying interactions in their favor (Meyer & Driskill, 1997). In addition to interpersonal skills, Corsaro (1990) found schoolchildren become skilled at tactics to avoid work by leaving the scene, complaining about a personal problem, and pretending not to hear.

In college, your interactions with instructors and professors inside and outside of the classroom are predictive of your occupational knowledge. The more interactions you have with instructors, the more knowledge you develop about an occupation of interest and the types of organizations you could work (Taylor, 1985). The interaction with professors has been shown to be very influential for many college students. Cordes, Brown, and Olson (1991) found accounting students intent on becoming an accountant perceived more social cues, classroom task significance, and autonomy than students who had not chosen a career path or did not intend to become an accountant. In addition, Feij (1998) argued schooling and education were a significant influence for work socialization and career development. The educational system assists in the development of childhood and interpersonal communication and later on in life adolescents and young adults with an increased interest level for a given occupation or college coursework are far more likely to seek out and gain additional information from professors as well as recognize the significance of class activities and assignments.

Finally, educational institutions provide you with opportunities to participate in co-op work experiences (e.g., internships) to enrich the academic learning experience and further develop your expectations about organizational life. Moore (1986) found participation in educational activities allows you to develop and learn the "social procedures" and norms for socially acceptable organizational interactions. Co-op and internships have shown the potential for you to further develop and learn appropriate communication norms and interactions while participating in the organizational setting through experiential learning (Van Maanen & Barley, 1984).

Part-Time Jobs

The socialization value of part-time work experience is relatively mixed. Knowledge gained from part-time jobs is highly based on the relevance of the job. Experiencing paid work for the first time helps adolescents define themselves, develop their self-identity, and find their place in the work world (Vondracek & Porfeli, 2003). Further, work experience can provide valuable learning experiences that have led researchers to believe knowledge gained from the *correct* job experience and learning how to develop work relationships to be valuable (Greenberger, Steinberger, Vaux, & McAuliffe, 1980).

However, the experiences acquired through part-time job experience are, at best, undetermined. Research has shown many part-time jobs fail to socialize young adults into the organizational network (Greenberger et al., 1980). In turn, these employees fail to develop close communicative relationships with their coworkers. Further even if young adults develop relationships in part-time positions, research has shown those relationships are destined to have little impact on future career plans as only a limited number of part-time jobs obtained by students lead to full-time vocations after finishing school (Greenberger et al.; Steinberg, Greenberger, Vaux, & Ruggiero, 1981). One explanation is the demands of part-time jobs vary drastically depending on the quality of the position (Loughlin & Barling, 2001).

In contrast to the socialization expectations of part-time positions, research conducted on the influence of co-op experiences, such as high school students working on the school newspaper, have a positive influence on career decisions (Forrester, 1985); although these experiences can be framed under the influence of education. Much like students who take advantage of interactions with instructors or professors in college, co-op positions can provide positive experiences, not only creating a learning experience but providing an influence for a student's desired vocation. Stone, Stern, Hopkins, & McMillon (1990) found high school students whose jobs made use of their skills and provided them with opportunities to learn increased the students' motivation to do good work and decreased their cynicism about their job. However, the opposite experience was reported by some college students in Clair's (1996) exploration of the "real job" colloquialism. That said, internships, whether organized through an educational institution or not, can provide positive experiences and valuable learning opportunities for those involved.

Peers

Peers and significant others have also had a noteworthy impact on VAS. After-school activities and other organized voluntary groups and non-school-related activities provide numerous socialization opportunities for adolescents (Levine & Hoffner, 2006). Organizations such as Scouts and organized sports provide structured group opportunities and assist in developing decision-making, problem-solving, self-management of emotions, impression management, team spirit, team unity and spirit between peers, and other communication skills (Auster, 1985; Fine, 1987). Furthermore, athletic activities allow for relationship development between player and coach and peer/team communication (Larson & Verma, 1999). While the specific nature of the socialization effects on peers from team sports and extra-curricular school activities on children's and adolescents' expectations of communication at work and in certain occupations is somewhat unknown, research by Larson and Varma and Fine have led scholars the likes of Jablin (2001) to assert such a relationship may exist.

Studies between peers and their influence on occupational aspirations show a positive relationship. Teenagers spend a majority of their time with friends (Csikszantmihalyi & Larson, 1984). As a result, many of their discussions include their future educational and occupational plans (Blyth, Hill, & Theil, 1982; Montemayer & Van Komen, 1980). Peterson and Peters (1983) report peers advise each other and "function as significant others who confirm or disconfirm the desirability" (p. 81) of personal occupational choices. Furthermore, Tangri (1972) found peers are less likely to advise their friends to enter into traditionally sex-role stereotyped occupations and/or occupations not viewed as prestigious. While the research on both part-time jobs and peers is somewhat mixed, it is clear some positive influence for VAS exist. The last influence on VAS has been mass media. While the research on this area is yet to explore many of the digital influences, the research on traditional media influences is rich.

Mass Media

Jablin's (1987) concept of vocational anticipatory socialization gives considerable weight to role models from mass media outlets, specifically that of television given the time frame of the research. Mass media can provide information on a wide range of vocations through entertainment-based programming, news networks, and news shows. Early studies of children's media use (Noble, 1975; Wolfe & Fiske, 1949) confirm children learn from television exposure, assign meaning to those lessons on television, and attempt to connect them with their own experiences. Several scholars have explored the impact of television portrayals on that of children and adolescents' vocational choice.

Much of the research has reported on how television transmits an inaccurate image of both the communicative traits and communication practices in organizations as well as the inaccurate portrayal of occupations and individual behavior (see Hylmö, 2006). Furthermore, female characters have been underrepresented on television since its inception (Elasmar, Hasegawa, & Brain, 1999). Hylmö discovered that movies targeting girls tend to focus on glamorizing careers in the fashion, film, or music industries. This same pattern holds true for ethnic group representation and ethnic television characters portrayal rely heavily on stereotypes (Elasmar et al.; Greenberger et al., 1980). Television shows often present organizational talk as predominantly social focused on family and marriage issues, romantic relationships, and generic small talk as opposed to task-related (Katzman, 1972; Turow, 1974). Furthermore, organizational managers or superiors are regularly portrayed as incompetent or spending the bulk of their conversational time giving orders, advising others, and engaging in aggressive communication behaviors (Theberge, 1981).

Additionally, inaccuracies portrayed on television include the overrepresentation of prestigious occupational endeavors and occupations, white-collar occupations, and professional occupations all while less prestigious occupations are underrepresented (DeFleur & DeFleur, 1967; Theberge, 1981; Turow, 1980). Furthermore, Hylmö (2006) argued parents and girls' images in films tend to symbolize blue-collar jobs as temporary situations, while white-collar or artistic jobs are an ideal reality to aspire. In short, television inaccurately portrays organizational life as "a caricature of the actual world of work" (Peterson & Peters, 1983, p. 81).

In addition, Lichter, Lichter, and Rothman (1994) found many primetime television shows focus on superior-subordinate conflicts within an organization. Specifically, authority figures in the workplace are portrayed as mentally inferior to their subordinates, receive the brunt of ridicule, and tend to lose in authoritative conflicts. Additional findings indicate television represents workplace conversations focused on extraneous topics. Work issues are rarely discussed and if television characters do broach the topic of work, the conversation contains little content. Typical workplace discussions represented on television focus on family issues, marriage issues, romantic relationships, and generic small talk (Katzman, 1972; Turow, 1974). This inaccurate representation on television is of greater concern because the language we use, the education we receive, and the norms and values society teach and reinforce through mass media are all part of a socialization process through which we develop and embrace our sense of self.

In fact, King and Multon (1996) found one third of children surveyed select the same occupation for themselves as one of their favorite television characters. Children who aspire to occupations frequently portrayed on television are also heavy viewers of entertainment television (Wright et al., 1995). Wroblewski and Huston (1987) concluded that popular television shows are a significant influence on the occupational aspiration and attitudes about the legitimacy of occupations for children. Further supporting this assertion, O'Conner (1998) found medical and legal students report television characters had a positive influence on their career choices. More recently, popular television series like *Crime Scene Investigator* (*CSI*) and its offshoots (e.g., *CSI Miami, CSI Las Vegas*) have been linked to the increase in college students seeking criminal justice and forensic degrees ('CSI' sparks, 2003). However, *CSI* focuses on a glamourized perception of how each character does their job and excludes the tedious and ordinary aspects of the job (Houck, 2006). Another show, *Rescue 911*, inaccurately depicts a dispatcher's job as exciting and heroic. Real dispatchers pointed out they actually spend much of their time dealing with mundane problems and situations (Shuler & Sypher, 2000).

Outside of television messages, the depiction of sex roles is inaccurate or, at a minimum, incomplete. Many messages have been found to reinforce stereotypical sex-role occupations. For example, research analyzing children's literature found children's books contain occupational, racial, and sexual stereotypes (e.g., Ingersoll & Adams, 1992; Perse, 2001; Purcell & Stewart, 1990). Adya and Kaiser (2005) argued that not only print media but electronic media influences and enhances gender stereotypes that are typically focused on physical images instead of career choices. Unfortunately, these media stereotypes "do not appear to be random in nature" as they are "frequently patterned and presented in persuasive ways" (Jablin, 2001, p. 741). Unfortunately, these distorted images may well persist through early adulthood and continue until individuals enter into their chosen occupation.

Television, while entertaining, disseminates negative information about workplace communicative behaviors. Many of these messages contradict the messages parents, peers, and educational systems have invested years instilling into children. Even though television can be an important source of learning about work for adolescents, many media outlets present limited and distorted images of the work world (Hoffner et al., 2006). While television comedies often give the positive perspective of occupational aspirations (e.g., enjoyable, easy), dramas were often the source of a negative view (e.g., not enjoyable, difficult, stressful) (Hoffner, Levine, & Toohey, 2008). As a result, the entertainment value of mass media may serve to reinforce certain types of communication (Chesebro, 1991).

While little research has been focused on social media, with respect to shaping adolescents' vocational and occupational aspirations, Ellison, Wohn, and Greenhow (2014) have argued Facebook relationships and other forms of social media could expand the social capital of individuals impacting their life and career aspirations in a positive fashion. The language we use, the education we receive, and the norms and values society teach are all part of a socialization process through which we develop and embrace a sense of self.

Organizational Anticipatory Socialization. Once you have chosen a career, you will need to decide where you would like to work. While the option of self-employment is a consideration for some, the vast majority of us will work for an organization or institution. As a job seeker you will receive information about potential employment from organizational resources, recruitment materials, job advertisements, and interpersonal communication. Typical organization resources include the job announcement, company websites, annual reports, and the interview process (Jablin, 2001). Typical recruiting materials job seekers consume are job advertisements and job fairs (especially college students going to job fairs held on university campuses). Job advertisements can be found on the organization's webpage as well as through professional organizations and popular web pages (think hotjobs, indeed, etc.).

A second major source of employment and job information is from the interview itself. Past research has questioned the accuracy of job information received by interviewees through interpersonal communication (see Jablin, 1984; Wanous, 1992). In response to these findings, the early 1980s saw several academics calling for realistic job previews (RJPs). Jablin (2001) argues that with over 40 studies proposing reasons why RJPs should work, RJPs should reduce organizational turnover and improve recruits' attitudes. The results of RJPs were rather inconsistent based on Jablin's review of the RJP literature. While intuitively, one would think employers would provide accurate information to potential employees and should be ethical in their information-giving, many employers are more interested in filling a spot as opposed to finding the right person for a job.

A final area of research you should consider during the job search process is person-job (P-J) fit and person-organization (P-O) fit. P-J considers if the person applying for the job has the proper skills, knowledge, and ability to perform the job the organization is filling. P-O considers a more organizational cultural approach (see Section 3 of this unit) regarding if the person interviewing for this position fits the organization. Both P-J and P-O are from the viewpoint of the organization. That said, you as job seeker should spend some time considering is the job that I'm applying for one that I really want to do, and secondly is this an organization that I like and will be happy working for? Once you begin to consider if the job and organization is a good fit for you personally, you have formally entered the pre-entry stage of organizational assimilation.

Here are some of the questions you should consider asking yourself:

- ▶ If you are offered the position, is this an organization that you would like to work for?
- ▶ If you are offered the position, is this a job that you would like to have?
- ▶ Do you like your potential coworkers?
- ▶ Do you like your potential new boss?

ORGANIZATIONAL ENTRY AND ASSIMILATION

The organizational assimilation process begins at the point you enter and start to begin to integrate into the culture of the organization that you accepted a position. Assimilation is the "ongoing behavioral and cognitive processes by which individuals join, become integrated into, and eventually exit an organization" (Jablin & Krone, 1987). In the entry phase the new employee is learning and negotiating their new role in the organization. This entry process is marked by two somewhat competing forces occurring simultaneously. First, you, the new employee, want to individualize your role in the organization and your work environment. Second, the organization is attempting to socialize you, the new employee, into the standardized work procedures of the position that you were hired to execute. These two forces have typically been studied under the pretense of the organizational efforts to influence the actions of the employee (**role-taking**) and the attempts of the new employee to influence or individualize their role and work environment (**role-making**) (Jablin & Krone).

In the entry phase it is not uncommon for newcomers to be surprised at the lack of feedback from upper management and quite often the lack of communication from and at the higher levels of the organization. Further, new employees are very likely to experience higher levels of uncertainty revolving around unclear job requirements, lacking of formalized training, the new organizational culture, and from written and

unwritten organizational rules. For this reason, organizational newcomers have been found to utilize a number of information seeking tactics as identified by Miller and Jablin (1991). The seven most common information seeking tactics utilized by newcomers to obtain information about the organization as well as individualized job performance feedback is:

1. Overt questions: used when the information seeker is comfortable soliciting information and will involve direct informational targets to gain insight about the uncertainty.
2. Indirect questions: used if the information seeker is uncomfortable seeking information from the given source about the uncertainty.
3. Third party tactic: substitutes a third party as a primary source of information. This is typically used when the information seeker is uncomfortable going directly to the primary source and another individual is used to gain information about the uncertainty.
4. Testing limits: refers to the creation of situations that the target of the information must respond to. In doing so, the information seeker attempts to gain insight about specific behaviors, attitudes, or issues.
5. Disguising conversations: a direct attempt to mask information seeking by the information seeker. Individuals may attempt this in order to be perceived as nonchalant to the information target. This can be accomplished through humor or use of subtle requests.
6. Observing: typically used in salient situations when the information seeker desires to learn while maintaining some unobtrusiveness.
7. Surveillance: is an inconspicuous approach used to monitor organizational functions (Miller & Jablin, 1991; see also Kramer, 2004).

In order to interpret organizational life in the new organization you, the newcomer, can rely on predispositions, past experience, and the interpretations of others. Thus, the organizational encounter phase encompasses both learning about the organization and your role in the organization.

As you continue on the assimilation journey, three phases of influence occur between you, the new employee, and the organization. Consider this process a give-and-take as both entities (you and others in the organization) interact and get to know each other.

Role-Development is the process a new employee goes through as they learn the communication norms or interaction with coworkers, and as they define and develop their organizational roles (Major, Kozlowski, Chao, & Gardner, 1995). Leader Member Exchange (LMX) theory divides role development into three interrelated phases. First, **role-taking**. During role-taking the organization will request a variety of activities of the new member or employee. By observing how the new employee responds to these requests, organizational leadership will evaluate the talents, skills, and motivation of the new employee. Second, **role-making**. During role-making the new employee should begin to *take ownership* of their role in the organization and seek to modify the nature of their role and manner their job is performed. In doing so, the new employee can offer new skills, more effort and time in the role-making process. In addition, the organization can offer formal rewards as well as informal resources such as information, support, and attention to the employee. By exchanging these resources and rewards, organizational leadership and the employee work together to develop and modify the new employee's organizational role. Third, **role-routinization**. Role-routinization is the point when the role of the new employee and the expected behaviors of the new employee and organizational leadership is understood and agreed upon by the employee and organizational leadership. While all developmental processes are unique during assimilation, the role-routinization point is marked by the employees' successful transition from organizational or group outsider to insider. It is important to note, however, that each development process is unique and there is no set time period for this process. However, many employees and organizations have an expectation that role-routinization be met within 60 to 90 days of hire.

METAMORPHOSIS

At this point you, the employee, is no longer a newcomer. At the metamorphosis stage you have successfully transitioned into a group or organizational insider. This is not to suggest, however, that the relationship between you, the individual, and the organization is static as there is always some measure of flux and uncertainty in the employee's understanding of organizational roles and culture. Additionally, employees who transfer between work groups, division, or are promoted within the organization will be forced to cope with new job requirements, new social relationships, perhaps a new location. Kramer (2010) argues that these transitions within the organization would cause the employee, regardless of tenure in the organization, to reenter the organizational entry phases on some level and work back toward metamorphosis.

ORGANIZATIONAL DISENGAGEMENT OR EXIT

Much like organization entry, organizational exit is a process, not an event. Exit has a lasting impression and influences both those who leave an organization, or location, and those who are left behind. As with all other socialization processes communication plays a critical role in the disengagement process. Three primary areas have been studied; first preannouncement, second announcement and actual exit, and third post exit (Jablin, 2001). Regardless of your job or position in an organization, you will exit a job and/or organization in one of the following ways: retirement, resignation, firing, layoff, or transfer/promotion.

© Andrey_Popov/Shutterstock.com

In the case of retirement, resignation, and or transfer/promotion the process is typically marked by a preannouncement phase where some employees may share confidentially with coworkers their plans, but the majority of research has focused on private interpersonal and intrapersonal communication. Once the employee announces their intent to exit, the interaction with coworkers begins. Of primary concern is how and if a relationship will be maintained at the time of exit. Regardless of the reason for separation, exit is primarily about relationship maintenance and the desire to maintain any relationship with the parting employee. This is the case regardless of reason for organizational exit.

CONCLUSION

The goal of this section was to review the socialization process from the view of a new employee seeking, choosing, and assimilating into a new career. The content of socialization is clearly and obviously communication centered and focused. Socialization models help us understand the process of organizational socialization and how new employees move from vocational and organizational choice, to organizational entry, into metamorphosis, and eventually disengagement. Embedded in the concept of organizational socialization is the idea of a variety of ongoing and continuous communication processes through which socialization occurs using a variety of communication channels.

Discussion Questions

1. Which of the five VAS influences have had the most influence on your vocational or occupational choice?

2. Are there other influencers or influences that impacted your career or vocational choice?

3. How long do you believe it takes to reach the metamorphosis stage after entering a new organization?

4. For past positions that you have left, how did you maintain your relationships with former coworkers or bosses?

Adya, M., & Kaiser, K. M. (2005). Early determinants of women in the IT workforce: A model of girls' career choices. *Information Technology & People, 18*(3), 230–259.

Asmussen, L., & Larson, R. (1991). The quality of family time among young adolescents in single-parent and married-parent families. *Journal of Marriage and the Family, 53*(4), 1021–1030. doi:10.2307/353005

Auster, C. J. (1985). Manual for socialization: Examples from Girl Scout handbook 1913–1984. *Qualitative Sociology, 8*(4), 359–367. doi:10.1007/bf00988845

Barber, B. L., & Eccles, J. S. (1992). Long-term influence of divorce and single parenting on adolescent family- and work-related values, behaviors, and aspiration. *Psychological Bulletin, 111*(1), 108–126. doi:10.1037/0033-2909.111.1.108

Blyth, D. A., Hill, J. P., & Theil, K. S. (1982). Early adolescents' significant others: Grade and gender differences in perceived relationships with familial and non familial adults and young people. *Journal of Youth and Adolescence, 11*(6), 425–450. doi:10.1007/BF01538805

Brint, S., Contreras, M. F., & Matthews, M. T. (2001). Socialization messages in primary schools: An organizational analysis. *Sociology of Education, 74*(3), 157–180.

Chesebro, J. W. (1991). Communication, values, and popular television series—A seventeen-year assessment. *Communication Quarterly, 39*(3), 197–225. doi:10.1080/01463379109369799

Clair, R. P. (1996). The political nature of the colloquialism, "a real job": Implications for organizational socialization. *Communications Monographs, 63*(3), 249–267. doi:10.1080/03637759609376392

Cordes, C., Brown, J., & Olson, D. E. (1991). The role of social information processing in the career selection process. *Akron Business and Economic Review, 22*(3), 7–19.

Corsaro, W. A. (1990). The underlife of the nursery school: Young children's social representatives of adult rules. In G. Duveen & B. Lloyd (Eds.), *Social representatives and the development of knowledge* (pp. 11–26). Cambridge, UK: Cambridge University Press. doi:10.1017/cbo9780511659874.002

Crites, J. O. (1969). *Vocational psychology: The study of vocational behavior and development.* New York: McGraw-Hill.

'CSI' sparks interest on campus. (2003, August 18). Retrieved from http://www.msnbc.com/news/954104.asp#BODY

Csikszantmihalyi, M., & Larson, R. (1984). *Being adolescent: Conflict and growth in the teenage years.* New York: Basic Books.

DeFleur, M. L., & DeFleur, L. B. (1967). The relative contribution of television as a learning source for children's occupational knowledge. *American Sociological Review, 32*(5), 777–789. doi:10.2307/2092025

Dunn, J. (1988). *The beginnings of social understanding.* Harvard University Press. doi:10.4159/harvard.9780674330610

Elasmar, M., Hasegawa, K., & Brain, M. (1999). The portrayal of women in US prime time television. *Journal of Broadcasting & Electronic Media, 43*(1), 20–34. doi:10.1080/08838159909364472

Ellison, N. B., Wohn, D. Y., & Greenhow, C. M. (2014). Adolescents' visions of their future careers, educational plans, and life pathways: The role of bridging and bonding social capital experiences. *Journal of Social and Personal Relationships, 31*(4), 516–534. doi:10.1177/0265407514523546

Feij, J. A. (1998). Work socialization of young people. In P. J. D. Drenth, H. Thierry, & C. J. deWolf (Eds.), *Handbook of work and organizational psychology* (Vol. 3, pp. 207–256). Hove, England: Psychology Press/Lawrence Erlbaum Associates, Inc. Publishers.

Fine, G. A. (1987). *With the boys: Little league baseball and preadolescent culture.* Chicago: University of Chicago Press.

Forrester, M. A. (1985). High school journalism influences professionals. *Communication: Journalism Education Today, 19*, 12–14.

Gibson, M. K., & Papa, M. J. (2000). The mud, the blood, and the beer guys: Organizational osmosis in blue-collar work groups. *Journal of Applied Communication Research, 28*(1), 68–88. doi:10.1080/00909880009365554

Goodnow, J. J. (1988). Children's household work: Its nature and functions. *Psychological Bulletin, 103*(1), 5–26. doi:10.1037//0033-2909.103.1.5

Goodnow, J. J., Bowes, J., Dawes, L., & Taylor, A. (1988). Would you ask someone else to do this job? The effects of generation, gender and task on household work requests. *Unpublished manuscript, Macquarie University.*

Goodnow, J. J., & Warton, P. M. (1991). The social bases of social cognition: Interactions about work and their implications. *Merrill-Palmer Quarterly, 37*(1), 27–58.

Greenberger, B. S., Steinberger, L. D., Vaux, A., & McAuliffe, S. (1980). Adolescents who work: Effects of part-time employment on family and peer relations. *Journal of Youth and Adolescence, 9*(3), 189–202. doi:10.1007/bf02088464

Hoffner, C. A., Levine, K. J., Sullivan, Q. E., Crowell, D., Pedrick, L., & Berndt, P. (2006). TV characters at work: Television's role in the occupational aspirations of economically disadvantaged youths. *Journal of Career Development, 33*(1), 3–18.

Hoffner, C. A., Levine, K. J., & Toohey, R. A. (2008). Socialization to work in late adolescence: The role of television and family. *Journal of Broadcasting & Electronic Media, 52*(2), 282–302. doi:10.1080/08838150801992086

Houck, M. M. (2006). CSI: Reality. *Scientific American, 295*(1), 84–89.

Hylmö, A. (2006). Girls on film: An examination of gendered vocational socialization messages found in motion pictures targeting teenage girls. *Western Journal of Communication, 70*(3), 167–185.

Ingersoll, V. H., & Adams, G. B. (1992). The child is "father" to the manager: Images of organizations in U.S. children's literature. *Organizational Studies, 13*(4), 497–519. doi:10.1177/017084069201300401

Jablin, F. M. (1982). Organizational communication: An assimilation approach. In M. E. Roloff & C. R. Berger (Eds.), *Social cognition and communication* (pp. 255–286). Beverly Hills, CA: Sage.

Jablin, F. M. (1984). Assimilating new members into organizations. In R. N Bostrom (Ed.), *Communication Yearbook 8.* Beverly Hills, CA: Sage.

Jablin, F. M. (1987). Organizational entry, assimilation, and exit. In F. M. Jablin, L. L. Putnam, K. H. Roberts & L. W. Porter (Eds.), *Handbook of organizational communication: An interdisciplinary perspective* (pp. 679–740). Newbury Park: Sage.

Jablin, F. M. (2001). Organizational entry, assimilation, and disengagement/exit. In F. M. Jablin & L. L. Putnam (Eds.), *The new handbook of organizational communication: Advances in theory, research, and methods* (pp. 732–818). Thousand Oaks, CA: Sage. doi:10.4135/9781412986243.n19

Jablin, F. M., & Krone, K. J. (1987). Organizational assimilation. In C. R. Berger & S. H. Chaffee (Eds.), *Handbook of communication science* (pp. 711–746). Newbury Park, CA: Sage.

Jahn, J. L. S., & Myers, K. K (2015). "When will I use this?" How math and science classes communicate impression of STEM career: Implications for vocational anticipatory socialization. *Communication Studies, 66*(2), 218–237. doi:10.1080/10510974.2014.990047

Katzman, N. (1972). Television soap operas: What's been going on anyway? *Public Opinion Quarterly, 36*(2), 200–212. doi:10.1086/267992

King, M. M., & Multon, K. D. (1996). The effects of television role models on the career aspirations of African American junior high school students. *Journal of Career Development, 23*(2), 111–125. doi:10.1007/bf02359291

Kramer, M. W. (2004). *Managing uncertainty in organizational communication.* Mahwah, NJ: Lawrence Erlbaum Associates, Inc. Publishers. doi:10.4324/9781410609854

Kramer, M. (2010). *Organizational socialization: Joining and leaving organizations.* Cambridge, UK: Polity.

Larson, R. W. (1983). Adolescents' daily experience with family and friends: contrasting opportunity systems. *Journal of Marriage and the Family, 45*(4), 739–750. doi:10.2307/351787

Larson. R. W., & Verma, S. (1999). How children and adolescents spend time across the world: Work, play and developmental opportunities. *Psychological Bulletin, 125*(6), 701–736. doi:10.1037//0033-2909.125.6.701

Levine, K. J., & Hoffner, C. A. (2006). Adolescents' conceptions of work: What is learned from different sources during anticipatory socialization? *Journal of Adolescent Research, 21*(6), 647–669. doi:10.1177/0743558406293963

Lichter, S. R., Lichter, L. S., & Rothman, S. (1994). *Prime time: How TV portrays American culture.* Washington DC: Regnery.

Lindholm, J. A., Astin, A. W., Sax, L. J., & Korn, W. S. (2002). *The American college teacher. National norms for the 2001-2002 HERI faculty survey.* Los Angeles: Higher Education Research Institute, University of California.

Loughlin, C., & Barling, J. (2001). Young workers' work values, attitudes, and behaviours. *Journal of Occupational and Organizational Psychology, 74*(4), 543–558.

Major, D. A., Kozlowski, S. W. J., Chao, G. T., & Gardner, P. D. (1995). A longitudinal investigation of newcomers' expectations, early socialization outcomes, and the moderating effects of role development factors. *Journal of Applied Psychology, 80*, 418–431.

Medved, C. E., Brogan, S. M., McClanahan, A. M., Morris, J. F., & Shepherd, G. J. (2006). Family and work socializing communication: Messages, gender, and ideological implications. *The Journal of Family Communication, 6*(3), 161–180. doi:10.1207/s15327698jfc0603_1

Meyer, J., & Driskill, G. (1997). Children and relationship development: Communication strategies in a day care center. *Communication Reports, 10*(1), 76–85. doi:10.1080/08934219709367661

Miller, V. D., & Jablin, F. M. (1991). Information seeking during organizational entry: Influences, tactics, and a model of the process. *Academy of Management Review, 16*, 92–120. doi: 10.2307/258608

Montemayer, R., & Van Komen, R. (1980). Age segregation of adolescents in and out of school. *Journal of Youth and Adolescence, 9*(5), 371–381. doi:10.1007/bf02087675

Moore, D. T. (1986). Knowledge at work: An approach to learning by interns. In K. M. Borman & J. Reisman (Eds.), *Becoming a worker* (pp. 116–139). Norwood, NJ: Ablex.

Myers, K. K., Jahn, J. L. S., Gailliard, B. M., & Stoltzfus, K. (2011). Vocational Anticipatory Socialization (VAS): A Communicative Model of Adolescents' Interests in STEM. *Management Communication Quarterly, 25*(1), 87–120. doi:10.1177/0893318910377068

Noble, G. (1975). *Children in front of the small screen.* London: Constable.

O'Conner, M. M. (1998). The role of the television drama ER in medical student life; Entertainment or socialization? *Journal of the American Medical Association, 280*(9), 854–855. doi:10.1001/jama.280.9.854

Perse, E. M. (2001). *Media effects and society.* Mahwah, NJ: Lawrence Erlbaum Associates, Inc. Publishers. doi:10.4324/9781410600820

Peterson, G. W., & Peters, D. F. (1983). Adolescents' construction of social reality: The impact of television and peers. *Youth & Society, 15*(1), 67–85. doi:10.1177/0044118x83015001005

Piotrkowski, C. S., & Stark, E. (1987). Children and adolescents look at their parents' jobs. In J. H. Lewko (Ed.), *How children and adolescents view the world of work* (pp. 3–20). San Francisco: Jossey-Bass.

Purcell, P., & Stewart, L. (1990). Dick and Jane in 1989. *Sex Roles, 22*, 177–185.

Shuler, S., & Sypher, B. D. (2000). Seeking emotional labor: When managing the heart enhances the work experience. *Management Communication Quarterly, 14*(1), 50–89. doi:10.1177/0893318900141003

Signorelli, N. (1993). Television and adolescents' perceptions about work. *Youth & Society, 24*(3), 314–341. doi:10.1177/0044118x93024003004

Steinberg, L. D., Greenberger, E., Vaux, A., & Ruggiero, M. (1981). Early work experience for students in high school and college. *Youth & Society, 12*, 403–422.

Stone, J., Stern, D., Hopkins, C., & McMillon, M. (1990). Adolescents' perception of their work: School supervised and non-school-supervised. *Journal of Vocational Education Research, 15*(2), 31–53.

Tangri, S. (1972). Determinant of occupational role innovation among college women. *Journal of Social Issues, 28*(2), 177–200. doi:10.1111/j.1540-4560.1972.tb00024.x

Taylor, M. S. (1985). The roles of occupational knowledge and vocational self-concept crystallization in students' school-to-work transition. *Journal of Applied Psychology, 73*, 393–401.

Theberge, L. (1981). *Crooks, conmen and clowns: Businessmen and TV entertainment.* Washington, DC: Media Institute.

Turow, J. (1974). Advising and ordering in daytime, primetime. *Journal of Communication, 24*(2), 138–141. doi:10.1111/j.1460-2466.1974.tb00379.x

Turow, J. (1980). Occupation and personality in television dramas: An industry view. *Communication Research, 7*(3), 295–318. doi:10.1177/009365028000700302

Van Maanen, J. (1975). Breaking in: Socialization to work. In R. Dubin (Ed.), *Handbook of work, organization and society.* Chicago: Rand McNally.

Van Maanen, J., & Barley, S. R. (1984). Occupational communities: Culture and control in organizations. In B. M. Staw & L. L. Cummings (Eds.), *Research in organizational behavior* (Vol. 6, pp. 287–365). Greenwich, CT: JAI.

Vondracek, F. W., Lerner, R. M., & Schulenberg, J. E. (1986). *Career development: A life-span developmental approach.* Hillsdale, NJ: Lawrence Erlbaum Associates, Inc. Publishers.

Vondracek, F. W., & Porfeli, E. J. (2003). The world of work and careers. In G. R. Adams, M. D. Berzonsky, & M. D. Malden (Eds.), *Blackwell handbook of adolescence* (pp. 109–128). Malden, MA: Blackwell.

Wanous, J. P. (1992). *Organizational entry: Recruitment, selection, orientation, and socialization.* Reading, MA: Addison-Wesley.

Wolfe, K. M., & Fiske, M. (1949). Why children read comics. In P. F. Lazerfeld & K. M. Stanton (Eds.), *Communication Research, 1948–1949.* New York: Harper & Row.

Wright, J. C., Huston, A. C., Truglio, R., Fitch, M., Smith, E., & Piemyat, S. (1995). Occupational portrayals on television: Children's role schemata, career aspirations and perceptions of reality. *Child Development, 66*(6), 1706–1718. doi:10.2307/1131905

Wroblewski, R., & Huston, A. C. (1987). Televised occupational stereotypes and their effects on early adolescents: Are they changing? *Journal of Early Adolescence, 7*(3), 283–297. doi:10.1177/0272431687073005

ORGANIZATIONAL CULTURE

Greg G. Armfield

Objectives

- ► Describe what organizational culture is.
- ► Compare and contrast the prescriptive and descriptive view of organizational culture.
- ► Analyze Schein's approach to the study of organizational culture.

The concept of organizational culture took business and the academic community by storm in the last 40 to 50 years. The speed at which organizational culture emerged as a significant lens for communication scholars and other academics to examine or otherwise engage with organizations and institutions was astounding (Eisenberg & Riley, 2001). The metaphor of culture clearly resonated with both academics and practitioners. It just makes sense to see organizations as a complex arena of stories and values. The culture metaphor opened up new and fruitful areas of research. Organizational culture quickly became a part of everyday talk around watercoolers and in carpools. Many organizational employees began proclaiming "the culture here won't allow us to" or "our culture is work hard, play hard." The first part of this section will review the major elements of organizational culture and how to analyze an organization's culture when you are looking for a job. The second part of this section will review the organizational process which will be highly beneficial to you as you integrate into full-time employment in organizations or work in an internship or COOP position prior to full-time employment.

ORGANIZATIONAL CULTURE DEFINED

ORGANIZATIONAL CULTURE

a complex system of symbolic resources, worldviews, values, and norms.

It is undeniable that organizations exist within cultural environments. In organizational studies the culture that an organization exists within is referred to as the organizational environment. Within each organization there exists a culture that is unique only to the organization. While some organizations may have weak cultures, the organizational culture is still active. Research focused on organizational culture is typically exploring a very successful culture (e.g., Southwest Airlines, Disney, Google). To say that an organization's culture has an influence on the communication within an organization is an understatement.

Culture is used to describe groups of people, geographic regions, or localized cultures. Examples include Third World cultures, African American culture, Hispanic culture, the culture of an inner city, East coast or West coast culture, and even Southern or Southwest cultures. But, we can focus even more on local cultures in cities and towns. Recall Morgan's definition of culture in Unit One of this text: "culture is a complex system of symbolic resources, worldviews, values, and norms of appropriate enactment." To frame this definition, with respect to organizational communication, the existence of a culture occurs when people share a common frame of reference for interpreting and acting toward one another and the world in which they live (Papa, Daniels, & Spiker, 2008). Organizational culture is reflected in the customs, communication, and other observable features of a community. This includes rites, rituals, celebrations, legends, myths, and heroic sagas.

Over time organizations create their own culture through symbolic interaction (Mead, 1934). In other words, through organizational communication, organizational members create and recreate the cultural system that is used as their social context (Giddens, 1984). In this context, organizational members understand how they should interpret their experiences, which in turn gives members a social context for creating meaning. Further, organizational culture provides members with a way to change the organization through communication (Papa, Daniels, & Spiker, 2008).

Schein (1990) provided a multidimensional definition of organizational culture. First, culture is "a pattern of basic assumptions." Second, culture is "invented, discovered, or developed by a given group." Third, the group "learns to cope with its problems of external adaptation and internal integration" that has "worked well enough to be considered valid, and therefore is to be taught to new members as the correct way to perceive, think, and feel in relation to those problems" (p. 111). A final and very simplistic, but at the same time descriptive definition of organizational culture is, "The way we do things around here" (Deal & Kennedy, 1982).

SHARED

a common way of understanding and interpreting an organizational phenomena.

In short, the three common characteristics of organizational culture are: (1) It is **shared**—the members of the culture share common ways of understanding and interpreting organizational phenomena. This does not mean all organizational members are forced to think the same way. But organizational culture does provide a means or lens through which understanding and interpretation of organizational events can

take place in a similar way. (2) It is **intangible**—constructed through human interaction, but not concrete at its core. Culture consists of values, assumptions, norms, and is a framework for understanding, none of which are tangible. For example, to change a dress code or a daily ritual within an organization is only changing the reflection of the culture and not the culture itself. For example, a University President encouraging students and faculty alike to wear school colors on Friday does not change the core values of the university. However, it does change the way we as employees or students might reflect as a value or norm. Specifically, the norm to new students and faculty would be reflected as wear Crimson on Friday. (3) It affects **human behavior**—this is one of the more important notions of culture. Organizational culture is not a managerial, financial, or operational decision. It is a construction of human interaction that affects and is affected by the behavior of all members of the organization. Culture provides a lens for interpreting organizational events as members experience them on a day-to-day basis. However, the example of wearing school colors on Fridays would affect human behavior for students and employees. Obviously, organizational culture is very complex.

INTANGIBLE

constructed through human communication.

HUMAN BEHAVIOR

constructed from human interaction.

THE BIG PICTURE

One of the most important concepts about organizational culture is that organizational culture is a lens used to understand the way organizational members interpret, interact with, and make sense of organizational reality (Louis, 1980). As a member of a culture you may have been enculturated with the values and assumptions of the group. As you go through your daily life those values and assumptions help you to make sense of what is going on around you. You tend to learn to make a positive perspective from these cultural assumptions. In order to understand how and why organizational members behave as they do, one must understand the organizational culture that guides and constrains them. By studying the culture of an organization researchers have revealed why Enron failed (watch *Enron: The Smartest Guys in the Room*). Compare the culture of Enron or that of Volkswagen being charged with falsifying emissions tests for diesel cars, Uber, or the Weinstein Company overlooking the allegations of sexual harassment and abuse of employees by Harvey Weinstein to that of Google, Zappos, Disney, Patagonia, or Southwest Airlines. You will gain a clear picture of the importance of a well-developed and ethically based culture.

THE PRESCRIPTIVE VIEW

One of the first ways organizational scholars explored organizational culture was like a prescription. After observing and accounting for several highly successful and productive strong organizational cultures, Deal and Kennedy (1982) found several features in common among these organizations. Strong organizational cultures have:

▶ *Values*—beliefs and visions that members hold for the organization.
▶ *Heroes*—individuals who had come to exemplify the organization's values.
▶ *Rites and Rituals*—ceremonies through which an organization celebrates its values.
▶ *Cultural Network*—a communication system through which cultural values are instituted and reinforced. (Deal & Kennedy, 1982)

By providing a prescription for organizations to follow, many organizations took the ideas that successful companies either had or had implemented and mimicked them. However, several were unsuccessful. Why? Well, in short, one fix is not always correct, because a culture is the result of the interactions of individuals. In other words, it is a result of the overall health of communication inside an organization, and healthy communication is not easy or simply mimicked. For example, if a manager is unethical, racist, or sexist, no organizational set of rules will improve the organization until the bad seed (that unethical manager) is properly dealt with.

THE DESCRIPTIVE VIEW

A second way to study organizational culture involves understanding that culture is something an organization *is*, as opposed to the prescriptive approach, which looks at culture as something an organization *has*. The former being a prescriptive approach and the new view being a descriptive approach. Four issues highlight the distinction between prescriptive and descriptive approaches to culture. First, organizational culture is complicated. Organizational culture simply cannot be reduced to several simple concepts. Scholars have found organizational culture is revealed through rites of passages, degradation, enhancement, renewal, conflict reduction, and integration (Beyer & Trice, 1987); ceremonies (Dandridge, 1985); values and belief systems (Quinn & McGrath, 1985); metaphors (Smith & Eisenberg, 1987); stories (Boje, 1991; Meyer, 1995); and communication rules (Shockley-Zalabak, 1991, 1994). In short, culture is a highly complex phenomenon.

Second, organizational culture is emergent. Organizational culture is socially created through the communicative interactions of the members; not merely transmitted through communication. This idea is central to the communicative focus on culture as culture is not merely transmitted through communication; communication is "constitutive of culture" (Eisenberg & Riley, 2001, p. 294). Organizational communication is interactional between members, contextually embedded in organizational situations, episodic (nameable as distinct events), and improvisational (there are no scripts that guide organizational members) performances.

Third, culture is not unitary. Organizations do not have a single culture because of the existence of subcultures that may co-exist in harmony, conflict, or indifference to the global organizational culture (Schein, 2010). Martin (2003) states subcultures are emergent from personal contacts or demographic similarity. These subcultures can become a breeding ground for the emergence of shared meaning (Louis, 1980). Recall that culture is constantly being recreated.

Finally, culture is often ambiguous, fragmented, and hard to pin down. This is especially true for organizations that are rapidly changing and adapting to internal or external influences. In fact, several organizational cultures exist in a state of flux and are continually adapting to multiple realities. Examples of this include companies that are being acquired, organizations that are merging and the cultures are trying to be merged, or organizations that are subject to extreme government regulation.

Now that you understand why the prescriptive approach was flawed, we will look at how you would explore an organizational culture from a descriptive view. Remember, all organizations have a culture, but many will not be as strong as Disney or Pixar, or as visibly different as flying Southwest Airlines compared to American Airlines (which are both based in the same city). To understand the descriptive approach to organizational culture, we need to turn to the scholarship of Edgar Schein and his model of organizational culture.

Schein (2010) defines organizational culture as: "a pattern of shared basic assumptions that the group learned as it solved its problems of external adaptation and internal integration, that has worked well enough to be considered valid, and therefore, to be taught to new members as the correct way to perceive, think and feel in relation to those problems" (p. 103). In order to further explore organizational culture, one must understand the three layers that, based on Schein's (2010) research, will reveal organizational culture. Schein's model is best depicted like an onion where you explore different layers to reveal the organizational culture (see Figure 4.3). The outer layers of the model are the most visible (artifacts) followed by values (which are observable) and assumptions (which you really should experience).

The key to determining culture is figuring out what is demonstrated by the organizational artifacts and figuring out what the underlying meaning behind those artifacts is, which reveals an organization's culture. Artifacts are the most visible level of an organization's culture. However, these artifacts are often very difficult to decipher and hard to assign meaning (Schein, 2010). Just because something is observable, does not mean it is directly related to the organizational culture. Artifacts include architecture, furniture, technology, dress, written documents, art, forms of address, decision-making style, communication during meetings, and network configurations. For example, if everyone in an academic department called each other by their formal names, such as Professor Smith or Dr. Smith, how would you interpret this observation? Maybe the colleagues hold each other in high esteem. Maybe formality is a rule throughout the university. Perhaps faculty members are trying to set an example for students. Or, perhaps the faculty members dislike each other so intensely they are trying to maintain a distant relationship and therefore call each other by their surname. In short, the outer layer is difficult to decipher as any of these conclusions could be true (but only one is), and not all interpretations have a direct reflection on the department's culture.

The second layer is espoused values. This level reveals the organizational preferences for what "ought" to happen and shares those values among all organizational members. Several organizational values are often brought forth from organizational

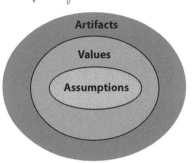

Figure **4.3**

© Kendall Hunt Publishing Company

© AR Pictures/Shutterstock.com

heroes or founders. For example, many of the values Walmart still claims to stand for today were principles brought forth by founder Sam Walton. At Walmart, new hires are socialized with the story of Sam Walton and how Walmart started as one store. The following are examples of organizational values:

► An organization that values hard work will expect their employees to put in 60-plus hours a week.
► An organization that values innovation and creativeness will likely be more open to change and expect their employees to work at improving different facets of the organization.

While it is understood that all members of the organization should share organizational values, we all know that sometimes they do not. For example, an organization may have an open door policy and emphasize the value of upward vertical communication. However, there will be managers in the organization that will not practice an open door policy. He or she may have a "figurative" open door and through understanding the organizational culture for your workgroup (some would consider this a subculture) you begin to understand that you do not go into your manager's office without an appointment. Another example of espoused values might be equality. For example, I am sure you have noticed how parking permits are assigned at many universities and organizations. If equality is the value set forth by leadership, why do some employees get priority parking, like professors and administrators, on many campuses? Why do faculty get closer spots to buildings and why does upper administration get assigned parking spots? Wouldn't it be more fair or equal if the first person on campus, regardless if they were an administrator, student, or faculty, could park in the closest spot? If parking was open or first come, first served, then the practice of equality would be practiced with respect to parking. Just because the leadership of an organization articulates a value does not mean it is a "real" value of the organization.

The relationship between level one and two is that values are inherently intangible, cognitive constructs and not always articulated by organizational members. In this way, values may or may not be "visible" in artifacts and behaviors. Other times, organizational members may articulate a value that contradicts the espoused values and behaviors an organization proclaims to stand for. Can an organization that does not recycle really proclaim to be environmental friendly? In these cases you are looking at a "fantasy value," one that is proclaimed, but not practiced. The final level is that of the core assumptions that organizational members hold about the world and how it works. These assumptions tend to be taken for granted, because they have been reinforced time and time again as the organization or group deals with internal and external problems. These assumptions are uniformly held and reveal "the way we are" or "the way we do things around here." The six assumptions are the nature of reality and truth, time, space, human nature, human activity, and human relationships. All six assumptions deal with how organizational members view the world, they are not a function of an organization.

The nature of reality and truth looks to determine what is real and how reality is determined. External reality refers to reality that is determined in an empirical fashion, such as standardized tests determine a level of topic understanding. As a college student, a college admittance test (e.g., the SAT or ACT) was used to partially determine your placement in courses and in the competition for scholarships. Another type of reality, social reality, is used when groups reach consensus on observations or decisions. Finally, individual reality is one's own acquired experiences, information learned and/or knowledge gained. I often like to hang around older people to hear and learn from their stories and experiences. This is a way to gain knowledge, but each individual chooses to share, or not share, their individual reality. There are other ways cultures have determined what is reality and truth. For example, truth is what works; let's try it and see what works. I have observed many children learn from this simple process. Another example is truth as established by the scientific method (Schein, 2017).

The second assumption, the nature of time, deals with the symbolic nature that people use for talking about orderliness of social life. Las Cruces, and New Mexico in general, is often joked to be the land of mañana. I was once asked by a new resident of Las Cruces, "I know this is the land of mañana, but does that really mean one year?" Several of us laughed and replied, maybe! However, time is critical because it is invisible, taken for granted, but at the same time imposes social order. One approach to the nature of time that was brought up in the section on culture in Unit One is that of monochronic versus polychronic time. As you recall, monochronic time is the idea of focusing on one thing at a time. For example, you might have multiple assignments due next week, but you only work on one at a time. As opposed to monochronic time, polychronic time is to work on items, perhaps differing class assignments, simultaneously or at the same time. The saying to kill two birds with one stone reflects a polychronic time belief. The nature of time reflects the symbolic nature of time in American culture. We use time to order our social life. Many people operate on a "not enough time to . . ." mind set. Or, we attend a function and walk away thinking to ourselves, well that was a waste of time. We also frame our friends and colleagues as a persona that is always on time, or always late. In short, in American culture we place a high value on time, yet it is invisible and in part taken for granted (Schein, 2017).

The third assumption, the nature of space, incorporates symbolic meaning. Recall earlier in Unit One Morgan discussed physical space between two or more people. The nature of space also incorporates the social meaning of space, which includes the use of walls or office partitions. Space is used to show power. The larger one's desk or office is the more important they are. Assigned parking spots are a sign of special ownership. If you are given an office space and decorate it with personal possessions, it shows that you have taken ownership of the space. Finally, space also consists of body language, which was mentioned in Unit One (Schein, 2017).

The fourth assumption, the nature of human nature and motivation, includes the basic human instincts and how we determine what is or is not inhuman behavior. Granted human nature is inherently complex and human nature changes with your life cycle as we mature. A few of the approaches to human nature include Maslow's (1954) hierarchy of needs, which explains how an employee or people in general are motivated and which needs must be satisfied (e.g., food and safety) before we focus on larger gratifications. Another example of human nature is one's belief that people are intrinsically good or bad. Finally, one's belief about what is most important in life. Have you ever been asked to name the three most important things in your life? Was family first or was work? Or did you answer that a higher power is most important in your life? All of this is a reflection on how you, as a human, view human nature (Schein, 2017).

The fifth assumption is the nature of human activity or how humans act in relation to their environment. Schein (2017) summarized three orientations that researchers have identified. The first is the doing orientation. This is identified by the saying "getting things done" or "let's do something." The Nike slogan "Just Do It" is a great framing of the doing orientations. The belief here is that nothing is impossible. Managerial functions of power can include manipulation and control (Schein, 2017). The second orientation is the extreme of the doing orientation. The being orientation is a subservient belief looking at nature as the powerful force and humanity as subservient to nature. Organizations with this outlook tend to find a niche that allows them to survive and adapt to the external reality rather than try to create or dominate a portion of the market or environment. The third, and final, orientation is being-in-becoming. This approach serves as a middle ground between the doing and being orientations emphasizing a harmony of nature and humanity. The focus is on what the person *is* rather than what a person can *accomplish*. Human development is the key with a focus on coexisting with nature (Schein, 2017).

The sixth and final assumption, the nature of human relationships, encompasses several approaches to how individuals develop and maintain interpersonal relationships inside the organization. All six assumptions deal with how organizational members view the world; they are not a function of an organization. Earlier in the section on culture, in Unit One, we discussed collective versus individualistic cultures. This is also reflected in our organizations (Schein, 2010). A second issue in the human relationship orientation is how higher and lower status people form relationships and what the relationship should be among team members and peers. Many of these rules and norms are deemed to be "situationally appropriate" (Schein, 2017, p. 100). Schein (2016) identified four relationship levels among organizational members that are influenced by the country, religion, and ethnicity of organizational employees. These four levels vary from: (1) no relationship or negative relationship; (2) civility or the acknowledgment of relationships; (3) working relationships and the recognition that individuals are unique persons; to (4) strong emotional friendships to include love and intimacy (Schein, 2017).

These assumptions are not specific to organizational culture, but revolve around how people view the world and humanities, relationship to it. Schein (2017) believes that examination of these assumptions reveals a coherent paradigm that guides a strong and united culture. However, the cultural assumptions might be fragmented and contradictory, thus revealing a problem of adapting to external and internal organizational problems. Regardless, it is important to explore the underlying assumptions of any group or organization in an attempt to identify the paradigm from which the group views organizational life. But, one cannot claim to have described or understood a group's culture unless they have made significant empirical observations of the organization. In short, organizational culture, much like social culture, is deep, wide, very complex, and covers all aspects of life.

Can an organizational culture exist if a group of individuals do not agree on the six assumptions above? Absolutely. However, the result will be a fragmented culture that is not a strong culture. In addition, lack of agreement among organizational members on these assumptions is more likely to result in the existence of several possibly dysfunctional subcultures.

While Schein's model can be viewed as an oversimplified reality of organizational culture and the role of communication in creating and sustaining that culture, it is an important descriptive approach to culture. At a time when researchers and theorists increasingly see culture as a fragmented and often ambiguous phenomenon, Schein's model brings clarity to the complexity of organizational cultures. Schein's model also provides a helpful heuristic view for looking at the multiple indicators of organizational culture and how these indicators might or might not be indicative of more enduring assumptions and values of an organization. The final part of this section will review the organizational socialization and, specifically, the organizational socialization process as one chooses a career; and once they get a job, assimilate into the organizational workplace.

CONCLUSION

Organizations exist within environmental and cultural influences. There is little argument that culture also exists within organizations (Papa et al., 2008). However, to fully understand how an organization works (much less why), organizational members must make themselves aware of both influences. Nothing outstanding may be seen in either type of culture initially, but as a "peon" or "little" when you enter an organization, few cultural factors will reveal themselves as you initially see them. For this reason, I encourage you to use Schein's model for exploring organizational culture so you will be open and aware of the communication networks and the culture that influences all of your organizational interactions.

Discussion Questions

1. What are the primary differences between the two views of culture (Prescriptive and Descriptive)?

2. Describe organizational culture.

3. Describe the four levels of Schein's cultural analysis.

References

Adler, R. B., & Elmhorst, J. M. (2008). *Communicating at work: Principles and practices for business and the professions* (9th ed). Boston: McGraw Hill.

Beyer, J. M., & Trice, H. M. (1987). How an organization's rites reveal its culture. *Organizational Dynamics, 15,* 5–24.

Boje, D. M. (1991). The storytelling organization: A study of story performance in an office-supply firm. *Administrative Science Quarterly, 36,* 106–126.

Dandridge, T. C. (1985). The life stages of a symbol: When symbols work and when they can't. In P. J. Frost, L. F. Moore, M. R. Louis, C. C. Lundberg, & J. Martin (Eds.), *Organizational culture* (pp. 141–153). Beverly Hills: Sage.

Deal, T. E., & Kennedy, A. A. (1982). *Corporate cultures: The rites and rituals of corporate life.* Reading, MA: Addison-Wesley Publishing Company.

Eisenberg, E. M., & Riley, P. (2001). Organization culture. In F. M. Jablin & L. L. Putnam (Eds.), *The new handbook of organizational communication: Advances in theory, research, and methods* (pp. 291–317). Thousand Oaks, CA: Sage.

Giddens. (1984). *The constitution of society.* Cambridge: Polity.

Louis, M. R. (1980). Surprise and sense making: What newcomers experience in entering unfamiliar setting. *Administrative Science Quarterly, 25,* 226–252.

Martin, J. (2003). *Organizational culture: Mapping the terrain.* Thousand Oaks, CA: Sage.

Maslow, A. H. (1954). *Motivation and personality.* New York, NY: Harper Row.

Mead, G. (1934). Mind, self, and society. Chicago: University of Chicago Press.

Meyer, J. C. (1995). Tell me a story: Eliciting organizational values from narratives. *Communication Quarterly, 43,* 210–224.

Papa, M. J., Daniels, T. D., & Spiker, B. K. (2008). *Organizational communication: Perspectives and trends.* Los Angeles: Sage.

Quinn, R., & McGrath, M. (1985). The transformation of organizational cultures: A competing values perspective. In P. Frost, L. Moore, M. Louis, C. Lundberg, & J. Martin (Eds.), *Organizational culture* (pp. 315–334). Newbury Park, CA: Sage.

Schein, E. H. (1990). Organizational culture. *American Psychologists, 45,* 109–119.

Schein, E. H. (2010). *Organizational culture and leadership* (4th ed.). San Francisco, CA: Jossey-Bass.

Schein, E. H. (2016). *Humble consulting: How to provide real help faster.* San Francisco, CA: Jossey-Bass.

Schein, E. H. (2017). *Organizational culture and leadership* (5th ed.). Hoboken, NJ: John Wiley & Sons.

Shockley- Zalabak, P. (1991). *Fundamentals of organizational communication.* New York: Longman.

Shockley- Zalabak, (1994). *Fundamentals of organizational communication* (2nd ed.). New York: Longman.

Smith, R. C., & Eisenberg, E. (1987). Conflict at Disneyland: A root metaphor analysis. *Communication Monographs, 54,* 367–380.

Organizational Conflict Management: A Focus on Practical Skills

By Shawn Werner

Objectives

► Identify the communication tools and practices for creating a healthy organization culture.
► Discuss the differences between a primary and secondary group.

By now, it should be clear that effective communication skills are essential to maintaining interpersonal relationships. In organizations, the communication skills that people seem most interested in mastering are related to conflict management. A quick Google search for "workplace conflict" will yield thousands of links to articles and books related to the subject.

This section will outline communication practices and tools for creating an environment where conflict management is both encouraged and executed competently, as well as introduce practical skills for managing conflict within organizations. Though organizational conflict management is the focus here, it is worth noting that many of the skills covered in this section can be applied to relationships and contexts well beyond the organization.

WHAT IS CONFLICT MANAGEMENT?

Conflict in organizations is a common occurrence and is due in large part to the differences in personalities and values of organizational members. There are several potential responses to organizational conflict, but the following two terms are used most frequently: *conflict management* and *conflict resolution*. **Conflict management** acknowledges that conflict is ongoing in relationships. It emphasizes that acquiring skills to manage conflict can have potential benefits and positive outcomes such as increased productivity at work, cohesiveness in groups, improved task completion,

CONFLICT MANAGEMENT

ongoing practice of conflict skills in order to produce positive outcomes.

and positive changes in interpersonal relationships (Amason & Schweiger, 1997). Conflict resolution, on the other hand, has the primary goal of ending a conflict (Jandt, 2017) and, in some cases, it may require third-party mediation or arbitration, particularly when conflict has become discriminating or threatening. This section will introduce skills related to conflict management rather than conflict resolution in order to highlight the continuous process of maintaining and improving organizational relationships and climate.

TOWARD A POSITIVE GROUP CLIMATE: ESTABLISHING VULNERABILITY-BASED TRUST AND SHARING WORKING-STYLE PREFERENCES

POSITIVE GROUP CLIMATE

group environments in which communication is supportive, productive, and caring.

In order to adequately apply conflict management skills within the organization, it is first helpful to take steps toward establishing a *positive group climate*. A **positive group climate** refers to a group environment in which the communication practices are perceived by the individuals in the group as being supportive, productive, and caring. In contrast, a *negative group climate* is comprised of individuals who perceive that they are under-valued, untrusted, and unsupported (Rothwell, 2012). It stands to reason then that promoting skills that will help to create a positive group climate, rather than a negative group climate, will better enable organizations to embrace and advance effective conflict management skills.

This book covers the concept of organizational culture and the idea that the organization is a structure that employees create and recreate through their interactions. Essentially, it is the employees who give the organization a purpose through their communication with each other over time (Giddens, 1984). Though leaders within organizations should be the first to model effective communication behaviors, all employees have the ability to implement communication skills at work that can influence others who are both above and below them in the workplace (e.g., Bohns & Flynn, 2013). The following are communication practices and tools that organizational employees can

© sirtravelalot/Shutterstock.com

use in order to help shape a positive group climate where effective conflict management is both valued and encouraged.

Work to Establish Vulnerability-Based Trust

The presence of trust is critical to building a positive group climate, because it plays a major role in establishing and maintaining productive and cooperative work-related behaviors (Dirks & Ferrin, 2002) and for engaging in organizational conflict management (Prusak, 2001). A common feature in definitions of trust is the idea of showing vulnerability. In his extensive work examining teams and teamwork, Patrick Lencioni (2002) goes one step further by introducing the concept of *vulnerability-based trust* as the key to developing a high-functioning team whose members can engage in constructive conflict.

Vulnerability-based trust exists within a workplace where employees, "comfortably and quickly acknowledge, without provocation, their mistakes, weaknesses, failures, and needs for help. They also recognize the strengths of others, even when those strengths exceed their own" (Lencioni, 2013, p. 10). Teams that lack vulnerability-based trust do things like jump to conclusions about each other's behaviors, hold grudges, and find reasons to avoid spending time together. If vulnerability-based trust is present on a team, members demonstrate transparency and honesty by saying things such as, "I was wrong," "I made a mistake," "Can you help me?," "You are better at that than me," "I'm sorry," and so forth (Lencioni). Moreover, they become more willing to express their opinions even when they know their points can be refuted. Thus, if organizations devoted the time and effort to building vulnerability-based trust, they would become safer places to communicate and manage conflict.

Lencioni (2013) acknowledges that the process of building vulnerability-based trust cannot happen overnight, and offers some tools that teams can use for the purposes of building vulnerability-based trust over time:

> ► *Personal histories exercises*—team members share their life stories and backgrounds in order to humanize each other.
> ► *Personality and behavior preference profiles*—team members provide profiles of their behavioral preferences and personality styles as a way to safely begin sharing their own vulnerabilities.
> ► *Experiential team exercises*—team members engage in team-building activities, such as a ropes course or scavenger hunts in order to establish trust through non-work-related teamwork.

**VULNERABILITY-
BASED TRUST**

trust that is established by acknowledging one's own mistakes, weaknesses, failures, and needs for help.

There are also two higher-risk tools recommended by Lencioni (2002): the **team effectiveness exercise** and the **360-degree feedback**. Both activities involve team members identifying their own contributions and areas for improvement on the team, as well as giving candid feedback to other team members regarding their strengths and weaknesses. Though critical to creating vulnerability-based trust, organizational teams may want to be cautious about starting with these two tools, especially if team trust going into to these exercises is low.

Meet to Share Working-Style Preferences

In addition to establishing vulnerability-based trust, organizational members should also commit to meeting face-to-face to share their *working-style preferences* with each other in order to move toward a more candid and productive work environment (Harley, 2013). Shari Harley, the author of the popular book, *How to Say Anything to Anyone* (2013) offers questions that team members can ask to better understand each other's **working-style preferences**:

WORKING-STYLE PREFERENCES

one's preferred ways of working and communicating with others.

- ▶ How do you best like to communicate? Via e-mail, voicemail, text, instant message, telephone, or in person?
- ▶ If we need to talk, do you prefer to work by appointment or would you prefer I drop by your desk or give you a call?
- ▶ If I have something to give you when you're not at your desk, where would you prefer I leave it? On your desk or chair, in your in-box, or with someone else?
- ▶ If I need to reach you outside of regular business hours, what method is best? What time is too early and what time is too late to call?
- ▶ What are your pet peeves? What types of things annoy you at work?
- ▶ How will I know when you are frustrated?

Additional questions members might ask are:

- ▶ What stresses you out or concerns you at work?
- ▶ If I need to approach you with a delicate topic, how would you like/not like me to do that?
- ▶ Tell me about your conflict style. How would you like to work out problems with me in general?

Discussing these questions can help contribute to building vulnerability-based trust and a positive group climate and could also go a long way toward minimizing miscommunications in organizations. Team members will have a clearer picture of how everyone likes to work, as well as valuable information about communication and conflict management preferences.

PRACTICAL SKILLS FOR MANAGING ORGANIZATIONAL CONFLICT

Once an organization has taken steps toward building a positive group climate by establishing vulnerability-based trust and sharing working-style preferences, members will be better positioned to focus on their conflict management skills. Below, I will share four practical skills that organizational members can commit to working on in an effort to improve their communication during conflict situations.

© baranq/Shutterstock.com

Practice Empathic Listening

Empathy has been defined as an ability to understand and accurately acknowledge the feelings of another and then respond in an attuned way (Soanes & Stevenson, 2010). In other words, practicing empathy enables team members to interact with each other in a thoughtful way in which they demonstrate appropriately responsive behaviors. Empathic listening involves listening with the other person in mind and attempting to imagine what they are feeling (Purdy & Borisoff, 1997), which positively affects conflict management. People who practice empathic listening may actually facilitate more constructive conflict management practices simply because they have a better understanding of the other's position (Davis, 1996).

Fred E. Jandt (2017), who is a well-respected scholar in the field of communication and conflict management, suggests the following for effectively practicing empathic listening:

EMPATHIC LISTENING

listening in order to understand the other person and imagine what they are feeling.

▶ *Control the environment to minimize noise and other distractions.*

> Reserve a private meeting room in the library instead of going to Starbucks or talking in the hallway next to your class.

▶ *Be totally present and in the moment.*

> Avoid meeting right before the difficult exam, after the stressful work shift, while feeling sick, and so forth, in order to fully focus and listen to the other peson.

▶ *Allow the speaker to speak without interruption.*

> Fight the urge to share information or ask questions until the other person has finished speaking.

▶ *Ask for help and clarification to understand speaker's meaning.*

> If any of the speaker's words or phrases are unfamiliar or unclear, ask the speaker to further define them for you.

▶ *Take notes if the conflict story is complex.*

> Ask the speaker permission to write down key points that may need to be remembered or revisited later.

▶ *Ask clarifying, not threatening, questions.*

Ask questions like, "Can you tell me more about that?" "What happened next?" "Is there anything else you would like to share about that?"

> ▶ *Identify and remember the issues in the conflict.*
>
>   Pay close attention to what the person thinks the conflict is about and their position on each issue.

> ▶ *Make frequent summaries of facts and issues to show the speaker you heard them.*
>
>   Start with statements like, "I heard you say . . ." or "So the issues that are bothering you are . . ." Jandt also notes that this allows the speaker to correct you, refine their comments, and focus on pertinent issues rather than less important details as well.

> ▶ *Identify and remember the feelings underlying the speaker's messages.*
>
>   Pay attention to the other person's verbal and nonverbal behavior that hint at what they might be feeling. If they say, "this is so hard to talk about" while crying, take note that they are upset and are having a difficult time discussing the situation.

> ▶ *Acknowledge the speaker's feelings.*
>
>   Make statements like, "I can see that this situation is upsetting you" or "I can tell that this is very difficult for you to talk about."

> ▶ *Avoid expressing opinions or evaluations that may influence how the speaker sees the conflict.*
>
>   Watch out for statements like, "You shouldn't feel that way" or "That's silly."

Practice Showing Respect

Like empathic listening, the ability to act in a respectful way toward the other person in a conflict situation is vital to effective conflict management. In the book *Crucial Conversations: Tools for Talking When Stakes Are High* (2012), the authors assert that successful people are those skilled at being both direct and respectful when dealing with conflict. Often that means that skilled communicators are the ones who go first and begin showing respect to the other person, even when that other person is behaving badly. One helpful motivator for being the first to show respect is the concept of a *self-fulfilling prophecy*. A self-fulfilling prophecy is the notion that a person can shape another person's behaviors through their false perceptions of that person (Rosenthal & Jacobson, 1968). For example, if John mistakenly believes Karla is a mean person, John will likely behave in line with his false perception of Karla whenever he interacts with her, which could actually elicit mean behavior from Karla. However, there is evidence to suggest that positive self-fulfilling prophecies can be more powerful than negative self-fulfilling prophecies (Madon, Guyll, Spoth, Cross, & Hilbert, 2003). Thus, if a person takes the lead in conflict management by showing respect to a person they may not feel deserves it, they are not just being the bigger person, they may actually be prompting positive changes in the other person's behavior moving forward.

© Rawpixel.com/Shutterstock.com

Lochner (2012) provides some helpful tips for how to show respect when communicating with others using the acronym *RESPECT*:

▶ *Recognize how your words are being received by others.* Be cognizant of the nonverbal behaviors that accompany your speech and look out for people's reactions to what you are saying.

▶ *Eliminate negative words.* Consider what words or expressions you use that may be offensive or can be misinterpreted by others and then make an effort to stop using them.

▶ *Speak with people—not at them, or about them.* Remember that communication is an exchange. Invite people to share their views, rather than being singularly focused on expressing your own perspective.

▶ *Practice appreciation.* Be sure to both show and tell people that you appreciate them through kind words and gestures.

▶ *Earn respect from others.* It is important to model respect in your communication with others in order to gain respect in return. Your behavior toward others should demonstrate how you would like to be treated.

▶ *Consider others' feelings before speaking and acting.* Take a moment to think about what you are saying and how it may make the other person feel. Focus on what is both kind and vital to communicate to others.

▶ *Take time to listen.* As emphasized earlier in this section, make listening a priority in communication. Pay close attention when others speak and allow them to share without interruption.

Practice Addressing Misunderstandings

The authors of *Crucial Conversations* (Patterson, Grenny, McMillan, & Switzler, 2012) also contend that people have a natural tendency to move toward silence (masking, avoiding, or withdrawing) or violence (controlling, labeling, or attacking) in conflict situations. Individuals are encouraged to *learn to look* for signs when they or the other party in conversations begin to show signs that they do not feel *safe* by moving toward silence or violence (Grenny, 2012; McCallie, 2015). One helpful skill to restore safety

CONTRASTING

a two-step skill where one addresses the other person's concerns and then clarifies their real intent.

during a Crucial Conversation is **contrasting** in which a person: (1) addresses the other party's concerns that respect may have been violated or that there was a malicious intent (e.g., "I didn't mean to say/do . . .") and then (2) clarifies their real purpose (e.g., "What I really meant to say/do was . . .") (Patterson, Grenny, McMillan, & Switzler, 2012).

Below are two examples of how contrasting can be used to restore safety in a conversation: when a person notices someone else is showing signs of silence or violence and when a person notices signs of their own silence or violence behaviors.

1. Marty walks into the office of his friend and coworker, Lisa. He tells her that he just got off the phone with his roommate who invited him on a last-minute camping trip and he will have to miss the team presentation the following day. As Marty continues talking he notices that Lisa is becoming flushed, breathing hard, and giving him very short responses. Rather than continuing to talk about his trip, Marty stops the conversation to restore safety by using contrasting:

    "You know what Lisa, I didn't mean to bombard you with this trip without discussing it with you first, I actually intended to come in here to find out your thoughts about the implications of my missing the presentation and whether it could be worked out or not. I think I may have gotten ahead of myself a bit."

2. As Marty and Lisa revisit the conversation about his trip, Lisa begins listing all of the reasons why Marty cannot miss the presentation. While she is going through the list, Marty starts feeling hot and begins clinching his jaw. After a minute he blurts out, "So, you really don't think you can handle one presentation without me there? Of course not! And that's why I never get to take any time off." Marty quickly realizes what he has said and again stops the conversation to restore safety with contrasting:

    "Lisa, I'm so sorry. I didn't mean to attack you or your work, I was just hoping to explore potential options that might allow me to miss the presentation tomorrow without negatively impacting the rest of the team. But I'm afraid I let my emotions take over for a minute there."

As illustrated in the examples above, contrasting is a quick and easy skill that organizational members can use to manage misunderstandings before they spiral away from them. Still, it is worth noting that contrasting will work best when practiced simultaneously with the skills outlined earlier in this section. Ultimately, safety can only be restored when a person demonstrates both verbally and nonverbally that they respect the other person and can empathize with their feelings.

Practice Self-Reflection

SELF-REFLECTION

thinking back on conflicts to determine what one did well and how one can improve.

Finally, because conflict management is a process, organizational members must commit to practicing *self-reflection* regularly. **Self-reflection** requires thinking back on conflict situations and determining what one did well and what one might do differently in the future. Self-reflection should be done soon after a conflict situation and be deliberate and thoughtful. Like all of the communication skills provided in this section, reflection is an integral step to improving the practice of conflict management in organizations.

Below are some questions to assist with reflecting on conflict management:

- ► What happened?
- ► What conflict management skills did I use?
- ► What did I do well? How?
- ► What could I have done better? How?
- ► What actions related to the conflict situation should I take now, if any?
- ► What skills do I need to work on in future conflict situations? How can I do that?

CONCLUSION

All of the communication tools and skills introduced in this section can assist organizational members in creating and maintaining a positive group climate where competent conflict management is valued. Teams should work to establish vulnerability-based trust and share working-style preferences, as well as practice empathic listening, practice showing respect, address misunderstandings, and reflect on their skills early and often. Committing to these practical skills will better equip organizational members to engage in productive conflict management both within and outside of the organization.

Discussion Questions

1. Imagine that you have become a team leader at work. What are two examples of things that you could do or say to your teammates to begin establishing *vulnerability-based trust* on your team? What are two examples of things you should avoid saying or doing if you are trying to establish *vulnerability-based trust* on your team?

2. Besides the sample questions provided in this section, what are three additional questions that you might ask your coworkers to get insight into their *working-style preferences* and potentially avoid unnecessary misunderstandings with them in the workplace?

3. Imagine that you are about to sit down for a meeting to discuss a delicate topic with a coworker. List five to seven things that you could do to practice *empathic listening* during your meeting.

4. What if you ran into a coworker that you supervise at a restaurant on a Saturday night and you innocently say to them, "Oh hey, I didn't expect to see you here!" Your coworker then quickly responds, "I know, I know, I should be working on that report that is due on Monday morning." How could you use *contrasting* here to manage this misunderstanding?

Amason, A., & Schweiger, D. (1997). The effect of conflict on strategic decision-making effectiveness and organizational performance. In C. De Dreu & E. Van de Vliert (Eds.), *Using conflict in organizations*. London: Sage, 101–115.

Bohns, V., & Flynn, F. (2013). *Underestimating our influence over others at work*. Cornell University, IRL School. Retrieved from: http://digitalcommons.ilr.cornell.edu/articles/1057

Davis, M. H. (1996). *Empathy: A social psychological approach*. Boulder: Westview Press.

Dirks, K., & Ferrin, D. (2002). Trust in leadership: Meta-analytic findings and implications for research and practice. *Journal of Applied Psychology, 87*(4), 611–628.

Giddens, A. (1984). *The constitution of society. Outline of the theory of structuration*. Cambridge: Polity Press.

Grenny, J. (2012, February 27). *Surprising lessons from 525 life-changing crucial conversations: New research reveals why our crucial conversations fail or succeed*. Retrieved from: https://www.psychologytoday.com/us/blog/crucial-conversations/201202/surprising-lessons-525-life-changing-crucial-conversations

Harley, S. (2013). *How to say anything to anyone*. Austin, TX: Greenleaf Book Group Press.

Jandt, F. (2017). *Conflict & communication*. Thousand Oaks, CA: Sage Publications.

Lencioni, P. (2002). *The five dysfunctions of a team*. San Francisco: Jossey-Bass.

Lencioni, P. (2013). *Overcoming the five dysfunctions of a team*. San Francisco, CA: Jossey-Bass.

Lochner, B. (2012). *Communicating respect*. Retrieved from http://www.cornerstone-ct.com/communicating-respect/1002–1007

Madon, S., Guyll M., Spoth, R., Cross, S., & Hilbert, S. (2003). The self-fulfilling influence of mother expectations on children's underage drinking. *Journal of Personality and Social Psychology, 84*(6), 1188–1205.

McCallie, Deeanna R. (2015). *Evaluating the effectiveness of crucial conversations® training on nurses' self-efficacy. DNP Projects*. 62. Retrieved from: https://uknowledge.uky.edu/dnp_etds/62

Patterson, K., Grenny, J., McMillan, R., & Switzler, A. (2012). *Crucial conversations: Tools for talking when stakes are high*. New York: McGraw-Hill.

Purdy, M., & Borisoff, D. (1997). *Listening in everyday life: A personal and professional approach*. Lanham, MD: University Press of America.

Prusak, L. (2001). Where did knowledge management come from? *IBM Systems Journal, 40*(4).

Rosenthal, R., & Jacobson, L. (1968). *Pygmalion in the classroom*. New York: Holt, Rinehart and Winston.

Rothwell, D. (2012). *In mixed company: Communicating in small groups* (8th ed.). Belmont, CA: Wadsworth.

Soanes, C., & Stevenson, A. (2010) *Empathy*. In A. Stevenson (Ed.), Oxford English dictionary of English (3rd ed.). New York: Oxford University Press.

Small Group Types, Functions, and Development

By Greg G. Armfield

Objectives

▶ Describe the differences between group types and functions.
▶ Explain the stages of group development.
▶ Analyze what it takes to communicate effectively within groups.

Small groups are an omnipresent part of society's social structure. Everyone has been a member of a small group, whether it be a voluntary or non-voluntary group. Typically, the very first group people are socialized into is a family. Additional groups include teams, study groups, religious circles, fraternities, sororities, decision-making groups, work groups, and student organizations, to name a few. However, more often than not, we find ourselves situated among a crowd of people with whom we interact and communicate on a daily basis. Extending well beyond speaking with a professor, friend, or parent, communication takes place amongst peers and colleagues for a myriad of reasons ranging from unified decision-making processes to comedic banter at a bar. Previous sections of this text illustrated how communication functions within the realms of dyadic interpersonal relationships, but what happens when we have more than two participants in a conversation? Unlike the dyadic communication, which takes place in interpersonal relationships, groups are formed when a third participant introduces themselves into a conversation.

Groups present very interesting and unique dynamics with regard to the human interaction experience. Without groups, the roles and social norms that we interact in and the structures we find ourselves in would have no basis for existence. It is through communication that groups are formed, maintained, and demonstrate patterns and relationships amongst three or more individuals. In order to understand the functions and roles of a group, it is important to define the differences between primary and secondary groups.

TYPES AND FUNCTIONS OF SMALL GROUPS

Group interactions are complex and include the personal lives of each individual and how those individuals function within the group. **Primary** groups do not serve any one express purpose, but rather, are formed through close relationships that are built on

PRIMARY

close personal relationships.

267

mutual interest and shared experiences (Olmsted & Hare, 1978). This type provides us with a sense of belonging and support (Alberts, Nakayama, & Martin, 2015). Examples of primary groups include family members, roommates, close friends that you regularly socialize with, and coworkers with whom you regularly share coffee breaks or lunch together. **Secondary** groups stray from the aforementioned closely personal relationships and include members who have casual and distant social relationships (Anderson & Martin, 1995). A secondary group may include classmates you meet with after school for a study session or coworkers with whom you enjoy working together on projects while on the job, but your interaction with these individuals are less frequent. Conversely, primary group members enjoy spending time together doing any number of things and typically exist to meet individual needs of inclusion, love, and affection. Both primary and secondary groups have permeable boundaries as individuals tend to move in and out of both primary and secondary groups.

You are likely to find yourself involved in several different secondary groups as part of your professional life. For example, many organizations accomplish work through committee or task groups. Committee tasks can range from information gathering to reporting or carrying out an assignment. While committees range in size, including 25 or more, most committees function optimally with six to 12 members. Groups larger than a dozen, specifically larger groups consisting of 15 or more members, tend to see a noteworthy productivity drop-off.

Group Functions

Regardless of the group type, members of groups often serve multiple roles. Groups can also serve one or many purposes and these purposes define the type of group that individuals serve. Members of these groups all serve a purpose, but more importantly, the group serves an important function. The four most common group functions are task-oriented, problem-solving, decision-making, and idea generation or brainstorming.

During any given day, employees are assigned tasks or duties that need to be completed. Examples of group tasks include work on assembly lines, a budget committee, or special event planning. **Task-oriented groups** are formed to work together to complete a specific task such as a problem-solving group or decision-making group. Often these group members work together to establish communication norms and solve problems. Group communication can be social but tends to be procedural or to clarify questions a group member might have.

A **problem-solving group** attempts to discover a solution to a problem by analyzing the problem thoroughly and deriving potential solutions (Beebe & Masterson, 2012). Also described as a problem-solving group, the **decision-making group** has the added function of deciding which solution will be implemented, when and how it will be put into effect, how progress will be monitored, how changes in the solution will be handled, and how the program involving the solution will be evaluated (Adams & Galanes, 2011). Furthermore, the decision-making group focuses heavily on identifying possible choices, the consequences of each choice, and making a choice that best fits the needs and goals of the group or organization (Beebe & Masterson). Whereas a problem-solving group focuses on solving a problem, rarely do problem-solving groups enact choices to solve organizational problems. Often, they work in an advisory function. For example, a problem-solving group might analyze and make a recommendation on improving profits within an organization.

Perhaps not as evidently critical as the previous groups, **idea-generating or brainstorming groups** serve to discover a variety of solutions, perspectives, approaches, and consequences for any given scenario. Brainstorming groups grow when creativity is left uninhibited and given reign to freely flow through the minds of those participating. The ideas brought forth in this type of group should not be critically evaluated or judged for fear of stifling creativity. Brainstorming or idea-generation groups function outside of a hierarchical or tiered level of relevance. Figure 4.5 on the following page illustrates how each of these individual group functions could potentially serve a greater group, such as an automotive manufacturing plant.

Group Types

The interactive processes found in one group may vastly vary from those found in another group. That is to say, the way communication flows in a formal group is drastically different than the way communication flows in a support or networking group. Communication scholars have explored the flow of communication within an organization including communication styles within groups. Maintaining balance between objective productivity and interpersonal cohesion within groups is essential (Hardy, Eys, & Carron, 2005).

This section will focus on communication flow within five common group types: formal, advisory, creative, support, and networking groups.

Formal groups tend to be task-oriented, outcome-focused, and have a formal structure. Many formal groups also follow a strict communication protocol and set a rigid interactional pattern (Beebe & Masterson, 2012). *Robert's Rules of Order* (2011) is one such parliamentary procedure groups follow. Membership in a formal group is restricted or delegated. Attendance at meetings is expected and the group structure is clear and often somewhat rigid. Furthermore, power is typically vested in the chair (or president). Agendas are very common, as are rules for speaking, turn-taking, and voting. Formal groups are particularly common in governments and organizations with power structures, such as student government, legislative assemblies, Congress, congressional committees, shareholder meetings, and other organized bodies. A

TASK-ORIENTED GROUP

formed to complete a task such as a problem-solving or decision-making group.

PROBLEM-SOLVING GROUP

attempts to discover a solution to a problem.

DECISION-MAKING GROUP

has the added function of deciding which solution will be implemented, put into effect, how it will be monitored, how changes will be handled, and how the solution will be evaluated.

IDEA-GENERATING/ BRAINSTORMING GROUP

discover a variety of solutions, perspectives, approaches, and consequences for a given scenario.

FORMAL GROUPS

have a strict, formal structure.

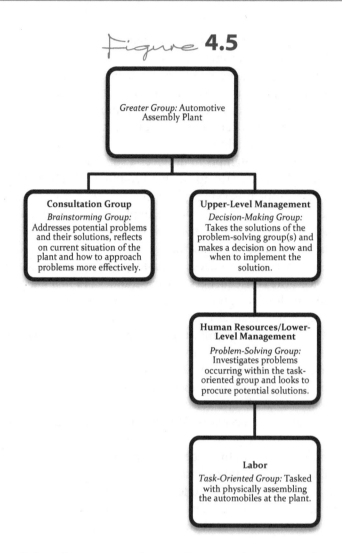

Figure **4.5**

characteristic of formal groups is their task-oriented, outcome-focused ideology where each individual member of the group is collectively focused on achieving some greater goal.

Similar to formal groups, **advisory groups** are also task-specific, usually evaluative with the intention of producing an outcome that is considered a "best solution" to a problem or event. Membership in advisory groups is still restricted with a formal structure and agenda. However, the rules for communication and discussion tend to be open, not rigid, and focused on weighing of evidence and alternatives prior to making decisions. Campus life gives birth to many advisory groups, including sororities and fraternity committees, homecoming committees, or review boards for student awards. Off-campus examples include organizational leaders, the President of the United States, who will surround themselves with individual advisors and/or advisory panels for a number of issues or concerns such as environment, security and so forth.

Creative groups function out of the necessity for alternative or creative solutions to complex problems. Creative groups are far less structured than the two groups discussed earlier. The aim of a creative group is to generate as many ideas as possible while simultaneously discouraging members from critically commenting on what has been brought forth. Not nearly as exclusive as a formal group, creative groups have a tendency to invite new members who they believe will assimilate quickly and further progress the consciousness-raising efforts employed by the group. Often, creative groups are referred to as focus groups, which are commonly used in industries to create new

ADVISORY GROUP

task-specific, evaluative function.

CREATIVE GROUP

less structure, idea-generation/ brainstroming.

products or reimage existing products for new or different uses. The advertising and marketing industries use focus groups to evaluate new campaigns. Because of the varied usage of creative groups, examples are as unique as its definition; spanning from the aforementioned focus groups to consciousness-raising groups who value awareness of gender equity, nationality, ethnicity, animal rights causes, and shared military experience.

Support groups, also commonly referred to as therapy groups, aspire to help, advise, and comfort members; share knowledge and information; and raise consciousness about specific issues. Support groups such as *Alcoholics Anonymous* (AA) have given those who aspire to help and those who are in need of help an outlet in contemporary society to address personal problems with those who have or are currently facing similar adversity (Beebe & Masterson, 2012). While AA groups tend to function as a closed group based on anonymity, other types of support groups are open. Thus, attendance in many support groups tends to be fluid as members can come and go as needed. Unique to support groups is the idea that every interlocutor has a desire or need to be involved, which subsequently poses several advantages over that of its non-voluntary admission practice. It is clear that group members can divide work, add unique perspectives to enrich what the group learns, gain insight from discussion information that might not have been gained in the absence of such discussion, and the motivation to continue learning can be enhanced.

Support groups exist in many forms, but the typical form can be defined as a therapy group designed to help individuals solve personal problems such as true support groups that enable social support for members dealing with individual crises (cancer, grief, AA). Additionally, learning groups (study groups) enable individuals and groups to acquire more information and/or understanding of a topic. The advent of the Internet has engendered a relatively new phenomenon in regard to group typologies and communication. We now turn our attention to contemporary networking groups, which have proliferated since the advent of the Internet.

Networking groups are formed with the express purposes of obtaining, building, and sustaining relationships on virtual platforms. A recent report showed that as many as 1.52 billion Facebook users log in daily and over 2.3 billion log in monthly making Facebook the largest social media platform in the world ("Company Info.," 2019). Like Facebook, membership in networking groups is not defined; members may join and leave as desired.

Now that we have defined the major types of groups and discussed the five most common group types—formal, advisory, creative, support, and networking groups—we will turn our attention to how groups form and develop.

Stages of Group Development

People join groups to meet needs (e.g., belonging to the community), and satisfy goals (e.g., learn or improve skills) (Hill, 2009; Shaw, 1981) or simply just to socialize with like-minded people (book clubs, chess club). Group formation does not spontaneously occur, but rather develops over a series of stages through which a collective of like-minded individuals subconsciously form; the most recognizable stage model of group development is Tuckman's: Forming, storming, norming, performing, and adjourning (1965).

During the **forming** stage of group development, "groups initially concern themselves with orientation accomplished primarily through testing" (Tuckman, 1965, p. 396). Forming is the initial stage of group development during which people come to feel valued and accepted. Identification with the group takes place but is slow and

SUPPORT GROUP

aspire to help, advise, comfort, share knowledge, and/or raise consciousness about specific issues.

NETWORKING GROUP

formed to express purposes of obtaining, building, and sustaining relationships on virtual platforms.

FORMING

first stage of group development; no conflict.

© Rawpixel.com/Shutterstock.com

uneasy, with members attempting to get a feel for the social setting and beginning to understand what their role in the group might be. Disagreement and hostility rarely surface, as group members are more flexible as they feel each other out and try to be polite to each other. Anderson (1988) suggests that as members of a new group, we should make appropriately benign self-disclosures and wait to see if they are reciprocated, while making efforts to be friendly, open, interested in other group members and refraining from aggressive or disagreeable comments. This means using active listening and empathizing skills to become better acquainted with other members of the group, and smiling, nodding, and maintaining good eye contact to make conversations a bit more relaxed.

STORMING

the stage when groups clarify goals and determine the roles each member will have in the group power structure; conflict emerges.

Successful efforts made in the forming stage inevitably lead to the **storming** stage. The storming stage functions as a mode to determine the roles each member will have in the group power structure. Tuckman's model characterizes conflict during this stage as "polarization around interpersonal issues" (1965, p. 396), which members heed ideological and fundamental differences among each other. In the forming stage, members are concerned about fitting in, whereas in the storming stage, members are concerned about expressing their ideas and opinions, as well as finding their place within the group. Ultimately, this results in primary and secondary tensions within the group (Bormann, 1990). Because members may not know their role in the group, communication can become excessively formal or hesitant. This may lead to emotional upsurges and antagonism. The flexible communication exhibited during forming may be replaced by snide comments, sarcastic remarks, or pointedly aggressive exchanges between some members. During storming, members may take sides or form cliques and coalitions. Alternative ideas, opinions, and ways of viewing issues surface during this crucial stage of group development.

NORMING

the stage when groups solidify each member's roles and the rules for behavior; conforming begins, less conflict.

Storming leads to **norming** and the solidification of the group's rules for behavior, especially those that relate to how conflict will be managed. As the group successfully completes the storming phase, it moves into a phase where members begin to apply more pressure on each other to conform. During this phase, the norms or standards of the group become clear. Tuckman (1965) notes that, "resistance is overcome in the third stage" (p. 396), allowing for

© fizkes/Shutterstock.com

group members to begin adopting the standards and adapting their communication styles to the norms of the group. Those who fail to comply with the established group norms are sanctioned, while those who have advanced in the power structure are privy to occasionally deviate from the norms.

Tuckman's original model concluded with the **performing** stage. Performing is when the group's skills, knowledge, and the abilities of all members are combined to overcome obstacles and meet goals successfully. "Roles become flexible and functional, and group energy is channeled into the task" (Tuckman, 1965, p. 396). During the performing stage, members *get in the groove*, and become more effective at creative problem-solving and task performance. Conversations are focused on problem-solving, sharing task-related information, and give little attention to relationship building. Successfully ascending through Tuckman's stages and arriving at the performing stage is the ultimate goal of every group, because it is here in which members gladly share information, solicit ideas from others, and work to solve problems. In other words, performing is when the group gets down to business.

Twelve years post hoc Tuckman's original publication, he revised the original model to include a fifth and final stage, adjourning. Tuckman and Jensen (1977) argued that scholars were building revised models based heavily on Tuckman's original concept, but with one major change, the addition of an exit stage. Along with Jensen, Tuckman revised his original theoretical framework introducing "the concept of a 'life cycle' model," which included an exit stage they called adjourning (Tuckman & Jensen, 1977, p. 425).

Adjourning, the final stage of development, is when group members begin to assign meaning to what they have done and determine how to end or maintain the interpersonal relationships that developed. Regardless of the life span of the group, group interaction and experiences will ultimately cease for some of the group members. Short-term project teams will face adjourning when they have completed their work within the specified time period. However, ongoing groups also experience endings when the team has reached a particular goal, finished a specific project, or lost members to reassignments or resignations. Both types of

PERFORMING

group overcome obstacles, meet goals, and get things done; most conflict is resolved.

ADJOURNING

group life cycle ends; groups begin making sense of the exit stage; many members maintain long-term interpersonal relationships.

groups (short-term and long-term) will be confronted with the same developmental challenges. Keyton (1993), in her research on the adjourning phases of groups, stressed the importance for groups to have a termination ritual that can range from an informal debriefing session to formalized celebrations with group members and their friends, family, and colleagues. Whatever form the ritual takes, Keyton believes such a ritual "affects how they (members) will interpret what they have experienced and what expectations they will take with them to similar situations" (p. 98).

Effective Group Communication

Despite the type of group, or how fast or slow the group bonds through the stage of group development, four basic tips will help all members of the group. First, patience. Be patient while members get to know each other and move through the bonding phase. A lot of people just want to skip through the forming stage and jump right to work (storming). Second, recognize and manage conflict. Ignoring conflict or not recognizing conflict between group members ends up being the worst case for most groups. I have worked for and with many conflict avoiders and I guarantee you from firsthand experience the group or organization always ends up in a worse place if they choose not to work through conflict. The ability to address conflict and work through conflict is the responsibility of a responsible leader. If conflict is not addressed, it is the direct result of poor leadership. (Note: Leadership is addressed later in this unit.) Third, be supportive and encourage full participation by all group members. Groups will always have members that interact less for a variety of reasons. You should ensure, especially for very important decisions, that everyone participates even if you have to directly ask for that group member's input.

Finally, stay focused on the group goals. Side conversations are distracting for all members and everyone should be focused on the group. One of the biggest critiques of group work is that it is ineffective. Group ineffectiveness is a direct result of the group not staying on task and group members failing to be fully focused and engaged in the group's goals.

CONCLUSION

Understanding how groups form and the unique dynamics that each group presents is crucial to your ability to effectively communicate within them. As groups are truly multifaceted and dynamic the process of group formation discussed here, while being recognized as one of the most popular, useful, and applicable to most groups, all groups will interact in unique and multifaceted ways. The next section will address how groups comes together to solve problems.

Discussion Questions

1. Discuss the differences between a primary and secondary group.

2. Discuss the different function that groups can serve.

3. Discuss the purposes that different types of groups serve.

4. Identify and describe each of the stages the groups go through according to Tuckman.

5. Identify and describe the constraints that groups may face during group development.

Acknowledgment

I would like to extend my sincere appreciation to Mario Selle for his previous contributions to an earlier printing of this content.

References

Alberts, J. K., Nakayama, T. K., & Martin, J. M. (2015). *Human communication in society* (4th ed.). New York: Pearson.

Adams, K., & Galanes, G. J. (2011). *Communicating in groups: Applications and skills* (8th ed.). Boston: McGraw-Hill.

Anderson, C. M., & Martin, M. M. (1995). The effects of communication motives, interaction involvement, and loneliness on satisfaction: A model of small groups. *Small Group Research, 26,* 118–137.

Anderson, J. (1988). Communication competency in the small group. In R. Cathcart & L. Samovar (Eds.), *Small group communication: A reader.* Dubuque, IA: Wm. C. Brown.

Beebe, S. A., & Masterson, J. T. (2012). *Communicating in small groups: Principles and practices* (10th ed.). Boston: Pearson.

Bormann, E. G. (1990). *Small group communication: Theory and practice* (3rd ed.). New York: Harper & Row.

Company Info. (2019). *Facebook Newsroom.* Retrieved from https://newsroom.fb.com/company-info/

Hardy, J., Eys, M. A., & Carron, A. V. (2005). Exploring the potential disadvantages of high cohesion in sports teams. *Small Group Research, 36,* 166–187.

Hill, C. A. (2009). Affiliation motivation. In M. R. Leary & R. H. Hoyle (Eds.), *Handbook of individual differences in social behavior.* New York: Guilford Press.

Keyton, J. (1993). Group termination: Completing the study of group development. *Small Group Research, 24,* 84–100.

Olmsted, M. S., & Hare A. P. (1978). *The small group* (2nd ed.). New York: Random House.

Robert, H. M., Honemann, D. H., & Balch, T. J. (2011). Robert's rules of order: Newly revised (11th ed.). Philadelphia: Da Capo Press.

Shaw, M. (1981). *Group dynamics: The psychology of small group behavior.* New York: McGraw-Hill.

Tuckman, B. W. (1965). Developmental sequence in small groups. *Psychological Bulletin, 63*(6), 384– 399.

Tuckman, B. W., & Jensen, M. A. C. (1977). Stages of small-group development revisited. *Group & Organization Management, 2*(4), 419–427.

Problem-Solving and Decision-Making in Groups

By Greg G. Armfield

Objectives

- ► Compare and contrast stages or steps in the unitary sequence model of decision-making.
- ► Critique the constraints of effective decision-making.
- ► Critique the state criticisms of unitary models.
- ► Analyze structuration theory.

PROBLEM-SOLVING IN GROUPS

Contrary to Daniel Defoe's claim that "only death and taxes are certain," problems, too, are certain. Problems arise at home and work, within any given social setting, and inevitably at school within the confines of Higher Education. We are confronted with problems on a daily basis; being intellectual beings, we find unique, clever, and often unorthodox ways to tackle them. As individuals, we find solutions to problems unimaginable; as groups, we have provided answers to some of the most complex scenarios that have unfolded in recent years. Groups rebuild entire countries, stifle hunger and starvation, enacted civil rights movements, and created the world in which we live in today.

Solving a problem, or **problem-solving**, is a fundamental function of many groups, and how groups come to a decision is oftentimes an extremely interesting process. Generally, groups either knowingly, or quite often unknowingly, progress through a linear sequence that starts by defining and analyzing a problem. Once the problem has been identified by the group (this is actually the very first step), the problem should be analyzed thoroughly, then criteria for an adequate solution is established, and finally the group begins to identify solutions that could work. These solutions are then evaluated and a decision is made based on what the group deems will appropriately solve the problem (Adams & Galanes, 2011). Thus, problem-solving is viewed as a process, and by many a linear process (Engleberg & Wynn, 2003). Each of the four steps will be detailed below and illustrated in Figure 4.6 below.

PROBLEM-SOLVING

how groups come to a decision.

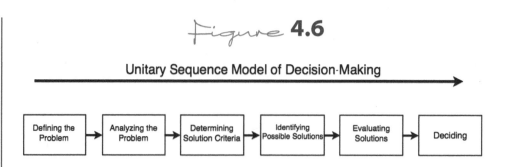

Figure **4.6**

Unitary Sequence Model of Decision-Making

Defining the Problem → Analyzing the Problem → Determining Solution Criteria → Identifying Possible Solutions → Evaluating Solutions → Deciding

Group problem-solving operates in the four identifiable phases as identified above. The first step, defining the problem, should begin by defining and stating the goals of the group as well as identifying the group's available resources and constraints (Adams & Galanes, 2011). Another consideration, this is often missed by groups, is to ensure the problem is important enough to solve as well as if this particular group is the right one for the job and has the right skillset. For example, a SWAT (Special Weapons and Tactics) team, for instance, should not bother addressing infrastructure issues in Haiti, in the same way that a group of engineers would not be the best suited group for a raid on a drug farm.

A good approach to the first step of **defining the problem** is to analyze the situation. A good approach to defining a problem is to state it in writing. This allows all group members to decide on a formal definition that should be stated as a question with only one central idea. Multiple ideas in one question lead to confusion and, as such, should be stated separately. This idea of mutual exclusivity is important when formulating the definition, "should the foreign language and social studies requirements be abolished at the university?" provides multiple ideas that most likely stem from different problems, beliefs, or issues. The use of specific and precise language aids comprehension of the problem, disallowing the mind to deviate from or misconstrue what is trying to be said. This issue would be better framed as two questions, one focused on the foreign language requirement, and the other focused on the social studies requirement. Finally, if the question the group poses is of fact, value, or policy, it more than likely satisfies a good definition of a problem.

Analysis of the problem entails finding out as much as possible about the problem and issues at hand as well as determine the criteria that must be met to find an acceptable solution (Adams & Galanes, 2011). First, a group must identify its audience, understand the history of the situation and its causes, and search for connections between the problem or opportunity and other issues involved. Three types of information are helpful in analyzing problems. First, begin by sharing the information that individual group members have acquired through their experiences. Second, examine published materials available through libraries, electronic databases, and the Internet. Oftentimes, the solution a group is looking for has already been established and, with a little research, an enormous amount of time can be saved. Finally, the group may want to consult experts for their ideas about a problem or conduct a survey to gather information from a particular target group. Stepping back and assessing the information the group has gathered provides insight to possible solutions and allows the group to determine the criteria for a plausible solution.

Once a group understands the nature of the problem, the third step is to determine what criterion should be established to ensure that any proposed solutions will solve the problem (Adams & Galanes, 2011). **Determining solution criteria** is a process of determining what test a solution should be able to pass in order to solve the given problem.

DEFINING THE PROBLEM

by analyzing the situation.

ANALYSIS OF THE PROBLEM

determine the criteria that must be met to find an acceptable solution.

DETERMINING SOLUTION CRITERIA

determining what tests a solution must pass in order to solve the problem.

© GaudiLab/Shutterstock.com

The criteria established then become the decisive factors in determining whether a solution will solve a problem. The group should ensure the criteria will provide a path for the best solution to be based on the information gathered to successfully solve the problem, and these criteria should be used to screen or choose the best solution.

Once the solution criterion is established, the fourth step is to **identify possible solutions**. The key to generating a series of creative solutions is to allow members freedom of expression. At this stage brainstorming and sharing of ideas is absolutely crucial in identifying these solutions. The key is to generate creative ideas that members are intrigued by; allowing them to further explore what could already be a great solution. Hirokawa (1987) states high-quality decisions are made by groups that are "careful, thoughtful, and systematic" (p. 10) in their evaluation options. It is very important to not judge the solutions during this stage.

After generating solutions, the group must **evaluate solutions** based on the solution criteria previously identified. Hirokawa (1988) argues that it is common for groups to begin by eliminating solutions that clearly do not meet important criteria and then to compare the positive features of the solutions that remain. The group needs to ask the following questions when evaluating a solution to circumvent any unintended or unforeseen problems that could arise from the solution. Does the solution actually solve the problem? Can it be done? If so, can it be done economically? Will the solution cause new problems? It is extremely important to explore the solution and ensure, to the best of the group's ability, the given solution will not create another problem.

The final step is to decide. Deciding is the ultimate **decision-making** process of choosing among the list of possible solutions and alternatives. In doing so, the group must come to a decision or conclusion as to which solution is the best. There are five methods that differ to the extent that each method requires members to agree with the decision and the amount of time it takes to reach a decision.

The **expert opinion** is established when all other alternatives have been eliminated, and the group member with the most expertise is asked to make the final decision (Adams & Galanes, 2011). This is quick and useful when one member is much more

IDENTIFY POSSIBLE SOLUTIONS

brainstorming and sharing of possible solutions.

EVALUATE SOLUTIONS

assessing each solution according to previously identified criteria.

DECISION-MAKING

the systematic process of evaluation and selecting the best solution.

EXPERT OPINION

is established when the group member with the most expertise makes the final decision.

**AVERAGE GROUP
OPINION METHOD**

each member of
the group ranks the
alternative solutions
and the highest
ranking becomes the
group choice.

**MAJORITY RULE
METHOD**

the group votes on
each alternative and
the one that receives
the majority vote is
selected.

**UNANIMOUS
DECISION METHOD**

uses continued
deliberation until
every member of the
group believes the
same solution is the
best.

**CONSENSUS
METHOD**

uses continued group
deliberation until
all members find an
acceptable decision
that they can support
and are committed to
help implement.

knowledgeable about the issue or has a greater stake in implementation of the decision. Alternatively, the **average group opinion method** is a decision-making process used when each member of the group ranks the alternatives that meet all the requirements and the one with the highest ranking becomes the choice. This approach can be very helpful when the group needs to make a quick decision or is under pressure to make a fast decision. This also works well for routine decisions that have very little to no consensus on the group. I have also witnessed this process used to rank solutions and frame a discussion about the top solutions. Quite often, a group will go with the average opinion methods and realize everyone is already in agreement and further discussion is not needed (Adams & Galanes, 2011).

Similar to the aforementioned method, the **majority rule method** encompasses the idea that the group votes on each alternative and the solution that receives the majority vote is selected (Adams & Galanes, 2011). This approach is considered the most democratic of all the methods; however, if the group is deciding on more than two solutions, one solution can earn the majority vote with less than 50% support from the group and the level or strength of objection coming from the opposition may be so great that more problems arise.

Although sometimes heavily tethered to groupthink (discussed in the latter portion of this section), the **unanimous decision method** practices continued deliberation until every member of the group believes the same solution is the best. This can be difficult to obtain, but when accomplished, members of the group will be committed to selling the decision to others and ensuring its implementation comes to fruition.

The **consensus method** builds on this idea, with continued group deliberation leading to a decision that all members find acceptable, can support, and are committed to help implement (Adams & Galanes, 2011). In fact, Rothwell (2014) noted that the consensus approach "tends to produce better decisions" (p. 272). This outcome may be attributed to the necessity of all members to endorse the decision. Furthermore, groups that make decisions based on **consensus** may believe there is a better solution than the decision that would have been agreed upon using unanimous decision.

© Flamingo Images/Shutterstock.com

Consensus is defined as a state of shared agreement (Saint & Lawson, 1997). Achieving true consensus in groups obliges agreement and approval from all members (DeStephen & Hirokawa, 1988). Consensus on which solution to implement is often arduous, but in doing so, the group has successfully fulfilled what it set out to do (Adams & Galanes, 2011). Using consensus produces a higher level of buy-in from all group members and, therefore, a higher level of support for the decision. Although majority rule method is widely used, selecting the consensus method is a wise investment if the group wants to gain everyone's support for the implementation of the solution. It is imperative the information gathered supports the chosen solution.

Other unitary sequence models of group development and decision-making exist. Fisher (1974), for example, discovered four phases that he argued unfold sequentially in time. Those phases are orientation, conflict, emergence, and reinforcement. Regardless of the unitary sequence used, all models assume that group decisions are made in a linear manner as the group progresses through each stage. Many scholars have argued that not all groups follow a linear path when making decisions and that some groups make decisions in cyclical patterns (see Poole, Seibold, & McPhee, 1985; 1996). We will return to the criticism of linear patterns of problem-solving later in the section after the discussion of the constraints groups face when making decisions.

CONSENSUS

a state of shared agreement.

CONSTRAINTS ON EFFECTIVE DECISION-MAKING

The idea that no group is entirely harmonious has been addressed in this section earlier, but the theoretical conceptualizations of the flaws that cause asynchrony within group settings remains to be addressed.

Groupthink

Groupthink occurs when members of a group come to consensus *not* because of mutual decision-making, but because the decision to not speak against the majority is a simpler option. Late psychologist Irving Janis coined the term, positing five conditions that

GROUPTHINK

group phenomenon that occurs when a group of people form a consensus in order to avoid conflict.

© Jacob Lund/Shutterstock.com

foster groupthink. Janis believed groupthink could take place if the group was highly cohesive; the group was of a mutual mindset (e.g., all Republican or Democrat); the group poorly gathered factual data; leadership within the group was highly influential (or coercion exists); and finally, a tendency to avoid conflict arose because of a high-stress situation (Janis, 1972). Groupthink, thus, is the outcome when members fail to provide critical analysis and open dialogue regarding decision-making, oftentimes just to avoid conflict or a potentially uncomfortable interaction.

The **Abilene Paradox** is one of the most common cited examples of groupthink where a family agrees with a suggestion for dinner, simply because the family members were unable to manage agreement or because of utter laziness. Harvey (1974) discusses the case of a family that is sitting around playing dominoes when the father suggests that they drive to Abilene, TX, two hours away from their home, for dinner. The wife agrees, and because the wife agrees, so does the son and mother-in-law. After making the trip there and back, a four hour round trip, the father mentions how nice the drive and dinner was, when his wife states, "it was long and hot and I would have rather stayed home." The father goes on to say that he only made the suggestion to please her, when the mother-in-law and son agree that they also would have rather not gone to Abilene (Harvey, 1974, p. 63). At the very core of the so-called Abilene Paradox is "the ability to manage agreement, not the inability to manage conflict" (Harvey, 1974, p. 66).

As we have come to find out groups are subject to many interpersonal problems (specifically those which are affiliative and egocentric); not to be overlooked, however, are the problems that arise when group members offer no input for fear of *rocking the boat*. Intrinsic to the standard unitary sequence models described earlier, which assumes groups follow a linear path when forming or making a decision, are constraints hindering the process. Constraints consist of, but are not limited to, group indecisiveness, personality clashes, and the ego of multiple leaders, which are just a few of the interactional conflicts that can prolong the decision-making process. Cognitive, affiliative, and egocentric constraints can exist in all groups and test the mental strength and will of members who are involved.

Cognitive constraints occur when a group feels under pressure as a result of a difficult task, a shortage of information, or there simply is not enough time to deal with the problem. Signs of cognitive constraints are comments such as: "How do they expect us to get this done in a week" or "we've got a ton of material to sift through." Overcoming these constraints requires a group to assure itself the task is important enough to give necessary time and to compensate for the difficulty. A group might need to overhaul the method used to produce a certain product, which would inevitably take lots of time. The group can overcome the anxiety brought about by time constraints by justifying the constraint is necessary and thusly labeling the time as well spent. In an ideal situation a group is forever harmonious and all acting members work synchronously to see a solution come to fruition. Ideal situations, however, are few and far between. As a result, **affiliative constraints** will begin to take a toll on the group. Occurring when some or all members of the group are more concerned about maintaining relationships than they are about making a high-quality decision, these constraints can be mortally detrimental to the group. Signs of affiliative constraints include reluctance to speak among each other, backing down for no apparent reason, and reluctance to show disagreement. Working through these constraints is often a matter of practicing the interpersonal skills we covered in Unit Three of this book or covered in the last section of this unit on organizational conflict. Once a group sees that constructive argument is healthy and good-natured, the group is more likely to

ABILENE PARADOX

the ability to manage agreement, not the inability to manage conflict.

COGNITIVE CONSTRAINTS

occur when a group feels pressure as a result of a difficult task, a shortage of information, or pressure of a timeline to solve a problem.

AFFILIATIVE CONSTRAINTS

occur when some or all group members are more concerned about maintaining relationships than they are about making a high-quality decision.

be honest with its opinions. Should a member assume the role of *devil's advocate,* this family of constraints can easily be eliminated.

Although not present in every group, **egocentric constraints** are often the bane of a group's success. When members of the group have high needs for control or are driven by other personal needs, the ego of the individual begins to dictate the way the group functions. These people see issues in terms of a "win-lose" situation and feel that getting the group to accept their position is a "win." If the group chooses another alternative, they have suffered a personal loss. What drives these egocentric individuals is not necessarily a strong preference for one alternative but the need to be "right." These constraints can be extremely difficult to overcome, but egocentric individuals are not incapable of rational thinking. Inviting them to verbalize the information upon which they are basing their conclusions can sometimes help them modify their position and focus on solving the problem at hand.

CRITICISMS OF UNITARY MODELS

Regardless of the unitary sequence model used, all models assume that group decisions are made in a linear manner, by the group progressing through each stage. Many scholars, however, argue that not all groups follow a linear path when making decisions and that some groups make decisions in cyclical patterns (see Poole, Seibold, & McPhee, 1985; 1996). In your experiences you have likely encountered a group that skipped right to norming, or perhaps the group already knew their assigned roles and progressed from forming directly to storming. Quite often my experience in academic groups has been one of quickly moving through the first three of Tuckman's stages (Forming, Storming, Norming) and participants jump to performing. If, or when, conflict arises the group will move backward to address norming and come to consensus regarding group norms then return to performing. The idea here is that established norms and rules are constantly changing and shifting directions depending on the context in which they are observed (Giddens, 1986).

Structuration theory (ST), originally conceptualized by sociologist Anthony Giddens in 1979, suggests human behavior is socially constructed and social systems are produced and reproduced through the group structure by the application of generalized rules and resources in human/organizational/group interaction (Giddens, 1986). This observable pattern of interaction and relationships among people within a group or organization is a **system**. An example of a system would be the interactions within a group. For example, students interacting with professors, and professors interacting with colleagues, department heads, or deans.

Giddens (1986) argues that the foundational structures of groups and organizations must be examined in order to make sense of a group or organizations communication. In ST, **structure** is comprised of the rules and resources that are recursively used to produce and reproduce communicative action in a social setting, specifically that of a group. During group interactions the group produces and reproduces the group structure through the use of agreed-upon communicative rules and resources used to interact with one another (Poole & McPhee, 2005). Furthermore, these interactions work to reaffirm the agreed-upon rules and resources through interactions that are stabilized across time and space.

Rules indicate the manner in which something ought to be done and help individuals decide whether a particular behavior or action will be interpreted negatively or positively (Poole & McPhee, 2005). Yet, rules go beyond describing what an employee

EGOCENTRIC CONSTRAINTS

when a member or members of the group have high ego needs for control or are driven by other personal needs.

STRUCTURATION THEORY (ST)

argues human behavior is socially constructed and social systems are produced and reproduced.

SYSTEM

an observable pattern of interactions.

STRUCTURE

the rules and resources used to produce and reproduce a social system such as a group.

RULES

indicate what should (ought) be done; rules are written or unwritten.

can and cannot do; rules guide interaction among group members. For instance, Professor Jones may outline in his syllabus that late work will be accepted under the pretense that a 10-point deduction will be enacted for each day the assignment is late. Within Professor Jones's structure, late work is accepted, but penalized. On the other hand, Professor Torres's syllabus indicates that late work is inexcusable, and an automatic "0" will be accrued for assignments not turned in on the due date. In both examples the rules are written. But in many organizational settings rules are unwritten or implied. For example, many college campuses have dress codes for all employees, including instructors and professors. In those dress codes, typically open-toed shoes are not allowed. If you work in maintenance or landscaping this would be strictly enforced, as not having proper footwear would be a health and safety risk. However, how many professors have you seen wear sandals or Birkenstocks? Dress codes can be overlooked for many faculty positions as rules on many campuses are not always enforced or may be in contradiction with an unwritten rule that has culturally been in place for years. Furthermore, many group norms are not written, but just accepted, such as the 5-minute rule for attendance. In other words, don't be more than 5 minutes late. Anything beyond 5 minutes is considered absent. Another example of a rule that may be written or unwritten is a K–12 teacher that considers students late if they are not sitting in their desk or chair when the bell rings. In other words, if you are standing next to your desk and the bell rings, you are late.

NORMS

rules that group members express; but are often unwritten.

RESOURCES

any number of materials, possessions, attributes, or power used to exert control or influence over group members.

STRUCTURATION

the production and reproduction of a social system through the use of rules and resources.

DUALITY OF STRUCTURE

the idea that structure is both the medium and the outcome of a recursive process.

Norms are the rules group members agree upon as what is to be expected in order to remain in good standing (Poole & McPhee, 2005). Oftentimes norms are unwritten. For example, the 5-minute rule discussed above is an unwritten rule in many organizations, and a norm for many faculty groups on a college campus. In addition, a norm of a college student might be having his/her work turned in on the due date or arriving to class at the scheduled time. It is important to note rules and norms are often unwritten and go unstated within groups and organizations.

The **resources** found within a structure could be any number of materials, possessions, attributes, or power used to exert control or influence over group members or the actions the group takes (Poole & McPhee, 2005). The most common types of resources in an organizational group include status, money, special knowledge, or a formal leadership position within the organization. Another example might be the experiences a group member had while at a previous job, a political position held in local government, the relations a person has with people of power or status, or the expenditure capabilities of the group.

Structuration occurs when members produce and reproduce a social system, such as a group, through the use of rules and resources in interaction (Poole & McPhee, 2005). Examples of social systems include organizational hierarchies, small groups, family communication patterns, and the production and reproduction of social systems through the application of structures through communicative interaction. Unique to structuration theory is the **duality of structure**, wherein Giddens states structures "are both the medium and outcome of the practices they recursively organize" (1986, p. 25). The beauty of structuration lies within the ever-expanding boundaries to which groups conform. Structuration is an ongoing process, where the duality of structure suggests that neither the medium nor outcome can exist without the other, while rules and norms are never static but the system continues to reproduce itself, even if it looks like nothing has changed (Giddens, 1986). The reality is that a group is continuing to reproduce the same social system by reinforcing the same social system through rules and resources. If the rules and resources change, so will the way a group functions. A university system intrinsically practices structuration through its daily functions organized around the members that will continue to reproduce and reinforce

Visual Representation of Structuration Theory in Group Decision-Making

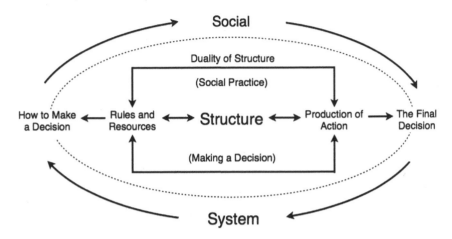

the duality of structure by influencing structure in a circular fashion, unless a rule or resource or some other system interference occurs.

Communication scholar Marshall Scott Poole (1990) has spent a good portion of his career applying Gidden's theory to real-world situations and has developed a multiple sequence model largely based on structuration. Adaptive Structuration Theory by Poole (1990) posits that groups may skip steps of decision-making processes or only take them in part. As discussed previously, Tuckman's unitary sequence model is linear and suggests that groups follow a predetermined path when making decisions, while "Poole's model views group decision-making as a set of parallel activities which evolve simultaneously and function to form different patterns over time" (Fisher & Stutman, 1987, p. 105). These patterns through the multiple sequence model as structuration theory describes are in turn dynamic and allow groups to find their own way for decision-making. Figure 4.7 illustrates how structuration theory functions in a cyclical, continuous motion.

CONCLUSION

Understanding small groups and interactions in small groups is important since your participation in a small group is inevitable. Groups are everywhere, operate in every organization, and their importance is increasing. By understanding group decision processes, group participants can learn how to communicate more effectively in them. Group communication is more complex and typically more task-oriented than dyadic communication. Compared to public speaking, group communication is less formal, the sender and receiver alternate roles more frequently, and feedback is more immediate.

Understanding how groups form and the unique dynamics that each present is crucial to effectively communicating within them. Groups regularly face conflict and endure many trials, but it is when a group comes together to solve a problem that no one individual could solely solve that the benefits of working in a group emerge. As an entity that is truly multifaceted and dynamic, as there is never a set method for solving problems, groups lend intuitive minds a unique outlet for crafting creative and innovative solutions in an efficient and timely manner.

Discussion Questions

1. Identify and describe each of the stages for problem-solving as discussed in the section.

2. Identify and describe the constraints that groups may face when making a decision.

3. Describe the difference between the unitary sequence model of group formation and the cyclical pattern of group formation.

4. Describe the Abilene Paradox.

5. Define structuration theory and each of the major components identified by Giddens.

Acknowledgment

I would like to extend my sincere appreciation to Mario Selle for his previous contributions to an earlier printing of this content.

References

Adams, K., & Galanes, G. J. (2011). *Communicating in groups: Applications and skills* (8th ed.). Boston: McGraw-Hill.

DeStephen, R., & Hirokawa, R. (1988). Small group consensus: Stability of group support of the decision, task process, and group relationships. *Small Group Behavior, 19,* 227–239.

Engleberg, I. N., & Wynn, D. R. (2003). *Working in groups: Communication principles and strategies* (3rd ed.). Boston: Houghton Mifflin.

Fisher, B. A. (1974). *Small group decision-making: Communication and the group process.* New York: McGraw-Hill.

Fisher, B. A., & Stutman, R. K. (1987) An assessment of group trajectories: Analyzing developmental breakpoints. *Communication Quarterly, 35,* 105–124.

Giddens, A. (1979*). Central problems in social theory: Action, structure, and contradiction in social analysis.* Berkley, CA: University of California Press.

Giddens, A. (1986). *The constitution of society.* Berkley, CA: University of California Press.

Harvey, J. B. (1974). The Abilene Paradox: The management of agreement. *Organizational Dynamics, 3*(1), 63–80.

Hirokawa, R. Y. (1987). Why informed groups make faulty decisions. *Small Group Behavior, 18,* 3–29.

Hirokawa, R. Y. (1988). Group communication and decision-making performance: A continued test of the functional perspective. *Human Communication Research, 14,* 487–515.

Janis, I. L. (1972). *Victims of Groupthink.* Boston: Houghton Mifflin.

Poole, M. S. (1990). Do we have any theories of group communication? *Communication Studies 41*(3), 237–247.

Poole, M. S., & McPhee, R. D. (2005). Structuration theory. In S. May and D. K. Mumby (Eds.), *Engaging organizational communication theory & research: Multiple perspectives* (pp. 171–195). Thousand Oaks, CA: Sage.

Poole, M. S., Seibold, D. R., & McPhee, R. D. (1985). Group decision-making as a structurational model. *Quarterly Journal of Speech, 17,* 74–102.

Poole, M. S., Seibold, D. R., & McPhee, R. D. (1996). The structuration of group decisions. In R. Y. Hirokawa and M. S. Poole (Eds.), *Communication and group decision-making* (2nd ed., pp. 114–146), Thousand Oaks, CA: Sage.

Rothwell, J. D. (2014). *In mixed company: Communicating in small groups and teams* (9th ed.). Boston: Cengage.

Saint, S., & Lawson, J. (1997). Rules for reaching consensus. San Diego: Pfeiffer.

Leadership

By Greg G. Armfield

Objectives

▶ Evaluate the positive and negative attributes of leaders.
▶ Describe leadership styles, approaches, and theories.
▶ Consider how you are becoming a leader.

At some point everyone will be asked or required to step up and lead in some form or fashion. While there is no universally agreed-upon definitions of what leadership is, I can assure you leadership is not yelling directions or generally bossing people around. This is called an omnipotence fallacy. Those who think they are all-powerful and can do whatever they want are more likely to have been placed in a position of power, but they did not earn the position through gaining the respect of others. Nor is leadership being a know-it-all (omniscience) like Sheldon Cooper from *The Big Bang Theory*. Power hungry leaders will very often be found to have a heightened sense of entitlement, and quite often these people will exhibit narcissistic traits.

A good general definition of **leadership** is, "A process whereby an individual influences a group of individuals to achieve a common goal" (Northouse, 2007, p. 5). Breaking down this definition recognizes the leadership is first a process, not a trait or characteristic, that one individual has or does not have. A process indicates becoming a leader involves a series of steps, taken in order, to achieve a goal or outcome. Next, leadership involves influencing an individual or a group of individuals. A leader influences and persuades multiple audiences, not just their subordinates, as to the correct direction the company should move, as well as the mission of the organization to ultimately achieve an agreed upon goal. Having a common goal between a leader and follower implies a mutual agreement and emphasizes the importance of ethical responsibility. In addition, anytime communication is used to influence others, ethical standards must be adhered to (Rost, 1991). Furthermore, Burns (1978) argued that leaders should have an ethic of caring and pay attention to the leader-follower relationship.

LEADERSHIP

"a process whereby an individual influences a group of individuals to achieve a common goal" (Northouse, 2007, p. 5).

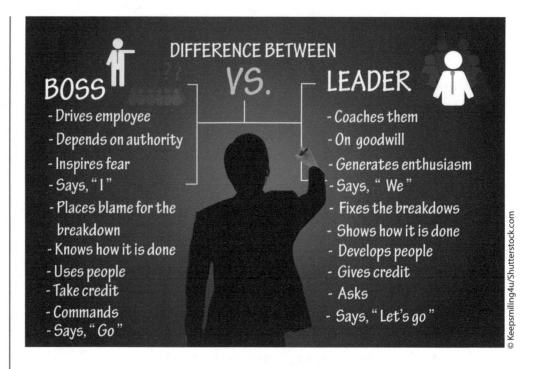

DIFFERENCE BETWEEN

BOSS **VS.** **LEADER**

- Drives employee
- Depends on authority
- Inspires fear
- Says, "I"
- Places blame for the breakdown
- Knows how it is done
- Uses people
- Take credit
- Commands
- Says, "Go"

- Coaches them
- On goodwill
- Generates enthusiasm
- Says, "We"
- Fixes the breakdows
- Shows how it is done
- Develops people
- Gives credit
- Asks
- Says, "Let's go"

© Keepsmiling4u/Shutterstock.com

© Natasa Adzic/Shutterstock.com

A second definition that applies to leadership is from Warren Bennis' book *On Becoming a Leader*. Bennis (1989) states, "The point is not to become a leader. The point is to become yourself, and to use yourself completely—all your gifts, skills, and energies—to make your vision manifest. You must withhold nothing. You must, in sum, become the person you started out to be, and to enjoy the process of becoming" (pp. 111–112). This is the philosophy I encourage you to embrace throughout your lifetime, as becoming a leader is a process. You are never finished; always and continuously work toward being a better person and a better leader. With that in mind, the next section will review three leadership styles.

While there is no single agreed upon definition of leadership, or what a leader should be, there are several philosophies of leadership that over time have received an abundance of attention. Research has focused on positive and negative attributes of leaders. The GLOBE study assessed 62 different societies in order to establish a list of positive and negative universal leadership attributes. In doing so House, Hanges, Javidan, Dorfman, Gupta (2004) built a perspective of leader attributes that have been recognized internationally as positive or negative (see Table 4.1). Next, I will review some of the most prominent and important approaches to leadership that have developed over time, beginning with three different leadership styles and approaches before we turn our attention to three major theories of leadership, and finishing with a discussion of creating a personalized leadership approach.

YOUR PERSONAL LEADERSHIP STYLE

Why is it important to understand your personal style of leadership? Because, as a leader, you set the tone of the organization you are leading or on a smaller level, the group or division that you lead. As you read the following pages in this section, reflect on the productive ways you have, or could have, helped group members perform at a

Table 4.1
Universal Leadership Attributes

Positive Leadership Attributes

Administratively skilled	Encouraging	Motivational
Builds confidence	Excellence oriented	Motivator
Communicative	Foresighted	Plans ahead
Coordinator	Honest	Positive
Decisive	Informed	Team builder
Dependable	Intelligent	Trustworthy
Dynamic	Just	Win-win problem solver
Effective bargainer		

Negative Leadership Attributes

Asocial	Irritable	Nonexplicit
Dictatorial	Loner	Ruthless
Egocentric	Noncooperative	

Source: House, R. H., Hanges, P. J., Javidan, M., Dorfman, P. W., & Gupta, V. (Eds.) (2004). *Culture, leadership, and organizations: The GLOBE study of 62 societies.* Thousand Oaks, C.A. Sage Publications.

higher level. How could you have provided structure or boundaries for followers or group members in the past so that they could work effectively?

Your personal philosophy, which influences your leadership style, should be built off your own individual set of unique habits. Much like how you balance work and play in your personal life, leaders should have a sense of balance in their personal leadership approach much like one should have a balance between being a task-oriented or relationship-oriented leader. While many of us will exhibit a blend of approaches, most leaders will lean toward one style. For example, task-oriented people are goal-oriented. They want to achieve and their work is where they find meaning. Reaching a goal is a positive expression of who they are. They facilitate goal accomplishment, initiate structure, organize work, define responsibilities, and schedule work activities. Task-oriented leaders thrive from the production orientation and technical aspects of a job. Their focus is primarily on how the job will be done.

The culture a task-oriented leader will seek to provide is structure, it is one that clarifies rules and norms, and promotes a standard of excellence among all. Task-oriented leaders will set the tone in a productive way and help group members perform at their highest levels of excellence. Providing structure gives people a sense of security, direction, and stability.

While all leaders will not obviously be successful every time or in every situation, most would consider Michael Jordan a great leader on the basketball court. Yet, Nike ran an advertisement quoting Michael Jordan:

> I've missed more than 9,000 shots in my career. I've lost almost 300 games. Twenty-six times I've been trusted to take the game-winning shot and missed. I've failed over, and over, and over again in my life. And, that is why I succeed (Zorn, 1997).

In doing this, Nike and Michael Jordan reinforced that not all leaders are successful 100% of the time. In fact, the most successful entrepreneurs have failed at some point;

but they didn't think of themselves as failures. They learned from their mistakes and became a better person, entrepreneur, and leader. The following sections will review leadership styles, approaches, and theories. Consider which one(s) you most align to.

LEADERSHIP STYLES

Lewin, Lippitt, and White (1939) were one of the first groups to conduct research on the impact of leadership styles on small-group behavior. From their research, three distinct styles emerged: authoritarian, democratic, and laissez-faire.

AUTHORITARIAN LEADERS

exert influence and control over others.

Authoritarian Style

Authoritarian leaders perceive subordinates as needing direction and, therefore, exert influence and control over group members. Their communication is directive and top-down. An authoritarian leader will set the agenda of the organization and direct the organization based on what they perceive is best for the organization. They give praise and criticism freely, but the praise and criticism are based on their personal standard. The weaknesses of this approach are that followers tend to be submissive and dependent on the leader. This approach doesn't allow for followers to grow or to express individuality. It can also lead to organizational discontent and hostility. The strengths of this approach are that the organization can be efficient and productive. It is also argued that more can be accomplished in a short period of time as long as the followers are in alignment (Northouse, 2015).

© alphaspirit/Shutterstock.com

DEMOCRATIC LEADERS

are capable of working with others without exerting control or power.

Democratic Style

Democratic leaders perceive subordinates as capable of working on their own without the excursion of any control or power over them. Leaders that utilize a democratic style *work with* followers and treat them fairly in an egalitarian manner. In this way the leader speaks to followers on the same level, not talking down to followers. The weaknesses of this approach are that this style takes more time and commitment than an authoritarian approach, and this approach can lead to lower productivity and organizational inefficiencies. The advantages of this approach include greater group member satisfaction, commitment, and cohesiveness among followers. Followers tend to have a higher level of motivation and greater creativity and originality. Democratic leaders also develop a culture of friendliness, mutual praise, support, and group mindedness (Northouse, 2015).

LAISSSEZ-FAIRE LEADERS

takes an extremely hands-off approach and do not exert control or influence over others.

Laissez-Faire Style

Laissez-faire leaders perceive subordinates as needing little direction, influence, or control. In fact, their influence as a leader is nominal. Think of this as a country club approach to leadership. Laissez-faire leaders take a hands-off approach to leadership and do not exert any control or influence over groups or outcomes. Many argue laissez-faire leadership has few, if any, positive outcomes. Weaknesses include members who feel directionless, unmotivated, and disheartened. However, this style can work if the followers are highly motivated, understand their role in the organization, and need little to no direction or oversight (Northouse, 2015).

All three of the leadership styles—authoritarian, democratic, and laissez-faire—reflect a philosophy of leadership that are based on our assumptions about human nature in relation to how we as individuals believe followers of subordinates need to be influenced. A laissez-faire leader assumes people are self-motivated and need little to no influence to complete a task. The opposite, in turn, is an authoritarian leader who believes leaders need high influence to get followers to complete a task. Democratic leaders are the middle-of-the-road. They believe a moderate amount of influence is needed to encourage and direct followers. Understanding how our philosophy of leadership influences our style of leadership is the first step in becoming a more competent leader.

LEADERSHIP APPROACHES

The following section will review some of the major approaches and theories of leadership that have been developed over time.

Trait Approach

Referred to as The "Great Man" or trait theory, it was originally argued that leaders were born not formed. For example, to be a great leader one might have thought that you had to be tall, good–looking, and male; thus a "Great Man" or great leader. Today, trait theory focuses on the unique set of traits that each leader has. The emphasis is on the leader-follower context and their working relationship. While the "Great Man" theory has been thoroughly criticized and trashed, the reality of the modern approach to the trait approach is that all people are born with a unique set of traits that can be built upon, modified, and changed.

Strong successful leaders the likes of George Washington, Harriet Tubman, Eleanor Roosevelt, Winston Churchill, Mother Teresa, Nelson Mandela, Bill Gates, or Oprah Winfrey all share the following traits: visionary, strong-willed, diligent, inspirational, purpose-driven, role model, symbol of hope (Northouse, 2018). From these exceptional leaders we can gain a better understanding of traits that are important for effective leadership. Additional traits of successful leaders include intelligence (IQ), emotional intelligence (EQ), confidence, charisma, determination, sociability, integrity, honesty, competent, forward-looking, inspiring, fair-minded, broad-minded, courageous, straightforward, imaginative, honest, inspiring, visionary, and a strong sense of purpose have all been argued to be traits that successful and prominent leaders have mastered. One of the next approaches to leadership was the ability approach.

Ability Approach

Ability refers to the capacity or one's capacity to learn. Everyone has the natural capacity to learn how to do or accomplish something. Did you play a musical instrument when you were younger? The more you practiced, the better you became. That is your natural capacity or ability to learn. We can develop our abilities as a person or a leader through hard work and practice. For example, you can become a better speaker by practicing the art of speechmaking. John Wooden, who has won the most NCAA

TRAIT APPROACH OR THE GREAT MAN THEORY

argues leaders are born.

ABILITY APPROACH

the capacity to learn.

Men's Basketball Championships, taught his players the value of hard work and developing one's abilities through practice. His goal was to practice game simulations so that his players would instinctively do the right thing, make the correct play, and perform well when under great pressure. Another approach that was explored after trait approach is the behavioral approach.

Behavior Approach

BEHAVIOR APPROACH

what leaders do. It's the actions of a leader.

The behavior approach is about the actions of a leader. When you are a leader, you act like one. It is what leaders do when they are in a leadership role. Leadership requires both task and process behaviors. Task-focused leadership is when leaders focus on the task at hand that needs to be performed, whereas process-focused leaders are focused on learning together with their followers and sharing the experience with others (Howell & Costley, 2001). Task-focused leaders find meaning in their work, they want to achieve, and they typically like to make "to-do" lists. Accomplishing goals and getting things done is one of the reasons they exist. They identify heavily with what they have accomplished. Process-focused leaders are more about the progression toward a goal (task), their (individual) development, and the development of their team or the organization while working toward the goal. A phrase I like is, *it's about the journey, not the destination.* If you think about that statement, it really speaks to the ideas that the journey you are on, or in this case the journey of becoming a good leader, is more important than the ultimate goal of being a good leader.

In reality, effective leaders combine both task and process behaviors in the best possible way to become the best leaders possible. The idea is that everyone learns together. Some people learn to lead, some learn to follow, and some learn to support; but everyone has the same experience and partakes in a learning experience (Howell & Costley, 2001). Similar to ability and behavioral approach is the skill approach.

Skill Approach

SKILL APPROACH

to know how to do something and be competent in a given skill.

A skill means that you know how to do something and are competent. When you look at leadership as a skill or competency, the ability to become a leader is now available to everyone. If you learn from experience, leadership can't be a trait, it is a skill or competency that is acquired through experience. Given that leadership skills are a learned competency, leaders are able to demonstrate their skills (Katz, 1955). The skills approach, in what few studies that have explored them, tend to be discussed within three different groups: administrative, interpersonal, and conceptual. Northouse (2018) argues that the administrative grouping includes a leader's ability to manage people, manage resources, and show technical competence. Interpersonal grouping includes a leader's ability to be socially perceptive, demonstrate emotional intelligence, and manage interpersonal conflict. Finally, the conceptual grouping includes a leader's ability to provide strategic planning, create an organizational vision, and solve problems (Northouse, 2018). The next approach we will cover is the strength-based approach.

Strength-Based Approach

STRENGTH

an attribute that can account for success.

Similar to ability, behavior, and the skill approaches, the strength-based approach identifies attributes or qualities that an individual has developed which account for consistently successful performances. Linley (2008) explains a strength as a capacity that enables extraordinary work. Further, Buckingham and Clifton (2001) argue a strength is the ability of an individual to consistently demonstrate outstanding work. This approach to leadership has been practiced by 3M for years. More recently Facebook and Google have been utilizing this approach to teamwork.

The challenge leaders face is to identify or realize what their leadership strengths are as well as those strengths of their followers. One issue we face in identifying our strengths is that we often are timid or even shy when trying to acknowledge our own strengths or positive attributes. Northouse (2015) points out that in Western or "American" culture it is often viewed as self-serving or conceited to acknowledge or talk about our own strengths. "In fact, focusing on [one] self is disdained in many cultures, while showing humility and being self-deprecating is seen as virtuous" (Northouse, 2015, p. 49).

Gallup has identified four domains of strength using a 177-item questionnaire. The four domains—executing, influencing, relationship building, and strategic thinking—have been researched by Gallup and were the brainchild of Donald O. Clifton over 40 years ago (Clifton & Harter, 2003). Effective teams enjoy a wide range of strengths represented on their teams. Leaders need to identify and engage their followers' strengths. Knowing your followers' strengths allows the leaders to place followers in positions that they will succeed in and promote a positive work environment, which in turn will have a positive impact on individual and organizational work performance. While the strengths-based approach is a new area of research, the approach provides a unique path to becoming a more effective leader. Tom Rath's (2007) Strengths-Finder 2.0 has continued to carry on this line of research. The last approach discussed in this section is the relational approach.

To watch a video about Strength-Finder 2.0: https://www.youtube.com/watch?v=qS1mT_NmDoM

Relational Approach

Leadership as a relationship may strike you as a funny notion. However, the relationship leaders have with followers is the result of the collaborative process between a leader and follower. The relationship approach is centered on the communication between leader and follower. The key to relational leadership from a communication standpoint is that the communication between leader and follower is an interactive process. In

RELATIONAL APPROACH

centers on the communicative relationship between a leader and a follower.

© fizkes/Shutterstock.com

comparison, an authoritative leader will use a top-down, one-way communication approach. In short, relationship leaders believe three things:

1. Treating followers with dignity and respect.
2. Building relationships and helping people get along.
3. Making the work setting a pleasant place to be.

Following these three items is an integral part of being a relationship leader (Northouse, 2018).

Relationship-oriented people find meaning in being rather than in doing. Instead of seeking out tasks, relationship-oriented people want to connect with others (Blake & Mouton, 1964). They have strong orientation in the present and find meaning in the moment. Relationship leaders are more focused on an employee orientation that focuses on taking an interest in workers as human beings, valuing follower uniqueness, and giving special attention to their personal needs. In doing so, relationship leaders show a concern for their followers, building trust, providing good working conditions, maintaining a fair salary structure, and promoting good social relations (Bowers & Seashore, 1966). All leaders have preferences when it comes to work based on task and relationship. Your style preference influences your leadership style. Understanding your personal styles of work and play can provide a better insight into your personal leadership style. Developing your style of leadership will be discussed later in this section.

LEADERSHIP THEORIES

From the styles and approaches that have been studied for years, several theories of leadership have emerged. The first of the major theories of leadership was developed by Bernard Bass (1990).

**TRANSFOR-
MATIONAL
LEADERS**

have a visible positive
impact on followers.

Transformational Leadership

Transformational leadership, also known as charismatic leadership, is one of the most researched leadership theories (Aldoory & Toth, 2004; Barbuto & Burbach, 2006). Charismatic leadership is rooted in Weber (1947), but the development of transformational leadership has its significant beginnings in Burns (1978) and was notably extended by Bass (1985). Based on the positive impact on followers. Bass (1985) argues there are four components of transformational leadership: idealized influence, inspirational motivation, intellectual stimulation, and individualized consideration.

Idealized influence, or *charisma* (Bass, 1985). The leader is viewed as a strong role model and followers seek to emulate the leader (Northouse, 2007). "These leaders usually have very high standards of moral and ethical conduct and can be counted on to do the right thing" (pp. 181–182). They gain followers' trust and are able to encourage others to follow their mission or vision and generally engage moral higher reasoning (Avolio, 2005; Bass & Steidlmeier, 1998). Although often conflated with charismatic leadership, researchers caution that transformational leadership is not just due to charisma. "Because charisma is a relationship and not a personality characteristic of leaders, charisma exists only because followers say it does or followers behave in specific ways" (House, Spangler, & Woycke, 1991, p. 366). Thus, transformational leadership relies heavily on the perception of followers.

© Gustavo Frazao/Shutterstock.com

Followers are inspired to commit to a leader's vision of a "more desirable future" (Avolio, 2005, p. 196) through the use of symbols and pathos as a result of the second factor, which is *inspirational motivation*. The leader takes the focus off of self-interest and places it on team effort. Inspirational leaders are not afraid to take risks to achieve their vision and are able to motivate others to join them on the journey. This is done through *intellectual stimulation*, the third factor, asking followers to be creative and innovative. In so doing, followers should also continuously challenge their own beliefs and the beliefs of the leader and organization. The goal of sharing diverse ideas is to generate "the highest levels of creativity from one's followers" (Avolio, 2005, p. 197). Transformational leaders ultimately encourage followers to look at problems in new ways (Avolio & Gibbons, 1988). Transformational leaders "are distinguished by their risk-taking, goal articulation, high expectations, emphasis on collective identity, self-assertion, and vision" (Aldoory & Toth, 2004, p. 159). However, these factors are dependent on the relational aspects of leader communication.

Transformational leadership is about the relationship between the leader and the followers, which makes the final factor, *individualized consideration*, a key characteristic. Leaders appear supportive by listening to the needs of followers and communicating expressively. The leader might delegate so followers begin to take their own initiative. Leaders who get to know those they work with can be supportive where necessary, but challenging also to help followers in their own development as leaders. Transformational leaders attempt to motivate followers into action to the point of no longer needing to rely on the leader. Such efforts to help mold others as leaders might be difficult under America's current political system and climate, but it makes sense that the President should help Congressional representatives be more innovative rather than divisive.

Although some view transformational leadership as an "either you are or you are not" dichotomy, Avolio and Gibbons (1988) argued that is a matter of degree and can appear at all levels of an organizational hierarchy. "The leader's enthusiasm for an objective can become infectious. The sense of inner-direction, if translated properly by the leader, will attract followers who agree with the leader's end values" (p. 288). It also should be viewed as an ongoing process, allowing that some leaders might move toward becoming transformational leaders, and likewise, transformational leaders have to work to maintain a commitment to improving one's self (Bennis & Nanus, 1985) and continuously challenge themselves. Transformation leaders work to stimulate and encourage creativity by exploring new ways of doing or learning things. In doing so, they quite often challenge the status quo. Transformational leaders offer individualized encouragement and support to followers, developing supporting relationships and establishing an open line of communication, leading to a free flow of idea sharing and recognition of each individual's unique contribution. In doing so, transformational leaders are able to articulate a clear vision and their passion and motivation toward their vision is essentially contagious. Transformational leaders focus not only on bringing their vision to fruition, but also on helping each of their followers succeed as well.

While there are several theories of leadership that have developed over time, the two most centrally related to communication are leader member exchange (LMX) theory and servant leadership. In addition to being communication centered, the styles, approaches, and theory reviewed up to this point have all looked at the leader-follower relationship from the perspective of the leader. LMX focuses on the interactions between the leader and follower as they are engaged in a relationship. The focuses of communication and the origination of the theory is the individual relationships between the leader and *each* follower; whereas other leadership theories and styles focus on the relationship between the leader and followers as a group. LMX conceptualizes leadership as a process centered on the interactions between a leader and each follower.

Leader Member Exchange (LMX)

Originally called Vertical Dyad Linkage (VDL), VDL focuses on the link, or relationship, formed between the leader and each (individual) follower. Early studies on VDL explored the individual relationships between leader and follower by focusing on the quantity of interactions between the leader and follower. Those followers that communicated more often with the leaders were classified as in-group members, and those who communicated less often were seen as out-group members. Earlier research also found that subordinates were either in the in- or out-group based on the quantity of interaction with the leader. Further, it was found that in-group members were able to exert more influence than out-group members.

Graen and Uhl-Bien (1995) depicted this dyadic relationship similar to Figure 4.8. For LMX, the dyadic relationship between leader and follower is the focal point of the theory. While LMX has undergone several revisions, LMX argues all other leadership theories focus on the leader-follower dynamic in a way that all followers in a group are treated as a collective and all followers are the same. By exploring the dyadic relationship between the leader and follower as an interpersonal dyadic relationship, LMX recognizes that differences exist between a leader and each of their followers.

One might think that looking at leadership as a dyadic relationship between the leader and follower is unusual. And, in a way it is. LMX is the only theory to frame leadership as a dyadic relationship between leader and follower. In doing so, the focus is on the communication, which is an interaction and interactive, between the leader and follower. Thus, the dyadic relationship between leader and follower (see Figure 4.8) is the focal point of the leadership process. In focusing on the relationship between leader and follower, the leadership process is centered on the interaction

Figure **4.8**

| Leader | Dyadic Relationship | Follower |

Source: Adapted from Graen, G. B., & Uhl-Bien, M. (1995). Relationship-based approach to leadership: Development of leader-member exchange (LMX) theory of leadership over 25 years: Applying a multi-domain perspective. *Leadership Quarterly,* 6(2), 219–247.

between leader and follower. This focus on communication interaction is unique to LMX. No other leadership theory focuses on this interaction.

Later studies involving LMX explored the quality of LMX and of group interactions. High quality exchanges were found to increase organizational effectiveness. As leaders developed a quality relationship with each organizational member, those members felt as if they were part of the in-group, which can benefit organizational goals and progress.

LMX provides a descriptive process (see Northouse, 2019) for leaders to develop quality relationships with all organizational members and make all followers feel like in-group members. LMX theory is also a very unique theory in that it is the only leadership approach focused on dyadic relationships as a leadership process. This is noteworthy because LMX directs our attention to the importance of communication in leadership and there is a large body of research that substantiates communication practices are positively related to organizational outcomes.

Regardless of your personal style or preference, or the theory (e.g., LMX or Transformational) that best aligns with your preferred leadership style, all leadership has a moral dimension, because leaders influence the lives of others. Ethical leadership is defined as the influence of a moral person who moves others to do the right thing in the right way for the right reasons (Ciulla, 2003). Earlier in Unit One, Section 5, we discussed general approaches to ethics and several ethical theories. Here I want to briefly review ethics with respect to leadership and introduce my favorite leadership theory, servant leadership.

Despite the numerous scandals in the business and public sectors, organizational leaders have an obligation to work for the common good (Northouse, 2018). I argue that ethical leaders should:

- ▶ Treat other people with respect
- ▶ Respect other people's values
- ▶ Allow other people to be themselves
- ▶ Approach others with a sense of unconditional worth
- ▶ Value individual differences.

While ethical leadership has many dimensions, Northouse (2018) summarizes ethical leadership as character, actions, goals, honesty, power, and values. To be an ethical leader, you need to pay attention to who you are, what you do, what goals you seek, your honesty, how you use power, and what you value. The one theory that has the strongest altruistic ethical overtones is servant leadership.

Servant Leadership

Servant leadership was originally developed and defined by Robert Greenleaf (1977) as a "natural feeling that one wants to serve, and serve *first*" (p. 7). Later, the person makes a conscious choice that brings one's aspiration to lead. The difference manifests itself in the care taken by the servant—first to make sure that other people's highest

© Marijana Batinic/Shutterstock.com

priority needs are being served. Greenleaf (1977) argues that the best test is: Do those served grow as persons? Do they (those served), while being served, become healthier, wiser, freer, more autonomous, more likely themselves to become servant? And, What is the effect on the least privileged in society; will they benefit, or, at least, will they not be further deprived? (p. 7).

Servant leadership is somewhat of a paradox as some scholars treat it as a trait but most, including me, view it as a behavior. Further, the action of being a servant leader is service and influence. Until recently, servant leadership was very prescriptive in its approach to leadership. However, the past 10 to 15 years has seen scholars working to provide more clarification of the assumptions and concepts that underlie servant leadership by identifying the key characteristics that make up a servant leader. Spears (2002) identified 10 characteristics based on Greenleaf's writings that are viewed as central to the development of a servant leader (see Table 4.2).

Table **4.2**

Ten Characteristics of Servant Leaders Based on Robert Greenleaf's Writings

Listening	Acknowledging the viewpoint of followers and validating these perspectives.
Empathy	"Standing in the shoes" of another person and attempting to see the world from that person's point of view.
Healing	Helping followers become whole, servant leaders are themselves healed.
Awareness	Understanding oneself and the impact one has on others.
Persuasion	Creates change through gentle, nonjudgmental argument.
Conceptualization	The ability to be a visionary for an organization.
Foresight	The ability to predict what is coming based on what is occurring in the present and what has happened in the past.
Stewardship	Carefully managing the people and organization one has been given to lead. Holding the organization in trust for the greater good of society.
Commitment to the Growth of People	Treating each follower as a unique person with intrinsic value beyond what he/she contributes to the organization.
Building Community	Allowing followers to identify with something greater than themselves that they value.

In addition to the 10 characteristics identified by Spears (2002), several scholars have focused on understanding the concepts of servant leadership, a process needed to understand the theoretical concepts presented. One of the most comprehensive collections of this work was presented by van Dierendonck (2011). Van Dierendonck summarized the key characteristics of servant leadership as empowering and developing people, humility, authenticity, interpersonal acceptance, providing direction, and stewardship.

© Ted Pendergast/Shutterstock.com

As the servant leader nurtures others, the ethical responsibility in serving both an organization and others involves removing any existing inequalities and social injustices that exist. It is also typical for servant leaders to exert less institutional-ized power and control, while shifting more authority to followers much in the way Southwest Airlines did under leaders prior to Gary Kelly. Servant leadership is rooted in a contradiction of historical authoritarian beliefs of leaders being directors, as ser-vant leader serves the higher purpose or serves the organization (Liden, Wayne, Zhao, & Henderson, 2008).

Servant leadership is most often found in nonprofit organizations and reli-gious organizations (e.g., Mother Teresa). It can be applied and used at all levels of management and in all types of organizations (e.g., Southwest Airlines, Starbucks, Nordstrom, Marriott, REI). While different from other approaches reviewed here, Liden, Panaccio, Hu, and Meuser (2014) have found the three outcomes of successful practice of servant leadership by organizations is follower growth, increased organiza-tional performance, and a positive societal impact. To date, hundreds of studies have been published on servant leadership. Eva, Robin, Sendjaya, van Dierendonck, and Liden (2019) have found a consistent, positive relationship between servant leader-ship and highly valued outcomes for all types of organizations at the individual (cit-izenship), team (performance and potency), and organizational (customer service/satisfaction and return on investment) level. In short, servant leadership provides a philosophy and characteristics that you can learn and practice in the organizational setting as well as in your personal life. Following the principles of servant leadership will have a significant impact on how you think and act, which in turn have a positive impact on you, your followers, and the organization you serve. Furthermore, selecting or training leaders who practice servant leadership is "especially well-suited for an organization that desires long-term growth and benefits for all stakeholders" (Eva et al., 2019).

The focus of servant leadership is for leaders to put the follower and the organi-zation first. They should focus and attend to their followers by empowering, trusting, and developing them, while taking care of and nurturing the growth of their followers. Servant leaders must understand that "going beyond one's self-interest" is the core characteristic of servant leaders (Greenleaf, 1977, p. 7). For followers, leaders, and organizations to achieve their full potential all involved must recognize that all organizational employees must feel empowered to handle tasks and decisions on their own without fear of reprimand (Eva et al., 2019). Developing, nurturing, and allowing a culture of servant leadership will result in increased loyalty, customer satisfaction, and in turn a better return and stronger bottom line for the organization.

Discussion Questions

1. What attributes would you add to the list of positive leadership attributes and negative leadership attributes?

2. Compare and contrast the leadership styles.

3. Compare and contrast the leadership approaches.

4. Compare and contrast the leadership theories.

References

Aldoory, L., & Toth, E. (2004). Leadership and gender in public relations: Perceived effectiveness of transformational and transactional leadership styles. *Journal of Public Relations Research, 16,* 157–183. doi:10.1207/s1532754xjprr1602_2

Avolio, B. J. (2005). *Leadership development in balance: Made/born.* Mahwah, NJ: Erlbaum.

Avolio, B. J., & Gibbons, T. C. (1988). Developing transformational leaders: A life span approach. *The Jossey-Bass management series. Charismatic leadership: The elusive factor in organizational effectiveness.* In J. A. Conger and R. N. Kanungo (Eds.), (pp. 276–308). San Francisco: Jossey-Bass.

Barbuto, J. E., Jr., & Burbach, M. E. M. (2006). The emotional intelligence of transformational leaders: A field study of elected officials. *The Journal of Social Psychology, 146,* 51–64. doi:10.3200/SOCP.146.1.51-64

Bass, B. M. (1985). *Leadership and performance beyond expectations.* New York: Free Press.

Bass, B. M. (1990). From transactional to transformational leadership. *Organizational Dynamics, 18,* 19–31.

Bass, B. M., & Steidlmeier, P. (1999). Ethics, character, and authentic transformational leadership. *The Leadership Quarterly (10)*2, 181–217.

Bennis, W. (1989). *On becoming a leader.* New York: Addison Wesley.

Bennis, W. G., & Nanus, B. (1985). *Leaders: The strategies for taking charge.* New York: Harper & Row.

Blake, R. R., & Mouton, L. S. (1964). *The managerial grid.* Houston, TX: Gulf.

Bowers, D. G., & Seashore, S. E. (1966). Predicting organization effectiveness with a four-factor theory of leadership. *Administrative Science Quarterly, 2,* 238–263.

Buckingham, M., & Clifton, D. (2001). *Now, discover your strengths.* New York, NY: Free Press.

Burns, J. M. (1978). *Leadership.* New York: Harper & Row.

Ciulla, J. B. (2003). *The ethics of leadership.* Belmont, CA: Wadsworth/Thomson Learning.

Clifton, D. O., & Harter, J. K. (2003). Investing in strengths. In K. S. Cameron, H. E. Dutton, & R. E. Quinn (Eds.), *Positive organizational scholarship* (pp. 111–121). San Francisco, CA: Berrett-Koehler.

Eva, N., Robin, M., Sendjaya, S., van Dierendonck, D., & Liden, R. (2019). Servant leadership. A systematic review and call for future research. *The Leadership Quarterly, 30,* 111–132.

Graen, G. B., & Uhl-Bien, M. (1995). Relationship-based approach to leadership: Development of leader-member exchange (LMX) theory of leadership over 25 years: Applying a multi-domain perspective. *Leadership Quarterly, 6*(2), 219–247.

Greenleaf, R. K. (1977). *Servant leadership: A journey into the nature of legitimate power and greatness.* New York, NY: Paulist Press.

House, R. H., Hanges, P. J., Javidan, M., Dorfman, P. W., & Gupta, V. (Eds.). (2004). *Culture, leadership, and organizations: the GLOBE study of 62 societies.* Thousand Oaks, CA: Sage Publications.

House, R. J., Spangler, W. D., & Woycke, J. (1991). Personality and charisma in the U.S. presidency: A psychological theory of leader effectiveness. *Administrative Science Quarterly, 36*, 364–396. doi:10.2307/2393201

Howell, J. P., & Costley, D. L. (2001). *Understanding behaviors for effective leadership.* New York, NY: Pearson.

Katz, R. L. (1955). Skills of an effective administrator. *Harvard Business Review, 33*(1), 33–42.

Lewin, K., Lippitt, R., & White, R. K. (1939). Patterns of aggressive behavior in experimentally created "social climates." *Journal of Social Psychology, 10,* 271–299.

Liden, R. C., Panaccio, A., Hu, J., & Meuser, J. D. (2014). Servant leadership: Antecedents, consequences, and contextual moderators. In D. V. Day (Ed.), *The Oxford handbook of leadership and organizations* (pp. 357–379). Oxford, UK: Oxford University Press.

Liden, R. C., Wayne, S. J., Zhao, H., & Henderson, D. (2008). Servant leadership: Development of a multidimensional measure and multi-level assessment. *Leadership Quarterly, 19,* 161–177.

Linley, A. (2008). *Average to A+: Realizing strengths in yourself and others.* Coventry, UK: CAPP Press.

Northouse, P. G. (2007). *Leadership: Theory and practice* (4th ed.). Thousand Oaks, CA: Sage Publications.

Northouse, P. G. (2015). *Introduction to leadership: Concepts and practice* (3rd ed.). Thousand Oaks, CA: Sage Publications.

Northouse, P. G. (2018). *Introduction to leadership: Concepts and practice* (4th ed.). Thousand Oaks, CA: Sage Publications.

Northouse, P. G. (2019). *Leadership: Theory and practice* (8th ed.). Thousand Oaks, CA: Sage Publications.

Rath, T. (2007). *Strengths-finder 2.0.* New York: Gallup Press.

Rost, J. C. (1991). Leadership for the twenty-first century. New York, NY: Praeger.

Spears, L. C. (2002). Tracing the past, present, and future of servant-leadership. In L. C. Spears & M. Lawrence (Eds.), *Focus on leadership: Servant-leadership: Developments in theory and research* (pp. 1–16). New York, NY: Wiley.

Weber, M. (Henderson, A. M., & Parsons, T. (Trans)). (1947). *The theory of social and economic organization.* New York: Oxford University Press.

van Dierendonck, D. (2011). Servant leadership: A review and synthesis. *Journal of Management, 37*(4), 1228–1261.

Zorn, E. (1997, May 19). *Without failure, Jordan would be false idol.* Retrieved from http://articles.chicagotribune.com/1997-05-19/news/9705190096_1_nike-mere-rumor-driver-s-license

FIVE
Unit

Communication Contexts in Action

The study of human communication is complex, as has been made clear through the previous four units. It is our hope that you have found the material included in these units interesting, and more importantly, helpful in your own experiences. In this final unit, we present some chapter-length manuscripts devoted to specific contexts that may be of interest to many students. To begin, Dr. Kenneth Hacker discusses how persuasive communication operates. This section covers a brief history of persuasion along with many of the psychological processes associated with the cognition of persuasive messages. In the second unit, Dr. Anne Hubbell presents the fascinating research area focused on deception. If you have ever wondered about why people lie, how well people can detect lying, or even about the ethical dimensions of deception, then you will enjoy this section. Dr. Hubbell continues in this unit with an important section on Health Communication. More and more, scholars and health care practitioners are understanding the need to better understand how communication is an integral part of our health-care system. This section addresses how we understand health-related messages among other important topics. Finally, Dr. Danielle Halliwell addresses the increasingly vital concept of digital media literacy. In this section, you will learn about what this concept is along with some key strategies for developing your own digital media literacy. These are just a few of the many exciting areas that communication scholars study. We hope you enjoy this journey!

Persuasive Communication

By Kenneth L. Hacker

Objectives

▶ Introduce you to the study and practice of persuasion.
▶ Understand the main theories and principles of persuasion.
▶ Facilitate your interests in both recurring and new forms of persuasion.

You can easily recognize how important persuasion is in your life by simply noticing how often during the day someone is trying to get you to believe something or do something—or you are the one trying to persuade someone else. "Can you get that door for me?" "You know, you really should vote for Bernie." "Being a communication major is a good choice." "How about a movie tonight?" These are all attempted acts of persuasion, and you encounter such acts all day long. Persuasion is crucial to personal and professional success, so there are many good reasons to pay careful attention to how it works.

Persuasion, like every other social science concept, has multiple definitions in studies, articles, and books. For this chapter, we define **persuasion** as using deliberate and strategically designed messages that are intended to change beliefs, attitudes, or behaviors, or any combination of the three. Attempted persuasion can be successful or unsuccessful and we will look at what makes persuasive efforts most effective. We will also look at ethics issues with persuasion and how to be a critical receiver of persuasive messages. While much of human communication is persuasive communication, we are not treating them as synonymous. Persuasion is communication intended for shaping, reinforcing, or changing how people think or behave.

It is very easy to grasp the importance of understanding persuasion once you realize that your personal success in so many areas of your life is related to how persuasive you can be. This can range from getting a date to convincing a professor that you are justified in requesting a grade change. It is important to realize that the process of persuasion is a dynamic and fluctuating process. One person is trying to get another person to believe or do something while the latter is attempting to convince the persuader that they are not interested. Persuasion is not as easy as we may think, once we recognize the fact that the persuasion process is a dynamic

PERSUASION

using deliberate and strategically designed messages intended to change beliefs, attitudes, or behaviors, or any combination of the three.

relationship between influence behavior and resistance behaviors. Doing effective persuasion in any social context requires a focused mindset that keeps your eye on the prize while also monitoring how and when you need to modify your messages. As you read the chapter on nonverbal communication, you will notice that nonverbal behaviors provide a good source of feedback that helps you assess how well you are relating to another person. It is more likely that you are being persuasive when your listener is nodding approval with your statements than when she/he is just staring at you. Effective persuasion depends on real-time adjustments in your strategies. These adjustments are your responses to the feedback that you receive from your message receiver.

As we get started in our brief lesson in persuasion, consider some questions to think about as we move forward. For example, why are some people far more successful than others who have less qualifications or talent than they do? How are some people able to connect to other people so much better than others who seem to lack that ability? On what basis was the winner of the presidential election of 2016 chosen? In times that you have been effective with your persuasion efforts, what did you do differently from times when your persuasive efforts did not work so well?

A BRIEF HISTORY OF PERSUASION THEORY AND PRACTICE

Most likely, there are more ancient roots for the study of persuasion than the ancient Greeks. However, like the development of democracy, the ancient Greeks did more systematic work of developing persuasion techniques than any other people before them. In ancient Greece, each citizen had to speak for themselves in the courts of law. Lawyers were not an option. The same was true in the Greek democratic assemblies. You did not have a representative speak for you. All of this meant that there was a premium on developing your speaking and persuasion skills. If you were not persuasive, you might lose your possessions or home to someone who was (Pratkanis & Aronson, 2001).

COMMONPLACE

general persuasion techniques.

PLATO

Greek philosopher.

ARISTOTLE

Greek philosopher and student of Plato.

ETHOS

persuader nature and creditability.

LOGOS

message arguments and logic.

PATHOS

emotional appeals.

While the citizens did not have lawyers, the ancient Greeks (over 2,500 years ago) could hire communication experts known as Sophists to help them become more persuasive. These were the how-to consultants of the day. One topic of the Sophists was what they called "**commonplaces**" or general persuasion techniques that could be used for multiple purposes (Pratkanis & Aronson, 2001, p. 12). Two things commonly said by the Sophists in ancient Greece that are repeated today are "Humans are the measure of all things," and "There are two sides to every issue" (Pratkanis & Aronson, 2001). Because the Sophists did not believe in absolute truth, some Greek philosophers like **Plato** criticized them for their word trickery (Pratkanis & Aronson). Plato said they were more interested in winning arguments than in truth (Perloff, 2003). He may have been correct.

Plato's student, **Aristotle** (fourth century B.C.) held a position different than that of both the Sophists and the absolutists like Plato. Aristotle described persuasion as something that helps people discover important facts and also important methods of persuading (Perloff, 2003). Three important aspects of persuasion, according to Aristotle are (1) **ethos** (persuader nature and credibility), (2) **logos** (message arguments and logic), and (3) **pathos** (emotional appeals). We know today that the Greeks were correct about these three elements of persuasion always being important and working together.

Like the Greeks, the ancient Romans after them believed that persuasion is essential to individual and collective life. Debate was emphasized as the best way to make sound decisions (Pratkanis & Aronson, 2001). However, the Roman society had lawyers and politicians who could speak for citizens. One of the famous Roman lawyers (and leaders of the Roman Empire) was the persuasion expert, Marcus Tullius Cicero. Cicero stressed the importance of having both wisdom and eloquence. One without the other could produce problems (Pratkanis & Aronson, 2001). In both ancient Greece and ancient Rome, the study of persuasion was a central component of higher education (Everett, 2001). We'll say more about Cicero later.

While the old origins of persuasion are important and interesting, we should note how very different persuasion is today in contrast to days so long ago. For example, the amount of persuasive messages we each encounter every day is dramatically higher than people in the past. The presence of persuasive messages today can be seen as advertisers track and find you online and even on your phone. We have modern-day Sophists today, those who consult others in how to be persuasive. They have a tradition that goes from ancient Greece through the Romans, into the European days of kings and queens, and right into our contemporary presidential election campaigns. In the 16th century, Niccolo Machiavelli famously taught Italian princes how to gain power and keep power with various persuasion techniques (Perloff, 2003). In 1820, reformers in the United States used persuasion to raise public awareness of the dangers of binge drinking (Perloff). Persuasion was central to the slavery abolitionists of the 19th century, to the movement for women's voting rights in the early 20th century, and for civil rights activism in the 1960s. Today, it is central to political campaigns, activist causes such as environmentalism, and various forms of governmental communication such as messages sent from the United States government to other nations (something known as public diplomacy).

Persuasive messages today travel faster and more widely than ever before. We have persuasion consultants in more areas of communication than ever before—in politics, in social media marketing, in political activism, in public relations, and in advertising. Two important areas of study that will help you become better at persuasion are (1) the technologies of persuasion, and (2) the specialized areas of persuasion practice. Whatever profession you decide to enter, you are very likely to be involved in various kinds of persuasive activities. This means you should gain a grasp of the basic principles of persuasion as soon as you can.

BELIEFS, ATTITUDES, VALUES, AND BEHAVIORS

Let's take a look now at the basic components and processes of persuasion. We can think of persuasion as all influence, whether intentional or not, but for the sake of clarity (and being practical), we will talk only about intentional persuasion. Thus, you begin the process of persuading another human being by knowing that you are trying to influence them. You are making conscious decisions about trying to change their minds about something or trying to change their behaviors. In this conscious and deliberate process we call persuasion, you are attempting to change the beliefs or attitudes of the other person. Beliefs are things they believe are true. For example, I may believe that a Toyota Tundra truck is expensive. Attitudes are positive or negative orientations toward something. If I have a negative attitude about Toyota trucks, that is how I feel about them. Attitudes come from the beliefs we have of a subject. The subject is known as the attitude object. The main objective for changing attitudes is to change behaviors. What we have stated so far can be summed up in Figure 5.1 on the following page.

MARCUS TULLIUS CICERO

Roman orator, lawyer, and politician. See Unit Two as well for other references to Cicero.

INFLUENCE

the beginning process of persuading.

BELIEF

things believed to be true.

ATTITUDE

positive or negative orientation toward something.

BEHAVIOR

action.

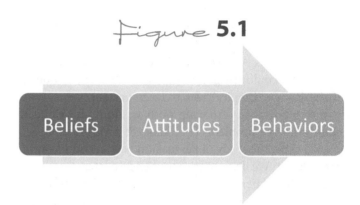

Source: Kenneth L. Hacker

You can think of attitudes as summations of the beliefs you have about an object. The more positive beliefs than negative beliefs, the more positive the attitude. My attitude about the Toyota Tundra can be seen as the aggregation of my beliefs about the truck.

If only things were this simple, persuasion would be very easy. But some long-term factors in the receiver's mind make things more complicated. They are called **values**. Values are things that people hold dear. For example, you might value prestige. Prestige is a value to you. If persuasive messages work against the values of a receiver, even if belief change is causing attitude change, the receiver may reject changes in behavior. Thus, a fundamental and simple starting model of persuasion is what we can call the belief-attitude-value model (Figure 5.1B below).

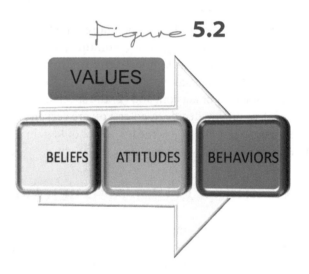

Source: Kenneth L. Hacker

VALUES

things that people hold dear.

Values affect the persuasive process which changes attitudes and behaviors. If the attitude change process is consistent with receiver values, the process is much smoother than a situation where the process violates his or her values. For example, if a person values protecting the environment and saving money by having a vehicle that gets good gas mileage, you can help them develop a positive attitude about the vehicle you are selling when you tell them about its nice features. Note that this requires that the product or buying the product is consistent with their values. However, if you are violating their values of environmental protection and saving money by trying to sell them a gas-guzzling, large SUV, the positive features might not produce a great deal of attitude change.

Thus far, we can see there are some very fundamental points about persuasion we have to clarify before we can even get close to the more complicated aspects of persuasion:

► The persuader seeks to gain specific changes in the mind of the person receiving the persuasive messages. This includes changes in beliefs and attitudes.

► Persuasion involves changes in what a receiver is thinking and feeling and perhaps in some of the observable behaviors.

► Persuasion that is intended to change behaviors must work through changes in beliefs and attitudes that are related to specific behaviors.

► Persuasion rarely involves direct effects from messages. Most of the time, persuasion occurs as message receivers respond in their own minds to messages sent to them by persuaders. Thus, a great deal of persuasion involves what is known as self- persuasion. This basic view of persuasion is shown in Figure 5.3 below:

Figure **5.3**

Source: Kenneth L. Hacker

As we will see, persuasion is a complex process because it involves many other processes such as human perception, thinking, feeling, relating new thoughts to old thoughts, and interpreting the content of persuasive messages. Staying with the basics, however, reveals that attitudes are our main focus point in the design of persuasive messages. We want to shape or change attitudes in our favor, meaning change the attitudes in favor of the behavior we are encouraging.

The three constant **goals of persuasion** are (1) attitude shaping, (2) attitude rein-forcement, and (3) attitude changing (Perloff, 2003). **Attitude shaping** is the easiest form of persuasion because you are informing your audience with new information and they have little resistance to what you are claiming. Shaping can be done with generat-ing beliefs ("This product tastes good.") or with what you see below as conditioning, or pairing something already liked with something new. **Attitude reinforcement** is confirm-ing what people already believe and giving them reasons to act on what they believe. This is commonly done in religion and politics. **Attitude change** is the most challenging kind of persuasion. For example, Whites in the United States, during the 1960s, had to be persuaded that open discrimination and prejudice toward Blacks were no longer acceptable.

EARLY PSYCHOLOGY STUDIES OF PERSUASION

The earliest scientific research on persuasion was done in psychology in the early 1900s. Those studies gave us useful information about attitudes, conditioning, and basic human psychological tendencies such as our need for mental balance or consistency. Before psychologists had the concept of "attitude" in their theories of

GOALS OF PERSUASION

attitude shaping, attitude reinforcement, and attitude changing.

ATTITUDE SHAPING

informing your audience with new information.

ATTITUDE REINFORCEMENT

confirming what people already believe and giving them reasons to act.

ATTITUDE CHANGE

to modify or change an individual's perception.

persuasion, efforts to change human thoughts or behaviors were limited to primitive notions about changing beliefs and behaviors. People were thought to be pushed and pulled by ideologies, dominating forces, animal instincts, and passive learning (Perloff, 2008). With Gordon Allport's psychology research on attitudes, it was possible to talk about changes in thinking and feeling that affect changes in behaviors. For example, if an advertiser was trying to get you to buy their new product, they would first have to get you to develop a positive attitude about the product. The earliest uses of the term "attitude" referred to postures or physical arrangement such as someone being in an "attitude of prayer" (O'Keefe, 2002). Since 1935, when Allport theorized about attitudes, the concept has generally referred to an individual's general evaluation of an object. The thing evaluated, the "attitude object," can be a person, an event, a policy, a product—anything that can be evaluated (O'Keefe).

For decades, we have viewed attitudes as important factors leading to certain behaviors. Thus, if we change a person's attitudes, we are likely to change their behavior. For example, if I seek to convince you to quit smoking, I will need to help you develop a more negative attitude about cigarettes and smoking. One of the earliest approaches to attitude change for persuasion was changing beliefs in order to change attitudes. This involves identifying the beliefs that together form an attitude. For example, if we wish to change your attitude about Hillary Clinton, we have to first identify what you believe about Ms. Clinton. If your beliefs are mostly positive, you will have a positive attitude about her and our challenge is to reinforce those positive beliefs and maybe add some more to the collection. If your beliefs about Clinton are mainly negative, we have to change those beliefs in order to make your attitude more positive. In election examples like this, that attitude toward a candidate is believed to be significantly related to how likely you are to vote for them. Generally, you are most likely to vote for the candidate for which you have the most positive attitude. We should note that many experts argue that the formation of attitudes involves feelings as well as beliefs (O'Keefe, 2002).

MAIN THEORIES OF PERSUASION

Historically, the theories of persuasion developed over time and progressed from early rhetorical theories (Greeks, Romans) to modern theories of how the brain processes messages and forms networks of association and images of products, people, events, and institutions. Here we will cover only the theories of persuasion that are most used in communication research and applied persuasion efforts.

Classical Conditioning Theory

CLASSICAL CONDITIONING

the process of using messages to pair a new concept with concepts that are already liked.

Classical conditioning is the process of using messages to pair (repeatedly associate) a new concept (new product for example) with concepts that are already liked. Coca-Cola has used this approach to persuasion very successfully for decades as they have paired the soft drink with things that are valued by Americans such as patriotism, ethnic diversity, and family relationships (Perloff, 2008). Levi jeans have been associated (paired) with youth and rebellion. Marlboro cigarettes were successfully paired with rugged, individualist cowboys by advertising that showed cowboys alone with their Marlboros.

© Diana Indiana/Shutterstock.com

Successful pairing of an attitude object such as a product and something already valued requires knowing that the positive object (the already-valued stimulus) is likely to arouse immediate positive responses and associating the attitude object repeatedly so that the positive responses to the new object of evaluation become almost as automatic as the positive responses to the thing that is already valued or liked. Politicians running for office, for example, often stand in front of American flags or wear blue suits, white shirts, and red ties. This is an effort to pair the candidate with the red, white, and blue symbols that are liked and valued by Americans.

Pairing, or associating a new stimulus (the one you are selling) with an already favored one is illustrated in the model in Figure 5.4 below.

Figure **5.4**

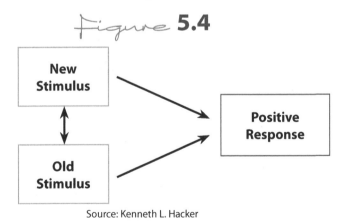

Source: Kenneth L. Hacker

The double arrow in the model indicates repeated association or pairing over time. Once this occurs many times over time, the new stimulus has a response similar to the old stimulus. Below is an example still used in advertising to persuade people to buy perfume or cologne (see Figure 5.5).

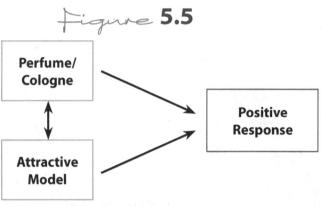

Figure **5.5**

Source: Kenneth L. Hacker

Classical conditioning works so well that it often involves more imagery than words. Very little text is necessary to sell cologne, perfume, beer, cigarettes, and other products that are very high in demand. The association and pairing process, of course, depends on lots of repetition and time.

Social Judgment Theory

Social Judgment Theory notes that receivers of persuasive messages have three basic ways of responding to any message. This theory says that receivers of persuasive messages do not evaluate an argument solely on the merits of what is said, but rather compare what is argued with what they already believe (Perloff, 2008). Another way of saying this is that receivers compare their attitudes toward a subject to what attitude they perceive in the persuasive messages.

Social Judgment Theory says that we all have a continuum of possible evaluations for any message we hear. This continuum ranges from acceptance to non-commitment, to rejection (Perloff, 2008). You can visualize this continuum as follows (see Figure 5.6):

Figure **5.6**

Social Judgment Latitudes		
Acceptance	Non-commitment	Rejection

Source: Kenneth L. Hacker

SOCIAL JUDGMENT THEORY

receivers have a continuum of possible evaluations for any message we hear.

LATITUDE OF ACCEPTANCE

arguments you agree with.

LATITUDE OF REJECTION

arguments you believe are objectionable.

LATITUDE OF NON-COMMITMENT

arguments you do not have a strong view about yet.

These three types of responses are called latitudes—latitude of acceptance, latitude of non-commitment, and latitude of rejection. Messages you agree with fall into your latitude of acceptance. Your latitude of rejection includes all those arguments you believe are objectionable. Your latitude of non-commitment are arguments you do not have a strong view about yet (Perloff, 2008). Note that an increase in one's latitude means a decrease in the other two. For example, a bigger latitude of acceptance means a small latitude of non-commitment, a small latitude of rejection, or both.

In order to use this theory effectively, you need to meet two basic challenges. First, you must be certain your messages are not automatically being rejected. Such rejection will occur if what you are advocating fall into the receiver's latitude of rejection (those positions that the receiver is already opposed to). Second, you must assure your arguments fall into the receiver's latitude of acceptance. However, you must make sure that your acceptable argument is not so easily accepted that it produces no meaningful attitude change. In other words, it must get your audience thinking about the need for change.

Cognitive Dissonance Theory

One of the most important sets of early theories in psychology concerned research which indicated that humans have inborn tendencies to maintain equilibrium or consistency with their thoughts, feelings, and behaviors. The predecessors to **Cognitive Dissonance Theory** were Balance Theory and Congruity Theory. All three theories stressed the need that humans naturally have for consistency of beliefs, feelings, attitudes, and behaviors (O'Keefe, 2002). Balance Theory and Congruity Theory said that all people need consistency in their thoughts, feelings, and actions. Cognitive Dissonance Theory turned out to be the most useful of the consistency theories and is still widely used today in many persuasion applications.

This theory was formulated by Leon Festinger in 1957. Since then, it has been the most useful theory of persuasion based on principles of cognitive consistency (O'Keefe, 2002). Inconsistency produces a discomfort called **dissonance**, according to Cognitive Dissonance Theory. An example given by Festinger is a person knowing that smoking cigarettes causes lung cancer, but the person continues to smoke (O'Keefe). Festinger predicted that dissonance would motivate a person away from dissonance and toward consistency. In the smoking example, the person might quit believing that smoking causes cancer or might quit smoking.

In a situation of cognitive dissonance, high dissonance is likely to motivate change to make things more consistent and balanced, while low levels of dissonance may not motivate a person toward change (O'Keefe, 2002). The persuader then attempts to use messages to generate cognitive dissonance in the message receiver and follow that feeling of dissonance with changes in attitudes or behaviors. Generally speaking, receivers are more likely to try staying with their existing attitudes than to change them. This means that in the smoking example, a smoker confronted with the fact that smoking can cause lung cancer (or heart disease), may seek out other beliefs to lower the severity of the new information. For example, he/she may say, well yes, smoking causes cancer, but it helps me relax or lose weight. Besides, everyone has to die from some cause. This process of attempting to reduce dissonance is called rationalization. The receiver attempts to reduce dissonance by rationalizing and the persuader attempts to minimize the rationalization process. For example, the persuader might say "You know we all have to die from some cause, but dying with an oxygen machine and getting chemo is not the best way to go."

Why is it that a law school student might endure grueling treatment by professors in front of hundreds of other students and still come to think positively about those professors? This is an example of how cognitive dissonance works. The student changes attitudes about the professors from negative to positive because he or she has invested years of work getting through law school. Liking the professors is part of justifying the amount of effort it took to get through law school (Perloff, 2003). Should a parent pay a child each time the child leaves the TV to go outside and get some exercise? This theory says no. Again, persuasion is going to follow dissonance. Paying a child to exercise removes the need for the child to develop a positive attitude about exercising. Getting the child to exercise by a very small reward or requiring it will create dissonance between two beliefs—I am exercising and I do not like to exercise. As long as the behavior of exercising continues, the attitude toward exercising will become more positive (Perloff, 2003).

COGNITIVE DISSONANCE THEORY

stresses the need that humans naturally have for consistency of beliefs, feelings, attitudes, and behaviors.

DISSONANCE

an inconsistency that produces discomfort.

For you to use this theory effectively requires dealing with three big challenges. First, you have to show and call out the inconsistencies in your receiver's beliefs. Note that a behavior psychologically is represented as a belief. Thus, smoking is "I smoke." If you effectively show inconsistency, you may be able to induce dissonance. For example, you might tell a friend, "You are an environmentalist but you do not recycle as good environmentalists do." The second challenge is preventing rationalization by the receiver to block or lessen their feeling of dissonance. For example, when your friend says, "Yes, I should recycle but I am not able to," you can reply, "OK let me help you find the containers or let me bring you one."

Cognitive Response Theory

COGNITIVE RESPONSE THEORY

explores the effect of indirect effects on attitude change.

Cognitive Response Theory provided an important finding about how indirect the effects of messages are on attitude change. One of the most practical sets of findings in the research which produced this theory is the sequence of responses that are necessary for any successful act of persuasion. You will see that this is consistent with what you read about in the section about public speaking regarding persuasive speaking. This sequence is called the Hovland/Yale Model of Persuasion and is shown below (see Figure 5.7):

Figure **5.7**

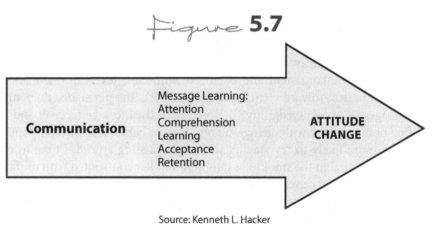

Message Learning:
Attention
Comprehension
Learning
Acceptance
Retention

Communication

ATTITUDE CHANGE

Source: Kenneth L. Hacker

The steps under "message learning" are sequential moving down the list. Each step depends on all steps above it. Nothing in persuasion works unless attention, the first step, is achieved. Attention is not enough; the audience must comprehend what is being said and so on. Of course, this looks more simple than what actually occurs because message receivers do not simply accept everything along the way from attention to retention. There are many points of resistance along the way. This led researchers to replace the concept of message learning with that of cognitive response. The theoretical focus became what is shown below (see Figure 5.8).

Figure **5.8**

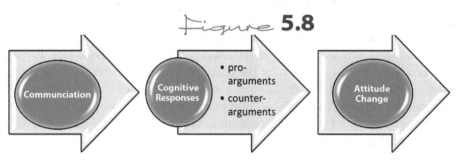

Communciation

Cognitive Responses

• pro-arguments
• counter-arguments

Attitude Change

Source: Kenneth L. Hacker

Like Social Judgment Theory, Cognitive Response Theory informs us about how message receivers have mental reactions to what a persuader tells them and how those responses (not the message themselves) drive attitude change. Pro-arguments are internal responses that argue along with the persuader. Counterarguments are the opposite. Persuasion is working when pro-argumentation is high.

Cognitive and affective (emotional) responses to your persuasive messages are essential to how effective you are as a persuader. It is also important to remember that while your audience is processing what you say, they are also cognitively responding to opposing claims from competing sources (Pratkanis & Aranson, 2001). As we hear persuasive messages, various cognitive and emotional responses run through our head in relation to those messages. Sometimes we think carefully about what is being said and at other times we respond with very little in-depth thinking (Pratkanis & Aronson). This latter kind of processing is explained by a theory derived from Cognitive Response Theory. Both theories explain how successful persuasion involves promoting positive responses and disrupting negative responses. The second theory is called the Elaboration Likelihood Model.

Elaboration Likelihood Model

Findings from Cognitive Response Theory preceded a theory that added what was discovered about the mediating role of internal responses to messages. However, the psychologists who developed the **Elaboration Likelihood Model** (ELM) of persuasion, Richard Petty and John Cacioppo, realized that Cognitive Response Theory only explained active responses to persuader messages. It did not account for those moments when a message receiver was not thinking critically about certain messages (Perloff, 2008). The ELM explained both critical thinking internal responses and responses based on mental shortcuts. The term "elaboration" is used to describe cognitive responses to messages that actively evaluate the quality of arguments that are presented.

The ELM is what is known as a dual-process model or theory of persuasion. It says that there are two main mechanisms determining how messages affect attitude change (Perloff, 2008). The ELM explains two basic "routes" or ways that we psychologically process incoming persuasive messages—a central route and a peripheral route. The **central route** is careful assessment of what is being said or presented. Responses in the central route are what the theory calls "arguments"—claims that can be objectively assessed. The **peripheral route** is responding to persuasive messages with little critical thinking and reacting more on the basis of what are called "cues"—bits of information like how attractive the persuader is and how much credibility they appear to possess (Pratkanis & Aronson, 2001).

To illustrate how easily we can process messages with little in-depth or critical thinking, consider the following facts. Advertising containing words like "new," "improved," and "easy," can be used to increase product sales (Pratkanis & Aronson, 2001). What is known as "bundle pricing" can also be used to increase the sales of a product. You can better sell the product with the price of two for $1 instead of fifty cents each (Pratkanis & Aronson). On April 12, 2016, Presidential candidate Donald Trump appeared with his family on a CNN Town Hall session in New York. Trump was disfavored in the polls by about 70% of American female voters. The pundits, interviewing each other after the town hall, talked about how much of a nice family man Trump had appeared to be on stage with his family. Could this kind of public presentation be persuasive? According to the ELM, it certainly could be.

ELABORATION LIKELIHOOD MODEL

a dual-processing model that explains both critical thinking internal responses and responses based on mental shortcuts.

CENTRAL ROUTE

careful assessment and critical thinking of what is being said or presented.

PERIPHERAL ROUTE

responds to persuasive messages with little critical thinking.

Effective use of the ELM requires using strong arguments for receivers who are motivated to think critically about what you are claiming. It requires the use of cues for those who are not so motivated. Sometimes, it is best to use both routes to add persuasive appeals to your overall presentation as possible, being careful to not let cues dominate when they should not.

Heuristic-Systematic Model

There were some criticisms of the ELM that led to a theory that offers a few alternative views about the persuasive process. Both theories are useful. The **Heuristic-Systematic Model** (HSM) of persuasion is another dual-process model of persuasion. This theory of persuasion also says that there are two main forms of processing messages. The "**systematic**" processing is like the central route in the ELM. The "**heuristic**" processing is like the "peripheral route" of the ELM. With heuristic processing, message receivers are likely to use shortcuts of processing (called cognitive shortcuts or heuristics in psychology) to evaluate message claims. An example of a shortcut or heuristic is the belief applied to the message that says "Experts are always right" (Perloff, 2003).

The main distinguishing feature of the HSM, in contrast to the ELM, is that the HSM tends to stress a parallel processing or simultaneous processing of the two routes of message evaluation (Perloff, 2003). The HSM also argues that people, in general, are easily drawn to heuristic processing because it is common for people to use shortcuts in daily activities and tend to use minimal information to process messages during the day (Perloff, 2003). To effectively use the HSM requires that you follow the guidelines for using the ELM but that you also apply heuristics to your arguments—rules of thumb, common knowledge, and cognitive shortcuts.

While the ELM and HSM explain how message receivers may not be motivated to think critically about message quality at times, another theory describes a time when people are motivated to think about the details of persuasive arguments and not likely to be persuaded by more superficial information. These theories concern reasoned action and planned behavior.

Theory of Reasoned Action and Theory of Planned Behavior

We now look at two theories designed to produce behavioral change and can offer methods of measuring changes in attitude and intentions toward certain behaviors. The reasoned action view of persuasion assumes the beliefs that people hold about either attitude objects or actions affect how they will behave in regard to objects (Yzer, 2013). Reasoned action does not mean rational action, but rather having specific beliefs that form intentions to act in certain ways. With both the **Theory of Reasoned Action** (TRA) and the **Theory of Planned Behavior** (TPB), it is assumed that beliefs affect behaviors by shaping intentions and that behaviors result from intentions (Yzer). The TRA is shown very simplistically in the following model (see Figure 5.9):

HEURISTIC-SYSTEMATIC MODEL

a parallel processing model consisting of a systematic and heuristic route.

SYSTEMATIC

like ELM's central route.

HEURISTIC

like ELM's peripheral route.

THEORY OF REASONED ACTION

assumes that beliefs affect behaviors by shaping intentions and that behaviors result from intentions.

THEORY OF PLANNED BEHAVIOR

assumes that beliefs affect behaviors by shaping intentions and that behaviors result from intentions.

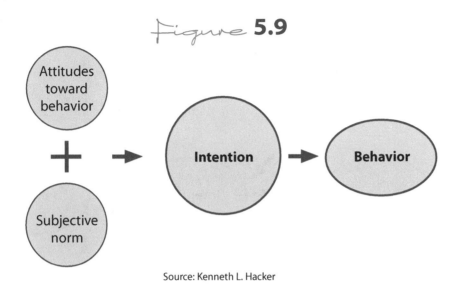

Source: Kenneth L. Hacker

Attitudes toward behaving a certain way toward the object (what you are promoting or working against) are formed by collections of beliefs about the new behavior. Subjective norms are beliefs about what other people who influence you a great deal think about the behavior. Together the attitude toward the behavior and the subjective norm create an intention to perform the advocated new behavior. For example, let's say we are trying to get someone to become a vegetarian. The attitude involved is the attitude about becoming a vegetarian. The subjective norm is the result of what influential others say about becoming a vegetarian and also how likely the audience is to comply with these other people in general (Perloff, 2008).

Our job using the TRA to persuade you to become a vegetarian involves providing you with positive and strong beliefs about how good this behavior will be for you. Furthermore, our challenge involves convincing you that people you trust and listen to are in favor of you becoming a vegetarian. This theory has a good track record of being useful in many different types of persuasion situations. To use it effectively, you need to learn a great deal about the person you are trying to persuade and what people around them tell them about the behavior that you are advocating to them. While the TRA is very useful, there is a possible factor that blocks intentions from producing desired behavior and that factor is how well or easily the person has the ability to perform the new behavior they wish to perform. This is where the TPB offers an additional element to the TRA and makes the combination more useful.

What if you have persuaded your friend to lose weight by giving them lots of credible health information that leads to them having a strong positive attitude about losing weight? Assume you have also helped them to understand that the people they turn to the most for advice in their lives also believe that losing weight is clearly something they should do. What would predict that this person with a nice positive intention to lose weight might do nothing to shed those pounds? This is where the TPB becomes a better alternative to the TRA.

The TPB has all of the principles of the TRA but the critical element of perceived behavioral control (PCB). PCB is a third cause of intention formation in this theory as shown on the following page (see Figure 5.10).

Figure **5.10**

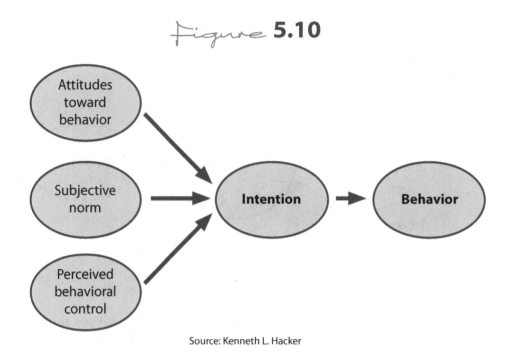

Source: Kenneth L. Hacker

The TPB says that the perceived behavioral control is a third cause of behavioral intention. Thus, a persuader not only needs to persuade a person that an advocated behavior is a good thing to do and that important others agree, but also that it is possible for the person to accomplish the new behavior. In the weight loss example, the person needs to also know they can add more exercise and subtract more calories from their daily habits.

Now that we have reviewed the traditional views of persuasion, we can take a brief look at some newer approaches to persuasion. These include automatic ways of moving people toward certain behaviors and some new work being done with computer networking.

MICRO-LEVEL APPROACHES TO PERSUASION

Micro-level persuasion is done in the peripheral route of message processing described above in our discussion about the ELM. It is fairly mindless and fast responding to signals and messages. We review some of these fascinating areas of research and application and begin with Cialdini's six methods of gaining compliance from another person.

Cialdini's Fixed Action Patterns

Psychologist Robert Cialdini believes that people today are too busy to do lots of critical thinking as described in the central route processing of the ELM and the systematic processing of the HSM. Instead, he finds that most people are doing superficial processing of persuasion messages and therefore can be easily moved toward certain behaviors with simple cues in the persuasion environment and messages. Here are the patterns he discovered (Cialdini, 2001).

1. **Reciprocity.** When you do something for another person, they have a sense of obligation to also do something for you. Food servers have learned that helping their customers with even something as simple as giving them a mint can increase tips. If delegates to the conventions of the two main political parties are offered nice hotel rooms and free meals, the givers are probably hoping for votes in return.

2. **Consistency and Commitment.** This pattern is grounded in the consistency assumptions we discussed above in the section on Cognitive Dissonance Theory. This persuasion technique uses commitments to get follow-up commitments and then compliance with larger requests. For example, a charity may call you and thank you for your $10 donation from last year. Then they will ask you to donate $10 or $15 this year. Political campaigns that simply ask a person if they are planning to vote on Election Day can increase voting turnout because of consistency pressures.

3. **Social Proof.** Here is the secret of the Facebook organization. We assume that what our friends think is correct is actually correct and what they prefer is better than what people we do not know prefer. The actions of those we like are guides for our decisions. Yet even what crowds or people that we do not know are doing serves as a guide for what we think is normal. Bartenders learn that if they "salt" their tip jar (put bills, not change in the containers), they can increase how much they make in tips. Like monkey see, monkey do, people copy each other.

4. **Liking.** The more you are liked, the better your chances at persuasion. Tupperware gave up on stores after they found that home parties bring together people that like each other to talk about buying their products. Businesspeople know the value of business lunches. Studies show that people become more favorable about certain subjects when they dine with someone else and talk positively about the topics, than they would without the meal.

5. **Authority.** Outward signs of power and authority have positive effects on gaining compliance. Experimental findings show that people are more willing to comply with a request from someone wearing a uniform than someone in regular clothing.

6. **Scarcity.** When people are told that something is limited or time is short for making up their mind, they are more likely to purchase something than if they are not told these things. Studies on medical messages show that letters telling patients how many years of life they will lose if they keep smoking are more effective than letters that tell them how many years of life will be gained if they quit smoking. In short, we want what we think is being taken from us. Do you really think you need to go to that "midnight madness" sale at the mall?

RAPID COGNITION

Rapid cognition is also known as "thin slicing." In the past, if you walked into a Nordstrom's department store, you would see a man in a nice suit playing pleasing music on a piano. Why? The store believed that this made you feel like you were in a special place (Perloff, 2003). The store began phasing this out in recent years, however, in favor of more contemporary recorded music.

RECIPROCITY

doing something for another person.

CONSISTENCY AND COMMITMENT

uses commitments and then compliance with larger requests.

SOCIAL PROOF

one assumes that what our friends think is correct and what they prefer is better than what people we do not know prefer.

LIKING

the more you are liked, the better your chances at persuasion.

AUTHORITY

outward signs of power and authority have positive effects on gaining compliance.

SCARCITY

when something is limited or time is short for making up their mind, they are more likely to purchase something.

RAPID COGNITION

thin slicing.

THIN SLICING

making judgments
with very little
information and time.

SOCIAL MEDIA

websites that allow
users to create and
share content or
participate in social
networking.

SOCIAL INFLUENCE

a behavioral change
that one person
causes in another,
intentionally or
unintentionally, as
a result of the way
the changed person
perceives themselves
in relationship to the
influencer.

SOCIAL NETWORKS

a network of social
interactions or
relationships.

GOING VIRAL

a message that
diffuses rapidly
through online and
off-line networks of
communication.

**INFLUENTIALS OR
INFLUENCERS**

people who affect the
spread of messages of
behaviors more than
others in the network.

Other examples of rapid cognition have been described by Malcolm Gladwell (2005) in his classic book called *Blink: The Power of Thinking Without Thinking*. Rapid cognition is also referred to as "**thin slicing**" or making judgments with very little information and time. Studies show that lawsuits against physicians are more common against doctors the patients felt treated them poorly or ignored them. Psychologists discovered that the tone of voice for a surgeon can predict whether that physician is more or less likely to get sued. The surgeons with dominating voices were the ones most likely to be sued and the ones with more concerned voices were less likely to be sued.

Marketing experts use thin slicing continuously to increase sales of products. Louis Cheskin, a marketing expert working in the 1940s, discovered that people often transfer the feelings from one item to another. This is called sensation transference. Margarine was a product that was not liked in the United States. Americans did not want to eat it or buy it. Cheskin experimented with various forms of sensation transference and made margarine acceptable and popular by coloring it yellow to look like butter, and wrapping it in foil (which is associated with high quality). Adding a crown symbol, the "Imperial" brand name sealed the impression of high quality.

Networks of Influence

Because of the rapid adoption and usage of **social media**, a newer type of persuasion is becoming more common. This is the use of **social influence** in **social networks**. The most common example is the "Like" procedure and the emojis on Facebook. These tools were designed with research showing that people are more likely to take the advice of their friends (and their "friends' friends") than the advice of people they do not know.

One hot persuasion topic today is how persuasive messages can "go viral" on the Internet. **Going viral** means that messages are diffused rapidly through online and off-line networks of communication. It concerns how far and how intensely people are sharing specific content. Many attempts to make content on the Internet go viral fail. In fact, most attempts fail (Scott, 2015). The common ingredients in the successful cases appear to be content that is fun or shocking, a network of people who like the content, and links that make it all very easy to share (Scott). While we often hear about how wide and fast bad news travels, studies show the opposite with new networks of communication like Internet-based networks.

Research indicates that content is more likely to go viral if it is positive (Berger & Milkman, 2011). On the other hand, studies also show that content that arouses intense emotions (like anger or awe) can go viral despite being positive or negative (Berger & Milkman). Types of emotions are also important, not just whether the content is positive or negative. Research shows that positive and negative emotions linked to arousal (such as awe or anger) are positively related to going viral while emotions linked to sadness are negatively related to virality (Berger & Milkman).

Influentials or "**influencers**" in a social network like Twitter are defined as people who affect the spread of messages of behaviors more than others in the network (Bakshy, Karrer, & Adamic, 2009). However, there are traits about these people that also affect how influential they are. These traits can include knowledgeability and social position (Bakshy et al., 2009). Marketing experts who exploit social networking sites (SNS) like Facebook, recognize a very simple fact about networked influence, that is, individuals tend to like what is liked by their friends (Bakshy et al., 2009). We mentioned this above in discussing the liking principle of gaining compliance.

© metamorworks/Shutterstock.com

As with any kind of communication measurement, caution is urged with what social media metrics aimed at measuring influence are truly measuring. For example, influencing another person to simply pass along a link or a message does not indicate other kinds of influence such as changing their political opinion (Bakshy et al., 2009). Many messages like links or Tweets are not passed on at all after being received (Bakshy et al.). Still, researchers seek to find out what might characterize consistent members of networks who have higher rates of diffusing messages than other members (Bakshy et al.). Researchers have found that past influence on others and the number of followers on Twitter can predict future influence of network members (Bakshy et al.). A study of Second Life network influentials shows that the rate of content adoption by network members increases with an increase in the number of friends adopting the content (Bakshy, Karrer, & Adamic, 2009).

There are many reasons for studying social influence online. One reason is that online social influence affects more than online behaviors. Online social influence involves friends inducing other friends to behave in certain ways (Anagnostopoulos, Kumar, & Mahdian, 2008). Influence in social networks can result from a process of induction, whereby the behavior of one user is triggered by the behaviors of other users (Anagnostopoulos et al.). With social influence, ideas, norms, or objects like products can diffuse through a social network in ways that create what are commonly known as viral marketing or messaging and cascading effects (Anagnostopoulos et al.).

Networks and social networks have always been important to human communication and persuasion. Today's computer-based networks and social networking increases, however, make your use of social media and online networks a crucial part of your larger-scale efforts to do persuasion.

BECOMING A MORE EFFECTIVE PERSUADER

Improving your persuasive skills, like improving all communication skills generally, requires knowledge and practice. This chapter provides you with very basic knowledge and you will do well to take one or two courses that deal only with persuasive communication. Practice should include putting what you learn from theories and research into direct applications, self-analysis of how you do, and then making plans to get better. A few basic areas of practicing can be very helpful. First, work on understanding your audience and paying attention to their main concerns. Second, work on having a positive relationship with the person or group receiving your messages. Third, remember that persuasion is interactive and that you must keep adjusting your messages in relation to the listener responses. Below is a list of more practical areas for your persuasion development.

1. Learn how to develop and present your credentials, expertise, and credibility.
2. Try being more dialogic than monologic. Speak directly to listener concerns.
3. Recognize always that persuasion, like communication, is a complex dynamic process with effects fluctuating right in front of you. Your job is to guide the ebbs and flows of responses in your favor.
4. Learn and practice how to "connect" with your audiences. Know their values, concerns, and needs before you attempt to change their attitudes. Be sure that issues you discuss are relevant to your listeners.
5. Work on both the credibility of who you are (expertise or knowledge) and the credibility of what you say (good arguments, good sources). Both work very well together.
6. Form a positive relationship with an individual or audience before you attempt to persuade them.
7. Always remember that persuasion is a dynamic process. Like the theories above describe, responses to your message are not all positive or all negative. They are sometimes in your favor and sometimes working against you. Your big challenge is to generate a stream of positive responses that is far more substantial than the occasional negative response you may gain.

THE FOUR STRATEGEMS OF PERSUASION

Pratkanis and Arsonson (2001) offer four key principles to effective persuasion that you can add to the recommendations above. They call these the "four stratagems of persuasion."

1. Attempt what is known as pre-persuasion. Assert control of the situation in which you will be providing your persuasive messages. Frame (define) the issues at hand in your favor. Ancients talked about how a person who defines a debate is likely to win the debate. Work with that wisdom.
2. Establish a favorable image of yourself as a persuader. You do this by being credible, authoritative, trustworthy, and likable.
3. Deliver messages to your audience that are focused on what you consider to be the main topic at hand. Use distraction to disrupt

counterarguments or not paying attention to your main points. Vivid imagery can be useful for this.

4. Arouse audience emotions and connect those emotions to the course of action you are advocating.

These four strategies are not exhaustive, but they are consistent with the proven practices of ancient persuaders and the principles of effective persuasion discovered in social and behavioral science. Aristotle describes pre-persuasion efforts as having a thorough understanding of one's audience and their concerns (Pratkanis & Aronson, 2001). This included detecting their emotional dispositions using the strategies. Aristotle also talked about what he called "**atechnoi**" or the facts and events that the persuader cannot control. You can think of atechnoi as the playing field you are entering as you get ready to persuade. Cicero, the great Roman persuader, lawyer, and leader of Rome, said that the duties of a persuader ("**officia oratoris**") include establishing personal credibility, teaching with sound arguments, and moving the audience with emotions (Pratkanis & Aronson). Pre-persuasion for Cicero included a clear grasp of "**statis**" or the status of the issues to be discussed. Cicero said the persuader must define the situation in ways most favorable to his/her arguments (Pratkanis & Aronson). Today, we refer to this as framing the debate.

ETHICAL ISSUES IN PERSUASION

Whenever you are going to affect another person's mind and life with your messages, as you do in persuasion, you need to set boundaries on what is morally acceptable and what is not in how you design and use your message strategies. Is it ethical, for example, to deceive your audience with misleading or false facts about your competition?

There are two moral extremes to consider with persuasion. One, made famous by Machiavelli in the 16th century, simply assumes that the ends justify the means. The other extreme is a more absolute position which says that evil means produce evil ends. This was argued by the well-known revolutionary in India, Mahatma Ghandi.

Another view, stated by Jewish scholar Martin Buber, says that you should treat people like a "thou" rather than like an "it." He meant that ethical communication involves concern for the other party. In this view, if you use persuasion for your benefit with no regard for the well-being of the person you are persuading, you are being unethical.

BECOMING A MORE CRITICAL RECEIVER OF PERSUASIVE MESSAGES

It is common today to hear about how over-communicated we are as a society or how uncivil our public discourse has become. While there is some truth to these complaints, it is also true that all human history has had problems with ethical persuasion. Simple slogans and imagery in political campaigns did not begin recently; its goes back to our very first presidential election campaigns.

To be effective with a critical thinking approach to persuasion, you must begin with the realization that you cannot resist messages very easily if you do not have subject knowledge. It is good to become knowledgeable about a topic before you expose yourself to persuasive messages about it. You also have to do what is called central route processing in the ELM and systematic processing in the HSM. Think about the

ATECHNOI

facts and events that the persuader cannot control.

OFFICIA ORATORIS

persuader.

STATIS

the status of the issues to be discussed.

source of persuasive messages. Do they know what they are talking about? Are they trained or educated in the subject matter they are discussing? Think about the quality of the evidence that is presented. Are data from credible sources and are claims backed by important and verifiable evidence? What are their motivations for trying to persuade you?

CONCLUSION

This section has covered some of the main principles of persuasion theory that will help you understand the processes of persuasion, and also how to become both a better practitioner of persuasive messages and a more critical consumer of persuasive messages. Your development of your skills will depend on learning more about the research done on persuasion and also practicing your skills in various social situations.

Like any other communication skill, persuasive skills take self-observation, watching what works for others, educating yourself on research concerning how the mind and persuasion work, and carefully planning the steps of each persuasive challenge you face.

As for the theories we have reviewed in this section, it is assuring to know that they can be used together in all kinds of interesting combinations and that no single theory of persuasion is a key to all your persuasion challenges in a given application. Just as you should use multiple channels of communication when you interact with others about important topics, you should use multiple theories of persuasion if you are involved in a big persuasion task.

Discussion Questions

1. Name some contexts or situations of everyday life where you find yourself being persuaded or where you are doing the persuasion.

2. Talk about particular situations where you just wish you could be more persuasive.

3. In 1960, how was presidential candidate John F. Kennedy, a Catholic, able to persuade about 400 Protestant and anti-Catholic pastors about how he was no threat to the nation as the first possible Catholic American President? Research President Kennedy at the following website: https://www.jfklibrary.org

4. Think about some "meme" you have heard about going around the Internet. What made it go viral and was it persuasive?

5. When did you last purchase a product that you really did not need? Why did you buy it?

6. Who is someone in your life that you view as being very persuasive? What skills do they have that make them change the beliefs, attitudes, or behaviors of others so easily?

7. What ethical problems do you see in the persuasive techniques used by some famous persuaders today?

Anagnostopoulos, A., Kumar, R., & Mahdian, M. (2008). Influence and correlation in social networks. *Proceedings of the 14th ACM SIGKDD international conference on knowledge discovery and data mining, 7–15.*

Bakshy, E., Karrer, B., & Adamic, L. (2009). Social influence and diffusion of user-created content. *Proceedings of the 10th ACM conference on Electronic commerce, 325–334.*

Berger, J., & Milkman, K. (2011). What makes online content viral? *Journal of Marketing Research, 49,* 192–205.

Cialdini, R. (2001). *Influence: Science and practice.* Boston: Allyn and Bacon.

Everett, A. (2001). *Cicero: The life and times of Rome's greatest politician.* New York: Random House.

Gladwell, M. (2005). *Blink: The power of thinking without thinking.* New York: Little, Brown, and Company.

O'Keefe, D. (2002). *Persuasion theory and research,* (2nd ed.). Thousand Oaks, CA: Sage Publications.

Perloff, R. (2003). *The dynamics of persuasion* (2nd ed.). New York: Routledge.

Perloff, R. (2008). *The dynamics of persuasion,* (3rd ed.). New York: Routledge.

Pratkanis, A., & Aronson, E. (2001). *Age of propaganda: The everyday use and abuse of persuasion.* New York: W.H. Freeman and Company.

Scott, D. (2015). *The new rules of marketing and PR.* Hoboken, NJ: John Wiley & Sons.

Yzer, M. (2013). Reasoned action theory: Persuasion as belief-based behaviour change. In J. Dillard & Shen (2013), *The Sage Handbook of Persuasion.* Thousand Oaks, CA: Sage Publications, 120–136.

Deceptive Communication and the Ethics of Lying

By Anne P. Hubbell

Objectives

- ▶ Define deception.
- ▶ Explain how children develop the ability to lie.
- ▶ Identify reasons individuals give for lying.
- ▶ Differentiate among the four dimensions along which information can be distorted within deceptive messages.
- ▶ Describe why humans are ineffective at detecting deception.
- ▶ Explore two ethical perspectives to lying behavior.

When my daughter Madi told her first lie, my husband was surprised, upset, and concerned. I, however, was ecstatic! The ability to lie demonstrates higher level thinking in adults and the presence of what we call **theory of mind** (Astington & Edward, 2010). Basically, if you have theory of mind, you can understand how another person feels about or views a situation. A lie is based on theory of mind because it means you can understand someone else's perspective enough to do something or say something in order to alter their perspective. We also use the phrase *false belief* when we talk about deception and theory of mind because for an individual to lie, they must know what another person's true belief is and how to change this into a false belief. So, when my daughter started lying, she was showing that her cognitive abilities were developing nicely, even though lying is not the communication behavior parents want to encourage in children. In order to better understand deception among humans, even children, this section will include discussion on children and lying, why and how we lie, whether we can detect lies, and ethical theories and perspectives on deception.

THEORY OF MIND

the ability to understand how another person feels, views, or thinks about a situation.

BUT FIRST, A DEFINITION AND RATES OF EVERYDAY LYING

Sometimes what we call "deception" was an accident. Our memories are faulty and our own biases can distort what and how we store information. This means that someone may tell a story in a way in which we would not agree but they may not be

DECEPTION

when an individual purposefully changes information in order to fool another or create a false belief.

PROLIFIC LIARS

research has shown that teenagers report more lies per day than other age groups.

4 YEARS OF AGE

children begin to demonstrate Theory of Mind.

purposefully lying. Deception only occurs when there is intent. **Deception** occurs when an individual purposefully changes information in order to fool another or create a false belief. Also, it is not just deceit about anything, only the distortion of relevant information makes a message deceptive (McCornack, 1992). If I want to deceive you, I have to change or alter the information which is important, or relevant, to the conversation we are having. For example, if a child wishes to avoid punishment for breaking a dish, the child may throw the broken dish away and pretend they know nothing about it when questioned by a parent. By doing so the child avoids punishment because the relevant information, the broken dish, is never to be seen again!

Regarding how often we lie, a substantial number of studies have tried to determine lie frequency. The findings seemed to indicate that we lie about one to two times a day (DePaulo, Kashy, Kirkendol, Wyer, & Epstein, 1996). More current research, however, has shown most people do not report lying every day with the exception of prolific, or high-volume, liars (Serota, Levine, & Boster, 2010). The most **prolific liars**, in fact, have been found to be teenagers (high-school students) who reported lying about four times a day (Levine, Serota, Carey, & Messer, 2013). This leads us to how children and teenagers develop the ability to lie.

CHILDREN AND LYING

My favorite video clip on deception is one where comedian Richard Pryor is talking about a child lying about breaking something. Although it is an old video, it is hilarious because it shows how children first create unsophisticated lies to protect themselves from harm or avoid punishment. This is true in the literature on deception as well. Until children reach about 4–5 years of age, they may not be able to understand how to be deceptive. In a foundational study on children and the development of theory of mind and deception ability, Peskin (1992) used two puppets and stickers to explore the ability of children aged 3–5 and their ability to deceive. Peskin used a dark blue and a light blue puppet and without telling the children in the study which puppet was "bad" and which was "good," each puppet was assigned the role of being good or bad. Children were asked to pick from three types of stickers: one was sparkly; one was of a cartoon character; and one was brown and beige. Most children picked the sparkly sticker as their favorite. After picking a favorite sticker, the children interacted with the good and bad puppets. When they interacted with the bad puppet, the bad puppet would ask the children to reveal which sticker they liked the most. Once a child would tell the bad puppet their preference, the bad puppet would take the favored sticker. The good puppet, in contrast, would pick one of the other stickers and not pick a child's favorite. What Peskin found was children at 3 years of age could not hide their preference for the sparkly sticker from the bad puppet. They were more likely to physically try to keep the sticker for themselves or take it from the bad puppet but they could not act to fool the bad puppet. However, at **4 years of age**, children started to be able to tell the bad puppet they wanted one of the lesser preferred stickers and at 5 years of age, their ability to deceive improved. What Peskin found was that theory of mind developed at around 4 years of age and at age 4, children were able to start creating messages or act in a way which would deceive or fool the bad puppet. Before 4 years of age, the children were dramatically unable to do so.

Some of the research on the development of lies in children and young adults has shown girls tend to be able to control nonverbal "leaks" or clues to deception in their face earlier than boys (e.g., Feldman & White, 1992). A leak or clue is also called a cue to deception. It is something which we think will indicate someone is lying, like a

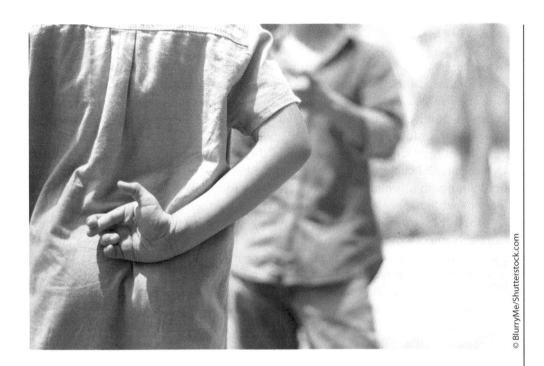

smile or looking away when a lie is told. Later in the section we will talk more about whether these cues are true indicators of a lie.

When we are talking about children and deception, however, the Feldman and White (1992) study is another one of my personal favorites on this topic and in my Deception class we actually redo the experiment. In their study, Feldman and White had 5–12-year-old boys and girls drink one of two drinks: one which tasted good and one which tasted awful. The children then had to pretend to like or dislike the drinks. Adults in the Feldman and White study (undergraduate students) were the observers and watched videos of the children talking about whether they liked or disliked what they had tasted. The observers believed the older girls showed improved ability to mask or prevent nonverbal leakage cues from showing on their faces when they talked. Boys, however, seemed to show more leakage cues with age; younger boys were better at masking cues in their faces than were the older boys. Similar studies have been conducted and have comparable findings. These findings are still viewed skeptically, however, as the observers may have had a bias and expected girls to be better at masking emotion or deception than boys. When I replicate this study in my Deception class we often find that the "deceivers" who drink the good or bad drink can easily fool the rest of the class. They tend to be good at lying about what they drank.

The research on children and lying has shown that as children age they become even better at deception, although most parents may wrongly assume they are good at detecting their children's lies. By the time children reach 10–11 years of age they have acquired "adult-like deception skills" (Knapp, McGlone, Griffin, & Earnest, 2016, p. 104) but their lies are still relatively detectable by adults. Then from 13–18 children become excellent liars. For example, in a study by McAfee, Inc. in 2013 on teenagers' Internet use, only 17% of the parents surveyed were aware of inappropriate Internet searches conducted by their teens. Yet, 57% of the teenagers stated they actively used the Internet to search for inappropriate content. Also, 22% of the teenagers admitted to hiding their Internet activity from parents. Most of the parents were unaware of their teenagers' Internet use as the teenagers were well able to deceive their parents.

SO, WHY DO WE LIE?

Before we get to the "why" it is important to talk about a few terms which are consistent across much of the research on deception. For example, in deception research we look at *high-stakes* or *low-stakes* lies and we also look at *anti-social* and *pro-social* lies. When you think about the "stakes" of lying, think about the game of poker. Deception is key to successful poker-playing. A high-stakes bet is one where a poker player puts out a lot of their chips, maybe even all of them. Let's use Denise as an example. Say Denise puts all her chips in as her bet but she has a terrible hand of cards. She is lying or bluffing with this high-stakes bet. She wants to appear confident and so she bets a lot in hopes that other players will fold, give up, and then Denise wins!

The same is true for conversational lying behavior. If a friend lies about something extremely important to you, that is a **high-stakes lie**. The lie does not have to matter to your friend, the speaker, but if the subject or information is important to you, the receiver of the lie, it is high-stakes. If you find out your friend lied to you, you may be hurt so badly that you may not trust your friend again. Your friendship may end. Therefore, a high-stakes lie is one which, if revealed, can have severe consequences. A **low-stakes lie** is the opposite. It may irritate you if you find out your friend told a low-stakes lie (e.g., they said you looked great in a new pair of jeans when they knew you did not), but most likely the friendship will not end because of the lie. We often call a low-stakes lie a "white" lie.

Pro-social and anti-social lies can have the same impact on relationships as high- and low-stakes lies. A **pro-social lie** can be considered a message we tell to be polite. So, if we go back to the example in the last paragraph, say you ask your friend (let's call him Bob), if you look good in a pair of jeans you are trying on. Bob responds with, "Sure, you look great!" Bob says this because he does not want to hurt your feelings. Although a lie, this can be considered pro-social as it is done with an intent to do no harm. An **anti-social lie**, in contrast, may be done to hurt another person. If Bob told you he liked how you looked in the jeans because he wanted you to look bad in front of other people, his behavior would be a cruel way to intentionally hurt you. Such deception is anti-social because the intent is to hurt another person. Much like high-stakes lies, anti-social deception, if discovered, can damage relationships.

All lies, however, are not told to hurt other people even if many lies we recall are those told to hurt or betray us. Because of this we do not want to see ourselves as deceivers, yet we all lie from time to time. Sometimes we do so to avoid hurting another person's feelings or to help them feel better.

To better understand why we lie we can turn to two of the most highly referenced deception studies. The first comes from researchers Turner, Edgley, and Olmstead, who, in 1975, conducted a "**diary study**," where 130 participants wrote down details about any conversation which went beyond a casual, "Hello" and where "important matters were at issue or stake" (p. 71). The results Turner et al. found demonstrate that most people (55.2%) reported lying to protect "face" for themselves or others. A person's "face" is how they portray themselves. For example, it may be that we want to be perceived by others as friendly, confident, strong, and/or intelligent. When someone lies to protect "face" they do so to protect the way a person is viewed by others and potentially prevent embarrassment of themselves or another person. Turner et al. found the second most common reason research participants gave for lying was to avoid conflict (22.2%). Other reasons were to keep a conversation going, end a conversation, attack a person's "face," or exploit or take advantage of the other person in

---

HIGH-STAKES LIE

a lie about something which is important to the receiver of the lie. These lies can have severe consequences if they are discovered.

LOW-STAKES LIE

often considered a "white" lie. These lies are often about something which is not important to the receiver of the lie.

PRO-SOCIAL LIE

this type of lie is often considered a "polite" lie. It is a low-stakes lie told to protect someone else from being hurt.

ANTI-SOCIAL LIE

this type of lie is told to hurt or harm another person.

DIARY STUDY

a study where research participants write about behaviors, like lying, on a daily basis. Diary studies usually include several days of data from each research participant.

5.11
Reasons for Lying

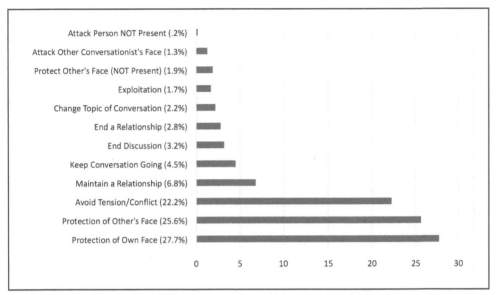

(Source: Turner, Edgley, & Olmstead, 1975; NOTE: percentages are from article but sum to 100.1%, perhaps because authors rounded numbers when they listed them as having only 1 decimal place)

the conversations. Also, there were a few instances of the conversational participants in the study telling a lie about someone who was not part of the presentation; that person was not there. Results from Turner et al.'s study are in Figure 5.1.

Turner et al.'s (1975) study was replicated by DePaulo, Kashy, et al. (1996) in what has become another of the most heavily referenced research studies on deception. DePaulo, Kashy, et al. used two samples, students and community members, who for 7 days wrote about conversations which were 10 minutes or longer. The findings from this study were similar to Turner et al.'s work in that most people reported lying for self-serving reasons but those reasons were more likely to protect oneself from embarrassment or harm than to take advantage of another person. The second most common reason for lying was "other-oriented" (DePaulo, Kashy, et al., 1996, p. 986). The results were slightly different, though, in one of the groups they tested. Women talking to other women in DePaulo, Kashy, et al.'s study tended to tell more other-oriented lies than self-oriented lies than the other two groups in the study (men and women talking or men talking with other men). Also, DePaulo, Kashy, et al. found that participants in the study overwhelmingly reported lying to fake positive feelings rather than negative feelings. Participants in the study were more likely to pretend to like something than they were to pretend they did *not* like something.

These results seem to indicate we lie most often to protect ourselves and others from embarrassment or harm. Such lies can be part of the **politeness norms** (Brown & Levinson, 1987) we enact to be cooperative communicators. If someone asks us if they look fat in an outfit, it is not appropriate in American culture to say "YES!" unless you have developed the type of relationship where this is acceptable. Now with a better understanding of why we lie, we can look at how we lie, which we talk about next.

POLITENESS NORMS

expectations of how a person should behave in order for them to be considered appropriate, or polite, communicators.

HOW WE LIE

Both Turner et al. (1975) and DePaulo, Kashy, et al. (1996) also looked for messages created in conversations reported by research participants. From these and other studies we started to look at types of lies including exaggerations, blatant lies, white lies, changing the subject, and/or not answering (called "withholding" in some research). Researchers were finding deceivers were sophisticated in their verbal deception but we still lacked a theoretical framework with which to examine lying behavior.

In 1992, McCornack published one of the first theories on deceptive communication. It was called **Information Manipulation Theory** (IMT). McCornack later added to the theory and published Information Manipulation Theory 2 (IMT2) (McCornack, Morrison, Paik, Wisner, & Zhu, 2014) which will be discussed later in the section. The first version of IMT and the first published test of IMT were published as lead articles in a highly respected communication journal, *Communication Monographs.* IMT did not include message types but instead, McCornack, Levine, Solowczuk, Torres, & Campbell (1992) stated: "IMT posits that in ordinary conversations, individuals monitor information that they disclose along four different primary dimensions: amount, veracity, relevance, and clarity" (p. 17).

In IMT, McCornack used Grice's (1989) **cooperative principle** to show how we can vary information in messages to successfully deceive. The cooperative principle was defined by Grice as "Make your conversational contribution such as is required, at the stage at which it occurs, by the accepted purpose or direction of the talk exchange in which you are engaged" (Grice, 1989, p. 26, as cited in McCornack, 1992). Using Grice's cooperative principle and maxims of conversation as a foundation of IMT, McCornack (1992) proposed that lies can vary along four dimensions:

1. Important or information relevant to the other person in the conversation is left out (called a **quantity violation** in IMT) by a deceiver;
2. A deceiver may completely change the information in a message or tell a complete lie (called a **quality violation** in IMT);

INFORMATION MANIPULATION THEORY (IMT)

individuals can purposefully alter relevant information to make it deceptive along four different dimensions: amount, truthfulness, relevance, and clarity.

COOPERATIVE PRINCIPLE

expectations of how people should communicate with others. People should communicate only what is needed to be communicated, they should not lie, they should stay on topic (not change the subject), and they should communicate clearly and unambiguously.

QUANTITY VIOLATION

when a deceiver leaves out some of the relevant information. Also often called a "white" lie.

QUALITY VIOLATION

when a deceiver tells a complete lie.

© Sue Smith/Shutterstock.com

3. A deceiver could change the subject away from the topic which is relevant to the other person in the conversation (called a relevance violation in IMT);

4. A deceiver could answer in an ambiguous, or unclear way (called a manner violation in IMT).

According to McCornack (1992) and IMT, an individual may be more or less ambiguous, more or less completely untruthful, more or less a "little" deceptive, and more or less change the subject away from what another person in a conversation thinks is relevant. In the first test of IMT, McCornack, Levine, et al. (1992) created two scenarios, "Committed Chris" and "Upstate Terry," to explore how forms of the deceptive messages were perceived in terms of their relative honesty and competence within the two different scenarios. My favorite of the scenarios is "Committed Chris" (McCornack et al., 1992, p. 27). Basically, in this scenario you are asked to put yourself in the place of having a relationship with "Chris" (male or female Chris, does not matter). You and Chris are in a committed relationship that is not currently going well, so Chris has started hanging out with someone else and began a relationship with them. You suspect something is up so you say to Chris, "'lately you've been acting really distant'" (p. 27) and (in the study) you receive one of these responses (NOTE: all responses from McCornack et al., 1992, pp. 28–29):

Honest Message: "I haven't really been honest with you . . ." (Chris goes on to tell about the other person they are dating).

Quantity Violation (white lie, some relevant information left out): "Yes, I have."

Quality Violation (total lie): "No, I don't know what you mean, I think I have just been under a lot of stress recently, with all these exams and papers and stuff."

Relevance Violation (changing the subject message): "Why would you say something like that? You know, sometimes I wonder how you feel in this relationship. I mean, all we ever seem to do is fight recently."

Manner Violation (ambiguous message): "I've been going out."

The participants in this first test of IMT reported the honest message form was the most honest and competent, followed by the quantity (white lie) violation. The quality violation (complete lie) was also perceived as less honest but more competent, or appropriate, than the relevance (changing subject) and manner (ambiguous) message forms. So, the ratings of competence in a cheating situation were: (1) honest message (most competent); (2) quantity violation; (3) quality violation; (4) manner violation; and (5) relevance violation.

Some of my research (my Master's thesis and Dissertation mostly) came from IMT but I applied the message forms to different situations. Essentially, I found that we are sophisticated in our perception of the relative acceptability of lying behavior. In low-stakes lying situations it becomes more acceptable to tell a white-lie (quantity violation) than it may be to tell the truth. Quality violations or complete lies tend to not be acceptable in lower-stakes lying situations and changing the subject (relevance violation) or being ambiguous (manner violation) were somewhere between completely lying or telling a white lie. There is still more work to be done but what we are finding is in line with the research by Turner et al. (1975) and DePaulo, Kashy, et al. (1996) in that there are times when our reason for lying may be to protect ourselves or another person from harm and in those situations we may tell little white lies, or those lies which are relatively acceptable.

RELEVANCE VIOLATION

when a deceiver changes the subject away from a relevant topic.

MANNER VIOLATION

when a deceiver's message is unclear or ambiguous.

DECEPTION DETECTION

Having covered children and lying as well as the how and why we deceive, we get to the question numerous researchers have spent years exploring, "How do we catch someone lying?" The answers are not what you expect. We anticipate we can tell if someone is lying through nonverbal behaviors, or what we call leakage cues. Decades of research, however, has shown us there are no reliable nonverbal cues to deception and that truth-tellers' and deceivers' behaviors are nearly identical (DePaulo, Lindsay, et al., 2003).

For example, when you ask someone how they know if someone is lying, the common answer is by looking at a person in the eyes. The belief that individuals cannot maintain eye contact when lying is a widespread belief. The Global Deception Research Team (2006) found that in 51 out of 58 countries eye contact was the top behavior people would use to determine if they were being deceived. Ironically, we learn to be exceptionally good at maintaining eye contact when lying. We will even deliberately use eye contact to seem more believable (e.g., Mann et al., 2012). So, eye contact and other nonverbal cues, or clues to deception, you have looked for in the past are not reliable indicators of deception.

Also, another piece of bad news, we are terrible lie detectors. Some individuals will claim they are exceptional at detecting lies, but in a meta-analysis of 206 studies on deception detection, the average ability to detect lies was only 54% of the time (Bond & DePaulo, 2006). The likelihood of detecting someone lying is only slightly better than chance. It may be even worse than that, however. The **veracity effect** (Levine, Park, & McCornack, 1999) influences our judgments to make us even less likely to be able to detect when we are being deceived. The *veracity effect* is the tendency for individuals to more often judge a message as truthful rather than deceptive. For example, if we go back to our friend Denise, the poker player, we can ask her to participate in a little study we are doing on this. Perhaps we videotape her answering a list of 10 benign questions. We ask her to lie in half (five) of her answers and tell the truth in her other five answers. Then, say we have a research participant serve as an observer and watch the video. The observer tells us when they believe Denise was truthful or lied. The results would resoundingly show the observer would rate most of Denise's messages as truthful. Perhaps eight of the 10 messages were judged as truthful, only two as lies. Just by chance alone, then, the observer would be more likely to have judged the truthful judgments correctly but missed many lies. There were five lies and the observer may have only caught two at best. The veracity effect, therefore, is that our truth-detection accuracy level is significantly higher than our lie-detection accuracy. Our truth-detection accuracy may reach as high as 90% but our lie-detection accuracy may be less than 50%, even closer to 10 to 25% (Levine, Kim, & Blair, 2010). We can catch people telling the truth because we want to believe them and rate more statements as truthful. We do not catch lies because we do not anticipate lies as often as we do truth.

The reason given for the veracity effect is the **truth-bias** (McCornack & Parks, 1986). Truth-bias is the tendency for us to want to believe other people, even when we have evidence which may indicate deception. The truth-bias is one of the most robust or strongest effects found in the deception literature. Many of the students in my Deception classes are troubled by the findings about our poor ability to detect deception and by truth-bias. Some have even said that this makes them seem like "fools" and I completely disagree. Truth-bias shows we believe in other people and even if they are not always truthful, we want to continue to believe in them. If someone successfully betrays you and you find out later, who is the most functional of the two of you? It is you, your trust and belief in another person makes you a healthy

Global Deception Research Team Findings: If you want to know more about what they found: https://www.ncbi.nlm.nih.gov/pmc/articles/PMC2957901/

VERACITY EFFECT

the tendency for individuals to more often judge a message as truthful rather than deceptive.

TRUTH-BIAS

the tendency for us to want to believe other people, even when we have evidence which may indicate deception.

relational partner, even if that leads to you being betrayed. The person who lied is the person who failed as a relational partner, not you. The belief in other people, the truth-bias, makes us poor at detecting deception but it also aids us in cooperative communication and allowing ourselves to become close to others.

Another reason we may be bad at detecting lies is based on the inaccurate belief that liars have more cognitive load or anxiety when they lie. Substantial research efforts have gone into the assumption it is harder to tell a lie than to tell the truth. Yet, According to *IMT2* (**Information Manipulation Theory 2**), McCornack et al. (2014) posits it is often easier to tell a lie than to tell the truth. Deception often solves difficult problems. If your professor asks you why you did not turn in an assignment on time it may feel easier to tell a white-lie than admit you simply forgot the assignment. IMT2 adds more to our understanding of the cognitive processing of lies, and I am greatly simplifying it here, but the theory helps in understanding why people can get away with lies. We are looking in the wrong place, we are looking for cues, like having to look away when lying, which indicate the difficulty of creating a deceptive message. Yet, as lying may at times be easier than telling the truth, such cues may not exist.

There is still hope, however! There have been studies looking at other methods of detecting deception. In a seminal article by Levine, McCornack, Morrison, and Ferrara (2002), research participants were asked to talk about a time they were lied to and found out about the lie. The participants reported primarily the revealing of lies through another person (third party) telling them they had been deceived (32%) (see Figure 5.12). Participants also discovered lies through physical evidence (18%) of deception or a combination of methods used to discover a deception (30.9%).

Of the combinations of methods employed to catch a deceiver, the most effective combination was the use of third party information and solicited confessions. Nonverbal and verbal behavior cues were rarely used alone to successfully discover a lie but often used in combination with third party information, solicited confessions, and physical evidence.

INFORMATION MANIPULATION THEORY 2

the second version of IMT. One addition is about the ease of lying versus telling the truth. According to IMT2, it is often easier to lie than to tell the truth.

Figure **5.12**

Methods Which Led to Discovery of Deception

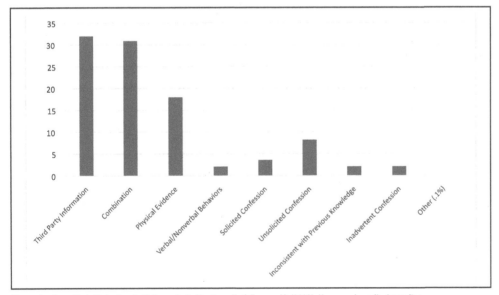

Chart taken from: Park, H., Levine, T., McCornack, S., Morrison, K., & Ferrara, M. (2002). How people really detect lies. *Communication Monographs, 69*(2), 144–157. doi: 10.1080/714041710.

In the same study by Levine, McCornack, et al. (2002), they also found only 14.9% of lies were discovered within a conversation. The majority of discovered lies were uncovered more than an hour after a conversation ended (80.9%). Of those lies discovered after an hour passed, 60.3% were unearthed after more than a day passed and 39.7% were discovered after over a week had gone by.

The short answer, then, to the question of how to detect lies is to listen to what others tell you, find evidence of deceit, use a combination of methods to determine if you have been lied to, and do not jump to conclusions. Give it time. Do not rely on eye contact or someone telling you something they saw online about deception detection; instead, employ multiple approaches to determine deceit.

IS IT OK TO LIE? AND ETHICS

This brings us to the final discussion in the section—what about ethics and is it OK to lie? To look at ethics and lying, we need to frame our discussion through two ethical theories: Utilitarianism and Deontology.

UTILITARIANISM

in order to determine if a behavior or decision is ethical, one must evaluate the consequences of the behavior or decision. The goal is to the greatest good for the most people.

Utilitarianism is focused on the evaluation of consequences of one's actions and the desire to do the greatest good (Johnson, 2015). If the consequences of an action harm another person then the behavior would be deemed unethical. If we use utilitarianism to evaluate the act of lying, high-stakes and anti-social lies would emerge as the least ethical or perhaps completely unethical deceptive act. It is not as simple as this, however. To examine the ethical dimensions of a deceptive act under utilitarianism, you have to examine all the possible consequences of an act and all the individuals who may be hurt by telling the truth or deceiving.

When looking at utilitarian ethics and deception, if a lie is told in order to protect someone else or to achieve the greatest good for the most people, it could be considered more ethical than telling the truth. Let's go back to Bob who we used in an earlier example. If Bob is dating Isabella but has decided that he now wants to date Sophia, Bob may lie to Isabella about going on a date with Sophia. To understand if the lie is unethical we need more information. Hypothetically, say that we know the following:

1. Bob and Isabella have not been getting along for some time.
2. Isabella has been reluctant to make a commitment to Bob.
3. Isabella and Bob have an open relationship and can see other people.

DEONTOLOGY

this ethical perspective focuses on an individual fulfilling their duty or responsibility to others.

We still may not have enough information, we need to think about each of the people in the situation and the consequences of Bob's lie. If Isabella and Bob are currently in a sexual but uncommitted relationship and not using protection like condoms, then the greatest good very well may be for Bob to tell the truth. If Isabella and Bob are not in an intimate relationship and are only casually dating, it may only serve to hurt Isabella's feelings if Bob tells the truth. Another consequence may be that Sophia knows nothing about Isabella and she may also be hurt by Bob being untruthful or dishonest.

No situation is simple, however, so evaluation of the relative morality or ethics of a deceptive act under utilitarianism hinges on understanding the consequences for all those involved. If you are evaluating a situation from the perspective of utilitarian ethics, you need to know how each person is impacted in order to analyze a situation and determine the outcome which either harms the least amount of people and/or helps the most people.

IMMANUEL KANT

Kant is one of the best-known ethical theorists. He took an exceptionally strong stand on lying being unethical and unacceptable behavior.

Deontology, in contrast to utilitarianism, is focused on duty or responsibility and deontology ethicists have strong perspectives on deceptive behavior. **Immanuel Kant**

(1724–1804) was a philosopher who was dogmatic about the unacceptability of lying. In his essay "On a Supposed Right to Lie from Altruistic Motives" (published in 1949), Kant states: "For a lie always harms another; if not some other particular man, still it harms mankind generally, for it vitiates the source of the law itself" (para 7). On lying, Kant was clear, it was not OK, it was an unethical behavior. Kant was strongly influenced by his Christian beliefs (Knapp et al., 2016) and the writings of Catholic church leaders like St. Thomas Aquinas who stated that all lies, even those which are not verbal, are unacceptable and are considered sins (Westerfelhaus, 2014).

Kant even offered the highly debated example of a "murder at the door" (for an excellent discussion on this see Varden, 2010). In Kant's example of a murder at the door, a friend comes to your home to hide from someone who wishes to kill them. The friend hides and the murderer comes to your door asking for your friend. According to Kant, you must tell the truth to the murderer, you must give up your friend to them. The intent seems clear that Kant believed all lies to be unacceptable, unethical. Yet, as discussed by Varden and others, Kant's insistence of telling the truth in this situation may be misinterpreted. Still, applying Kant to our Bob-Isabella-Sophia example, Kant would most likely tell Bob to tell the truth to both Isabella and Sophia, regardless of the consequences.

Another philosopher who also believed in duty and individual responsibility to be fundamental to ethics, but was critical of Kant's work, is Sir W. D. Ross (1877–1971). His list of duties is still widely used and is as follows:

- ► Fidelity: the duty to keep promises
- ► Reparation: the duty to compensate others when we harm them
- ► Gratitude: the duty to thank those who help us
- ► Justice: the duty to recognize merit
- ► Beneficence: the duty to improve the conditions of others
- ► Self-improvement: the duty to improve our virtue and intelligence
- ► Nonmaleficence: the duty to not injure others

(Freeley & Steinberg, 2014, p. 114)

SIR W. D. ROSS

an ethical theorist who also believed that duty and responsibility are fundamental to ethics. He put forward a list of "duties" which can be used to evaluate the ethics of deception.

The duties put forth by W. D. Ross focus on our responsibilities to others and are a more day-to-day perspective of ethics and how to communicate ethically with others. With regard to deception, W. D. Ross stated, "If, as almost all moralists except Kant are agreed, and as most plain men think, it is sometimes right to tell a lie or to break a promise . . . " (Ross, 1930, p. 28). At times an individual's duties will conflict. For example, perhaps Bob does not tell Isabella about wanting to date Sophia because he does not want to hurt Isabella. Bob may also believe that the relationship with Isabella is pretty much over so telling her may hurt any chance they could have of eventually being friends. This could be considered the duty of nonmaleficence, our responsibility to do no harm. Yet, if Bob is breaking a promise to Isabella to go to the movies with her, he is violating the duty of fidelity. We often face conflicts with the responsibilities we have to others and Ross (1930) shows some understanding of how ethical challenges may result in some form of deception. The debate on the ethicality of lying is robust but comes down to trying to do what you believe is the right thing to do.

CONCLUSION AND THOUGHTS ON DECEPTION

Writing this section has been a wonderful experience and my hope is that writing in this first-person manner has made the section feel like a discussion, rather than a textbook section. There is an abundance of research on deception and ethics and in this section we only touched on a small amount of what is out there, waiting for you to find. I encourage you, though, to not let your truth-bias lead you to believing all you read about deception. Ironic but true, there are many lies about deception, particularly about cues to deception. I also encourage you to consider taking a class on ethics as there are centuries of debate and conversation on the ethics of human thought and behavior. In the end, I hope I leave you a little wiser about deception and a little more accepting of yourself and others with regard to lying. We all lie or have lied but hopefully our lies were told to help and not hurt others. We also believe others, even when they lie to us. To be human is to trust and believe in the good of other people, even deceiving Bob in the earlier example. I leave you now to go check in with my daughter, Madi, whom I discussed at the beginning of the section, and her brother, Jonathan, and Max, my husband. Inevitably one of them will probably tell me a white lie today or tomorrow, especially if I ask them if I look OK in my jeans.

Discussion Questions

1. Think about a time you saw a child lie. How old was the child and were they able to lie well? Compare that to the findings of Peskin (1992) talked about in this section. Do you think children at 4 years of age can have theory of mind?

2. What do you think about the study on Internet use? Do you think teens are good at lying to their parents about their Internet use? Why or why not?

3. What do you think about the truth-bias? Do you think there are some people who you may have more of a truth-bias with? Family? Friends?

4. Remember a time when you have been lied to and you caught the other person in a lie. Which of the methods included in Figure 5.12 helped you find out about the lie?

5. Thinking of the same time you caught someone in a lie, did you catch the person during the conversation, as they lied? If not, how long did it take you to discover the lie?

Astington, J. W., & Edward, M. J. (2010). The development of theory of mind in early childhood. *Encyclopedia on Early Child Development*. Retrieved from http://www.child-encyclopedia.com/social-cognition/according-experts/development-theory-mind-early-childhood

Bond, C. F., Jr., & DePaulo, B. M. (2006). Accuracy of deception judgments. *Personality and Social Psychology Review, 10,* 214 –234. doi:10.1207/s15327957pspr1003_2

Brown, P., & Levinson, S. (1987). *Politeness: Some universals in language use.* Cambridge, U.K.: Cambridge University Press.

Depaulo, B., Kashy, D., Kirkendol, S., Wyer, M., & Epstein, J. (1996). Lying in everyday life. *Journal of Personality and Social Psychology, 70*(5), 979. doi:10.1037/0022-3514.70.5.979

DePaulo, B. M., Lindsay, J. J., Malone, B. E., Muhlenbruck, L., Charlton, K., & Cooper, H. (2003). Cues to deception. *Psychological Bulletin, 129,* 74 –118. doi:10.1037/0033-2909.129.1.74

Feldman, R., & White, J. (1992). Detecting deception in children. *Journal of Communication, 30*(2), 121–128. doi:10.1111/j.1460-2466.1980.tb01974.x

Freeley, A. J., & Steinberg, D. L. (2014). *Argumentation and debate, critical thinking for reasoned decision making, 13th ed.* Boston, MA: Wadsworth/Cengage Learning.

Global Deception Research Team. (2006). A world of lies. *Journal of Cross-Cultural Psychology, 37,* 60 –74. doi:10.1177/0022022105282295

Grice, P. (1989). *Studies in the way of words.* Cambridge, MA: Harvard University Press.

Johnson, C. (2015). *Meeting the ethical challenges of leadership: Casting light or shadow* (5th ed.). Thousand Oaks, CA: Sage Publications.

Kant, I. (1949). On a supposed right to lie from altruistic motives. Retrieved from https://www.unc.edu/courses/2009spring/plcy/240/001/Kant.pdf

Knapp, M., McGlone, M., Griffin, D., & Earnest, W. (2016). *Lying and deception in human interaction* (2nd ed.). Dubuque, IA: Kendal Hunt Publishing.

Levine, T., Kim, R., & Blair, J. (2010). (In)accuracy at detecting true and false confessions and denials: An initial test of a projected motive model of veracity judgments. *Human Communication Research, 36*(1), 82–102. doi:10.1111/j.1468-2958.2009.01369.x

Levine, T., Park, H., & McCornack, S. (1999). Accuracy in detecting truths and lies: Documenting the "veracity effect." *Communication Monographs, 66*(2), 125–144. doi:10.1080/03637759909376468

Levine, T., Serota, K., Carey, F., & Messer, D. (2013). Teenagers lie a lot: A further investigation into the prevalence of lying. *Journal of Communication Research Reports, 30,* 211-210. doi:10.1080/08824096.2013.806254

Mann, S., Vrij, A., Leal, S., Granhag, P., Warmelink, L., & Forrester, D. (2012). Windows to the soul? Deliberate eye contact as a cue to deceit. *Journal of Nonverbal Behavior, 36*(3), 205–215. doi:10.1007/s10919-012-0132-y

McAfee's Digital Deception: Exploring the Online Disconnect between Parents and Kids Study. (2013). Retrieved from https://www.mcafee.com/au/about/news/2013/q2/20130604-01.aspx

McCornack, S. (1992). Information manipulation theory. *Communication Monographs, 59*(1), 1–16. doi:10.1080/03637759209376245

McCornack, S., Levine, T., Solowczuk, K., Torres, H., & Campbell, D. (1992). When the alteration of information is viewed as deception: An empirical test of information manipulation theory. *Communication Monographs, 59*(1), 17–29. doi:10.1080/03637759209376246

McCornack, S., Morrison, K., Paik, J., Wisner, A., & Zhu, X. (2014). Information Manipulation Theory 2: A propositional theory of deceptive discourse production. *Journal of Language and Social Psychology, 33*(4), 348–377. doi:10.1177/0261927X14534656

McCornack, S., & Parks, M. R. (1986). Deception detection and relationship development: The other side of trust. In M. L. McLaughlin (Ed.), *Communication Yearbook, 9,* Newbury Park, CA: Sage Publications.

Park, H. S., Levine, T. R., McCornack, S. A., Morrison, K., & Ferrara, M. (2002). How people really detect lies. *Communication Monographs, 69,* 144–157. http://dx.doi.org/10.1080/714041710

Peskin, J. (1992). Ruse and representations: On children's ability to conceal information. *Developmental Psychology,* *28*(1), 84–89. doi:10.1037/0012-1649.28.1.84

Ross, W. (1930). *The right and the good.* Oxford, U.K.: Oxford University Press.

Serota, K., Levine, T., and Boster, F. (2010). The prevalence of lying in America: Three studies of reported deception. *Human Communication Research, 36, 1–24.* doi:10.1111/j.1468-2958.2009.01366.x

Turner, R., Edgley, C., & Olmstead, G. (1975). Information control in conversations: Honesty is not always the best polity. *Kansas Journal of Sociology, 11*(1), 69–89. doi:10.17161/STR.1808.6098

Varden, H. (2010). Kant and lying to the murderer at the door…One more time: Kant's legal philosophy and lies to murderers and Nazis. *Journal of Social Philosophy, 41*(4), 403–421. doi:10.1111/j.1467-9833.2010.01507.x

Westerfelhaus, R. (2014). Aquinas, Thomas. In T. Levine (Ed.), *Encyclopedia of Deception* (pp. 31–33). Thousand Oaks, CA: Sage Publications.

Health Communication

By Anne P. Hubbell

Objectives

- ▸ Connect the components within the Extended Parallel Process Model.
- ▸ Differentiate between danger control and fear control.
- ▸ Identify the components within the Transtheoretical Model.
- ▸ List the elements included in Motivational Interviewing.
- ▸ Apply the practical suggestions on how to communicate more effectively with health care practitioners.

First, let's consider two scenarios. In the first scenario, a young, single mother, Carrie, who has been diagnosed with HIV enters a clinic recommended by her physician. The clinic is well-known for providing services for HIV patients who struggle with being able to afford their medications and need emotional and financial help. Carrie is embarrassed to walk into this clinic and she is nervous that they will not be able to help her. The receptionist greets her warmly and escorts her to a small office where she is introduced to a young man. He is going to be her case manager and he is going to help her, explains the receptionist. He begins by asking the usual questions—when was she diagnosed, what medications is she taking, who is her physician, what is her viral load (a way of measuring the progression of HIV)? This takes some time, and Carrie is getting uncomfortable as she has to go pick up her daughter from her friend's house. Finally, the young man pulls out several brochures with contact numbers for other agencies that can offer Carrie some assistance. He helps her fill out some applications for assistance and tells her about other assistance programs for which she can apply. She leaves feeling like she knows better how to take care of herself and her daughter.

Carrie's scenario sounds perfect, but could it be better? In the second scenario, another single mother, Sharon, receives the same advice and support as did Carrie, but she is working with a case manager who is trained to use the Risk Behavior Diagnosis Scale (RBDS). The RBDS is a survey used by Sharon's case manager. It has easy-to-answer questions about Sharon's behaviors and helps the case worker determine what Sharon does to manage her disease (her use of medicine and how often she sees her doctor) as well as how she protects others from contracting it. After Sharon answers the questions on the survey, the case manager can then better understand what other services or support Sharon needs. By asking the questions on the RBDS, the case worker determines that Sharon has not been taking her medications. The case manager could assume that Sharon is not taking her meds because she cannot afford them, but that is only one part of the problem. As they go through the answers to the survey, the case manager finds that Sharon is lacking in what is called "self-efficacy." Sharon does not believe she can fight HIV, even with the medications. She is feeling fatalistic and believes she will die soon even if she takes better care of herself. Her case manager, though, has training on how to talk to Sharon about her feelings and brings out more information for her on the group therapy meetings they have for others like her who have, in many ways, given up on themselves. Sharon promises to return for the group meeting and, whether she does or does not, the case manager makes a note in her file to continue to try to work on her feelings of self-efficacy; her belief in her ability to fight HIV.

Although fictional characters and clinics were used for these scenarios, they are loosely based on true research conducted by Kim Witte, PhD, and colleagues. The scenarios used here are relatively similar to scenarios she and colleagues use in their book, *Effective Health Risk Messages* (2001). Further, the scenarios demonstrate that training in health communication can aid health care practitioners in gaining crucial information needed to treat their patients.

Because of the importance of communication in a health care situation, in this section we will first discuss two theories often used in health communication research and training, then we will give suggestions on how health care practitioners can improve their communication with patients, and we will end with a discussion on how patients can be more effective communicators with their practitioners. The theories included in this section will focus on health communication campaigns or efforts to try to encourage people to enact healthy as opposed to unhealthy behaviors (e.g., stop smoking).

THE FEAR APPEAL AND THEORIES IN HEALTH COMMUNICATION

The Creation of the Fear Appeal and the Extended Parallel Process Model

Most people enact at least some unhealthy behaviors. It may be as minor as chewing their nails on up to becoming addicted to meth. Although individuals have always tried to encourage loved ones to take care of their health, the first organized research efforts in the United States focused on improving health started in the 1950s. One of the first examples of a health campaign came from Yale University where campaigns were created to try to compel high school students to brush their teeth (Janis & Feshbach, 1953; Witte, Meyer, & Martell, 2001). The belief at that time was that if you scared an audience with a message, or "fear appeal," they would want to change their behaviors. So the high school students received fear appeals, or threatening messages, that varied from gentle to severe. Gentle messages included information about how not brushing could lead to them getting cavities while severe, or more threatening, messages included them losing all their teeth from not brushing or even going blind from an associated disease. The Yale researchers found that they could arouse fear by exposing the potential consequences of unhealthy behaviors with a caveat. When strong fear appeals were used, the students thought the message was persuasive, but they were more persuaded to brush their teeth from the gentlest fear appeals, also called the "minimal-fear message" (Haefner, 1965, p. 142).

This famous study was conducted again in 1965 (Haefner, 1965). Similar messages were used with a larger sample of students, however, the researcher had different findings than the earlier study. In Haefner's study, he found that stronger fear appeals were more effective than weaker fear appeals at getting students to brush their teeth regularly. With more analyses, Haefner proposed that the differences in the two studies may have been that in the earlier study they used students with a higher socioeconomic status than those in the 1965 sample. Thus, those who were of lower socioeconomic status may be more persuadable by stronger fear appeals. Those of higher socioeconomic status may be more persuaded by weaker fear appeals.

From these and similar studies, there was confusion about how to change behaviors using fear appeals. Some believed fear appeals did not work, while others believed that too much fear was bad, and others were trying to figure out how levels of fear impacted differing behaviors. Even though the debate was ongoing among health communication researchers, many organizations still embraced the ability of a strong fear appeal to change behaviors.

This belief blossomed into some famous anti-smoking health campaigns. One was extremely threatening, or scary, and showed the power of a single picture. The campaign used a picture of a woman covered in black tar and smoking a cigarette. Only the words "If what happened on your inside happened on your outside" accompanied the picture as the campaign was focused on visually representing the tar inside the woman's lungs from smoking; the graphic picture was sufficient to frighten. Other graphic anti-smoking advertisements have included showing people who smoked in body bags or people who had cancer talking out of holes in their throats. These frightening anti-smoking ads—although the most famous perhaps of all health communication campaigns—were not extremely effective. This was because smokers ignored the scarier ads or reacted to them by smoking more.

Because of the failure of many of what we call "fear appeal" campaigns like the harsh anti-smoking campaigns, many organizations began to believe that fear appeals do not work. What they did not understand, however, was that you had to have the right amount of fear and, with that, the person who received the message had to feel

EXTENDED PARALLEL PROCESS MODEL

focuses on understanding the people who were the target of a message.

SUSCEPTABILITY

when an individual believes they could be at risk of experiencing a threat.

PERCEIVED SEVERITY

the belief that a threat could have serious consequences.

SELF-EFFICACY

the belief that the individual has control over their own health or destiny.

RESPONSE EFFICACY

a person's perception of whether the recommended response is reasonable or easy to do.

the power to be able to fight the threat or enact the recommended behavior (i.e., efficacy). So, many fear appeal campaigns failed.

The **Extended Parallel Process Model** (EPPM) was created by Witte (1992) in response to previous health communication theories being unable to determine why health communication campaigns succeeded or failed. Witte incorporated variables from earlier theories in EPPM as well as a focus on understanding the people who were the target of a message. Such an understanding of the target audience *before* creating a health communication campaign, or a fear appeal, will result in a targeted campaign. One focused on what is needed to persuade the target audience to do what is recommended. Also included in EPPM was a model that showed how too much threat could lead to failure of the message to change behaviors and how to balance that with efficacy (remember Sharon from the scenarios?).

Witte's (1992) EPPM contains two dimensions—a threat and the ability to fight the threat (efficacy). The threat dimension of a message includes both perceived **susceptibility** to and severity of the threat. The more an individual believes they could be at risk of experiencing a threat, the greater the perceived susceptibility (i.e., "I could get cancer from smoking"), whereas **perceived severity** centers on the belief that a threat could have serious consequences (i.e., "Smoking can kill me"). The ability to fight a threat is called efficacy. Efficacy also contains two dimensions—self- and response efficacy. **Self-efficacy** is the extent to which an individual feels they are able to combat a threat (i.e., "I know I can stop smoking"). Self-efficacy is about personal power or one's belief that they are strong enough or smart enough to be able to do something. Response efficacy refers to a specific response to the threat that is recommended as a way to fight it (i.e., "I can join a support group to stop smoking").

Often, self-efficacy and response efficacy get confused. Self-efficacy is the belief that the individual has control over their own health or destiny, whereas **response efficacy** is their perception of whether the recommended response is reasonable or easy to do. So, for example, if a person does not think they can quit smoking at all they will not even consider the recommended response. If they think they can quit, they will evaluate whether the response is realistic for them to try. Sharon, in our scenario

from the beginning of the section, had low levels of perceived self-efficacy. We say "perceived" because they seem real but may not be. We can look at Sharon and see a strong, capable woman, but if she does not view herself in the same way she will have low self-efficacy. She will feel powerless and unable to fight HIV so she gives up and does not take her medication that is the recommended response (or response efficacy). By not taking her medications because she feels powerless to fight HIV, she is demonstrating low self-efficacy.

The four components of EPPM (severity, susceptibility, self-efficacy, and response efficacy) interact within an individual who is observing a message. As these components are considered by individuals, they will then process the fear appeal in one of three ways. First, they may not pay attention to the fear appeal so no fear is created and the message goes virtually unprocessed. The other two methods of processing the fear appeal are called fear control and danger control processing. **Fear control** processes are irrational responses to a fear appeal. When a person is in fear control they let emotions guide their response to a message (Witte, 1994; see also Lazarus, 1991a; Lazarus, 1991b; Rippetoe & Rogers, 1987). Fear control processing leads individuals to have strong perceptions of threat, but they do not think they have the ability to fight the threat (low response and self-efficacy). They may react by avoiding thinking about the threat, which is called defensive avoidance (Janis & Feshbach, 1953) and be less likely to fight the threat (Witte, 1998). So, when the anti-smoking campaigns focused on scaring smokers, smokers often responded by avoiding the ads, making jokes about them, or sometimes smoking more as a form of reactance. They were too scared, and they did not believe they could quit smoking—they had too little efficacy and too much threat (or fear)—so they were not going to quit; they were in fear control processing.

Danger control processing, though, is what you want to happen in response to a fear appeal or health communication campaign. If a person is using danger control processing, the message will encourage them to believe the threat is severe and that they are susceptible to it (both elements of threat), BUT they will also believe they have the ability to fight the threat (self-efficacy) and the recommended response is a reasonable way to do so (response efficacy). The person in danger control processing will rationally process the information in the health communication campaign and will be more likely to at least consider changing their behavior.

An example of an anti-smoking campaign more likely to create danger control processing is the "Don't Quit Quitting" ads from the American Cancer Society. There is also the "Great American Smokeout," which occurs every year on the third Thursday of November. These campaigns focus on building perceptions of efficacy among smokers in that they encourage them to keep trying to quit and to have a day set when they will quit. Smokers are well aware of the risks of smoking, but by giving them reasonable responses to the threat of smoking and by encouraging their beliefs they can do the recommended response (or quit), these campaigns have been extremely successful.

Risk Behavior Diagnosis Scale

The Risk Behavior Diagnosis Scale (RBDS) was created to apply the concepts of EPPM to better understand a patient's perceptions of efficacy and threat (Witte et al., 2001). It further gives the benefit of encouraging more interpersonal interaction between a patient and health care provider regarding specific behaviors and beliefs regarding diseases patients may have or be at risk of contracting. The RBDS assists health care practitioners through facilitating their understanding of patient perceptions of self- and response efficacy and the susceptibility and severity of threat. By understanding

FEAR CONTROL

irrational responses to fear appeals.

DANGER CONTROL

rational response to a fear appeal.

these perceptions, health care practitioners can then determine whether patients are in fear control or danger control processing. Then, practitioners have the ability, as in the example at the beginning of the section, to find out where a patient needs more information or support so that they can be moved toward danger control processing; that is, rationally evaluating the health threat or issue and taking positive steps to take care of themselves.

The RBDS includes 12 questions, three for each of the following: self-efficacy, response efficacy, susceptibility, and severity. A score is calculated based on the responses, and the score is used to then determine whether an individual is in danger or fear control processing. If a patient is in fear control processing, they will be irrationally processing information about a disease and are more likely to ignore information about the disease or even act in an unhealthier manner. Sharon, in our scenario, is an example of someone who may look like she is handling her HIV diagnosis, but when the case manager calculates Sharon's responses to the RBDS, he finds Sharon is not taking her medicines, seriously compromising her ability to control her HIV and stay alive. She is in fear control processing because she has low self-efficacy. By using the RBDS, the case manager can better understand Sharon's concerns and better help her manage her disease. For more information on the RBDS, go to https://www.msu.edu/~wittek/rbd.htm where you can find a handbook on how to use the RBDS.

Transtheoretical Model

The *transtheoretical model* (Prochaska & DiClemente, 1984) is like EPPM in that it focuses on understanding what an individual thinks about a message or health care issue before putting together a campaign to try to change behaviors. In essence, the transtheoretical model emphasizes meeting individuals "where they are" rather than assuming how they are going to behave when they receive a fear appeal or other message emphasizing changes in health behaviors. The transtheoretical model is also called a *stages of change* model because it focuses on the "stages of readiness that individuals pass through over time toward behavior change" (Bradley Wright, Sparks, & O'Hair, 2013, p. 267).

The transtheoretical model includes five stages. The five stages refer to what a person is thinking about a disease, health issue, or potential health communication campaign. If we use a non-smoking campaign as an example, the stages would be as follows (from Bradley Wright et al., 2013):

1. *Pre-contemplation stage:* individuals are not thinking about not smoking. They do not pay attention to any information on smoking because it is not even "on their radar" or important to them. They are unaware smoking can hurt them.
2. *Contemplation stage:* individuals know about the health issue so those in this stage may know smoking is hurting them, and they are thinking about whether or not they want to quit. They will weigh the pros and cons of quitting.
3. *Preparation stage:* here the smoker is making a plan to stop smoking; they are looking at what they need to do to quit and determining which method they prefer (e.g., the "patch," setting a quit date, etc.).
4. *Action stage:* in this stage, the smoker quits! They are taking action to change their behaviors.
5. *Maintenance/relapse stage:* after quitting, the smoker will reevaluate whether they want to continue their non-smoking or if they want to relapse and go back to smoking.

An organization or research group can use surveys, interviews, and/or focus groups to determine where their target audience is on the transtheoretical model. Say, for example, you are working on a grant and through this grant you want to encourage 16-year-olds in Las Cruces to stop smoking. A survey has been conducted and you know that 16-year-olds are in the preparation stage. They have a lot of peer pressure to smoke and say they enjoy smoking, but they are thinking about quitting smoking. A campaign focused on giving them easy alternatives that will help them stop smoking will be more effective for these 16-years-olds than a strong fear appeal. They need information that will help them stop; they do not need to be frightened into thinking about it. If they were in the pre-contemplation or even the contemplation stage, however, a small amount of threat will create a small amount of fear and may get them to start thinking about or get more motivated to quit smoking. If they were in the action stage then encouraging their positive behavior is needed—telling them they made the right choice and maybe convince them to help others (we often can persuade ourselves when we are persuading others).

Often, those creating health communication campaigns focus on the pre-contemplation, contemplation, and preparation stages, but when individuals are first trying to change their behaviors it is important to support them and if they relapse to help them to want to try again. The "Don't Quit Quitting" campaign put forward by the American Cancer Association is a brilliant example of supporting even those who fail at behavior change. This was based on research that determined that people often quit multiple times before they are able to successfully quit and remain a non-smoker.

Overall, when theories are used to create health communication campaigns, their chances for success greatly improve. Theories give us ways to measure attitudes and intentions so that we know what matters to our target audience and how to persuade or encourage them to start enacting healthier behaviors. The key to both of the theories discussed, and to the success of campaigns, is communication. Communication is often also the key to a health care practitioners', including doctors', ability to diagnose and treat patients.

PATIENTS, HEALTH CARE PRACTITIONERS, AND COMMUNICATION

Patient–Doctor Communication

As you read the header for this section—"Patient–Doctor"—this may seem off or strange. That is because much of the communication we experience with doctors trained in the United States is "Doctor–Patient" where a doctor asks questions and we, as patients, answer them. This is a highly efficient and effective method of interacting with patients. In many ways it is even more encouraged by the move of many physicians to use computers to enter data while talking to patients. The programs they use cue them to what information is needed and is data, not person, driven. This does not mean they are not efficient or even effective. For one, they can potentially cut down on time spent on each patient, and none of us like to sit for hours in a waiting room. They also will document symptoms so they can be tracked over time and a physician can easily look at trends. They can even pull up information to show the patient, greatly improving access to needed information. Technology also offers physicians a way to communicate with each other. The author's daughter, for example, was diagnosed with

© michaeljung/Shutterstock.com

a rare malformation within both her ears. It cannot be seen except through an MRI (Magnetic Resonance Imaging). After she was diagnosed by a specialist, her physician wanted to know more about how to help her so he sent her MRI via e-mail and had a teleconference with a specialist at one of the top clinics in the United States. This saved a lot of money and time for the family, and the specialist found an additional malformation that needed to be considered in her treatment.

Technology and computers greatly improve a physician's ability to care for their patients, but it can still encourage the doctor–patient or interview approach to their communication; thus, limiting the physician to working on what they can find with good questions. Because of limitations like this, the doctor–patient interview method of communication has been evolving into a more patient-centered approach.

One example that is highly communicative and becoming more popular is called **motivational interviewing**. This type of communication between patient and physician has been defined as "a directive, client-centered counseling style for eliciting behavior change by helping clients to explore and resolve ambivalence" (Rollnick & Miller, 1995, para 3; as cited in du Pré, 2010, p. 58). According to du Pré, motivational interviewing was first used in counseling and psychotherapy. It has been considered useful, however, in identifying patient issues and concerns. Patients may have underlying issues that prevent them from acting in a healthy manner and, thus, making good decisions. Motivational interviewing can help practitioners understand patients, and this has made it a useful new approach to communication in a patient–doctor interaction. When a practitioner uses motivational interviewing, they do not prescribe behaviors or medicines, instead they interview the patient as follows:

> . . . he or she does not presume to know what is best for the other person. Instead, the interviewer respects that people weigh a variety of factors when making decisions and that consequently they almost always have mixed feelings (ambivalence) about change. The interviewer's job is respectfully and nonjudgmentally to ask questions,

MOTIVATIONAL INTERVIEWING

a directive, client-centered counseling style for eliciting behavior change by helping clients to explore and resolve ambivalence.

(elicit) a person's feelings, to help clarify those feelings, and to assist the person in making choices (resolving the ambivalence) (du Pré, 2010, p. 58).

Motivational interviewing is particularly useful with incurable and/or painful diseases. For example, although there have been many efforts to understand how individuals cope with learning they have a terminal disease, each individual must come to terms with it on their own, and they do not follow the same steps in so doing. One person may withdraw and say nothing to anyone and another person may tell everyone they know but in a way that it sounds like they are talking about what they had for dinner the night before. Through motivational interviewing, the health care practitioner can better understand how the individual is experiencing their cancer and through understanding their experience, may be better able to help them manage the disease through pain medication, referring them to support groups, helping them tell their family, and/or referring them to a program like Hospice where they will receive quality end-of-life care. Without motivational interviewing, a health care practitioner may miss important signs, symptoms, or issues for which the patient needs help but does not know how to communicate their need.

So, how does a physician or health care practitioner conduct a motivational interview? du Pré (2010) summarizes several studies and offers suggestions on how to conduct such an interview (see Table 5.1). There are basically two parts to the interview. In the first part of the motivational interview the health care practitioner is trying to understand the patient and their concerns or problems. In the second part of the motivational interview, the health care practitioner attempts to offer patients alternatives for treatment and then work with them as they make their own personal choices. The health care practitioner, then, is a guide who can show the different ways to go, but they do not lead patients; patients remain the decision makers regarding their own health.

The first part of a motivational interview includes the following: establish "a respectful tone"; let the patient "set the agenda"; determine if the situation is important to the patient; investigate ambivalence; let the patient do the talking (listen);

Table **5.1**

Motivational Interviewing

Part 1 of the Motivational Interview	Part 2 of the Motivational Interview
Understanding the Patient	**Guiding the Patient through Health Care Decisions**
1. Set a Respectful Tone 2. Let Patient Set the Agenda 3. Gauge the Patient's Interest 4. Explore Ambivalence 5. Listen 6. Elicit-Provide-Elicit	1. Identify and Explore Multiple Options 2. Partner with Patient, Don't Persuade 3. Roll with Resistance 4. Determine the Patient's Self-Confidence and Self-Efficacy 5. Focus on Incremental (Small) Changes 6. Collaborate and Empower

From du Pré, 2010, p. 60

"elicit-provide-elicit" (du Pré, 2010, p. 60). First, a respectful tone means the health care practitioner has to approach the motivational interview with a positive and non-judgmental attitude; they must want to better understand the person they are interviewing. If they are in a bad mood or unable to truly be open to hearing what the patient has to say, they will not be able to conduct the motivational interview. Second, the practitioner has to let the patient say what matters to them. Questions that encourage open-ended responses like "How?" and "Why?" may encourage patients to open up and start talking about what is truly a concern and what is not. Third, if the patient is not interested in having the conversation, pushing it will only make the practitioner and patient more uncomfortable. An example question to determine this, given by du Pré (2010), was "On a scale of 1 to 10, how important is it to you to reduce your pain?" (p. 60). If a patient does not feel it is important, they may respond with a "1," and the interview at that point may not need to continue.

Investigating ambivalence, however, which is the fourth element of a motivational interview, may help in determining if the interview is worthwhile. Ambivalence is a complicated state and is common among patients in extreme pain and/or dealing with life-threatening illnesses. It is a state of feeling sometimes two contradictory feelings at the same time. For example, a person who is terminally ill may wish to not live any longer because the pain is unbearable, but they still want to live because they fear leaving their family will cause their family emotional pain. So, they may have two very different feelings they experience profoundly at the same time, causing them great stress. A motivational interview may help a health care practitioner to determine what mixed or ambivalent feelings a patient may be experiencing and could help the practitioner be better able to help the patient. So, for example, if the patient is in great pain, perhaps they are not complaining about it because they do not want to be a "pain" for their family. Through asking open-ended questions about pain and about how they think about pain and pain treatment, the practitioner may be better able to break down some of the resistance a patient may have to pain management. Or, they may be able to refer the patient to an individual better able to manage pain or the contradictory feelings the terminally ill patient has about whether they want to live or die.

None of this can happen, however, without the fifth element—listening. The patient has to do most of the talking or the interview has returned to being practitioner-centered and not patient-centered. In a presentation at the Western States Communication Association Annual meeting in 2013, the Top Student and Top Debut paper for the Health Communication Division was presented showing the different methods of interviewing women about them being diagnosed with breast cancer (Hine, 2013). The research was from a cancer research center in New Mexico, and the presenters acted out actual interviews between physicians and patients with breast cancer. The results were astounding. When traditional doctor-led interview methods were used, patients were given excellent information; however, it was not as detailed as when patient-led interviews occurred. When patients did most of the talking the physicians were better able to address concerns of the women and often found out more about their patients so they were better able to provide them with necessary information. Through listening to patients and providing answers to relevant questions, the patients were better able to understand the treatment options they were considering.

The fifth element of the motivational interview is "elicit-provide-elicit" (du Pré, 2010, p. 60). This involves the use of paraphrasing what a patient communicates. For this element of motivational interviewing, the health care practitioner asks the patient a question (i.e., "How would you describe your pain? How severe is it?"). The practitioner then waits for a response and tries to put it all together using paraphrasing and another question. So, he/she may say "It sounds like you are saying that your pain is severe, an '11' on a '10-point' scale. Do you think that it would help to increase the dosage of your medicine?" It is important to note that although the practitioner will talk about pain management with a patient in pain, the difference is through the motivational interview they are allowing the patient to communicate their concerns first so the physician knows the patient's main concerns or issues and can better address them.

After a health care practitioner listens and helps the patient identify what the issues and/or concerns are, the practitioner can then move to the second part of the motivational interview where they will offer the patient alternatives and help guide the patient to making a decision about how to proceed with treatment. There are six factors for this part of the interview, which include "identify multiple options"; "partner, don't persuade"; "roll with resistance"; "gauge the decision-maker's sense of confidence and self-efficacy"; "focus on incremental changes"; and "collaborate and empower" (du Pré, 2010, p. 60). First, the practitioner should offer the patient all of the alternatives to treatment or options. They can do this, though, without dominating the conversation. They should first ask the patient questions like "I see you have done a lot of research on the Internet; what types of alternatives to treatment have you looked at?" and "What did you think of them? What are the advantages and disadvantages that you found?"

The second factor in this part of motivational interviewing is focused on partnering with the patient rather than trying to influence them toward any particular treatment. For example, a patient with a terminal disease may or may not want to continue treatment. Many of us know individuals who have fought diseases like cancer for many years and are tired of fighting it. The toll that chemotherapy and radiation take on the body sometimes is not worth the fight, particularly if the individual with cancer feels they had a good life and want to just enjoy as much as they can with the time they have left. Others, though, will fight to the bitter end. These are important personal decisions and health care practitioners using motivational interviewing will encourage the patient to weigh all alternatives, but do so in a nonjudgmental manner; the patient will know best what they need and want. So, trust is essential to motivational interviewing; trust in the patient's ability to make good decisions that best suit them.

The third factor is for the health care practitioner to "roll with resistance" (du Pré, 2010, p. 60). Simply put, a practitioner should not try to argue with a patient. Sometimes a practitioner may feel strongly about a treatment, but the patient will refuse it. As practitioners take an oath to cure patients, it can be aggravating when a patient refuses or ignores treatment. In the motivational interview, however, it is not the practitioner's goal to persuade; it is to encourage the patient to persuade themselves of the best treatment. Research has shown when we convince ourselves a change is needed we are more likely to actually change. The non-smoking ads discussed earlier in the section illustrate this well. When a person makes a decision to stop smoking they will be better able to do this than if their partner forces them to stop smoking. That is why current non-smoking campaigns focus on empowerment and self- and response efficacy.

It is important, however, to determine if a patient has the self-confidence or self-efficacy needed to make decisions, which is the fourth factor in the second part of motivational interviewing. A health care practitioner can use surveys like the RBDS to estimate their patients' levels of self-efficacy regarding health care treatment decisions. If the patient does not feel comfortable or able to make decisions, the practitioner can then revert back to the first part of the motivational interview and ask questions

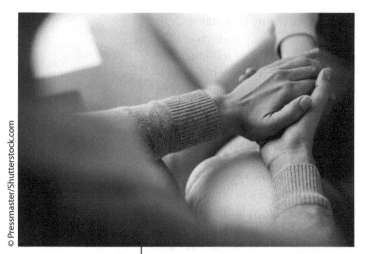

© Pressmaster/Shutterstock.com

to determine what is causing the lack of self-confidence. It may be that there are issues (e.g., being afraid they cannot afford the treatment) influencing a patient's ability to make decisions. If a practitioner knows this they can better address the concerns of the patient.

The fifth factor in the second part of the motivational interview is for the health care practitioner to not expect major changes through the interview. Instead, the practitioner should try to move the patient along a continuum toward improvement. For example, instead of expecting a patient who is overweight to completely change their behaviors overnight, it may be better to work on small changes a little at a time. It may be better to encourage them to try to exercise for 5 minutes a day instead of 30, for example.

Finally, and sixth, at the end of the motivational interview, the practitioner should remind the patient they are "partners in the process" and work to "empower" (du Pré, 2010, p. 60) the patient. If a patient believes they have a partner they can talk to as well as believe that they can take care of themselves, they may be better able to follow through on whatever treatment decisions they make. So, the patient who agrees to try to walk 5 minutes each day may feel able to do this and, if they fail, talk to the practitioner about the barriers that prevent them from this incremental change so it can be addressed.

Motivational interviewing takes time, though, so it is something that physicians or health care practitioners may only use when dealing with more serious illnesses or when they suspect more serious illnesses. Also, even with training, health care practitioners may not have the time or ability to effectively use motivational interviewing. Because of this, much research has focused on improving patient communication or on empowering patients to better communicate with their health care practitioners. du Pré (2010) also offers practical suggestions on how patients can more effectively communicate with their health care practitioners. They are as follows:

- ▶ *Write it down.* Write down your main concerns and questions. Bring two copies so your doctor can look on and keep a copy for future reference.
- ▶ *Rank-order your concerns.* Doctors like a list. You may not have time to go through all the items in one visit.
- ▶ *Think it through.* Assess your emotions and physical sensations in advance. Rehearse how to state your goals for the interview in a concise and straightforward way (preferably within 1 minute).
- ▶ *Prepare for the standard questions.* Be ready with answers to such questions as "What does it feel like? When? Where? For how long?"
- ▶ *Talk to the nurse.* Let the nurse know your concerns. He or she can help facilitate your visit.
- ▶ *Get to the point.* Use the first minute of a medical interview to suggest what you would most like to cover.
- ▶ *Take an active role.* Doctors usually understand patients' goals more clearly and share more information when the patients ask questions and state their concerns.

▶ *Acknowledge reservations.* If something prevents you from speaking frankly with a caregiver, let that person know ("I'm embarrassed," "I'm afraid," etc.).

▶ *Be assertive.* If your questions have not been answered or you do not agree with the advice given, state your feelings in a clear and respectful way.

▶ *Be succinct.* Caregivers have a legitimate need to keep transactions within reasonable time frames (du Pré, 2010, pp. 71–72).

Two further suggestions, here, are warranted. When dealing with a serious, terminal, or just plain scary or emotional health concern, it is best to *bring a trusted friend or family member with you* to help in asking questions and taking notes. Often when talking about a serious health issue it is hard to remember what a practitioner may be telling us so having another person there to help remember and think through options can help in making the best decisions regarding treatment plans. Also, if you have access to information via the Internet, it can assist in asking better questions regarding a health issue. It is crucial, however, to pick websites that are helpful and credible. Multiple searches and using websites sponsored by government organizations may provide the best quality and least biased information. Some websites that may offer useful information include: National Institutes of Health (http://www.nih.gov); Office of Disease Prevention and Health Promotion (http:// www.health.gov); Centers for Disease Control and Prevention (http://www.cdc.gov); U.S. Department of Health and Human Services (https://www.hhs.gov); and state departments of health like the New Mexico Department of Health (http://www.health.state.nm.us).

Discussion Questions

1. Looking at the discussion of the Extended Parallel Process Model (EPPM) and Fear Appeals, think about "danger control" and "fear control" processing. Apply these concepts to campaigns like the anti-meth campaigns you can access online (e.g., http://www.methproject.org/). After watching a few of the videos that are anti-meth or another graphic pro-health campaign, talk about whether you think the campaign would create "fear control" or "danger control" processing and why. Is the material too scary? Is it not scary enough? Is enough information available to help people take action as a result of seeing the campaign?

2. Look at the discussion of the Extended Parallel Process Model (EPPM) and Fear Appeals. Now think of some of the health improvement campaigns you have seen (e.g., anti-smoking, weight loss, prescription medications) and talk about one of them. Were the creators of the campaign trying to create an extreme level of fear, moderate level, or low level? How did the campaign make you feel or how did you react to it? Based on how the campaign influenced you would you say the level of fear it created (or did not create) was effective?

3. Look again at the two scenarios presented at the beginning of the section and also look at the Transtheoretical Model. What stage do you think "Carrie" is in? What evidence in the scenarios (you can look at them separately or together) tells you that she is in a particular stage? If you were her case manager, what would you want to do to help her?

4. In the Patient-Doctor Communication section we talk about "Motivational Interviewing." For about 5 minutes, role-play being the patient and doctor in a situation where you are enacting this type of conversation. First pick a disease the patient will have and then start the discussion. The "doctor" will not have all the medical information needed but can make up whatever is needed to facilitate

the discussion. After completing the role-play, consider these questions from both the patient and Dr. perspectives: (1) What was the hardest part of the conversation; which of the behaviors (e.g., "set a respectful tone," "roll with resistance") in the interview were most difficult?; (2) Which of these behaviors in the interview are the most important?; and (3) From the doctor's perspective, how hard is it to get through this conversation? Do you see doctors being able to do this? Why or why not?

5. Which of the suggestions for communicating better as a patient with health care practitioners would you now do as a result of learning about it in the text?

6. Which of the suggestions for communicating better as a patient with health care practitioners have you done in the past? How well did it work?

References

Bradley Wright, K., Sparks, L., & O'Hair, H. D. (2013). Health communication in the 21st century (2nd ed.). West Sussex, U.K.: John Wiley & Sons, Inc.

du Pré, A. (2010). *Communicating about health* (3rd ed.). New York: Oxford University Press.

Haefner, D. P. (1965). Arousing fear in dental health education. *Journal of Public Health Dentistry, 25,* 140–146. Retrieved from http://deepblue.lib.umich.edu/bitstream/handle/2027.42/65851/ j.1752-7325.1965. tb00484.x.pdf;jsessionid=4724D8391DA334CE58DB4BD32D8141F0? sequence=1

Hine, W. L. (2013). *Tell me a story or I'll tell you like it is: Narrative medicine and traditional biomedical interviewing approaches in women with breast cancer.* Paper presented at the Western States Communication Association Annual Meeting, Health Communication Division, Reno, NV.

Janis, I. L., & Feshbach, S. (1953). Effects of fear-arousing communications. *Journal of Abnormal Social Psychology, 48,* 78–92.

Lazarus, R. S. (1991a). Progress on a cognitive-motivational-relational theory of emotion. *American Psychologist, 46,* 819–834. Retrieved from http://psycnet.apa.org/?fa=main.doiLanding& doi=10.1037/0003-066X.46.8.819

Lazarus, R. S. (1991b). Cognition and motivation in emotion. *American Psychologist, 46,* 352–367. Retrieved from http:// www.ncbi.nlm.nih.gov/pubmed/2048794

Prochaska, J. O., & DiClemente, C. C. (1984). *The transtheoretical approach: Crossing the traditional boundaries of therapy.* Homewood, IL: Dow Jones/Irvin.

Rippetoe, P. A., & Rogers, R. W. (1987). Effects of components of protection-motivation adaptive and maladaptive coping with a health threat. *Journal of Personality and Social Psychology, 52,* 596–604. Retrieved from http://www.ncbi.nlm. nih.gov/ pubmed/3572727

Rollnick, S., & Miller, W. (1995). What is motivational interviewing? *Behavioural and Cognitive Psychotherapy, 23,* 325–335.

Witte, K. (1992). Putting the fear back into fear appeals: The extended parallel process model. *Communication Monographs, 59,* 329–349. Retrieved from https://www.msu.edu/~wittek/fearback.htm?False

Witte, K. (1994). Fear control and danger control: A test of the extended parallel process model. (EPPM). *Communication Monographs, 61,* 113–134. Retrieved from http://www.tandfonline .com/doi/abs/10.1080/ 03637759409376328?journalCode=rcmm20#preview

Witte, K. (1998). Fear as motivator, fear as inhibitor: Using the expended parallel process model to explain fear appeal successes and failures. In P. A. Anderson & L. K. Guerrero (Eds.), *Handbook of communication and emotion: Research, theory, application, and contexts* (pp. 423–450). San Diego: Academic Press.

Witte, K., Meyer, G., & Martell, D. (2001). *Effective health risk messages: A step-by-step guide.* Thousand Oaks, CA: Sage Publications.

Digital Literacy: What It Is and Why It Matters

By Danielle Halliwell

Objectives

- ▶ Explain the concepts of digital native and digital immigrant.
- ▶ Define the concept of digital literacy.
- ▶ Describe the seven competence areas in the Digital Literacy Global Framework.
- ▶ Discuss the importance of digital literacy in the modern workforce.

One morning a few years ago, my mom called me on my cell phone while I was getting ready for work. Our conversation went something like this:

ME:	Hello?
MY MOM:	Huh? Dani? Is that you?
ME:	Uhhh . . . yes?
MY MOM:	Oh, OK. I was trying to check the weather on my phone and must have answered your call without realizing it. I've about had it with this new smartphone.
ME:	Mom, you called me.
MY MOM:	No, I was trying to check the weather on my phone and then suddenly I heard your voice.
ME:	Yes, that's because I was answering your call. My phone rang, I saw it was you calling, and I answered it.
MY MOM:	What? I was just trying to check the weather. Are you sure?
ME:	Yes, mom. I promise you called me.

Eventually, my mom accepted that she was the one who had initiated the call and we said our goodbyes. Less than a minute after we hung up, my phone rang again. I will let you guess who was calling and what she had been "trying" to check on her phone.

I was not sure if I should just look up the weather report for my poor mother or immediately text my siblings a play-by-play so they could join me in teasing her. I am not proud to admit I chose the latter.

Perhaps I should have cut my mom a little bit of slack as she tried to figure out how to work her very first smartphone, but I am by far not the only person to find amusement in a parent's technology woes. The Internet is full of memes, subreddit discussions, and BuzzFeed lists poking fun at "parental technology fails," such as a mom mistaking the laughing-crying emoji for an expression of sadness in a text message reporting that her aunt passed away or a dad confusing his Facebook status field for the Google search bar. Similarly, in a standup routine several years ago, comedian Matthew Broussard described how he had become the default "tech guy" at work because he was the only person in the office under the age of 50. He humorously recounted how, more often than not, the computer "issues" that his older co-workers asked him to resolve were nonexistent; they simply did not know how to properly use the technology.

Many of you likely have similar stories about parents, grandparents, or older co-workers struggling to use a smartphone or not knowing how a particular app or social media site works. Indeed, it is generally assumed that teens and young adults are naturally more tech-savvy and "computer literate" than members of older generations (Judd, 2018; Smith, 2012). The belief that age is a key indicator of a person's digital competence can be traced to the distinction Prensky (2001) made nearly 2 decades ago between *digital natives* and *digital immigrants*. Prensky defined **digital natives** as a new generation of young students who grew up immersed in new technologies and, therefore, have an innate ability to effectively use the tools and devices of the digital age. **Digital immigrants**, on the other hand, are those who grew up prior to the widespread use of digital technologies and typically struggle to understand and appreciate the tech-savvy ways of digital natives. Thus, Prensky (2001) argued that because digital immigrants were not as well-versed in the "native language" of technology, they lagged behind younger generations in adopting new technologies and developing digital competence.

DIGITAL NATIVES

individuals who grew up surrounded by and using digital technologies.

DIGITAL IMMIGRANTS

individuals who grew up before the widespread adoption and use of digital technologies.

© Monkey Business Images/Shutterstock.com

Although Prensky's (2001) ideas concerning digital natives and digital immigrants were well-received by many scholars and educators, they have also been widely critiqued in the academic community. Much of the criticism is based on the considerable amount of evidence showing that young people do not inherently possess the skills to use digital technologies effectively and—by extension—are not necessarily more experienced with technology than members of older generations (Bennett, Maton, & Kervin, 2008; Judd, 2018; Wang, Hsu, Campbell, Coster, & Longhurst, 2014). For this reason, many researchers now argue that developing digital literacy skills involves much more than simply growing up with and frequently using new technologies (Kirschner & De Bruyckere, 2017; O'Neil, 2014). However, identifying what, exactly, digital literacy entails has not been an easy task, and a number of different definitions for the term have emerged over the years. The goal of this section, then, is to settle some of the confusion surrounding the concept of *digital literacy* and clarify what it means to be digitally competent in the 21st century.

WHAT IS DIGITAL LITERACY?

Author Paul Gilster is credited with introducing the idea of digital literacy—as it is understood today—in his aptly titled book, *Digital Literacy* (Gilster, 1997). Although the term "digital literacy" was used throughout the 1990s prior to Gilster's work, most of these earlier publications narrowly focused on technical skills or the ability to operate various technologies and software packages (Bawden, 2008). Gilster (1997), however, called for a broader conceptualization of digital literacy, arguing it should be based on "mastering ideas, not keystrokes" (p. 1). In line with this view, most current definitions of digital literacy emphasize intellectual skills such as the ability to think critically about and comprehend digital content, as well as how to use a wide range of technologies effectively and appropriately to accomplish specific outcomes (Spires, Medlock, & Kerkhoff, 2017; van Laar, van Deursen, van Dijk, & de Haan, 2018).

It is also important to mention the increased use in the last decade of the term *digital competence*, either in conjunction with or in place of digital literacy (Spante, Hashemi, Lundin, & Algers, 2018). As a result, there is an ongoing debate regarding how, if at all, *digital literacy* differs from *digital competence,* and whether the two concepts can or should be viewed as synonyms (see Iordache, Mariën, & Baelden, 2017; Spante et al.). Scholars have recently argued that the terms are conceptually different, with digital literacy defined as having the knowledge and awareness of various technologies and how to use them, and digital competence referring to the ability to strategically and appropriately apply this knowledge in order to achieve personal and professional goals (see Iordache et al.). Supporting this perspective, Spante and colleagues (2018) criticized the tendency for some researchers to treat the two concepts as inextricably connected, as evidenced by their observation that "definitions of digital competence sometimes involve digital literacy and vice versa" (p. 15). They also noted a tendency for studies to use the concepts of digital literacy and digital competence without clearly defining or explaining them, which they attributed to the fact that there are no universally agreed-upon definitions of either term.

Given the current lack of consensus regarding whether and how digital literacy and digital competence are distinct from one another, it is beyond the scope of this section to make an argument for using one term over the other. Further, although I appreciate the differences scholars have identified between the two concepts, I prefer to view them as interrelated ideas; that is, digital literacy is necessary to develop digital competence, and becoming digitally competent requires digital literacy. Thus,

DIGITAL LITERACY

the ability to define, access, manage, integrate, communicate, evaluate and create information safely and appropriately through digital technologies and networked devices for participation in economic and social life.

the position taken in this section is that digital literacy and digital competence go hand-in-hand, and both terms will be used to refer to ideas related to effectively performing tasks in digital environments. That said, it should be noted that the information presented in this section is drawn primarily from discussions of digital literacy because the concept has been in use longer and is currently more established in the literature (Spante et al., 2018).

Having explained the complicated background and evolution of digital literacy, we can now turn our attention to how it is defined. Researchers Law, Woo, de la Torre, and Wong (2018) from the Centre for Information Technology in Education (CITE) at the University of Hong Kong recently reviewed and synthesized the main ideas of several digital literacy frameworks for the purposes of developing a clear and concise understanding of **digital literacy**. Based on their analysis, they proposed the following definition:

> Digital literacy is the ability to define, access, manage, integrate, communicate, evaluate and create information safely and appropriately through digital technologies and networked devices for participation in economic and social life. It includes competences that are variously referred to as computer literacy, ICT literacy, information literacy, data literacy and media literacy (p. 3).

The above definition identifies the knowledge and skills associated with digital literacy, but it does not provide specific guidelines for assessing, or evaluating, the ability to perform these tasks. The Digital Literacy Global Framework, created and tested by researchers at CITE, is one instrument that can be used to measure common digital literacy skills.

Digital Literacy Global Framework (DLGF)

A variety of instruments and frameworks have been developed for the purpose of monitoring and assessing digital literacy. In general, these frameworks provide a list of skills or competences that represent what it means to be digitally literate. In June 2018, researchers from CITE (i.e., Law, Woo, de la Torre, & Wong) presented a report to the UNESCO Institute of Statistics in which they proposed a Digital Literacy Global Framework (DLGF). They developed the DLGF based on an extensive review of existing digital literacy frameworks and in-depth consultations with digital literacy experts across the globe. According to Law and colleagues (2018), its purpose is to provide a framework that "is intended to serve for monitoring, assessment, and further development of digital literacy" in adult populations in both economically-advanced and developing countries (p. 6). The DLGF consists of the following seven competence areas: devices and software operations, information and data literacy, communication and collaboration, digital content creation, safety, problem-solving, and career-related competencies.

DEVICES AND SOFTWARE OPERATIONS

a digital competence area focusing on the ability to operate both the physical components and software tools of digital devices.

The **devices and software operations** competence area focuses on the ability to operate digital devices and software tools. Specific skills include knowing how to: (1) identify and properly use the functions and features of the hardware tools (physical components) on different digital technologies, and (2) identify and make sense of the data, information, and digital content that are required to effectively use a device's software tools.

The **information and data literacy** competence area concentrates on the ability to locate, retrieve, evaluate, and manage information and digital content. Key skills include proficiency in: (1) browsing, searching, and filtering content in digital environments, (2) critically evaluating the credibility of sources of data and analyzing and interpreting digital content, and (3) organizing, storing, and processing digital content in a structured manner.

The **communication and collaboration** competence area is concerned with the capacity to effectively interact and collaborate with others using digital technologies and in online environments. Key skills include the ability to: (1) communicate via a variety of digital technologies and identify appropriate digital communication tools for a given context, (2) share digital content with others using appropriate digital technologies, (3) engage in participatory citizenship and seek opportunities for self-empowerment using appropriate digital technologies, (4) effectively collaborate with others and co-create resources and knowledge using digital tools, (5) understand behavioral norms and generational and cultural diversity while using digital tools and adapt to specific audiences in digital contexts, and (6) create and manage one's digital identity or identities, protect one's reputation in digital contexts, and responsibly manage the content one produces using digital technologies.

The **digital content creation** competence area emphasizes the ability to create, edit, and improve digital content while keeping in mind copyright and licensing regulations. Key skills include the capability to: (1) create and edit digital content using digital tools and to express oneself in a digital environment, (2) modify, improve, and integrate information into existing digital content in order to create new and relevant knowledge, (3) be aware of and understand how copyrights and licenses apply to digital content, and (4) develop a sequence of understandable instructions or programming languages for a computer system to solve a problem or perform a task.

The **safety** competence area deals with the ability to identify potential dangers and protect one's devices, content, and privacy in digital environments. Key skills include

INFORMATION AND DATA LITERACY

a digital competence area focusing on the ability to effectively locate, retrieve, evaluate, and manage digital content.

COMMUNICATION AND COLLABORATION

a digital competence area focusing on the ability to effectively interact and collaborate with others using digital technologies and in online environments.

DIGITAL CONTENT CREATION

a digital competence area focusing on the ability to create, edit, and improve digital content while keeping in mind copyright and licensing regulations.

SAFETY

a digital competence area focusing on the ability to identify potential dangers and protect one's devices, content, and privacy in digital environments.

the ability to: (1) understand threats and risks associated with digital technologies and apply appropriate security measures to protect devices and data, (2) understand the privacy policies that digital services use and protect privacy when using and sharing personally identifiable information in digital environments, (3) avoid potential dangers such as threats to physical and psychological health in digital environments and understand how to use digital tools to promote well-being and social inclusion, and (4) understand how using digital technologies impacts the environment.

PROBLEM-SOLVING

a digital competence area focusing on the ability to use digital tools effectively and creatively to resolve issues and produce innovative knowledge.

The **problem-solving** competence area addresses the ability to use digital tools effectively and creatively to resolve issues and produce innovative knowledge. Key skills include the capacity to: (1) identify and solve both simple and complex technical problems when using digital technologies, (2) identify and evaluate needs, concerns, and problems and address them using the appropriate digital tools and/or mediated responses, (3) creatively use digital technologies to individually and collectively create content and products and solve conceptual problems, (4) be aware of weaknesses in one's own digital competence and seek opportunities for improving digital skills, to support others with their digital competence development and improvement, and to stay up-to-date on new technological developments, and (5) select and use the appropriate tools, applications, or software to solve both technological and non-technological problems.

CAREER-RELATED COMPETENCES

a digital competence area focusing on the ability to operate the necessary digital tools and manage relevant data for a particular profession.

The **career-related competences** area is concerned with the ability to operate the necessary digital tools and manage relevant data for a particular profession. Key skills include competence with (1) identifying and effectively using the specialized digital technologies required in one's line of work and (2) interpreting, analyzing, and evaluating specialized data and digital content related to one's profession.

DIGITAL LITERACY IN THE 21ST-CENTURY WORKFORCE

With the widespread use of technology in the modern workforce, digital literacy has become a necessity in jobs at all levels and in nearly every field (Herold, 2018; van Laar et al., 2018). An analysis of technology use by employees in a Delaware health care system revealed that occupations at every rung of the organization's ladder—from an entry-level job that involves sanitizing patient rooms to a corporate position focused on managing the entire health system's digital data—require mastery of at least basic digital skills (Herold). Additionally, in their large-scale study of 7,800 European companies, Curtarelli, Gualtieri, Jannati, and Donlevy (2017) discovered that digital technologies are used in all types of occupations and across a broad spectrum of economic sectors. Specifically, nearly all of the workplaces they surveyed (98%) reported digital literacy is important in management positions and most (90%) stated employees in subordinate positions within their organization are required to use digital technologies to perform job-related tasks. A particularly noteworthy finding is that workplaces in sectors that typically are not associated with digital transformation—such as farming and construction—noted an increase in the use of digital tools over the last 5 years and were among the most likely to describe targeted efforts to invest in new technologies. In light of these findings, it makes sense that both researchers and industry leaders alike emphasize that digital literacy skills are crucial for securing initial employment and obtaining future promotions (Adams Becker, Pasquini, & Zentner, 2017; Herold).

When you consider the specific skills employers typically cite as the most valuable, the importance of digital literacy in professional contexts becomes even more evident.

© Frank Gaertner/Shutterstock.com

As we have established throughout this section, most jobs at any level require at least some degree of digital competence (such as the ability to use Outlook for e-mail). However, more and more companies are *also* seeking professionals with advanced and highly specialized digital skills. For example, recent data from LinkedIn shows the top two skills companies need the most in 2019 are cloud computing and artificial intelligence, followed by almost two dozen other sophisticated skills including game design, animation, and mobile application development. Further, along with a rise in job postings emphasizing relatively common "tech" skills (e.g., social media marketing, software testing, data analysis, etc.), the list also highlights how technological advances have created the need for new jobs using innovative and emerging skills such as audio production and natural language processing (Petrone, 2019).

Although the surge in jobs requiring sophisticated digital skills is promising in many ways, it also raises a few concerns for employers, job seekers, and the workforce as a whole. On the positive side, many occupations involving digital prowess and/or specializing in information technology (IT) provide products and services we rely on in our day-to-day lives for work, teaching and learning, socializing, completing domestic tasks, and entertainment and relaxation (Bosamia, 2013). Additionally, findings from a 2017 report published by the International Data Corporation indicates that IT jobs in data management, cyber security, IT infrastructure, software development, and digital transformation are vital to the sustainability and growth of the global economy. The report also noted these five IT areas are expected to add 1.2 million jobs in the United States by 2027, resulting in a 39% increase in national employment (International Data Corporation, 2017). Finally, at an individual level, occupations requiring specialized and highly sought after digital and IT skills generally pay well and provide opportunities for career advancement (International Data Corporation; Pattabiraman, 2019). In LinkedIn's recent study seeking to identify the most promising jobs in 2019, technology-driven jobs dominated the list. The median base salaries for the 15 jobs that made the list range from $200,000 for a "site reliability manager" with skills related to cloud computing, database management systems, and

DIGITAL DIVIDE

the division
between people
who have access to
and regularly use
technology and those
who have limited
or no access to
technology.

software development to $88,500 for a "customer success manager" with proficiency in cloud computing and Web-based software (Pattabiraman).

The emphasis on advanced digital literacy skills in the current job market also presents quite a few concerns that are important to consider. Chief among these are issues related to the **digital divide**, which refers to the division between people who have access to and regularly use technology and those who have limited or no access to technology (Elliott, 2019). The unequal access to the Internet and communication technologies largely stems from socioeconomic disparities; that is, individuals from high income families and/or communities have more opportunities to develop digital skills than individuals with low or middle class backgrounds (Chetty, Aneja, Mishra, Gcora, & Josie, 2017; Spires et al., 2017). In this sense, the ongoing digital transformation in contemporary workplaces tilts the job market in favor of individuals from economically-advantaged populations who have grown up using technology and have had more time to develop and practice digital literacy skills (Chetty et al.; Curtarelli et al., 2017). Excluding underprivileged groups from digitally-intensive employment opportunities often limits them to low-skill occupations and increases the likelihood of unemployment, which has the potential to widen the divide in the workforce between those who possess digital skills and those who do not (Curtarelli et al.).

Although numerous policies and action plans have been developed to increase digital participation and minimize the digital divide (including the DLGF discussed earlier in this section), problems of access continue to plague disadvantaged populations at community, state, national, and global levels (Curtarelli et al., 2017; Elliott, 2019; Law et al., 2018). Being aware of how unequal access to technology impacts your desired profession and the overall job market can help you identify which digital skills to include in your repertoire and whether they need to be refined, updated, or improved. Furthermore, ongoing efforts to strengthen your digital competence will allow you to avoid the pitfalls associated with a prominent challenge within the current workforce referred to as the *digital skills gap.*

UNDERSTANDING (AND OVERCOMING) THE DIGITAL SKILLS GAP

DIGITAL SKILLS GAP

a situation in which
employees lack the
digital skills necessary
to perform all of their
job duties completely,
properly, and
efficiently.

According to Curtarelli and colleagues (2017), a **digital skills gap** is a "situation in which the level of digital skills of the existing workforce in a workplace is less than required to perform a job adequately or to match the requirements of a job" (p. 81). In other words, a digital skill gap occurs when employees lack the necessary experience with and knowledge of the technologies needed to execute all of their job duties completely, properly, and efficiently (McGuinness & Ortiz, 2016). Previous research shows that deficits in digital literacy among workers is a consistent issue in organizations in all industries (Curtarelli et al.; Deloitte, 2019). For instance, in Deloitte's research report examining how organizations respond to the changes caused by digital tools, 72% of the senior leaders who were surveyed reported they did not believe their current employees had the necessary knowledge and expertise to carry out their company's digital strategy. Moreover, only 18% of the executives expressed that they believed people leaving or graduating from college possess the appropriate digital skills for their field.

The fact that many employers have little confidence in young job seekers' technology-related abilities is not entirely surprising considering students in every educational stage—from elementary school to college—generally exhibit low levels of digital competence (Bennett et al., 2008; Judd, 2018; Wang et al., 2014). For instance, there is evidence that students tend to rate their digital literacy skills as much higher than they actually are (ECDL, 2015; Judd; Wang et al.), resulting in what has been called a **digital overconfidence effect** (Porat, Blau, & Barak, 2018). Although college students frequently use communication technologies to accomplish personal and social goals, prior research shows they have limited experience and ability using digital tools to support their learning or academic goals (see Bennett et al., 2008; Judd, 2018). Overall it appears many young people are proficient with a variety of technologies when it comes to socializing, entertainment and leisure, and personal interests, but do not always exhibit the same level of digital competence in academic and professional contexts (Judd; Wang et al.).

Scholars have identified several reasons why many students (and young people in general) are not seasoned and innately skilled users of technology as the "digital natives" label suggests. Of course, having limited access to and experience with technology while growing up is cited as one of the most significant barriers to acquiring digital skills (Kim, Hong, & Song, 2018; Spires et al., 2017). It must be acknowledged, however, simply being exposed to the Internet and technology from an early age does not mean children will naturally develop digital competence. In many cases, even students who are immersed in media-rich environments at home do not have the technological expertise to use devices effectively for learning and professional development (Judd et al., 2018; Porat et al., 2018). Based on this evidence, most scholars support the belief that digital literacy skills are not inherently developed through technology use, but are attained gradually by way of formal instruction and practice in school settings (Kim et al.; Perez-Escoda, Castro-Zubizarreta, & Fandos-Igado, 2016). Thus, the tendency for students in grades K–12 to demonstrate subpar digital skills is often attributed to the lack of effective educational programs designed to promote the development of and an appreciation for digital literacy (Perez-Escoda et al.; Wang et al., 2014).

Although teachers are typically aware of the need to support their students' digital learning, many have cited various setbacks that interfere with efforts to introduce technology-based activities into the classroom (Cruz & Díaz, 2016; Perez-Escoda et al., 2016). Wang and colleagues (2014), for example, found that middle school science teachers experience five specific barriers to effective technology integration: (1) insufficient knowledge of technology integration strategies, (2) lack of time, (3) insufficient digital skills and knowledge, (4) students' lack of access to technology in the classroom, and (5) lack of support and resources due to school policy. Nearly all of the teachers reported that the main barrier they faced was their own lack of knowledge and ingenuity to effectively integrate technology, followed by the related issue of not having enough time to learn, test, and evaluate new integration strategies. Similarly, other studies have shown that most teachers are capable of using technology to accomplish administrative tasks (e.g., recording grades) and to develop curriculum materials (e.g., creating PowerPoint slides), yet they often express uncertainty about how to incorporate teaching strategies that require students to use digital technologies as a learning tool (Cruz & Díaz; Hsu, 2011; Hutchison & Reinking, 2010). Thus, even teachers who self-identify as "tech-savvy" lack the level of knowledge and digital prowess required for successful technology integration in the classroom (Wang et al.).

Without formal instruction designed to teach students how to engage with technology in productive, creative, and responsible ways, they are less likely to develop the appropriate knowledge and skills to successfully manage the digital environments they will encounter at college and in their career (Porat et al., 2018; Spires et al., 2017). In other words, by not adequately preparing students to be productive digital citizens, educational systems contribute to the digital skills gap in the workforce. Accordingly,

DIGITAL OVERCONFIDENCE EFFECT

the tendency for people to perceive their digital skills as higher than they actually are.

numerous scholars have urged those involved in education to devote more attention to digital instruction, with Porat at al. emphasizing that it is crucial "for schools in general, and for teachers in particular, to take responsibility for nurturing digital literacies of students, and to design learning and evaluation activities that develop these competencies" (p. 33). A key task involved with improving technology integration in classroom settings is to provide better training for teachers focused on improving their digital competence (Cruz & Díaz, 2016; Wang et al., 2014). Such efforts to strengthen educators' use of technological devices is vital because—as Cruz and Diaz (2016) aptly put it—"teachers cannot help students develop a competence that they themselves do not possess in depth" (p. 104).

My purpose for drawing attention to the gap in digital skills observed in student populations is not to criticize young people or to put a damper on their professional pursuits. Rather, I hope to inform college students about current trends that impact them so that they are better prepared for the challenges and opportunities that come with the digitization of the modern workforce. As an example, a friend who works in upper management for a tech company recently told me that 2 years ago he stopped hiring people right out of college to fill entry-level positions; now, he will only consider job candidates with at least 2 years of post-college work experience. The reasoning he gave is that recent college graduates "only know how to text and use social media" and "aren't ready" for the digital tasks his company requires. I challenged him about it and shared stories of the many accomplished, motivated, and digitally competent students I have had the pleasure of teaching and working with, but he could not be persuaded. In fact, he said in the 2 years since he implemented this hiring "rule" he has noticed greater productivity among entry-level workers and an increase in retention for the positions.

While my friend may be missing out on some extremely talented and creative job candidates, his decision to not consider anyone fresh out of college demonstrates just how serious companies are about hiring people who have professional experience using digital tools and working in digital environments. As technology continues to disrupt organizational processes and create an increased demand for sophisticated

digital skills, it is crucial for job candidates to focus on digital skill development and market themselves as digitally literate professionals. With the countless resources universities offer, college students are in a prime position to gain valuable experience using digital technologies and enhance their technological expertise. Below, I briefly discuss five ways students can sharpen their digital literacy skills throughout their college education:

1. **Seek positions on campus with a technology focus.** Many university clubs and organizations have positions such as public relations officers and social media coordinators that involve regular use of digital technologies. If available, you can also explore opportunities to get involved with the student newspaper, the college radio station, or other student-run media organizations.

2. **Ask professors about opportunities to practice digital skills.** It is commonly understood that learning should not be restricted to the classroom, and this is especially true for strengthening fundamental digital literacy skills. Ask your professors for advice about how you can gain more experience using technology or if they are aware of any specific opportunities outside of class to practice your digital skills. For instance, some professors may be looking for research assistants who can help with tasks such as gathering and organizing online sources, maintaining electronic records of research materials, and using data management software to enter and analyze data. Many departments are also open to recruiting responsible and dedicated students to help maintain and update the department's web page or manage its social media accounts.

3. **Take online classes—and make the most of them.** One of the overlooked advantages of online courses is that they enable students to learn and practice important digital literacy skills. Taking a course online requires the ability to effectively locate, filter, and organize information in an online environment. You can also gain experience using digital technologies to create and share digital content, collaborate with others in discussion boards, communicate professionally over e-mail, and manage your online reputation in a responsible manner. Additionally, it can be helpful to make sure your online professors know who you are by attending virtual or face-to-face office hours and doing your best work throughout the course. When it comes time to apply for jobs, having a reference who can speak highly of your digital skills and your online professionalism can make a difference.

4. **Strive to incorporate a digital component into course assignments.** Most course assignments involve using technology to some degree (e.g., using Word or PowerPoint, conducting online research, submitting documents electronically, etc.). However, you can further develop your digital skills by striving to incorporate technology into your assignments in more sophisticated and creative ways. For instance, if you have the freedom to select the topic or focus for an assignment, consider whether it is possible to pursue a topic related to technology. Students in my previous public speaking classes have presented speeches on topics such as smartphone addiction, the concept of "Twitter journalism," and privacy issues associated with digital media. For a "Relational Issue Analysis" paper in my interpersonal communication class, students often

focus on the challenges of online dating, problems related to "phubbing" (i.e., ignoring others by paying attention to one's smartphone), the perceived obligation to "keep up" with the social media activity of friends and family, and other topics examining the role of technology in relationships. In general, focusing on topics involving technology for course assignments can be a helpful way to increase your knowledge of current "tech" issues and strengthen your digital literacy.

5. **Seek ways to incorporate technology into your responsibilities at work.** If you have a job or an internship, you are likely already gaining some level of experience using digital tools to complete work-related tasks. If technology does not play a strong role in your job or internship responsibilities, ask your manager or supervisor if there are tasks you can help with that will allow you to improve your digital competence. For example, one of my former students worked part-time at a local bakery and managed all of the company's social media accounts as part of his job responsibilities. This position gave him the opportunity to practice using digital tools in a professional context and helped him develop valuable digital skills that he could highlight on his resume or in an interview.

The five tips discussed above are by far not the only ways you can become a more knowledgeable and capable digital citizen. Taking an active role in developing and improving your digital skillset can give you a competitive edge when seeking employment after graduation and will open doors for you throughout your career. Digital literacy skills are no longer optional; they are required for participation in all areas of society and are key to achieving personal and professional success.

Discussion Questions

1. How does Prensky (2001) explain the concepts of digital natives and digital immigrants, and why have his claims been critiqued by other scholars? Do you believe Prensky's descriptions of "digital native" and "digital immigrant" are valid today? Why or why not?

2. Define *digital literacy* and explain how it differs from basic technical skills.

3. Review the seven competence areas in the Digital Literacy Global Framework. Which areas are your strongest, and which ones do you feel need the most improvement? What are some specific strategies you can apply to improve your digital competence in these areas?

4. Explain the idea of the *digital skills gap*. How wide (or narrow) do you believe the digital skills gap is in your desired career or field?

Adams Becker, S., Pasquini, L. A., and Zentner, A. (2017). *2017 digital literacy impact study: An NMC Horizon project strategic brief.* Austin, TX: The New Media Consortium.

Bawden, D. (2008). Origins and concepts of digital literacy. In C. Lankshear and M. Knobel (Eds.), *Digital literacies: Concepts, policies and practices* (pp. 17–32). New York: Peter Lang.

Bennett, S., Maton, K., & Kervin, L. (2008). The 'digital natives' debate: A critical review of the evidence. *British Journal of Educational Technology, 39*(5), 775–786. doi:10.1111/j.14678535.2007.00793.x

Bosamia, M. (2013). *Positive and negative impacts of information and communication technology in our everyday life,* paper presented at the International Conference on Disciplinary and Interdisciplinary approaches to knowledge creation in higher education: Canada & India, Bhavnagar, India.

Chetty, K., Aneja, U., Mishra, V., Gcora, N., & Josie, J. (2017). Bridging the digital divide in the G20: Skills for the new age. *Economics: The Open-Access, Open-Assessment E-Journal, 12*(24), 1–20. doi:10.5018/economics-ejournal. ja.2018-24

Cruz, F. J. F., & Díaz, M. J. F. (2016). Generation Z's teachers and their digital skills. *Comunicar, 24*(46), 97–105. doi:10.3916/C46-2016-10

Curtarelli, M., Gualtieri, V., Jannati, M. S., and Donlevy, V. (2017). *ICT for work: Digital skills in the workplace.* Luxembourg: Publications Office of the European Union. doi:10.2759/4984

Deloitte. (2019). *Digital disruption index.* Retrieved from https://www2.deloitte.com/content/dam/Deloitte/uk/ Documents/consultancy/deloitte-uk-digital-disruption-index-2019.pdf

ECDL Foundation. (2015). *The fallacy of the 'Digital Native': Why young people need to develop their digital skills.* Retrieved from www.ecdl.org/media/TheFallacyofthe%27DigitalNative%27PositionPaper1.pdf

Elliott, L. J. (2019). The digital divide and usability. In *Critical Issues Impacting Science, Technology, Society (STS), and Our Future* (pp. 197–217). Hershey, PA: IGI Global.

Gilster, P. (1997). *Digital literacy.* New York: Wiley.

Herold, B. (2018, September 25). Jobs at all levels now require digital literacy. Here's proof. *Education Week,* Retrieved from https://www.edweek.org/ew/articles/2018/09/26/jobs-at-all-levels-now-require-digital.html

Hsu, S. (2011). Who assigns the most ICT activities? Examining the relationship between teacher and student usage. *Computers & Education, 56*(3), 847–855. doi:10.1016/j.compedu.2010.10.026

Hutchison, A., & Reinking, D. (2010). A national survey of barriers to integrating information and communication technologies into literacy instruction. In *Fifty-ninth yearbook of the National Reading Conference* (pp. 230–243). Milwaukee, WI: National Reading Conference.

International Data Corporation. (2017). *20 most significant ICT jobs you should consider to maximize your career potential, now and in the future.* Retrieved from https://mkto.cisco.com/rs/564-WHV-323/images/IDC_Cisco_ IB_3025.pdf

Iordache, C., Mariën, I., & Baelden, D. (2017). Developing digital skills and competences: A quick-scan analysis of 13 digital literacy models. *Italian Journal of Sociology of Education, 9*(1). doi:10.14658/pupj-ijse-2017-1-2

Judd, T. (2018). The rise and fall (?) of the digital natives. *Australasian Journal of Educational Technology, 34*(5). doi:10.14742/ajet.3821

Kim, H., Hong, A., & Song, H. D. (2018). The relationships of family, perceived digital competence and attitude, and learning agility in sustainable student engagement in higher education. *Sustainability, 10*(12), 4635. doi:10.3390/ su10124635

Kirschner, P. A., & De Bruyckere, P. (2017). The myths of the digital native and the multitasker. *Teaching and Teacher Education, 67,* 135–142. doi:10.1016/j.tate.2017.06.001

Law, N., Woo, D., de la Torre, J., & Wong, G. (2018). *A Global Framework of Reference on Digital Literacy Skills for Indicator 4.4.2* (Report No. UIS/2018/ICT/IP/51). Montreal, Quebec: UNESCO Institute for Statistics.

McGuinness, S., and Ortiz, L. (2016). Skill gaps in the workplace: Measurement, determinants and impacts, *Industrial Relations Journal, 47*(3), 253–278. doi:10.1111/irj.12136

O'Neil, M. (2014, April 21). Confronting the myth of the digital native. *The Chronicle of Higher Education,* Retrieved from https://www.chronicle.com/article/Confronting-the-Myth-of-the/145949

Pattabiraman, K. (2019). The most promising jobs in 2019. *LinkedIn.* Retrieved from https://blog.linkedin.com/2019/january/10/linkedins-most-promising-jobs-of-2019

Perez-Escoda, A., Castro-Zubizarreta, A., & Fandos-Igado, M. (2016). Digital skills in the Z generation: Key questions for a curricular introduction in primary school. *Comunicar, 24*(49), 71–79. doi:10.3916/C49-2016-07

Petrone, P. (2019*).* The skills companies need the most in 2019—and how to learn them. *LinkedIn.* Retrieved from https://learning.linkedin.com/blog/top-skills/the-skills-companies-need-most-in-2019--and-how-to-learn-them

Porat, E., Blau, I., & Barak, A. (2018). Measuring digital literacies: Junior high-school students' perceived competencies versus actual performance. *Computers & Education, 126,* 23–36. doi:10.1016/j.compedu.2018.06.030

Prensky, M. (2001). Digital natives, digital immigrants part 1. *On the horizon, 9*(5), 1–6. doi:10.1108/10748120110424816

Smith, E. E. (2012). The digital native debate in higher education: A comparative analysis of recent literature. *Canadian Journal of Learning and Technology, 38*(3), doi:10.21432/T2F302

Spante, M., Hashemi, S. S., Lundin, M., & Algers, A. (2018). Digital competence and digital literacy in higher education research: Systematic review of concept use. *Cogent Education, 5*(1), 1–21. doi:10.1080/2331186X.2018.1519143

Spires, H. A., Medlock, C., & Kerkhoff, S. N. (2017). Digital literacy for the 21st century. In M. Khosrow-Pour (Ed.), *Encyclopedia of information science and technology* (4th ed., pp. 2235–2242). Hershey, PA: IGI Global.

van Laar, E., van Deursen, A. J., van Dijk, J. A., & de Haan, J. (2018). 21st-century digital skills instrument aimed at working professionals: Conceptual development and empirical validation. *Telematics and informatics, 35*(8), 2184–2200. doi:10.1016/j.tele.2018.08.006

Wang, S. K., Hsu, H. Y., Campbell, T., Coster, D. C., & Longhurst, M. (2014). An investigation of middle school science teachers and students use of technology inside and outside of classrooms: Considering whether digital natives are more technology savvy than their teachers. *Educational Technology Research and Development, 62*(6), 637–662. doi:10.1007/s11423-014-9355-4

Exercises

EXERCISE 1.1A

Ice Breaker

Find one person who . . .

Avoids conflict	Likes music more than television	Explain to you, in a few words, how an electric motor works	Doesn't own a cell phone	Was born and raised in Las Cruces
Spend a weekend alone and love it	Briefly share a dream they have had in the past two weeks	Learn a country line dance	Listens to classical music	Exercises on a frequent basis
Always makes their checking account balance	Was born outside of New Mexico	Stand on one foot with their eyes closed for at least 5 seconds	Enjoys public speaking	Was born outside of the continent of North America
Role play a scene they encountered today	Complete the numerical sequence: 36, 30, 24, 18, _____	Doesn't want to have kids	Has more than two pets	Doesn't think they'll ever marry
Recite at least four lines from any poem from memory	Is an only child	Paints or draws in their spare time	Sends more than 40 text messages a day	In a fraternity or sorority
Has a gay best friend	Have more than two siblings	Have children	Enjoys musicals	Enjoys celebrity gossip
Plays team sports well	Is married	Takes pictures for fun	Sorts and categorizes objects such as: sports cards, rocks, shells, etc.	Dreams in color

EXERCISE 1.4A

Rules and Norms

Sometime during the next day or two, find opportunities to break 2–3 communication rules and norms that we take for granted. You must do this in an ethical way (e.g., don't use eye contact or touch to threaten a stranger), and without disrupting university business (e.g., don't run up and down the halls talking loudly during class periods).

Following are some norm-violating exercises you can use to test the ways in which norms are important in everyday life. The people with whom we interact—strangers, friends, and intimate companions—do not expect us to break the norms. When we do, we need a reason; therefore, you must follow up by telling your "victim" your reason for your norm violation. Remember, the assignment is to break NORMS, NOT LAWS!

On Your Own:

- ► Walk up to a stranger and ask for exact change so you can buy two stamps with which to send in your financial aid forms.
- ► Ask a stranger in the grocery store to squeeze the tomatoes for you to see if they're ripe. Tell him or her you've never been any good at it.
- ► Smile and wave at passers-by.
- ► Ask a stranger for his or her autograph.
- ► Hug a friend you don't usually greet with a hug.
- ► Clip your toenails on a busy staircase or in the lounge area of the dorm.
- ► Walk backwards down a busy sidewalk.

With a Classmate or Friend:

- ► Sit down with your books and study together in the middle of a busy sidewalk. Ignore the people who try to walk around you.
- ► One of you put on a dog collar and let the other lead you around campus. Ask someone to hold the leash for you while you tie your shoes, or go into a building. The person on the leash should talk only if the stranger asks questions.
- ► Eat a meal together in the student union using your most disgusting table manners (e.g., eating with your hands, putting your face in your soup bowl, slurping drinks loudly, belching, etc.).

Write down a few of your observations and bring them to class for discussion

EXERCISE 1.5A

Principle Based Ethics

Read the case study below and answer the questions. Then in teams of four to five, work through the case study and questions below. Your instructor will tell you which "side" you will be on and you will need to work with your group to formulate arguments. Then, your team will debate another team using those arguments.

ACME is a company which manufactures a medicine called Evercil. Evercil is used to treat Congestive Heart Failure (a terminal illness that is a horrible way to die) and is one of the most effective and powerful drugs on the market. Evercil is a miracle drug for patients suffering from CHF. They can get out of bed, even play with their grandchildren. They feel like they can breathe again! Patients and their doctors LOVE Evercil. The CEO of the company, Ms. Knowsalot, has just gotten a report from her medical researchers that says Evercil shortens patients' lives by 2–3 months. They live a lot better life, BUT they live a shorter amount of time.

Ms. Knowsalot has to decide what to do with the report. She could delay the announcement of the results of the report and do more research, or she could immediately announce to doctors, patients, and the FDA the report results. If Evercil goes off the market, patients will go back to living horrible lives and be unable to do anything but wait to die. Also, Ms. Knowsalot believes that ACME will have to fire over 1,000 people if Evercil goes off the market.

Within your team, answer these discussion questions:

1. Which of the principle based ethics apply to this case study?

2. Which ethical theories can be applied to this case study?

3. Should Ms. Knowsalot tell the truth about Evercil? Why? Why not?

4. Not communicating about something or communicating that Evercil is safe would be untrue (perhaps a lie), but save jobs and give patients a better quality of life. To tell the truth means that people at ACME will lose their jobs, their careers. Patients may live longer, though. Do either of these scenarios change the decisions you made? Why? Why not?

Contributed by Greg G. Armfield and Anne Hubbell

EXERCISE 1.7A

Narratives

1. Write down a story that you heard growing up. (Alternative: Ask a family member to tell you a story.)

2. Exchange stories with a classmate.

3. Discuss how the story informed your sense of:
   a. how the world works,

   b. your place in the world,

   c. how to act in the world,

   d. how to evaluate what goes on in the world.

4. Are the answers to the above aspects similar to your partner's? If so, why do you think this is the case? If not, why not?

EXERCISE 1.7B

Rituals

1. Make a list of as many rituals you participate in as possible.

2. Select one of these rituals to attend and participate in.
3. While at the ritual, make note of the sequence of communication events. (i.e., first this happened, then this, then this, etc.).
4. Interview another participant about what they think the ritual means.
5. Do you agree with the participant's analysis? If so, why? If not, why not?

EXERCISE 1.8A

Cultural Adaptation

Two cultural contexts that most everyone in your lab has experienced are a secondary education context (i.e., high school or a home schooling equivalent) and a post-secondary education context (i.e., college or university). To illustrate the concepts of cultural adaptation, culture shock and the symbolic nature of culture, please answer the following questions:

1. What are some of the rules, expectations, practices and patterns of communication in the university academic context that differ from those you experienced during your secondary education?

2. Which of the rules, expectations, practices and patterns of communication in a university academic context seemed strange or silly to you when you first encountered them?

3. Which of the rules, expectations, practices and patterns of communication in the university academic context were (or are) most difficult for you to adjust to?

4. Having experienced the university academic context, how do you feel now about the rules, expectations and communication practices in a secondary education context

From *Principles and Practice in Human Communication: A Reader and Workbook for Comm 265* by Eric Morgan and Elizabeth Lindsey. Copyright © 2007 by Kendall Hunt Publishing Company. Reprinted with permission.

EXERCISE 1.8B

Intercultural Conversation

For this exercise, you will interview an international student about the communication behaviors associated with his/her culture. You will have to conduct the interview for this assignment. The interview should last at least 15 minutes. Use the following guide for your interview.

What is your name?
Where are you from?
What language(s) do you speak?
Could you describe your country for me?
Could you describe your community for me?
What are some of the values of people in your culture?
What are some nonverbal communication differences between your culture and those you have experienced here?
How are gender roles viewed in your culture?
How important is family in your culture?
If I were to travel to your country for a study abroad program, what would I need to know about communication?
Is there anything else you would like to tell me about your country or culture?

Make sure to ask all the questions, but also enjoy the conversation.

After you have completed the interview, write a paper discussing these answers and what you learned from the interview.

EXERCISE 2.1A

Speech of Introduction

Prepare a 2–3 minute speech of introduction using the information you collected during your interview in Exercise 1-2. The speech should contain an introduction, body and conclusion. Use the space below to outline your speech prior to presentation.

EXERCISE 2.1B

Speech of Introduction—Interview

Your instructor will pair you with another student for informal interviews. You will use the information you collect from this interview to prepare a speech introducing your interview partner to your classmates. Below you will find some ideas to help you collect information during the interview.

1. Demographic information (e.g., hometown, place of birth, year in school, major, age, etc.):

2. Sports and hobbies (e.g., any sports, collections, cooking, computers, games):

3. Community activities (e.g., Big Brothers/Sisters, any volunteer work):

4. Social activities (e.g., parties, going out to dinner, dancing, etc.):

5. Goals and aspirations (e.g., career goals, personal growth goals, etc.):

6. Vacations and travel:

7. Odd fact (3 legged dog, unusual relative, strange job, etc.):

EXERCISE 2.1C

Speech of Introduction—Objects

This speech is designed to be a completely non-threatening, no-pressure situation to start the class with a successful first speech.

For this assignment introduce yourself with three objects. Two that say something about yourself and one that has a funny story associated with it.

a.   Keep in mind your story needs to be appropriate for a public audience. In other words, you may not want to disclose private or very personal information that might make some of your classmates uncomfortable.

b.   Your objects must also be appropriate for class display (i.e., not vulgar, too small or too large, etc.) and the story should not be about activities that would require your instructor to report you to the proper authorities.

In the speech you need to:

▶   Tell the audience your name and give background information about yourself.

▶   Present, separately, the two objects that give the audience insight into who you are as an individual.

▶   Finally, share the funny story that is associated with the third object.

This speech is judged on the following three factors:

1.   Did you stand up and attempt to deliver a speech? (50%)

   a.   Any substantial attempt is good for full points.

2.   Did you act as if you were having fun? (20%)

   a.   This is to emphasize the importance of presenting a good face when speaking, even if you are not having a good time or you do not feel like you are doing your best; acting as if you are relaxed and having fun makes the speech more appealing and effective to the audience.

3.   Overall, how good was your speech? (30%)

   a.   This is judged on: Content/Message, Delivery, and Organization.

4.   Try to speak for 2 minutes.

EXERCISE 2.1D

Speech of Introduction—Critique

Content/Message (amount of information, could it be understood? etc.)

Delivery (posture, gestures, distracting motions, eye contact, voice, etc.)

Organization

Recommendations:

<u>Keep doing well</u>   <u>Work to improve</u>

EXERCISE 2.1E

Audience Analysis Worksheet

Analyze the following audience factors (as they apply to your classroom audience) and decide how they will affect your upcoming informative speech.

1. Time Constraints:

2. Physical Environment:

3. Composition of the Audience:

    size of the audience

    average age

    gender (males to females)

    occupations

    education levels

    cultural, ethnic backgrounds

4. Their Prior Knowledge of the Subject:

5. Their Attitude Toward the Subject:

6. Their Attitude Toward You as the Speaker:

EXERCISE 2.3A

Informative Speech Organizational Patterns

There are four common organizational patterns for speeches (p. 79): (1) topical, (2) spatial, (3) chronological, and (4) cause and effect. Below are possible topics for speeches. Choose an organizational pattern that works the best for the topic. Try to use all four different patterns. Provide detailed reasons why you choose the organizational pattern that you did.

1. Student activities center

   Reason:

2. Different types of shoes

   Reason:

3. Common colds

   Reason:

4. Starting a student organization

   Reason:

5. Yellow teeth

   Reason:

6. History of U.S.A.

   Reason:

7. How to make good fried chicken

   Reason:

Choose one of the topics above and develop three main points using the organizational pattern you chose.

Topic:

Main points:

   I.

   II.

   III.

EXERCISE 2.3B

Informative Speech Worksheet

TITLE: _____

Specific Purpose: _____

Introduction:

    I.   Attention getting opening:

        _____

        _____

        _____

    II. Reason your audience would be interested in this speech:

        _____

        _____

        _____

    III. Establish your credibility:

        _____

        _____

        _____

    IV. Thesis statement:

        _____

        _____

        _____

        A. Main Point 1: _____

        B. Main Point 2: _____

        C. Main Point 3: _____

Transition to the body of the speech: _____

Body

    I. Main Point: _____

        _____

        A. Subpoint: _____

            _____

        B. Subpoint: _____

            _____

        C. Subpoint: _____

            _____

Transition: _____

    II. Main Point: _____

        _____

        A. Subpoint: _____

            _____

        B. Subpoint: _____

            _____

        C. Subpoint: _____

            _____

Transition: _____

    III. Main Point: _____

        _____

        A. Subpoint: _____

            _____

        B. Subpoint: _____

            _____

        C. Subpoint: _____

            _____

Transition to conclusion: _____

Conclusion

   I.   Restate thesis (summarize each main point below):

       _____

       _____

       A. _____

       B. _____

       C. _____

  II.   Clincher (provide a sense of closure; refer to introduction):

       _____

       _____

EXERCISE 2.3C

Persuasive Speech Worksheet

TITLE: _____

Specific Purpose: _____

Introduction:

   I.   Attention getting opening:

_____

_____

_____

   II. Reason your audience would be interested in this speech:

_____

_____

_____

   III. Establish your credibility:

_____

_____

_____

   IV. Thesis statement:

_____

_____

_____

   V. Overview (State the main points you will cover):

      A. Main Point 1: _____

      B. Main Point 2: _____

      C. Main Point 3: _____

Transition to the body of the speech: _____

Body

   I. Main Point: _____

         _____

      A. Subpoint: _____

             _____

      B. Subpoint: _____

             _____

      C. Subpoint: _____

             _____

Transition: _____

   II. Main Point: _____

         _____

      A. Subpoint: _____

             _____

      B. Subpoint: _____

             _____

      C. Subpoint: _____

             _____

Transition: _____

  III. Main Point: _____

         _____

      A. Subpoint: _____

             _____

      B. Subpoint: _____

             _____

      C. Subpoint: _____

             _____

Transition to conclusion: _____

Conclusion

    I.   Restate thesis (summarize each main point below):

        _____

        _____

        A. _____

        B. _____

        C. _____

    II. Call to action (refer to introduction; provide closure and make a call to action):

        _____

        _____

EXERCISE 2.3D

Persuasive Speech Worksheet—Monroe's Motivated Sequence

TITLE: _____

Specific Purpose: _____

Introduction:

   I.   Attention Step: Attention getting Oopening/create interest:

_____

_____

_____

   II.   Reason your audience would be interested in this speech:

_____

_____

_____

   III. Establish your credibility:

_____

_____

_____

   IV. Thesis statement/what do you want them to do as a result of your speech?

_____

_____

_____

      A. Main Point 1: _____

      B. Main Point 2: _____

      C. Main Point 3: _____

Transition to the body of the speech: _____

Body

    I. Main Point (need step/need for change): _____

          _____

        A. First reason there is a need for change: _____

             _____

        B. Second reason there is a need for change: _____

             _____

Transition: _____

    II. Main Point (satisfaction step; solution to problem): _____

          _____

        A. Define solution to problem: _____

             _____

        B. More detail on what solution is: _____

             _____

Transition: _____

    III. Main Point (visualization step; audience can see themselves in action): _____

          _____

        A. Exactly what can *they* do? Examples of what they can do: _____

             _____

        B. More on what they can do (if needed): _____

             _____

Transition to conclusion: _____

Conclusion/Call to Action Step:

    I.   Restate thesis (summarize each main point below):

        _____

        _____

        A. Main Point 1: _____

        B. Main Point 2: _____

        C. Main Point 3: _____

   II. Call to action (memorable finish):

        _____

        _____

EXERCISE 2.4A

Speech Karaoke

► A well-known speech makes a favorable impression on the audience, as speakers may invoke a range of styles or delivery methods. Using this activity illustrates the importance of delivery style and helps speakers find and develop their voice for presentations while reinforcing the effective speeches can move audiences to take substantial action and bring about positive change.

► Select a single section from a famous speech of no more than 250 words. Copy the text into a manuscript or visual aid (e.g., PowerPoint slide), which you will read from. During class, each student will read their speech from their prepared manuscript or visual aid just as one would sing the lyrics of a popular song during karaoke!

Contributed by William Hoffman, University of Kansas. Copyright © Kendall Hunt Publishing Company.

EXERCISE 2.4B

Impromptu Speech Evaluation

Speaker: _____ Date: _____

Specific Purpose: _____

_____

_____

Thesis Statement: _____

_____

_____

	Poor	Good	Excellent
1. Gives an impromptu speech using no notes and following the guidelines provided by the instructor.	1	1.5	2
2. Speaks clearly and audibly avoiding nonfluencies.	1	1.5	2
3. Delivers the speech appropriately and demonstrates vocal fluency, variety, and proper enthusiasm.	1	1.5	2
4. Delivers that speech using appropriate nonverbal skills.	1	1.5	2
5. Properly finishes within 1 to 2 minutes.	1	1.5	2

Contributed by Greg G. Armfield

EXERCISE 2.4C

Impromptu Persuasive Speech Evaluation

Speaker: _____ Date: _____

Specific Purpose: _____

_____

Thesis Statement: _____

_____

	Poor	Good	Excellent
1. Gives an impromptu persuasive speech using no notes and following the guidelines provided by the instructor.	1	1.5	2
2. Speaks clearly and audibly with good language avoiding verbalized pauses and nonfluencies.	1	1.5	2
3. Delivers the speech appropriately and well using good nonverbals, and proper enthusiasm, etc.	1	1.5	2
4. Clearly structures the speech using Monroe's motivated sequence (attention, need, satisfaction, visualization, and action).	1	1.5	2
5. Properly finishes within 1 (min) to 2 (max) minutes.	1	1.5	2

Contributed by Greg G. Armfield

EXERCISE 2.5A

Listening Evaluation

Write a candid evaluation of your three major strengths and three major weaknesses as a listener. Explain what steps you need to take in order to become a better listener. Please be specific.

EXERCISE 2.5B

Telephone Tree

Depending on the size of the class your instructor will divide the class into groups of 10 to 12. Ask for one volunteer from each group, alternatively you can choose a person. Take the student outside the classroom and read them something similar to the following: "to get to *The Cedar*, take Hillside to 13th Street. Go East on 13th Street. *The Cedar* is a brown building on the North side of 13th between Hillside and Oliver." Read it to them two or three times then let them read it. Instruct them to return to the classroom and whisper the message to the student sitting next to them. The message should be relayed to the next person until the last person has the message. The last person should then write the message on the board. Then have the original student state the original message. There is almost always a wide variation between the original message and the message received by the last student. Repeat for each group with different or varying messages.

Alternative messages can be longer or shorter. Typically, the more specific the message the more message variation that is experienced. Colors, directions, street names, etc. all tend to change.

Afterward, discuss the message distortion that took place between message sender and receiver.

EXERCISE 2.5C

"Who's on First" by Abbott and Costello

The historical comedy routine by Abbot and Costello provides an opportunity to practice attentive listening skills. The transcript and audio of their skit can be found at the following link:

http://www.baseball-almanac.com/humor4.shtml

More history on Abbot and Costello as well as answers for who is playing what position can be found at this link:

http://www.baseball-reference.com/bullpen/Who's_on_First%3F

There are videos of their skit available from several sources that are around five minutes long. Make sure you play one of the original Abbot and Costello videos, not a current remake. Abbott and Costello will be in black and white ☺

First

Second

Third

Short

Pitcher

Catcher

Left Field

Center Field

Right Field

Manager

EXERCISE 3.1A

Interpersonal Relationship Development Stages

Knapp's relational development model suggests that there are five stages in developing relationships: initiating, experimenting, intensifying, integrating, and bonding stage.

As a group or individually: (1) define each of the five stages and (2) pick at least one emoji to represent each of the five stages (a group of four will have 20 emojis in total). Provide detailed reasons why you think those emojis could fit each stage.

Initiating

Experimenting

Intensifying

Integrating

Bonding stage

EXERCISE 3.2B

Relationship Stages

Your lab instructor will assign your group a particular relationship to evaluate in terms of the stages of relationships. This will be a role play exercise in which your group will play parts of a mini-drama in a relationship

Relationship =

Relationship Development	Relationship Development
Stage =	Stage =

EXERCISE 3.5A

Opinions About Conflict

Each of the statements that follow represents an opinion about conflict. Indicate whether you agree (A) or disagree (D) with each statement.

1. _____ People should not talk about important topics when they are tired or feeling strong emotions.
2. _____ People should talk more in order to overcome conflict.
3. _____ There is always a winner and a loser in a conflict situation.
4. _____ People can work out their problems and conflicts without outside help.
5. _____ When couples fight, it means they have bad relationships.
6. _____ Unless someone asks for negative feedback, it should not be offered.
7. _____ Men and women think about conflicts differently.
8. _____ Fighting is bad for interpersonal relationships.
9. _____ Conflict can almost always be resolved.
10. _____ Organizations try to minimize conflict since conflict is counterproductive.
11. _____ Most people avoid openly discussing conflict situations.
12. _____ The most important aspect in dealing with conflict is to think about it rationally and objectively.
13. _____ Fighting is bad because it reveals our bad sides—our pettiness, our need to be in control, and our unreasonable expectations.

EXERCISE 4.1A

Media Richness Activity

In groups of 4 or 5 make a list of the current communication media used in organizations. Be specific and separate out all of the channel choices available given the ongoing convergence of the Internet.

1. Based on the definition of richness provided in the chapter, rank them from richest to leanest.
2. Reflect on the rankings provided in Table 10.2. What differences exist between your group's rankings and the scholar's rankings?
3. What media has not been explored?
4. How do you think the culture of higher education has influenced your rankings?

EXERCISE 4.3A

Exploring Organizational Culture

Using Schein's model of culture as a guide, perform a cultural analysis of an organization, a division of an organization, or a group that students in your lab section are familiar with. Examples include campus groups or organizations, departments, local organizations.

Begin by brainstorming the artifacts prevalent in the organization and the behaviors that are observable. At this point it is important not to evaluate comments, only to brainstorm. Make sure each artifact or observation is as descriptive as possible.

Move to Schein's second level by making assumptions about the organizational values. Make sure you can make a logical argument as to why our observations might lead to the assumptions of organizational culture. Why would these values lead to the identification of the artifacts and behaviors listed above?

Based on the six assumptions regarding the nature of: reality and truth, time, space, human nature, human activity, and human relationships, what environmental influences affect the organizational culture? What artifacts might conflict with the espoused values of the organization?

Finally, discuss the potential of subcultures to exist within the larger organizational culture.

EXERCISE 5.1A

Emotional Appeals

Your task is to find print advertisements which provide examples of each of the following emotional or motive appeals:

1. Altruism

2. Fear

3. Individuality

4. Conformity

5. Power, control or influence

6. Appeals to self-esteem

7. Appeals to love

8. Achievement

9. Financial Gain

10. Status

EXERCISE 5.1B

Emotional Appeal Impromptu Speech

Your instructor will assign an impromptu topic, and then distribute one of the emotional appeals discussed in the lesson. After you have your topic, note the emotional appeal you have been assigned. You will integrate this appeal in the persuasive impromptu speech.

Questions for Consideration:

1. How did the emotional appeal you used for this assignment shape the content of your presentation?

2. Do you think a different emotional appeal would be better suited for the topic you were given?

3. Is there a specific advertisement or persuasive message that you found memorable? What was memorable about it? Did the producers use a wide range of appeals?

Used strategically, emotional appeals are advantageous to the persuasive speaker. However, they are never a substitute for sound logic (i.e., Logos).

Contributed by William Hoffman, University of Kansas. Copyright © Kendall Hunt Publishing Company.

EXERCISE 5.2A

Deceptive Communication and the Ethics of Lying

The Revised Lie Acceptability Scale (Oliveira & Levine, 2008)

Please answer the following questions using the following:

1 = Strongly Disagree	2 = Disagree	3 = Somewhat Disagree	4 = Neither Disagree or Agree
5 = Somewhat Agree	6 = Agree	7 = Strongly Agree	

_____ 1.   Never tell anyone the real reason you do anything unless it is useful to do so.

_____ 2.   *(R) Lying is immoral.*

_____ 3.   It is ok to lie in order to achieve one's goals.

_____ 4.   What people don't know can't hurt them.

_____ 5.   The best way to handle people is to tell them what they want to hear.

_____ 6.   *(R) There is no excuse for lying to someone else.*

_____ 7.   *(R) Honesty is always the best policy.*

_____ 8.   It is often better to lie than to hurt someone's feelings.

_____ 9.   *(R) Lying is just wrong.*

_____ 10. Lying is no big deal.

_____ 11. There is nothing wrong with bending the truth now and then.

TOTAL (AFTER YOU HAVE REVERSE-CODED, see below): _____

BEFORE YOU TOTAL the numbers on this scale you need to REVERSE SCORE items 2, 6, 7, and 9!
SO, to Reverse Code you make these changes to the underlined and bolded responses above:
If your answer is a 1, change it to a 7
If your answer is a 2, change it to a 6
If your answer is a 3, change it to a 5
If your answer is a 4, DO NOT change your answer
If your answer is a 5, change it to a 3
If your answer is a 6, change it to a 2
If your answer is a 7, change it to a 1

After you have your total, see where you fit below:

- ► If your total is 11–25, you see lying as relatively unacceptable. The lower your score, the more you see lying as unacceptable.
- ► If your total is 26–51, you are relatively neutral with regard to the acceptability of lying. You may have an "it depends" belief about when it is OK to lie.
- ► If your total is 52–77, you are relatively OK with lying. The higher your total on the scale, the more acceptable you may see lying behavior.

Questions for Discussion on Exercise:

1. Where are you on Lie Acceptability? What do you think about your total on this scale? Is it an accurate assessment of what you think about lying? Why or why not?

2. Look back at the chapter and the discussion of Ethics. Here are definitions of two ethical theories to remind you:

   Utilitarianism is focused on the evaluation of consequences of one's actions and the desire to do the greatest good (Johnson, 2014). Do the most good for the most people!

   Deontology, in contrast to utilitarianism, is focused on duty or responsibility and deontology ethicists have strong perspectives on deceptive behavior. Lying is NEVER OK!

   Compare your result from the Lie Acceptability Scale to these two Ethical perspectives. Which one better describes your attitude toward Lie Acceptability? How does this definition fit with your perception of Lie Acceptability? Is it a good fit or not? Why or why not?

3. Now, in groups, consider the "Murderer at the Door" scenario discussed in the chapter. Let's say that you have a friend who has come to you to hide in your home. The friend, let's call him Bellamy, has done something terrible. Bellamy killed your friend, Clark. The killing, though, was in self-defense because Clark was trying to kill Bellamy. Bellamy protected himself. BUT, now that you have hid Bellamy, a Police Detective, Abby, has come to your door asking you to give up Bellamy. You know that Bellamy will be killed if taken into custody by the police.

   In your groups, share your perspectives on Lie Acceptability and on which Ethical Theory you connect with the most. Use these perspectives to discuss this scenario.

Answer these questions in your group:

1. List your group members and their perspectives on Lie Acceptability (unacceptable, neutral/it depends, and lies are acceptable) AND the Ethical Theory (Utilitarianism or Deontology) they connect with the most:

2. What should you do? Give up Bellamy or lie to protect him?

3. What is your justification (as a group) for this decision?

4. Going back to the Lie Acceptability Scale, what is a potential problem with this scale? Can this scale really tell us if we see lying as acceptable or unacceptable? Why or why not?

Oliveira, C. M., & Levine, T. R. (2008). Lie acceptability: A construct and measure. *Communication Research Reports*, 25(4), 282–288. Retrieved from https://msu.edu/~levinet/Oliveira&Levine(2008)_Lie_Acceptability.pdf

Contributed by Anne Hubbell, New Mexico State University

EXERCISE 5.3A

Health Communication Activity

You will be analyzing the fear appeals within an advertisement for a health campaign. Choose a health campaign that has a goal of: (a) reducing a negative behavior, (b) acquiring a healthy behavior, or (c) uses fear and danger to present a potential health risk. You may search magazines or the Internet for an advertisement. Be sure to choose an appropriate advertisement that includes the goals listed above. Health campaigns about STDs and Meth tend to have graphic images, please choose wisely and double check with your Instructor.

Once you have found an advertisement, use the Extended Parallel Process Model (EPPM) to answer the following questions. Consider yourself or the audience the health campaign is trying to target.

1. What is the threat or negative consequence the ad is trying to prevent?

2. Define perceived susceptibility. Does this ad provide perceived susceptibility? Explain.

3. Define perceived severity. Does this ad provide perceived severity? Explain.

4. Define self-efficacy. Does the ad provide self-efficacy? Explain.

5. Define response-efficacy. Does the ad provide response-efficacy? Explain.

6. Overall, how effective do you think this ad may be?

EXERCISE 5.3B

Health Communication and Ethical Challenges

Read the case study below and answer the questions. Then in teams of four to five, work through the case study and questions below. Your instructor will tell you which "side" you will be on and you will need to work with your group to formulate arguments. Then, your team will debate another team using those arguments.

> Monty is an 85-year-old man who has been a smoker his entire life. Six months ago, however, Monty quit smoking and started "vaping" so that he could be healthier. His doctor, Dr. Knowsitall, believes that "vaping" can be harmful as well and wishes to convince Monty to stop. Monty also has recently been hospitalized and diagnosed with lung cancer, stage 4, and they believe that Monty may only have about 8 months left to live. Monty believes that he should be able to do what he wants with his time left and can vape all he wants. Dr. Knowsitall disagrees because the vape may actually put harmful chemicals in the area around a person who is vaping and that can hurt others around Monty, perhaps even making Monty's disease progress faster and take his life sooner.

Within your Team, Answer These Discussion Questions:

1. Using the Transtheoretical model, what stage is Monty in? Why do you put him in this stage?

2. Is "vaping" harmful? Why or why not. Look up research online through your phone or laptop and support your opinion. (Hint: there is information available on whether it IS or IS NOT harmful, you can get information for both sides.)

3. Create six arguments from what you learned in #2 above. Three of the arguments are taking Dr. Knowsitall's side and three arguments are taking Monty's side. At least one of the arguments should be from the information you got online for #2 above. Put your arguments here and cite the ones you got online:

4. Each team now is assigned a "side" to take. Each team will debate a team which takes the opposing "side." So, if there are four teams in a class, two of the teams will be in support of Monty's opinion and two will be in support of Dr. Knowsitall's opinion. The instructor will decide on one of the following: (1) You can do this by pretending to be Monty versus Dr. Knowsitall; or (2) you can do this as a more professional debate and just debate the facts of the case and not take on the personalities of Dr. Knowsitall and Monty.

Contributed by Anne Hubbell, New Mexico State University

AFTER DEBATE Questions for Discussion

1. What was the most compelling argument you heard in the debate? Why was it compelling?

2. Can we connect any of the arguments to what we covered in the Health Communication chapter? Particularly Danger Control and Fear Control, which one of these is Monty demonstrating?

3. Based on this exercise, what do you think Monty should do? Why do you think this?

4. What do you think Dr. Knowsitall should do? Why do you think this?

Index